FEMINIST INTERPRETATIONS OF W. V. QUINE

RE-READING THE CANON

NANCY TUANA, GENERAL EDITOR

This series consists of edited collections of essays, some original and some previously published, offering feminist re-interpretations of the writings of major figures in the Western philosophical tradition. Devoted to the work of a single philosopher, each volume contains essays covering the full range of the philosopher's thought and representing the diversity of approaches now being used by feminist critics.

Already published:

Nancy Tuana, ed., *Feminist Interpretations of Plato* (1994)
Margaret Simons, ed., *Feminist Interpretations of Simone de Beauvoir* (1995)
Bonnie Honig, ed., *Feminist Interpretations of Hannah Arendt* (1995)
Patricia Jagentowicz Mills, ed., *Feminist Interpretations of G. W. F. Hegel* (1996)
Maria J. Falco, ed., *Feminist Interpretations of Mary Wollstonecraft* (1996)
Susan J. Hekman, ed., *Feminist Interpretations of Michel Foucault* (1996)
Nancy J. Holland, ed., *Feminist Interpretations of Jacques Derrida* (1997)
Robin May Schott, ed., *Feminist Interpretations of Immanuel Kant* (1997)
Celeine Leon and Sylvia Walsh, eds., *Feminist Interpretations of Soren Kierkegaard* (1997)
Cynthia Freeland, ed., *Feminist Interpretations of Aristotle* (1998)
Kelly Oliver and Marilyn Pearsall, eds., *Feminist Interpretations of Friedrich Nietzsche* (1998)
Mimi Reisel Gladstein and Chris Matthew Sciabarra, eds., *Feminist Interpretations of Ayn Rand* (1999)
Susan Bordo, ed., *Feminist Interpretations of René Descartes* (1999)
Julien S. Murphy, ed., *Feminist Interpretations of Jean-Paul Sartre* (1999)
Anne Jaap Jacobson, ed., *Feminist Interpretations of David Hume* (2000)
Sarah Lucia Hoagland and Marilyn Frye, eds., *Feminist Interpretations of Mary Daly* (2000)
Tina Chanter, ed., *Feminist Interpretations of Emmanuel Levinas* (2001)
Nancy J. Holland and Patricia Huntington, eds., *Feminist Interpretations of Martin Heidegger* (2001)
Charlene Haddock Seigfried, ed., *Feminist Interpretations of John Dewey* (2001)
Naomi Scheman and Peg O'Connor, eds., *Feminist Interpretations of Ludwig Wittgenstein* (2002)
Lynda Lange, ed., *Feminist Interpretations of Jean-Jacques Rousseau* (2002)
Lorraine Code, ed., *Feminist Interpretations of Hans-Georg Gadamer* (2003)

FEMINIST INTERPRETATIONS OF W. V. QUINE

EDITED BY
LYNN HANKINSON NELSON
AND JACK NELSON

THE PENNSYLVANIA STATE UNIVERSITY PRESS
UNIVERSITY PARK, PENNSYLVANIA

Library of Congress Cataloging-in-Publication Data

Feminist interpretations of W. V. Quine /
edited by Lynn Hankinson Nelson and Jack Nelson.
p. cm. — (Re-reading the canon)
Includes bibliographical references and index.
ISBN 0-271-02294-9 (cloth : alk. paper)
ISBN 0-271-02295-7 (pbk. : alk. paper)
1. Quine, W. V. (Willard Van Orman)
2. Feminist theory.
I. Nelson, Lynn Hankinson, 1948– .
II. Nelson, Jack, 1944– .
III. Series.

B945.Q54 F46 2003
191—dc21 2003007890

Printed in the United States of America
Published by The Pennsylvania State University Press,
University Park, PA 16802-1003

It is the policy of The Pennsylvania State University Press to use acid-free paper. Publications on uncoated stock satisfy the minimum requirements of American National Standard for Information Sciences—Permanence of Paper for Printed Library Material, ANSI Z39.48–1992.

Contents

Part III: Explications, Expansions, and Revisions of Quinean Positions

Acknowledgments

It would be hard to express the depth of our gratitude to the contributors of this volume who have given their work to it and waited patiently for its completion. We also owe special thanks to Nancy Tuana and Joseph Rouse for their wise guidance and support.

Family members and dear friends encouraged and supported our efforts, and we thank them.

We dedicate this volume to the memory of W. V. Quine, whose work continues to inspire and guide our own.

The following works included in this anthology are reprinted with permission:

Lynn Hankinson Nelson, Part I of the Introduction: reprinted with permission from Lynn Hankinson Nelson and Jack Nelson, *On Quine* (Belmont, Ca.: Wadsworth, 2000).

Lynn Hankinson Nelson, "Who Knows: From Quine to Feminist Empiricism": reproduced from *Who Knows: From Quine to Feminist Empiricism*, by Lynn Hankinson Nelson. Reprinted by permission of Temple University Press. Copyright © 1990 by Lynn Hankinson Nelson. All rights reserved.

Louise M. Antony, "Quine as Feminist: The Radical Import of Naturalized Epistemology": reproduced from *A Mind of One's Own: Feminist Essays on Reason and Objectivity*, by Louise Antony and Charlotte Witt. Copyright © 1992 by Westview Press. Reprinted by permission of Westview Press, a member of Perseus Books, L.L.C.

Lorraine Code, "What Is Natural About Epistemology Naturalized?": reproduced from *American Philosophical Quarterly* 33: 1 (1996).

Phyllis Rooney, "Feminist Epistemology and Naturalized Epistemology": parts of section II reproduced from "Putting Naturalizing Epistemology to Work, in *Epistemology: The Big Question*, ed. Linda Martín Alcoff, 288–93. Copyright © 1998 by Blackwell. Reproduced by permission of Blackwell.

Jack Nelson, "The Last Dogma of Empiricism?": reproduced from *Feminism, Science, and the Philosophy of Science*, ed. Lynn Hankinson Nelson and Jack Nelson, 59–78. Copyright © 1996 by Kluwer Academic Publishers. Reprinted with kind permission of Kluwer Academic Publishers.

Richmond Campbell, "Feminist Epistemology Naturalized": parts of this essay reproduced from *Illusions of Paradox*, by Richmond Campbell. Copyright © 1998 by Rowman & Littlefield.

Lynn Hankinson Nelson, "Feminist Naturalized Philosophy of Science": reproduced from *Synthese* 104 (3): 399–421. © 1995 by Kluwer Academic Publishers. Reprinted with kind permission of Kluwer Academic Publishers.

Preface

Nancy Tuana

Take into your hands any history of philosophy text. You will find compiled therein the "classics" of modern philosophy. Since these texts are often designed for use in undergraduate classes, the editor is likely to offer an introduction in which the reader is informed that these selections represent the perennial questions of philosophy. The student is to assume that she or he is about to explore the timeless wisdom of the greatest minds of Western philosophy. No one calls attention to the fact that the philosophers are all men.

Though women are omitted from the canons of philosophy, these texts inscribe the nature of woman. Sometimes the philosopher speaks directly about woman, delineating her proper role, her abilities and inabilities, her desires. Other times the message is indirect—a passing remark hinting at women's emotionality, irrationality, unreliability.

This process of definition occurs in far more subtle ways when the central concepts of philosophy—reason and justice, those characteristics that are taken to define us as human—are associated with traits historically identified with masculinity. If the "man" of reason must learn to control or overcome traits identified as feminine—the body, the emotions, the passions—then the realm of rationality will be one reserved primarily for men,[1] with grudging entrance to those few women who are capable of transcending their femininity.

Feminist philosophers have begun to look critically at the canonized texts of philosophy and have concluded that the discourses of philosophy are not gender-neutral. Philosophical narratives do not offer a universal perspective, but rather privilege some experiences and beliefs over others.

These experiences and beliefs permeate all philosophical theories whether they be aesthetic or epistemological, moral or metaphysical. Yet this fact has often been neglected by those studying the traditions of philosophy. Given the history of canon formation in Western philosophy, the perspective most likely to be privileged is that of upper-class white males. Thus, to be fully aware of the impact of gender biases, it is imperative that we re-read the canon with attention to the ways in which philosophers' assumptions concerning gender are embedded within their theories.

This new series, *Re-Reading the Canon*, is designed to foster this process of reevaluation. Each volume will offer feminist analyses of the theories of a selected philosopher. Since feminist philosophy is not monolithic in method or content, the essays are also selected to illustrate the variety of perspectives within feminist criticism and highlight some of the controversies within feminist scholarship.

In this series, feminist lenses will be focused on the canonical texts of Western philosophy, both those authors who have been part of the traditional canon, and those philosophers whose writings have more recently gained attention within the philosophical community. A glance at the list of volumes in the series will reveal an immediate gender bias of the canon: Arendt, Aristotle, Beauvoir, Derrida, Descartes, Foucault, Hegel, Hume, Kant, Locke, Marx, Mill, Nietzsche, Plato, Rousseau, Wittgenstein, Wollstonecraft. There are all too few women included, and those few who do appear have been added only recently. In creating this series, it is not my intention to rectify the current canon of philosophical thought. What is and is not included within the canon during a particular historical period is a result of many factors. Although no canonization of texts will include all philosophers, no canonization of texts that excludes all but a few women can offer an accurate representation of the history of the discipline, as women have been philosophers since the ancient period.[2]

I share with many feminist philosophers and other philosophers writing from the margins of philosophy the concern that the current canonization of philosophy be transformed. Although I do not accept the position that the current canon has been formed exclusively by power relations, I do believe that this canon represents only a selective history of the tradition. I share the view of Michael Bérubé that "canons are at once the location, the index, and the record of the struggle for cultural representation; like any other hegemonic formation, they must be continually reproduced anew and are continually contested."[3]

The process of canon transformation will require the recovery of "lost" texts and a careful examination of the reasons such voices have been silenced. Along with the process of uncovering women's philosophical history, we must also begin to analyze the impact of gender ideologies upon the process of canonization. This process of recovery and examination must occur in conjunction with careful attention to the concept of a canon of authorized texts. Are we to dispense with the notion of a tradition of excellence embodied in a canon of authorized texts? Or, rather than abandon the whole idea of a canon, do we instead encourage a reconstruction of a canon of those texts that inform a common culture?

This series is designed to contribute to this process of canon transformation by offering a re-reading of the current philosophical canon. Such a re-reading shifts our attention to the ways in which woman and the role of the feminine are constructed within the texts of philosophy. A question we must keep in front of us during this process of re-reading is whether a philosopher's socially inherited prejudices concerning woman's nature and role are independent of her or his larger philosophical framework. In asking this question attention must be paid to the ways in which the definitions of central philosophical concepts implicitly include or exclude gendered traits.

This type of reading strategy is not limited to the canon, but can be applied to all texts. It is my desire that this series reveal the importance of this type of critical reading. Paying attention to the workings of gender within the texts of philosophy will make visible the complexities of the inscription of gender ideologies.

Notes

1. More properly, it is a realm reserved for a group of privileged males, since the texts also inscribe race and class biases that thereby omit certain males from participation.

2. Mary Ellen Waithe's multivolume series, *A History of Women Philosophers* (Boston: M. Nijoff, 1987), attests to this presence of women.

3. Michael Bérubé, *Marginal Forces/Cultural Centers: Tolson, Pynchon, and the Politics of the Canon* (Ithaca: Cornell University Press, 1992), 4–5.

Introduction

Lynn Hankinson Nelson and Jack Nelson

1. W. V. Quine

At the time of his death in December of 2000, W. V. Quine was the Edgar Pierce Professor of Philosophy Emeritus at Harvard University. Quine was born in 1908 in Akron, Ohio. He attended Oberlin College as an undergraduate and earned his Ph.D. at Harvard, under C. I. Lewis. He was the preeminent American philosopher of the twentieth century.

Quine falls within, and is influenced by, at least three intellectual traditions: the empiricist tradition of John Locke, George Berkeley, David

Part 1 of our introduction draws extensively on sections of Nelson and Nelson (2000). We are grateful to Dan Kolak, the editor of the Wadsworth Series on Canonical Philosophers, for permission to reprint these sections.

Hume, the Vienna Circle, and, most importantly for Quine's development, Rudolph Carnap; the pragmatist tradition of William James, C. S. Peirce, John Dewey, and C. I. Lewis; and the tradition of modern mathematical logic, running from Bertrand Russell and Alfred Whitehead through Kurt Gödel and Alonzo Church. From the empiricist tradition comes Quine's lifelong concern with explicating the relationships between experience and our best going theories of the world. From the pragmatist tradition comes his advocacy of holism and the tentativeness of all of science. From mathematical logic comes his commitment to extensionality and to Alfred Tarski's theory of truth. Quine is the clear heir to the empiricist program for which Carnap set the agenda in the 1930s, 1940s, and 1950s. He is a product of this tradition. In our view, he is also its own severest critic and its ablest defender. But these views are not uncontroversial, as the essays collected here indicate.

Given the nature and the significance of Quine's positions, it is somewhat surprising that feminist philosophers have been rather slow to show interest in his work. In the 1980s, feminist critiques of the philosophy of science were largely directed at the logico-empiricist tradition, particularly the positions associated with Carnap, Carl Hempel, and Ernst Nagel. Arguably, Quine's positions constitute some of the most fundamental and far-reaching challenges anyone has offered to central tenets of this tradition. The 1990s saw more interest in Quine's work, as reflected in the number of contributors to Linda Martín Alcoff and Elizabeth Potter's collection *Feminist Epistemologies* who make substantive appeal to Quine's positions (Alcoff and Potter 1993),[1] and in the conference "Feminism and Naturalism," co-sponsored by the Philosophy departments at the University of Missouri-St. Louis and Washington University in September 1999.

But although relatively rare, feminist analyses that did engage Quine's positions in the 1980s constituted significant contributions to feminist philosophy of science and feminist epistemology. Helen E. Longino appealed to Quine's underdetermination thesis to argue for the plausibility of science critiques motivated by feminist perspectives (Longino 1987). Underdetermination is also a key premise of Longino's analysis and arguments in *Science as Social Knowledge* (Longino 1990), and of later articles in which she explores the viability of the traditional distinction between "cognitive" and "noncognitive" values (e.g., Longino 1995 and 1996). Alcoff explicated Quine's thesis of holism to argue that it makes the notion of "feminist social science" viable, rather than inherently contradictory as some feminist analyses were then suggesting (Alcoff 1987). Potter also appealed to holism as advocated by Quine and others in proposing a model of the relationships between gender politics and science (Potter 1988). Individually and collectively, these analyses demonstrated that the issues with which feminist scientists and science scholars are concerned are not limited to cases of "bad" science, and that positivism and relativism do not exhaust the options available to feminist theorists. Finally, in *The Science Question in Feminism*, Sandra Harding recognized Quine's arguments against the analytic/synthetic distinction as constituting a devastating challenge to key tenets of the logico-empiricist tradition of Carnap, Hempel, and Nagel (Harding 1986). At the same time, Harding was highly critical of other aspects of Quine's philosophy of science, particularly of what she argued to be a pervasive scientism within it.

Harding's critique of Quine's positions and of empiricism serves as important background to the essays in this volume. Contributors who view Quine's positions as having much to contribute to feminist philosophy of science and epistemology engage many of Harding's criticisms—although it will be clear that there are substantive differences in how they understand a number of Quine's positions and their implications. Contributors critical of one or more of Quine's positions, and those who seek to further develop Quinean naturalism or to offer alternative versions of naturalism altogether, also engage Harding's arguments. In general, they share Harding's concern that central features of Quine's philosophy of science straightforwardly preclude the kind and level of normativity feminist science studies calls for and invokes. Paul Roth, who advocates Quinean naturalism and its importance for feminist theorizing about science, concurs with the argument that naturalism rightly understood cannot provide the kind of normativity that contributors critical of it take to be important. But in Roth's view, this is not a failing of Quine's arguments for naturalized epistemology; it is what makes them sound and genuinely revolutionary.

Given these relationships, we review the major outlines of Harding's arguments. We set the stage for that discussion and for our introduction to the essays, themes, and agreements and disagreements in this volume by going back to the beginning, to Quine's "Two Dogmas of Empiricism" (Quine 1953). Here Quine offered his most significant challenge to logico-empiricist philosophy of science, as then understood, by rejecting both the analytic/synthetic distinction and verificationism. In doing so, he challenged the tradition's understanding of the philosophy of science and the tenability of its projects. Since its publication, philosophers have debated the soundness of Quine's arguments and argued about the extent of their implications for the philosophy of science and Anglo-American philosophy more generally. For Quine, the arguments of "Two Dogmas" served as the foundation of his subsequent work in the philosophy of science, and constituted the origins of others of his positions—including holism, the indeterminacy of translation, and his argument for naturalizing the philosophy of science (epistemology).

We spend time explicating these arguments and their relationships to the positions just mentioned for two reasons. First, although most contributors do not directly engage the arguments of "Two Dogmas" (but see Maureen Linker, Chapter 3 of this volume, for an extensive critique of them), they do engage the positions we maintain rely on its arguments, including holism and naturalism, and in some cases indeterminacy of translation. Second, we do not presume extensive familiarity with Quine's positions or the debates that have surrounded them. It goes without saying that not all contributors, let alone all Quine scholars or critics, will agree with our characterization of the structure, the implications, and the success of Quine's arguments in "Two Dogmas" or of the other positions we outline. Readers who wish can go directly to the second part of this introduction, where we discuss the essays in this volume.

Finally, a word about terminology. Quine often uses 'epistemology' when discussing the philosophy of science, that subdiscipline of philosophy that takes science, rather than knowledge in general, as its subject matter. Accordingly, we use 'philosophy of science' when discussing many of Quine's positions. But we also note that often Quine uses 'science' in an inclusive sense to include so-called common-sense theories and theorizing, as well as philosophy, indeed "the totality of our so-called knowledge or beliefs" (Quine 1953, 42).

"Two Dogmas of Empiricism"

I philosophize from the vantage point only of our own provincial conceptual scheme and scientific epoch, true; but I know no better.

—Quine, "Epistemology Naturalized"

Quine published "Two Dogmas of Empiricism" in 1951 in the *Philosophical Review*. In 1953 he included it as the second of nine essays in *From a Logical Point of View*. In it, he rejects outright both the analytic/synthetic distinction and verificationism, i.e., the verification theory of meaning applied to individual sentences.[2] The analytic/synthetic distinction has its roots in Hume's distinction between relations of ideas and matters of fact. The second dogma, verificationism, emerged as the basis of a strategy for completing one half of Hume's agenda—that of showing how all empirical knowledge flows from experience.[3]

Quine sets out to show that common, and superficially promising, defenses of the analytic/synthetic distinction invariably turn out to presuppose, rather than elucidate, the notion of analyticity. An investigation of the nest of interrelated notions—analyticity, synonymy, interchangeability *salva veritate*, and necessary truth—yields, Quine argues, an argument that "is not flatly circular, but something like it. It has the form, figuratively speaking, of a closed curve in space" (Quine 1953, 30).

Kant's view, Quine claims, can be taken to be that "a statement is analytic when it is true by virtue of meanings and independently of fact" (21). Quine finds meanings, in the sense of mental objects or ideas, to be "obscure intermediary entities" that are "well abandoned" in favor of an investigation of "the synonymy of linguistic forms" (23; cf. Quine 1966).[4] Instead of talking of meanings, he maintains, we can talk, given the notion of synonymy, of two linguistic forms—two sentences or two words—meaning the same if and only if they are synonymous. So we are making progress if we can give an account of synonymy. The progress is this: analytic statements fall into two subclasses—logical truths and statements that can be turned into logical truths by substituting synonyms for synonyms (23).

Quine's example of a logical truth is "[n]o unmarried man is married," and his general characterization of a logical truth is "a statement which is true and remains true under all reinterpretations of its components other than the logical particles" (22). An alleged example of a statement that is not a logical truth but yields one through the substitution of synonym for synonym is "[n]o bachelor is married," where 'bachelor' and 'unmarried man' are taken to be synonyms.

So, this first part of the closed curve seeks to explicate analyticity in terms of synonymy. But synonymy, Quine contends, "is no less in need of clarification than analyticity itself" (23). Quine rejects the view that synonymy rests on definition, according to which 'bachelor' is supposedly defined as, and is therefore synonymous with, 'unmarried man' (24). The problem, he points out, is that ordinary definitions, dictionary definitions, are not stipulations but reports on usage. "The lexicographer is an empirical scientist, whose business is the recording of antecedent facts" (24). He or she does not create usage or synonyms.[5]

Quine next turns to the notion of interchangeability of terms *salva veritate* as a possible explication of synonymy. The proposal is that expressions are synonymous if they are everywhere interchangeable without changing the truth or falsity of the containing statement. The problem here, Quine argues, is that such allegedly clear synonyms as 'bachelor' and 'unmarried male' are not so interchangeable. For example, 'unmarried male' cannot be substituted for 'bachelor' in

> 'Bachelor' has less than ten letters

without turning the above truth into the falsehood

> 'Unmarried male' has less than ten letters

(28). To make the substitutivity test work we have to limit substitutions to whole words. The word spelled b-a-c-h-e-l-o-r does not occur as a whole word in the above example, though its name does.

So far so good (assuming the notion of 'wordhood' is unproblematic). But to make the substitutivity test work—to prevent its declaring such co-referential but nonsynonymous expressions as 'the first President of the United States [under the Constitution]' and 'the second husband of Martha Washington' synonymous—we will have to consider substitutivity not only within such ordinary contexts as

> The first President of the United States was married to Martha Washington

but also within such contexts as

> Necessarily the first President of the United States was married to Martha Washington

for while the expressions 'the first President of the United States' and 'the second husband of Martha Washington' are intersubstitutable in the first context, *salva veritate*, they are not in the second.

> Necessarily the first President of the United States was married to Martha Washington

is presumably false while

> Necessarily the second husband of Martha Washington was married to Martha Washington

is presumably true.

But Quine now reminds us that to attach 'necessarily' to a statement is just to claim that the statement is analytic. That is,

> Necessarily bachelors are unmarried

is best understood as

> 'Bachelors are unmarried' is analytic.

So our curve in space has closed itself. We can explicate analyticity in terms of synonymy, synonymy in terms of intersubstitutivity *salve veritate*, including in contexts governed by 'necessarily,' and such necessity in terms of analyticity.[6]

Quine next turns his attention to his second target, verificationism. Historically, discussions of "Two Dogmas" have largely ignored the second dogma, perhaps because many defenders of the analytic/synthetic distinction have no sympathy for verificationism. And indeed at first it seems odd that Quine would see these two positions as paired or related dogmas. On reflection one might conclude that having rejected the analytic/synthetic distinction, Quine had no choice but to also reject verificationism, precisely because he does not want to abandon the meaningfulness of logic and mathematics. If the only criterion of meaningfulness is verification by sensory experience, then mathematics and logic appear to be meaningless, for there are no sensory experiences that can be taken to confirm or disconfirm the alleged truths of mathematics and logic. The view of logic and mathematics as consisting of important nonsense is one A. J. Ayer was willing to take in his explication and defense of verificationism in *Language, Truth, and Logic* (Ayer 1959). Being unwilling to follow Ayer, one might conclude that Quine has no choice but to reject verificationism as a theory of meaning.

But we suggest that this is not the motivation for Quine's rejection of verificationism. Quine does not take the truths of mathematics and logic to be unverified by the standards of verificationism. He notes that "[a]s long as it is taken to be significant in general to speak of the confirmation and infirmation of a statement, it seems significant to speak also of a limiting kind of statement which is vacuously confirmed, *ipso facto*, come what may; and such a statement is analytic" (41). That is, Quine grants that "the truth of statements does obviously depend both upon language and upon extralinguistic fact" (41). If we allow sentences to be candidates for truth and falsity taken one-by-one, it follows that we can explicate analytic sentences as the limiting case, those in which "the linguistic component is all that matters," i.e., where the role of extralinguistic fact is nil. Given verificationism, the truths of logic and mathematics and perhaps all commonly termed analytic statements are vacuously verified—verified "come what may" by way of experience. Hence were verificationism to stand, it would itself constitute a basis for an explication (and thus reinstitution) of the analytic/synthetic distinction, analytic statements being those that are verified come what may. So if the analytic/synthetic distinction is to be banished as an unsupportable dogma, so must verificationism. In fact, Quine asserts not just that the analytic/synthetic distinction is a consequence of verificationism, but also that "[t]he two dogmas are, indeed, at root identical" (41). We return to this issue below.

Quine holds verificationism to be closely connected with, if not equivalent to, radical reductionism—the view that "[e]very meaningful statement is . . . translatable into a statement (true or false) about immediate experience" (38). Quine's argument against verificationism and radical reductionism takes the form of what might be called "dismissal by charitable reinterpretation." Radical reductionism, he notes, goes back at least to Locke and Hume, who "held that every idea must either originate directly in sense experience or else be compounded of ideas thus originating" (38). Quine credits Tooke with improving on this idea by moving the focus from ideas to terms, allowing the doctrine to be rephrased "in semantical terms, by saying that a term, to be significant at all, must be either a name of a sense datum or a compound of such names or an abbreviation of such a compound" (38). But such a doctrine, Quine maintains, is "unnecessarily and intolerably restrictive in the term-by-term critique which it imposes. More reasonably, and without yet exceeding the limits of what I have called radical reductionism, we may take full statements as our significant units—thus demanding that our statements as wholes be translatable into sense-datum language, but not that they be translatable term by term" (38–39).

Devising a scheme for translating statements into sense-datum language was the goal of Carnap's *Aufbau* (Carnap 1928). Although Quine finds Carnap's attempt impressive, especially the constructions utilizing "the whole language of pure mathematics" (39), he believes the whole project is ultimately doomed to failure. This is because Carnap "provides no indication, not even the sketchiest, of how a statement of the form 'Quality *q* is at *x;y;z;t*' [a point instant] could ever be translated into Carnap's initial language of sense data and logic. The connective 'is at' remains an added undefined connective; the canons counsel us in its use but not in its elimination" (40). Carnap abandoned his radical reductionism project subsequently to publishing the *Aufbau*. In "Two Dogmas," Quine does not produce and criticize the arguments of those who continued to hold this view. Rather, he makes a "counter suggestion"—a charitable reinterpretation of the verificationism and radical reductionism of the *Aufbau*—namely, that "our statements about the external world face the tribunal of sense experience not individually but only as a corporate body" (41). This counter suggestion is, of course, holism—one of two key doctrines Quine was to spend the rest of his career elucidating and defending (the other being the explication of how experience does constrain theories—that is, of how we can have holism and empiricism).

The arguments that Quine gives against the analytic/synthetic distinction, the "closed curve in space" we have explored, are not decisive arguments. His strategy is rather to put the onus on those who want to rehabilitate the analytic/synthetic distinction. His challenge is this: If the analytic/synthetic distinction is to be maintained, then either the notion of meaning must be resuscitated and clearly enough explicated so as to provide grounds for deciding whether the "meaning" of one term is or is not included within that of another term (Kant's original notion); or the notion of cognitive synonymy must be explicated, without appealing to analyticity; or the notion of substitutivity *salva veritate* must be explicated, without appealing to contexts that presuppose analyticity but are strong enough to distinguish between co-extensionality and synonymy.

Since the publication of "Two Dogmas" Quine's critics have taken up this challenge, offering views of meaning or synonymy, or of modal operators such as 'necessarily,' that purport to break the "closed curve in space." Although we are of the view that none is successful, there is not consensus concerning this (see Linker, Chapter 3 of this volume).

We have noted that Quine's rejection of verificationism sparked far less discussion than did his rejection of the analytic/synthetic distinction. Those who reject Quine's holism do not generally do so in favor of some form of verificationism. Rather, they usually argue for or presuppose some version of a correspondence theory of truth, and a realism that grants to middle-sized physical objects, or molecules, or atoms and subatomic particles, or whatever, some status other than posits of our best going theories. That is, Quine's discussion of verificationism occurs, as it were, within the family of empiricist views that grants a special status to experience or some refinement of it (firings of sensory receptors); within *this* family, but not within the wider philosophical community, verificationism and holism exhaust the available options.

Finally, we return to Quine's claim, generally neglected in the literature, that the "two dogmas are . . . at root identical." If they are, then those who find verificationism implausible or unacceptable should take the same view toward the purported distinction between analytic and synthetic statements. Quine's argument to the effect that if verificationism can be defended then so too can the analytic/synthetic distinction is reasonably clear and has already been reviewed. Is there an implicit argument in the other direction? Perhaps. If there is an analytic/synthetic distinction, then it makes sense to distinguish the role of linguistic convention and the role of extralinguistic fact in determining the truth or falsity of a given statement. So if we are able to distinguish analytic statements from synthetic ones, it must be that we are able to identify the factors that determine their truth-values, the linguistic and nonlinguistic components, on a statement-by-statement basis. So for each synthetic statement we can identify the extralinguistic elements, the elements of experience that are relevant to its truth or falsity. But then we are free to identify the meaning of the statement with those extralinguistic elements. *And this is just what verificationism does*. So, in this sense, verificationism does follow from the analytic/synthetic distinction, if one is prepared to identify meaning with the experiences relevant to a synthetic statement's truth or falsity. Traditional empiricists were ready to do this; but Quine, at least in this respect, is not a traditional empiricist.

Holism, Indeterminacy of Translation, and Naturalizing Epistemology

We have noted that holism is Quine's alternative to the analytic/synthetic distinction and verificationism. But there is in "Two Dogmas" no full-blown argument for holism, no lengthy explication of it, and no exploration of how it transforms empiricism. We next briefly outline our understandings of the relationships between the arguments so far summarized, Quine's theses of holism and of the indeterminacy of translation, and his arguments for "naturalizing" the philosophy of science. Again, not everyone will agree with our analysis.

Although not argued for in "Two Dogmas," the classic statement of Quinean holism is given in the last section of that article, entitled "Empiricism without the Dogmas."

> The totality of our so-called knowledge or beliefs, from the most casual matters of geography and history to the profoundest laws of atomic physics or even of pure mathematics and logic, is a man-made fabric which impinges on experience only along the edges. Or, to change the figure, total science is like a field of force whose boundary conditions are experience. (42)

The first intertwined thesis of holism is that all of science (here, broadly construed to include "the totality of our so-called knowledge") is our own construction, and that even the apparently most disparate parts are, in fact, interconnected.

> A conflict with experience at the periphery occasions readjustments in the interior of the field. Truth values have to be redistributed over some of our statements. Reëvaluation of some statements entails reëvaluation of others, because of their logical interconnections—the logical laws being in turn simply certain further statements of the system, certain further elements of the field. . . . But the total field is so underdetermined by its boundary conditions, experience, that there is much latitude of choice as to what statements to reëvaluate in the light of any single contrary experience. (43)

The second intertwined thesis is that a recalcitrant experience can force an adjustment in the network of theories to which we are committed, to the totality of science. But such an experience cannot force a change of commitment to any *particular* belief or component sentence of science. This is because

> No particular experiences are linked with any particular statements in the interior of the field, except indirectly through considerations of equilibrium affecting the field as a whole. (43)

And this is the overarching thesis of holism: Our theories of nature face experience as a collective body, not sentence by sentence, not even particular theory by particular theory. There is no one-to-one relationship between most sentences of this body and specific experiences.

We suggest that this overarching thesis is a consequence of taking the verification theory of meaning seriously—the thesis that a chunk of language has empirical meaning only if there are experiences that will confirm or disconfirm it. There are no such confirming or disconfirming experiences for most individual sentences. There are for sentences taken collectively, for bodies of theory, for our whole going theory of the world. So, for the most part, it is only sentences taken collectively—bodies of theory, or our whole going theory of the world—that have empirical meaning.[7] Empirical meaning or content is spread across the sentences that together can be tested against experience.

In subsequent years, Quine offered a number of arguments for holism, and it emerged as a substantial doctrine (e.g., Quine 1960, 1966b, 1981a). Holism argues for the tentativeness of all theories and beliefs, from the most theoretical of the theoretical sciences to the most down-to-earth, common-sense theories and beliefs. In our view, but there are contributors who disagree, if holism holds, correspondence theories of truth go by the board and, with them, any possibility of construing empiricism as a theory of truth. Holism argues against the plausibility of "meta-level" theories of truth and for truth as immanent, *à la* Tarski. If there is a future for empiricism, it is as a theory of evidence: a theory about how the evidence provided by sensory receptors serves as the basis for warranted beliefs, and of how language contributes to "meaning," but not in a way that can be isolated on a sentence-by-sentence basis.

If holism holds, foundationalism also goes by the board; there are no Archimedean standpoints. We work, to paraphrase Quine, as scientists, laypersons, and philosophers, *from within*—from our vantage points within evolving bodies of theory that we inherit and seek to improve, on the basis of phenomenological experiences significantly shaped by these very same bodies of theory.[8] Working from within these theories, we indeed take the claims we find to be warranted to be true. But truth is immanent and the firmest of warrants is provisional (see, e.g., Quine 1981a).

Finally, if holism holds, and again not all contributors agree, the thesis of the indeterminacy of translation follows. As we outline below, its consequences are profound. As Joseph Rouse puts this point, Quine's thesis fundamentally challenges the "transparency and stability of meaning and experience" and, in this general respect, parallels challenges offered by feminist theorists Donna Haraway, Karen Barad, Judith Butler, and others (Rouse, personal communication).

In works as early as *Word and Object* (1960) and as late as *The Pursuit of Truth* (1990a), Quine explores the implications of holism for empiricism, i.e., for the relationship between experiences and theories. Noting years later that the notion of "experience" in "Two Dogmas" "still awaited a theory" (1981b), he subsequently worked to develop a physicalist notion of experience (e.g., as "the firings of sensory receptors" or "the triggerings of exteroceptors"), and he drew on anatomy, physiology, and empirical psychology to do so. This, we suggest, is holism at work. And he worked to develop an account of the relationship between, on the one hand, this nonlinguistic and nonphenomenological notion of experience and, on the other hand, obviously linguistic objects such as theories and hypotheses. In these efforts, Quine makes use of a stimulus response account of language acquisition to carve out a notion of an observation sentence, and ultimately that of observational categoricals, to argue that it is sentences of this kind that provide the link or bridge between the theoretical sentences of science, common-sense, and philosophy on the one hand, and experience construed in physicalist terms, on the other. Here we can only sketch this project, but the essays in this volume by Addelson, Antony, Duran, Linker, and Roth all address, to some extent, Quine's "theory of mind" and/or "theory of language."[9]

In Quine's account of language acquisition—both in the case of a child learning its first language and the field linguist attempting to construct a translation manual for a language entirely foreign to her (which Quine calls "radical translation")—the role of one-word sentences is pivotal. Such sentences include literally one-word sentences (i.e., sentences that cannot function as part of a longer sentence—Quine's example is 'ouch'), terms like 'red' that can function as a complete sentence, and multi-word sentences when construed holophrastically, i.e., as one-word sentences. Quine's contention is that, in both cases of language learning, one-word sentences (either literally one-word or multi-word understood holophrastically) are the first learned and initially keyed directly to sensory stimulation (experience physicalistically construed as, say, the firings of sensory receptors). There is, at this stage, no individuation or reference. Thus, for the infant, 'mama' is a feature-summoning or noting device on a par with 'water' (Quine 1969b, 7). For the linguist undertaking radical translation (i.e., translating a wholly foreign language), the question of whether 'Gavagai?,' which is typically assented to in the presence of observable rabbit-like phenomena, is really 'Ga va gai?' is deferred (Quine 1960, 35–52). (Although the linguist may impose her physical object ontology in this situation, translating 'Gavagai' as 'rabbit,' sensory stimulations do not warrant this; they only warrant a link with specific sensory stimulations equally compatible with 'Gavagai' signaling a rabbit-event or an instantiation of Rabbithood.)

Eventually, Quine suggests, the infant will catch on to the mechanics of individuation of her language community and learn to understand these initial sentences as incorporating reference and individuation. The linguist will solve the problem of how to translate the foreign language by importing her own conceptual scheme (Quine 1960, 1969c). And although beyond the scope of this discussion, we note that Quine famously or infamously maintains that "there is no fact of the matter" in terms of what the terms of our own language or those of a language we are attempting to translate refer to. In the case of our own language, we simply take our home language "at face value" (here again holism is at work). In the case of radical translation, we impose the same home language taken at face value (Quine 1969c, 47–49). But reference itself, given Quine's thesis of the inscrutability (or indeterminacy) of reference, has withered away.

Quine uses the ability for a multi-word sentence to be construed holophrastically and linked directly to the firings of one's sensory receptors in response to specific stimuli, and the ability of the same sentence to be made up of multi-words and incorporating reference, to carve out notions of observation sentences and observation categoricals (Quine 1990a; cf. Quine 1981a). The dual nature of these sentences, Quine maintains—that when construed holophrastically they are directly linked to sensory experience, and when not, contain theoretical terms that reappear in theory formulations—provides the link empiricists traditionally sought between a respectable notion of experience and the sentences of theories. It remains a matter of considerable debate, including among contributors to this volume, whether what we elsewhere call Quine's effort to "reconstitute empiricism"—to reconstitute the relationship between experience and theories in light of holism—is successful (Nelson and Nelson 2000).

We now turn to the relationships between the positions so far summarized and Quine's thesis of the indeterminacy of translation. We begin by noting that it is distinguished from the weaker thesis of the inscrutability of reference just discussed. Both theses are elusive, but we believe the following is a defensible interpretation of the thesis of indeterminacy of translation.

According to this thesis, it is possible to construct alternative translation manuals for translating one language into another, for example, Japanese into English, such that for any fairly extended passage of the language being translated, the manuals will yield different translations—different to the point that, in multiple instances, a sentence of the language being translated will go over into a *true* sentence of English in one scheme and a *false* sentence of English in the other scheme. *Overall* the translation manuals will be deemed equally acceptable, for they make, on the whole, equally good sense of the behavior, linguistic and otherwise, of the speakers of the language being translated. The difference between weak indeterminacy and strong is that in the former, but not the latter, truth is preserved, sentence by sentence.

Where does this strong thesis come from and what is the evidence for it? We elsewhere suggest that Quine takes the thesis to be, though strong and important, also obvious. It is an obvious consequence of his notion of empirical content—of his willingness, indeed eagerness, to identify empirical meaning or content, in the only clear sense he can give to this notion, with experience itself understood as the firings of sensory receptors, and with most individual sentences not enjoying, on their own, empirical content so understood. Put another way, Quine accepts the verification theory of meaning, but maintains that the relationship with experience is, in the case of most sentences, spread across the network of theories (this, again, is the thesis of holism). Strong indeterminacy of translation follows (Nelson and Nelson 2000).

Again, our recapitulation of Quine's argument is not uncontroversial. But we draw attention to Quine's remarks in response to Roger Gibson in *The Philosophy of W. V. Quine*:

> Gibson cites Føllesdal's interesting observation that the indeterminacy of translation follows from holism and the verification theory of meaning. Føllesdal mistrusts this defense because of doubts about verificationism, and I gather that Gibson agrees. But I find it attractive. The statement of verificationism relevant to this purpose is that "evidence for the truth of a sentence is identical with the meaning of the sentence"; and I submit that if sentences in general had meanings, their meanings would be just that. It is only holism itself that tells us that in general they do not have them. (Quine 1987, 155–56)

Holism precludes the assigning of meaning to individual sentences other than observation sentences and observation categoricals. As a result, translation is obviously indeterminate, for there will be multiple ways of translating sentences other than these special cases—and all of them will yield equally plausible though nonequivalent bodies of theory to be attributed to the native speakers of the language in question.[10]

Why is the strong indeterminacy of translation thesis controversial and troubling? Suppose two field linguists have been studying a new language for a number of years, and that they have developed two nonequivalent manuals of translation. Suppose also that the population whose language this is has theories of genetics, the sophistication of which are on a par with ours. Suppose that the nonequivalent translation manuals that these linguists have developed yield nonequivalent translations of these theories of genetics. Suppose also that the two field linguists (and their research teams, who have all gone bilingual) assure us that the genetic theories in question seems as good as ours—as sophisticated, as predictive of future experience, and as well integrated into the broader science of this population as our genetics is into our science.

If Quine is right, the alternative translations of this theory of genetics will constitute, in English, two different and *inconsistent* theories of genetics. The linguists will grant that both cannot be accurate translations of the theories in question. We will see that both cannot be true. And the population being studied, who we may presume have had their field linguists studying us, will produce multiple translation manuals for English to their language, with similar discrepancies. Overall, these manuals may well be equally acceptable. *And there is no fact of the matter concerning which manual is correct.*

Finally, we might as well picture ourselves as becoming field linguists studying ourselves, and developing alternative translation manuals for English to English while being bound only by the requirement of preserving stimulus meaning and the canons of holism. We will develop distinct manuals of English to English translation, and they will attribute to us distinct, nonequivalent, theories. This is the strong indeterminacy of translation brought home (see, e.g., Quine 1990a, 50).

Thus, the only apparent way of resolving the indeterminacy, by accepting one translation manual and rejecting all alternatives, has more arbitrariness about it than does accepting one's native tongue at face value, or so it seems. Strong indeterminacy holds that we could revise *any* significantly sized body of theory, throwing out some sentences and compensating for those by adding others, and end up with a theory that, on holistic grounds, is as good as the first.

Again, the implications of this thesis for notions of "meanings" and realism are profound, and both the thesis and its implications seem to us worthy of more exploration in feminist theory. As we outline below, the thesis also constitutes part of Quine's argument for naturalizing the philosophy of science. Before turning to these arguments, we summarize Quine's underdetermination thesis.

We have noted that feminists appealed to Quine's underdetermination thesis in the 1980s in their efforts to explain the issues raised in and by feminist science critiques. Some contributors to this volume do so as well. Although many, including Quine, view the thesis as relatively straightforward (whether they accept it or not) and distinct from the strong indeterminacy thesis just discussed (see, e.g., Quine 1990b), we are no longer sure.[11] Accordingly, we simply outline the grounds for the underdetermination thesis as Quine explicates them.

Quine takes theories to be underdetermined in at least three ways in addition to, or as elaborations of, general Humean underdetermination. Sensory experience underdetermines the theory of physical objects, macro, micro, and atomic and subatomic, in the sense that there may be (and presumably are) alternative posits that would connect past sensory experience with future sensory experience equally well. This is true, but esoteric. Given our actual scientific heritage we are unlikely to abandon our ontology of physical objects for one of events or numbers or whatever else. Second, even given our choice of physical objects as the primary constituents of the bridge science affords between past sense experiences and future sense experiences, the details of the bridge are underdetermined by experience. We can redistribute truth-values at will (perversely), or in response to a recalcitrant experience, while retaining our overall commitment, more or less, to the familiar physical objects and to the bulk of the sentences of our present theories. Finally, Quine's reconstructed notion of sense experience, be it as the firings of sensory receptors or the triggerings of exteroceptors, is *itself* a theoretical construct derived from our best going theories, of anatomy, physiology, neurology, and some branches of psychology. This theory of sense experience is itself, like all theories, underdetermined by available evidence (in the above senses). So we could, and future discoveries may lead us to, alter it; and thereby set the stage for a different science connecting, in different ways, our new versions of past sense experiences with our new versions of future sense experiences (see, e.g., Quine 1953, 1960, 1981c; see also Roth, Chapter 7 this volume).

As we noted earlier, we suspect there is more to underdetermination (specifically, more of a relationship with the strong thesis of indeterminacy), but what we have said is perhaps sufficient background for the essays included here. We conclude this section by relating the arguments so far summarized to those Quine offers for naturalizing the philosophy of science.

Quine's suggestion that traditional philosophy of science be abandoned in favor of self-conscious science, for a "reciprocal containment of science and epistemology," follows closely on the heels of his recognition that the project Carnap undertook in the *Aufbau* cannot be completed. It also reflects his doubts as early as 1936 that sentences of logic and mathematics are true by definition (Quine 1936). Both figure in the arguments of "Epistemology Naturalized" (Quine 1969a). In addition, Quine's rejection of the analytic/synthetic distinction makes the alleged nonempirical status of the philosophy of science or epistemology a nonstarter.

The opening pages of "Epistemology Naturalized" locate the sources of Quine's arguments for naturalizing the philosophy of science in the failure in the first half of the twentieth century to fulfill Hume's mandate of showing that every truth can be accounted for either on the grounds of meanings (for logic and mathematics) or on the grounds of sensory experience (for empirical truths). Quine's focus in this essay is, of course, the second project; but he begins by discussing the first. This enables him to later draw parallels between the failure of the first project (generally recognized by the time he published "Epistemology Naturalized") and the failure he sees as inevitable (but not yet generally recognized) for the second. Commentators too often ignore these opening pages (but see Roth, Chapter 7 this volume).

Quine notes that there were two focuses in studies into the foundations of mathematics. "Conceptual studies" were to show that the concepts of mathematics can be defined in the terms of logic. "Doctrinal studies" were to show that mathematical truths can be derived from the "obvious or at least potentially obvious . . . truths of logic" (1969a, 70). Obviously, the two projects are linked. If mathematical concepts are definable in the terms of logic, then the truths of mathematics are, in the end, truths of logic. If the latter are self evident, so are the former.

The project failed, on both the conceptual and doctrinal sides, Quine notes, because it turned out that mathematics does not reduce to "logic proper," but only to set theory (70). This was a deep disappointment for two reasons. "The end truths, the axioms of set theory . . . have less obviousness and certainty to recommend them than do most of the mathematical theorems we would derive from them. Moreover, we know from Gödel's work that no consistent axiom system can cover mathematics even when we renounce self-evidence" (70). Thus, the reduction of mathematics to set theory does not "reveal the ground of mathematical knowledge," does not "show how mathematical certainty is possible" (70).

Against this background, Quine turns to efforts to identify the foundations of (recognizably) empirical science.[12] Here, too, there is a conceptual project and a doctrinal project. The conceptual project, dating back to Hume, is to define sentences about physical bodies in terms of something directly linked to (or identical with) sensory experience. In this project, Quine sees progress. For Hume, bodies were to be identified with bundles of sense impressions, an approach Quine describes as "bold and simple" (73). The subsequent shift from impressions to sentences as the bearers of empirical meaning shifted the focus of the conceptual project. The goal was now to show that sentences about bodies derive from, or reduce to, sentences about immediate sensory experience.

But again it turned out that set theory was needed. And, as in the study of the foundations of mathematics, set theory compromised the conceptual project. Comparing the recourse to set theory with that of recognizing sentences as the bearers of meaning, Quine notes that "[t]he two resorts are very unequal in epistemological status. Contextual definition is unassailable. Sentences that have been given meaning as wholes are undeniably meaningful, and the use they make of their component terms is therefore meaningful, regardless of whether any translations are offered for those terms in isolation. . . . Recourse to sets, on the other hand, is a drastic ontological move, a retreat from the austere ontology of impressions" (73).

Quine's earlier discussion of studies into the foundations of mathematics is now brought to bear. The reason that recourse to set theory in studies of the foundations of empirical science was not generally recognized as a retreat from empiricism, Quine argues, is precisely because of the "deceptive hints of continuity between elementary logic and set theory" (73). These hints led Russell to be willing to define the conceptual project as that of accounting "for the external world as a logical construct of sense data," a project that Quine credits Carnap's *Aufbau* with coming "nearest to executing" (74). Even if Carnap's project had been successful, it would not have aided the *doctrinal* project. To show that the sentences of science can be so reconstructed does not show that these sentences "can be *proved* from observation sentences by logic and set theory" (74). "On the doctrinal side," Quine notes, "I do not see that we are farther along today than where Hume left us" (72).

Yet, Quine acknowledges, there were reasons to continue with the conceptual project, even in light of the failure of the doctrinal project and the retreat that recourse to set theory represented. One could still hope that the rational reconstruction of a sense datum language would "elicit" and "clarify" the sensory evidence for science, even if the steps between such evidence and scientific theories "fall short of certainty" (75). The reconstruction would contribute to understandings of how "all inculcation of meanings of words must rest ultimately on sensory evidence," for had Carnap or others succeeded, "the sensory content of discourse would stand forth explicitly" (75). It was not even necessary for Carnap to be able to demonstrate that the construction he arrived at was "the right one." "The question would have had no point. He was seeking what he called a *rational reconstruction*. Any construction of physicalistic discourse in terms of sense experience, logic, and set theory would have been as satisfactory if it made the physicalistic discourse come out right. If there is one way there are many, but any would be a great achievement" (75). But, for reasons earlier considered, Carnap did not succeed and Quine proposed holism as a countersuggestion to verificationism. With that proposal the stage is set for Quine's suggestion in "Epistemology Naturalized" that the conceptual project be abandoned altogether. "But why all this creative reconstruction, all this make-believe? The stimulation of his sensory receptors is all the evidence anybody has to go on, ultimately, in arriving at his picture of the world. Why not just see how this construction really proceeds? Why not settle for psychology?" (75). The turn to psychology (and Quine himself also appeals to linguistics and evolutionary theory in exploring questions traditionally of interest to the philosophy of science and epistemology) does represent a "surrender of the epistemological burden" to science; but this is appropriate given the abandonment of the doctrinal project.

> If the epistemologist's goal is validation of the grounds of empirical science, he defeats his purpose by using empirical science in the validation. However, such scruples against circularity have little point once we have stopped dreaming of deducing science from observations. If we are out simply to understand the link between observation and science, we are well advised to use any available information, including that provided by the very science whose link with observation we are seeking to understand. (75–76)

Suppose, however, that we lower our sights on the conceptual side, seeking only to show that sentences of science can be *translated* into sentences involving sense data, logic, and set theory. If possible, such a translation would further the Humean project by demonstrating "the essential innocence of physical concepts," showing them to be "theoretically superfluous." In so doing, "it would legitimize them—to whatever degree the concepts of set theory, logic, and observations are themselves legitimate" by demonstrating that "everything done with the one apparatus could in principle be done with the other" (76). The project might also retain a role for philosophy. "If psychology itself could deliver a truly translational reduction of this kind, we should welcome it; but certainly it cannot, for certainly we did not grow up learning definitions of physicalistic language in terms of a prior language of set theory, logic, and observation" (76). The problem, Quine notes, is that Carnap's project did not succeed *even in terms of translation*. The point at which it becomes clear that Carnap's translation will not succeed, Quine argues, "comes where Carnap is explaining how to assign sense qualities in physical space and time" (76). In "Two Dogmas," as we have seen, Quine argues that Carnap is unable to show how to translate a "statement of the form 'Quality *q* is at *x;y;z;t*' [a point instant] . . . into [his] initial language of sense data and logic" (40). Thus, Carnap is forced in subsequent writings to settle for "reduction forms," something far less than straightforward translation.

This is a far cry from the outcome that translation "of the sterner kind" would have generated. To give up the project of defining, via translation, physical concepts in terms of observation, logic, and set theory, is to give up "the last remaining advantage that we supposed rational reconstruction to have over straight psychology: namely, the advantage of translational reduction" (78).

As he did in "Two Dogmas," Quine suggests in "Epistemology Naturalized" that the source of the failure of the various projects just summarized is that most sentences do not have their own empirical meaning. The problem is not that "the experiential implications of a typical statement about bodies are too complex for finite axiomatization, however lengthy, but that the typical statement about bodies has no fund of experiential implications it can call its own" (79). Thus, if we persist in translation projects, we will need to focus on the "significantly inclusive portion" of a theory that has empirical meaning, axiomatizing "all the experiential difference that the truth of the theory would make" (79). This, Quine suggests, would be a "queer translation" because it would involve translating "the whole but none of its parts" and, indeed, perhaps 'translation' is not even the correct description. What we will have, in the end, might better be termed the "observational evidence for theories," their empirical meaning (79–80).

But we would do still better to give up translation projects altogether. This is because the indeterminacy of translation plagues "even ordinary unphilosophical translation, such as from English into . . . Chinese." Here, Quine repeats the argument earlier outlined, that "we can justify [the translation of sentences of English] into Chinese [or Japanese] only together as a body"—that there will be translations that will preserve the empirical implications of the theory we are translating (the observation sentences and observation categoricals it implies), and thus, there will be no grounds for saying one is correct. That is, if holism holds, indeterminacy of translation follows for everything but observation sentences and their kin. "If we recognize with Peirce that the meaning of a sentence turns purely on what would count as evidence for its truth, and if we recognize with Duhem that theoretical sentences have their evidence not as single sentences but only as larger blocks of theory, then the indeterminacy of translation of theoretical sentences follows. And most sentences, apart from observation sentences, are theoretical" (81).

In the end, then, holism and the indeterminacy of translation that it yields dictate the abandonment of the various conceptual projects to identify a foundation for science in sense data. In contrast to those who see "the irreducibility" involved as "the bankruptcy of epistemology," Quine suggests, "it may be more useful to say rather that epistemology still goes on, though in a new setting and a clarified status." Epistemology, "or something like it, simply falls into place as a chapter of psychology and hence of natural science" (82).

A question much debated since the publication of "Epistemology Naturalized" is whether the philosophy of science as Quine envisions it does or could carry normative import or force. As the summary of individual chapters to which we next turn indicates, there are deep disagreements, even among those who support Quine's arguments for naturalism, and certainly among those who are skeptical about Quinean naturalism, in terms of its answer. We would only briefly note that Quine's work subsequent to "Epistemology Naturalized" does suggest a normative role for naturalized philosophy of science, albeit not of the sort or to the degree that critics of his vision of naturalism believe are possible and necessary.

For example, the topics of Quine's "Natural Kinds" are two hallmarks of human reasoning—"our sorting of things into kinds" and induction—the relationship between things, and what explains them (Quine 1969d). Each, Quine argues, is a problem. On the one hand, it is an implication of research in psychology and linguistics that there is "nothing more basic to thought and language than our sense of similarity, our sorting of things into kinds" (160). Sorting by resemblance—in terms both "of a resemblance between the present circumstances and past circumstances" in which a word is used, and in terms of phonetic resemblance—is necessary to language learning. Moreover, induction itself depends on such sorting and "our tendency to expect similar causes to have similar effects" (116–17). On the other hand, "the notion of similarity or kind," so basic to human thinking and induction, "is alien to logic and set theory" (121) and "characteristically animal in its lack of intellectual status" (123). Moreover, "the relation between similarity and kind is less clear and neat than could be wished" (121).

Having spent considerable time in the essay to establish these several points, Quine's question is this: "For me . . . the problem of induction is a problem about the world; a problem of how we, as we now are (by our present scientific lights), in a world we never made, should stand better than random or coin-tossing chances of coming out right, when we predict by inductions which are based on our innate, scientifically unjustified similarity standard" (127). In brief, the answer Quine poses to this question notes first that natural selection might explain inductive reasoning and sorting by kind; both might be adaptations. At the same time, Quine argues, it is also a result of science that the first is fallible and the second is indefensible (i.e., undermined by our most serious theories). In the end, then, what makes natural selection "perhaps enough of an explanation" is that it can explain induction's "conspicuous failures" (127). Sorting by color seems endemic to the species and explicable in terms of its survival value (for example, it is useful for food-gathering). At the same time, our most serious theories of nature suggest that colors do "not qualify as kinds" and that the "distinctions that matter for basic physical theory are mostly independent of color contrasts" (127).

This sets the stage for the second part of Quine's answer to the question he has posed. Quine maintains that science both reveals innate similarity space and dispositions to induction, and possibly explains them using natural selection. At the same time, analyses of science's development and success, of the sort Quine here engages in, suggest that "things about [our] innate similarity sense that are helpful in one sphere [e.g., color to food gathering] can be a hindrance in the other [the search by science for 'more significant regularities']" (128). As a result, Quine suggests that

> Evidently natural selection has dealt with the conflict by endowing man doubly: with both a color-slanted quality space and the ingenuity to rise above it.
>
> He has risen above it by developing modified systems of kinds, hence modified similarity standards for scientific purposes. By the trial-and-error process of theorizing he has regrouped things into new kinds which prove to lend themselves to many inductions better than the old. (128)

This suggests that naturalized epistemology as Quine engages in it is an explanatory and a normative enterprise. "The career of the similarity notion," Quine maintains, "is a paradigm of the evolution of unreason into science" (138). This is a normative assessment, an evaluation of both common-sense theorizing and scientific theorizing. It draws on knowledge provided by the sciences and simultaneously assesses scientific theorizing on the basis of that very same knowledge. And this, we suggest, is holism at work and naturalism illustrated.

II. Feminist Interpretations of Quine

We noted at the outset of this introduction that analyses in the 1980s of Quine's positions offered by Linda Martín Alcoff, Helen E. Longino, and Elizabeth Potter constituted important contributions to feminist philosophy of science and epistemology.

The essays by Lynn Hankinson Nelson and Louise Antony (Chapters 1 and 2), published respectively in 1990 and 1994, were among the first to undertake more extensive explorations of Quine's positions in light of feminist scholarship. Antony and Nelson are concerned to analyze the implications of Quine's positions for feminist theorizing about science and vice versa. They are also concerned to defend the usefulness of Quine's positions to feminist science studies against feminist critiques of empiricism and "modern epistemology" offered in the 1980s.

Representative critiques were offered in essays by Jane Flax, Sandra Harding, and Nancy Harstock in Harding and Merrill Hintikka's ground breaking collection, *Discovering Reality* (1983); in Hilary Rose's "Hand, Brain, and Heart: A Feminist Epistemology for the Natural Sciences" (*Signs* 9, 1, 1983); and in Alison Jaggar's *Feminist Politics and Human Nature* (1983). Common to these analyses are arguments to the conclusion that empiricism is an inherently flawed doctrine—a doctrine that underwrites or propounds views of knowers, of evidence, and of science that are erroneous, that are incapable of accommodating the emergence and results of feminist science scholarship, and that function to insulate science from critical scrutiny. But, as earlier noted, Sandra Harding offered the most sustained and influential critique of empiricism in *The Science Question in Feminism* (Harding 1986).

Harding identified three general epistemological frameworks available to and drawn upon by feminist scientists and science scholars: feminist empiricism, feminist standpoint theory, and feminist postmodernism. Describing each framework as a hybrid that combined or attempted to combine feminists' questions, concerns, and findings, on the one hand, with those of an older, nonfeminist tradition, on the other, Harding explored how their advocates found themselves having to wrestle with a "parent" tradition not designed to accommodate or explain the issues emerging in feminist science critiques and scholarship.

Harding insisted on the contingency of her analysis, maintaining that each framework is unstable and would evolve in response to its own internal tensions, developments in the other two frameworks, and future developments in feminist science studies (cf. Harding 1994; Rooney, Chapter 5 this volume). She also maintained that each is best thought of as a "tool," useful or not depending on the specific domain being engaged. For example, Harding viewed feminist empiricism as the most useful tool when feminists were attempting to engage scientists—this because, in her account, feminist empiricism does not challenge traditional empiricist norms (25; but see Campbell, Chapter 9 this volume). Notwithstanding these qualifications, it is an implication of Harding's arguments that feminist empiricism is the least promising of these approaches, if in fact it is coherent. According to Harding, the problems at issue were within empiricism itself. "Empiricist conceptions of scientific method," she maintained, "create obstacles *for* and *in* feminist thinking about science" (36; italics in original).

In brief, Harding argued that the Marxist and postmodernist traditions in epistemology trace their roots to "emancipatory" projects. In contrast, she argued, empiricism is an inherently conservative tradition, committed to the view "that scientific method is sufficient to account for historical increases in the objectivity of the picture of the world that science presents," and rules out any relevance of movements of social liberation in fostering advances in knowledge (25–26).[13] Although Harding took Quine's challenges to the analytic/synthetic distinction as an advance, she attributed several other "dogmas" to twentieth-century empiricists, including Quine, that would make it difficult to construct a viable explanation of the emergence of feminist science scholarship. Finally, Harding maintained that epistemologies are as much *justificatory* as they are explanatory, and that these same dogmas would preclude justification of feminists' claims within and about the sciences.

The dogmas Harding attributed to empiricism include the distinction between the contexts of discovery and justification (25); the tenet that "the social identify of the inquirer is . . . irrelevant to the 'goodness' of the results of research," an assumption Harding linked to the context/discovery distinction as well as to the empiricist thesis that sensory evidence is the source and check point of knowledge (25); and the "sacred science dogma," which Harding described as the principle that "human understanding is decreased rather than increased by attempting to account for the nature and structure of scientific activity in the ways science recommends accounting for all other social activity" (38).

If feminist empiricism is necessarily committed to these dogmas, as Harding then assumed (i.e., if a framework *not* so committed is not *empiricist*),[14] some significant problems immediately arise. As she noted, these dogmas would require feminist empiricists to assume that bias of any sort, and surely political bias, is inherently compromising. But this would make it difficult to explain the emergence and findings of feminist science critique, which are obviously motivated and informed by feminist politics (i.e., bias), and difficult to explain how or why feminist perspectives are *more objective* than those they criticize. In addition, feminist empiricists would need to assume that the problems feminists identified in scientific research—for example, androcentrism—represent failures on the part of scientists to *adhere* to empiricist norms and methods, not flaws in the *norms or methods* themselves. Harding's characterization of feminist empiricism reflects both assumptions: "*Feminist empiricism* argues that sexism and androcentrism are social biases correctable by stricter adherence to the existing methodological norms of scientific inquiry . . . [and that] the women's movement produces not only the opportunity for . . . an enlarged perspective but more women scientists, and they are more likely than men to notice androcentric bias" (25, italics in original). We must note, Harding argued, the contradictions internal to such explanations. To explain feminist science studies on the basis of the women's movement or women's alleged abilities to more readily recognize androcentrism is in direct conflict with the empiricist assumption that "the social identity of the inquirer is irrelevant to the 'goodness' of the results of research" (25). Thus, Harding concluded, feminist empiricists will be unable to offer plausible explanations of the emergence and findings of feminist scholarship—or, if they do so, the explanations will "deeply subvert empiricism" by exposing the "empirical inadequacies in empiricist epistemologies" (25–26).

Part I: Early Feminist Analyses of Quine

Although we later identify what we take to be very significant differences in the details and general conclusions of Antony's and Nelson's arguments, we begin by noting some parallels. Both argue that the characterizations of empiricism with which critics such as Harding were working in the 1980s are outdated, and use Quine's positions to support this claim. Neither sees Quine as committed to the dogmas Harding attributes to empiricism; rather, each maintains that Quine fundamentally and successfully challenged these dogmas. Both offer arguments (but quite different ones) that Quinean naturalism and holism are compatible with and promising for feminist theorizing. This is not to say that Antony and Nelson take

Quine to be everywhere right. Each criticizes aspects of his work, albeit different aspects of it.

In "Who Knows: From Quine to Feminist Empiricism" (Chapter 1), Nelson frames her discussion of the implications of Quinean positions and feminist science studies for one another in terms of issues she takes to be central to Harding's critique of empiricism and to those other feminists offered. In one line of argument, she seeks to distinguish empiricism as *a theory of evidence* from empiricist theories of science *built from this theory*, such as those developed in logical positivism and postlogical positivism. In a second, Nelson argues that several of Quine's positions represent significant advances over positions maintained not only by the Carnap/Hempel/Nagel tradition but also by Kuhn, and that there are important parallels between Quine's positions and those suggested by the emergence and findings of feminist science studies. In particular, Nelson maintains, Quinean holism and naturalism call for empirically based studies of science and for explanations commensurate with actual scientific practice rather than "rational reconstructions" of it—precisely what research in feminist science studies indicates are needed. Nelson also maintains that naturalism and holism constitute viable and promising alternatives to two assumptions implicit in Harding's characterization of empiricism and feminist empiricism: that there is a need for a philosophy of science that can *justify* feminist claims, and that there is an epistemological chasm between feminists and their nonfeminist colleagues that cannot be bridged by evidence.

Among those of Quine's positions on which Nelson focuses are his arguments concerning the relationships between metaphysics and science, so-called common sense and science, and science and the philosophy of science (or epistemology). Each, she argues, can serve as an important resource for feminists; at the same time, each needs to be expanded or revised in light of the emergence and results of feminist science studies. For example, Nelson takes Quine's arguments that scientific theorizing and theories are interdependent with those of common sense to represent an important advance over views that portray science as uninformed by common-sense beliefs (but see J. Nelson, Chapter 8). She also argues that this feature of Quine's holism can serve as a model of evidential relationships that might explain the presence of androcentrism in scientific research, and the ability of feminist scientists to recognize it. In her view, holism also makes an unbridgeable chasm between feminists and nonfeminists implausible; there are many theories about which these groups will agree and these can be appealed to in attempting to adjudicate their differences.

But Nelson also maintains that Quine's account of "common-sense theory" is ahistoric and artificially limited, virtually exhausted as it is by what Quine calls "physical object theory." One obvious implication of feminist science scholarship, she argues, is that many kinds of "common-sense" beliefs inform scientific research; another is that so-called common-sense beliefs are no less dynamic than scientific hypotheses and theories. In a related line of argument, Nelson argues that the boundary Quine maintains between good science and (nonepistemic) values is no more real than the other traditional boundaries he challenges.

In her conclusion, Nelson supports Quine's argument for naturalizing the philosophy of science and argues for its relevance to feminist philosophy of science. Responding to Harding's arguments, she maintains that although Quinean naturalism is *not* justificatory, it is *normative;* it represents the abandonment of the traditional project to justify science—an abandonment she takes Quine to show is unavoidable (see also Roth, Chapter 7). But Nelson also argues that the individualism implicit in Quine's vision of naturalized epistemology is in fact undermined by his arguments against foundationalism and for holism. She maintains that these arguments, and research in developmental psychology, indicate that genuinely naturalizing epistemology requires abandoning individualism and taking communities or groups as the primary epistemic agents. She seeks to develop this project for the philosophy of science in "Feminist Naturalized Philosophy of Science" (Chapter 11).

At the outset of "Quine as Feminist: The Radical Import of Naturalized Epistemology" (Chapter 2), Louise Antony notes that she finds it "both unfortunate and ironic" that feminists interested in the philosophy of science and epistemology have "uniformly neglected" Quine's work and, for this and other reasons, have concluded that analytic epistemology is irrelevant at best to feminist science studies.[15] In her larger discussion, Antony offers several arguments for why feminists should draw on the resources of analytic epistemology, and seeks to illuminate what she takes to be "confusions" and "distortions" in feminist critiques of analytic epistemology. In particular, Antony maintains that contemporary naturalized epistemology—both as it conforms to what Quine envisioned and as it has moved beyond problematic aspects of Quine's work—provides the necessary and sufficient resources for justifying feminist claims.

Antony uses the question "How is bias properly conceptualized?," which figured prominently in Harding's analysis of feminist epistemologies, to frame these arguments. The question is a pressing one for feminists, Antony maintains, because exposing androcentric assumptions and other forms of bias is a central goal of feminist science scholarship—at the same time that feminists express skepticism about the possibility or desirability of *impartial* perspectives. Antony notes that, taken together, these features of feminist theorizing about science raise an important question: "Put baldly, if we don't think it's good to be *im*partial, then how can we object to men's being *partial*?"

Whether impartiality is possible, Antony argues, is an empirical question, an answer to which will need to rely on evidence supplied by empirical psychology and the cognitive sciences. But what can be said of analytic epistemology subsequent to the turn to naturalism is that work undertaken in it demonstrates that *partiality* or *bias* (of at least some sorts) conveys an "*epistemic advantage*." Citing Quine, Nelson Goodman, Hempel, Hilary Putnam, and Richard Boyd, Antony maintains that not only have they and others demonstrated that bias cannot be eliminated, they also demonstrate the "*positive value* of certain forms of it." And although Antony argues that the vindication of rationalism demonstrates the failings of Quine's behaviorism and his "theory of mind," she sees Quine's general argument for naturalism as important. It was the turn to naturalism, she contends, that allowed for questions within analytic epistemology concerning the plausibility of value-neutrality, and led to the view that such neutrality is "not sound epistemic policy." Antony argues that these developments in turn demonstrate that naturalized epistemology authorizes precisely the kind of critical assessment of epistemic norms that feminists call for.

This is not to say, Antony maintains, that analytic epistemology has answered all the questions that a proper conceptualization of bias needs to address. Epistemologists, including feminists, still need to address the question "*How do we tell the good bias from the bad bias?*" According to Antony, this project further illuminates the costs feminists incur when they reject analytic epistemology. For, she argues, we cannot expect an answer to this question to be provided solely through the empirical investigations into the processes through which knowledge is generated that feminists advocate. The question calls for a *normative* answer, and any such answer is impossible for an approach "that eschews the notion of *truth*—for any theory that tries to steer some kind of middle course between absolutism and relativism." Antony describes feminist standpoint theories and postmodernism as such approaches, and maintains that it is because the notion of truth remains central to the analytic tradition, including naturalized epistemology, that the tradition can maintain an "appropriately realist" conception of truth able to make sense of the distinction between "the world as we see it" and "the world as it is."

Thus, realist conceptions of truth make it possible to identify bias that is conducive to truth-seeking as "good," and bias that "impedes" truth seeking as "bad." Feminists, Antony argues, must be willing to talk about truth and falsity when critiquing epistemic ideals or particular theories that are sexist, racist, or in some other respect wrongheaded. Finally, Antony argues that the notion of truth is appropriately brought to bear on *epistemologies*—that what warrants acceptance of a feminist or any other epistemology is the belief that it is *likely to be true*. Here too, Antony maintains, naturalized epistemology has the advantage. It is likely to be able to "explain the facts" (including the "central" fact of "the long-ignored experiences and wisdom of women") and thus likely to be true.

Although Antony seems to dismiss feminist standpoint theory rather precipitously, particularly in light of her own arguments concerning the positive role of bias, we take her arguments concerning the recognition of the positive role of bias and other developments in analytic epistemology as making a strong case that more inclusive approaches in feminist theorizing about science and knowledge—in which the resources of analytic epistemology are seriously considered and evaluated—could contribute to feminist philosophy of science.

We earlier noted parallels between Antony's and Nelson's views concerning the relevance of Quine's naturalism and holism to feminist theorizing about science. We next note what we take to be fairly fundamental differences in their positions. Perhaps the most obvious is that Nelson holds that there is work done and remaining to be done by the *feminist* of 'feminist philosophy of science' and 'feminist epistemology,' i.e., that feminist science studies contribute unique insights into the nature of the sciences that have not in fact been embraced in analytic epistemology. In contrast, Antony sees the resources of analytic epistemology as not only important for feminist theorizing about science in the ways earlier outlined, but sufficient. There is, in her view, no need for distinctively feminist theories of science or knowledge. In addition, and we suspect related to the next difference we discuss, Antony takes naturalized epistemology to be a *theory* (and likely a true theory); Nelson views naturalism as a methodological approach to which the notions of 'true' or 'false' do not apply.

There is another difference that is a good deal "thicker," and we later suggest that it recurs in a number of essays in this volume. Antony argues that feminist philosophers' neglect and misunderstandings of analytic epistemology, including Quinean naturalized epistemology, have resulted in the perception that there is a need for distinctively feminist epistemologies (such as feminist standpoint theories) and in feminist interest in postmodernist approaches to science and knowledge. According to Antony, the resources of analytic epistemology—in particular its robust notions of truth and realism—are *necessary* to the defense and justification of feminist claims about science. In contrast, Nelson does not view Quine as an analytic philosopher (nor, arguably, did Quine, who has described his philosophy as "post-analytic").[16] We suggest that this disagreements is far more than a semantic quibble.

We noted in our summary of her chapter that Antony disavows Quine's behaviorism and what she calls his "theory of mind." We believe that it is these disavowals that enable her to both champion some of Quine's positions and not accept the full implications of Quinean holism, including the indeterminacy of translation.[17] If Quine's arguments for these theses are successful (and Antony does accept Quine's arguments for holism, from which we argue the strong thesis of indeterminacy follows), the notion of "meanings" as stable entities, the notion of "truth" as more than "immanent" (more than a predicate of a metalanguage attributable to sentences of an object language, as Tarski defined it), and a version of "realism" as robust as that advocated by "scientific realism," are nonstarters. Nelson assumes Quine's arguments to these several conclusions are successful. Antony, so it seems, does not. Similarly, Antony maintains that no epistemology that attempts to carve out a middle ground between "absolutism and relativism" can succeed. Nelson takes Quine to have developed just such an approach (as do a number of other contributors). Accordingly, their accounts of the resources Quine's positions afford feminist theorizing are significantly different.

Part II: Is Quinean "Naturalized Philosophy of Science" Philosophy of Science Enough?

We bring together the essays by Maureen Linker, Lorraine Code, Phyllis Rooney, and Kathryn Pyne Addelson because each is, to a significant degree, critical of Quine's vision of naturalized epistemology. In apparent contrast, the essays in Part III are generally supportive of the turn to naturalized philosophy of science that Quine envisions and maintain its usefulness, together with others of Quine's positions, for feminist theorizing.

But the contrast between the two sections is not as neat or straightforward as our organization of these sections suggests. Briefly put, Code offers a constructive alternative version of naturalism, Rooney seeks to demonstrate that those who describe themselves as naturalized epistemologists are not in fact engaged in the kind of research Quine called for or they say they ought to undertake, and Addelson seeks to develop Quine's vision of naturalized philosophy of science so that it actually reflects the pragmatism she attributes to him. Linker's chapter, although also constructive, argues for a "feminist rationalized epistemology" as an alternative to naturalized epistemology. Conversely, although generally supportive of Quine, most essays in Part III seek to extend or revise one or more of Quine's positions in light of feminist science studies. (The exceptions are Roth, Chapter 7 and Duran, Chapter 10.) Thus, what divides most essays in the two sections is not whether naturalism itself is viable, but whether Quinean naturalism (at least in its present form and as individual authors understand it) is viable for feminist theorizing.

There are other themes common to the essays in Part II. One is that the philosophy of science and/or epistemology, and certainly feminist research in these fields, must enjoy a healthy autonomy from the sciences if they are to yield the kind of critical, and not simply affirmative, stance toward the sciences that is called for. (The degree of autonomy the authors advocate differs.) Another is that Quinean naturalism does not seek such autonomy and, at least as some authors understand it, may be incapable of it.

In "The Case for a Responsibly Rationalized Feminist Epistemology" (Chapter 3), Maureen Linker argues that aspects of Quinean naturalism make it straightforwardly unsuitable for feminist theorizing about knowledge and science. Linker maintains that naturalized epistemology and holism of the sort Quine advocated and L. H. Nelson supports in Chapter 1 fail to allow for even "minimally satisfying" conceptions of meaning and truth—and certainly not conceptions able to underwrite the normative force of feminist claims. Linker advocates the development of a "rationalized feminist epistemology" as an alternative to naturalism on the grounds that it will allow for realist conceptions of meaning and truth sufficiently robust to justify the normative principles that motivate the empirical correctives feminists advocate.

Linker's main arguments—against the appropriateness of Quine's positions for feminist epistemology and in support of a rationalized feminist epistemology—are connected in her analysis through her sustained critique of Quine's arguments against the analytic/synthetic distinction and "meanings." She maintains that a core assumption of these arguments and of Quine's thesis of the indeterminacy of translation is that substitution criteria define the identity criteria for meanings. This assumption, she argues, is unwarranted, here building from arguments offered by J. J. Katz and from research in linguistics. Linker also maintains that a realist theory of meanings along the lines that Katz advocates—a theory that posits a realm of mind-independent sentences, senses, and sense relations—has significant advantages over Quine's denial of meanings. Among others, such a theory is able to explain data from linguistics that any viable theory of meaning *must* be able to explain and Quine's account cannot. These include the "infinite expressibility of the syntactic and semantic components of language," "literal meaning," and "the relationship of literal meaning to pragmatic meaning contexts." Moreover, Linker argues, the mind-independent objects that figure in Katz's realist theory of meanings constitute an objective source of language use and an objective constraint on it.

Linker uses several arguments to explicate the notion of a feminist rationalized epistemology. She argues that because Quine's arguments against the analytic/synthetic distinction are unsuccessful, so too are his challenges to "a priori truth" and to a distinction between science and the philosophy of science/epistemology. Thus, both remain available to the would-be rationalist. Second, Linker maintains that "a priori truth" allows for the objectivity of values and normative claims, and yields far more robust criteria for the assessment of claims and theories than those to which Quinean holism would limit us (coherence with sensory experience and with accepted theories). This is important, she maintains, because the "empirical correctives" feminists advocate in their analyses of science are *not identical with* the moral and political correctives that motivate their empirical investigations and recommendations. And neither Quinean naturalism nor feminist naturalism of the sort L. H. Nelson advocates can provide the grounds on which these moral and political principles can be defended. The justification of principles of "reason and fairness" requires a correspondence theory of moral and logical truth—something disallowed by naturalism but embraced by rationalism. Thus, a rationalist epistemology is better able to provide the grounds on which to defend feminists' normative claims—e.g., that "the exclusion and oppression of persons by institutions of knowledge and power is both morally wrong and at odds with the goal of truth production."

Lorraine Code begins "What Is Natural about Epistemology Naturalized?" (Chapter 4) by drawing a distinction between, on the one hand, naturalistic approaches to processes and institutions that generate knowledge that are likely to produce "potentially transformative consequences" (such as Foucault's) and, on the other, "the North American version of naturalism" that traces its roots to Quine's arguments. Code attributes three general features to Quinean naturalized epistemology that "thwart . . . [its] transformative possibilities." These include its "veneration of physical science" and its assumption that science is the only knowledge-producing institution "worthy of analysis"; its reliance on scientific psychology and cognitive science, which in turn precludes critical evaluation of these disciplines and "begs the question" concerning their epistemic status; and its problematic representations of physical and human nature. Code maintains that although there are "rich possibilities" for "a well-conceived naturalism" (i.e., a naturalism that responds to postmodern, postcolonial, and postpatriarchal critiques), Quinean naturalism is not well conceived in these senses. The first sections of Code's chapter are devoted to a critique of naturalized epistemology as Quine proposed it. In the last section, she argues for an alternative version of naturalism, which she maintains is more in keeping with the results of feminist scholarship and avoids many of the problems she attributes to Quinean naturalism.

Code sees research undertaken by Hilary Kornblith and others who look to empirical psychology for knowledge about "humans as cognizers" as representing precisely the sort Quine envisioned, and maintains that it suffers from some significant problems. For one thing, she contends, the scientism that informs both psychology and naturalized epistemology excludes many kinds of knowledge and subjects. Folk psychology and "the practices and wisdoms of extra-scientific, nonmainstream, marginalized people" are denigrated by empirical psychologists and cognitive scientists, and thus by naturalized epistemologists, who assume that only their own disciplines offer genuine explanations of knowledge and science.

As important, Code argues, and contrary to the assumption of both psychologists and epistemologists, the subjects who figure in the observer-observed laboratory experiments to which naturalists appeal are *not* "natural objects"; in effect, they have been "denatured." Given an underlying assumption that human beings form a "natural kind," given as well methodological commitments to "gloss over human differences and specificities," the "new human subject" that is the focus of psychological research is as much *the result* as it is the subject of such research. Its specificity, its historical and cultural "particularity," are set aside, resulting in the creation of a decidedly artificial "human subject." Moreover, Code maintains, "the rhetoric of the 'natural' claims a proximity to the 'real' that exercises a normative persuasion." This rhetoric, which Code argues figures in both the scientific research in question and epistemology, would suggest that no "stipulating" is occurring. But Code identifies factors that are set aside to demonstrate that psychologists and epistemologists make choices concerning what counts as "human natural identity," which expressions of it warrant empirical study, and so forth. Given scientism, Code argues, choices of the sort she details are unlikely to be reflected upon, let alone scrutinized, when psychologists and epistemologists assume that only scientific knowledge can provide "truly explanatory accounts" and when epistemology is taken to reduce to psychology.

Unlike many critics and advocates of Quinean naturalized epistemology, including some whose essays are included in this volume, Code does view this enterprise as normative. But she takes these dimensions to amplify the problems just noted. So practiced, Code argues, naturalized epistemology "will transform epistemology's justificatory strategies," but not in critically reflective ways.

Code next turns to the positive project of her chapter, that of identifying a kind of naturalism that would "reclaim" its emancipatory promise. She recommends "a revisioned naturalism," an epistemological approach the core assumptions of which are analogous with those that inform the discipline of ecology. Code maintains that the normative questions to be pursued in this epistemology will be concerned to investigate the implications for humans as potential knowers of living in certain environments, and the potential for cognitive practices that will create environments "where people can live well."

In "Feminist Epistemology and Naturalized Epistemology: An Uneasy Alliance" (Chapter 5), Phyllis Rooney introduces several distinctions to lay the groundwork for her argument that the alliance mentioned in her title is not only uneasy but should remain so. Rooney begins by drawing a distinction between what naturalist epistemologists *do* and what they *say* they ought to do. She argues that although naturalists are *committed* to making substantive use of scientific research in their theorizing about knowledge and science, they typically do not do so. Instead, it is the work of other philosophers, published in the main in philosophy journals, which is typically cited in naturalized epistemology. Nor, Rooney argues, is it common for naturalist epistemologists to engage with scientists, even those in empirical psychology and cognitive science on whose work they claim to rely.

Rooney builds from these arguments to introduce a distinction between what she calls the "noun-sense" of epistemology and the "verb-sense." According to this schema, those who subscribe to a noun-sense of epistemology take "a specific fixed theory of knowledge" as their goal and, in this and other ways, are committed to "final philosophizing"—in the case of epistemology, to "some 'final conception' of knowledge." In contrast, those who subscribe to a "verb-sense" of epistemology are concerned with *doing* epistemology and are more likely to devote critical attention to "particular kinds of motivating concerns, questions, and methods" that shape the way they do epistemology, rather than taking a final theory as their goal. Rooney uses this distinction to argue for what she takes to be important differences between naturalized epistemology and feminist epistemology as they are currently practiced. Those engaged in the former, she maintains, typically engage in epistemology of the noun-sense. Feminist epistemologists, on the other hand, typically engage in what she describes as verb-sense epistemology.

Rooney identifies a number of assumptions at work in naturalized epistemology that she takes to illustrate a commitment to a noun-sense of epistemology and other "non-naturalistic" features of work in the field. She cites assumptions of individualism, "that knowledge and knowing (and hence epistemology) are paradigmatically about having and acquiring beliefs," that scientific knowledge and practices are paradigmatic examples of knowledge and knowledge-producing activities, and that psychology can provide an accurate account of how people "actually arrive at beliefs." Rooney also argues that naturalized epistemology presupposes more "uniformity and generality" in scientific methods and practices than empirical investigations of scientific practice indicate is warranted. For the self-styled naturalist, Rooney contends, the problem with maintaining these assumptions is that they reflect philosophical preconceptions rather than empirical investigation.

In identifying what she takes to be differences between naturalized and feminist epistemologies, Rooney's analysis suggests that the approaches characterizing the latter are more naturalistic than those characterizing the former. Rooney argues that feminist epistemologists are more concerned with the nature and consequences of their practices—what she cites Helen E. Longino as identifying as the question of what it means "to do epistemology as a feminist"—than arriving at some specific theory of science or knowledge. She maintains that feminists engage with practicing scientists (something naturalists prescribe but rarely partake in), and assume a more critical stance toward scientific practice and theories, and philosophical theorizing about them, than do naturalists. Finally, Rooney maintains that feminists are typically more conversant and comfortable with the diversity and "messiness" of the knowledge-generating practices they study. Rooney takes these things to reflect feminists' engagements with practicing scientists, their attention to sociological and historical analyses of science, and their familiarity with debates within and across scientific specialties.

Rooney uses an extended case study to provide concrete examples to support her arguments. She concludes that, rather than feminists drawing on naturalized epistemology as some contributors advocate, naturalist epistemologists should look to feminist epistemology and feminist philosophy of science for "inspiration . . . and guidance."

At the outset of "Naturalizing Quine" (Chapter 6), Kathryn Pyne Addelson describes Quine's work "like all really good philosophical work [as] Janus-faced." Addelson credits Quine with exposing a number of problems in the assumptions and commitments of logical empiricism. At the same time, she argues that Quine preserves important aspects of that tradition and offers new solutions to its problems, including the research tradition of naturalized epistemology as its intellectual heir. Addelson's chapter as a whole reflects her positive and negative appraisals of Quine's work. She argues that the most significant and positive premise of Quine's arguments in "Epistemology Naturalized" is that knowledge is a natural phenomenon to be studied like all such phenomena. She also maintains that Quine clings to some dogmas even as he challenges others, and that the dogmas he retains both shape and limit his naturalized epistemology.

Among the dogmas and assumptions Addelson attributes to Quine and questions in her chapter are "that knowledge of nature and 'reality' is embodied in language" and particularly that knowledge of nature "is given in the discursive, representational use of language"; that science is a network of sentences; that science is "the authority" on nature, "including the relationship of the knower to the known"; and the dualism, criticized by Donald Davidson, "of conceptual scheme and experience."

Addelson's analysis of these assumptions and dogmas is by no means limited to critique; she works to extend Quine's own positions about science and naturalized epistemology in light of the *pragmatism* that she also finds within his work and seeks to develop.

In another constructive project, Addelson seeks to demonstrate that there can be a philosophy such that its notions of science and knowledge do not assume that knowers are individuals, that knowing is observational rather than participating, or that nature is "an object of study"—and she explores how such a philosophy might underwrite a naturalized epistemology that would enable scientists to understand their own practices in a more reflective way. Addelson offers several examples to demonstrate the possibility and coherence of the philosophy she envisions and to explore its normative dimensions.

In her most extensive example, Addelson uses historian Wamba-dia-Wamba's explication of the classic Kongo world picture ("cosmovision") to several ends. Here, Addelson argues, we have an example of a coherent worldview and set of practices that does not posit or create "individuals" in the sense assumed in Western (modern) societies, epistemologies, and sciences. Addelson argues that this worldview helps to demonstrate that the individuals that figure in Western worldviews are themselves constructed beings whose "collective enactment" is culturally specific. Addelson also uses the Kongo world picture as an example of a "presentational" rather than "representational" view of language that in turn entails a view of translation that does not reduce the "enactment" of the world or meaning to discursive representation able to be *translated or evaluated* on the basis of notions of "truth" and "falsity." Finally, she uses the Kongo cosmovision to "show people and their world as generated in collective action." From this perspective, Addelson maintains, one can interpret Quine's arguments concerning objects as "posits" and his talk of redistribution of truth values in "Two Dogmas" in far more pragmatic and fertile terms: in terms, that is, "of collective activity in making a world not as a linguistic game."

In her conclusion, Addelson builds from these arguments to use the notion of "sensitizing," which figures in the tradition of symbolic interactionism in sociology, to discuss how Quine's effort "to embody knowers as actors in making knowledge" might be developed in ways that would allow scientists to accommodate the philosophical insight that they are "producing the account of the relationships between knower and known."

We take an important argument common to the essays of Part II to be that epistemology and the philosophy of science, of any sort, are *active* and *interventionist engagements* with forms of knowing and knowledge-making—whether those engaged in these enterprises recognize or embrace this and recognize the responsibilities attendant to it. Seen this way, the philosophy of science and epistemology are inescapably normative, whether engaged in from philosophers' armchairs (in Rooney's sense of "noun-sense epistemology"), self-styled as "purely descriptive" (as some naturalists see their efforts), or self-consciously aimed at transformation, as these authors advocate.

Another common argument is that a philosophy of science or an epistemology worth undertaking and taking seriously will be, to a substantial degree, empirically focused on and grounded in empirical research. Each author maintains that a viable epistemology will make use of *and* critically engage at least research in those scientific disciplines that provide or claim to provide insights into knowledge-making. Taken together, the authors cite cognitive science, empirical psychology, cross-cultural studies, and linguistics among the sciences to be drawn on and/or to be critically engaged.

Yet there are differences in the implications the authors attribute to their analyses of the relationships between Quine's positions and feminist theorizing within and about the sciences. Linker advocates a rationalized rather than a naturalized epistemology on the grounds that only the former can underwrite the normative force of feminists' claims and projects. In contrast, Code and Addelson do not reject naturalism itself; Code takes Quinean epistemology to be insufficiently "emancipatory" or "transformative," and Addelson seeks to further develop it. And although Rooney argues that an alliance between naturalized epistemology and feminist epistemology should remain "uneasy," her central argument is that feminists engage in the kind of research and interaction with science that is called for and that naturalists say they "ought" to do but don't. This suggests that it is not the self-described project of naturalized epistemology that is problematic, but the failure by self-styled naturalists to execute it. In this argument, Rooney engages Code's arguments in Chapter 5, exploring their common uneasiness over an alliance with naturalized epistemology but offering somewhat different reasons for it.

There are also parallels and contrasts between the essays of this section and those of the first. We have noted that Linker directly engages L. H. Nelson's arguments in Chapter 1 concerning the usefulness of holism and naturalism for feminists. She also engages Antony's arguments.

Both Linker and Antony maintain that a realist conception of truth is necessary to underwrite the normative force of feminists' claims, and both take rationalism to be necessary to any such conception. But Linker advocates rationalism as an alternative to naturalism, while Antony maintains that naturalized epistemology *vindicates* rationalism, and the epistemology she argues for would seem to be informed by both. In contrast to the fallibilism Antony and Nelson attribute to Quine and to naturalized epistemology, Code and Rooney argue that aspects of Quinean naturalized epistemology are informed by scientism. Finally, Antony maintains that naturalized epistemology can provide "aid and comfort to feminists." In contrast, and as earlier noted, it is an implication of Code's and Rooney's analyses that naturalist epistemologists would do well to look to feminist epistemology and philosophy of science for models of genuine naturalism. In terms of this issue, Rooney engages Antony's arguments directly, maintaining that an alliance between feminist and naturalized epistemologies should "take the direction of influence in the direction opposite to that which Antony submits."

Finally, it seems to us that the essays by Code, Rooney, and Addelson raise the bar in terms of the criteria to be met by a genuinely naturalistic epistemology, and all four essays in this section raise the bar in terms of the criteria to be met by a responsible epistemology and responsible scientific practice.

Part III: Explications, Expansions, and Revisions of Quinean Positions

The essays by Paul Roth, Jack Nelson, Richmond Campbell, Jane Duran, and Lynn Hankinson Nelson are in general supportive of Quine's positions and see them as specifically relevant to feminist theorizing about science. But, as noted, there are also substantive disagreements among these contributors concerning the nature and implications of some of Quine's positions, and most seek to extend or revise some of them.

The first chapter of this part, Paul Roth's "Feminism and Naturalism: If Asked for Theories, Just Say 'No'" (Chapter 7), most clearly connects the chapters of this section with those of the preceding section. Like other authors in Part III, Roth advocates Quinean naturalism and argues for its relevance to feminist approaches to science. But Roth is also in agreement with the general claim that Quine's naturalized epistemology *cannot* be used to the normative ends that some so-called naturalist and feminist philosophers of science try to use it. As he indicates in his introduction, Roth's central argument is that Quine's arguments in "Epistemology Naturalized" are far more revolutionary—indeed, *that they sound the death knell of philosophical theories of science* than self-described naturalists in mainstream and feminist philosophy of science have come to terms with or embraced in their approaches to studying science.

In the first section of his chapter, Roth lays out what he takes to be the salient features of "philosophical theories," features he will go on to argue are not only not attributable to naturalized philosophy of science or epistemology, but also vitiated by Quine's arguments. According to Roth, philosophical theories are solutions to conceptual puzzles, unable to be falsified by experience, and proposed without the aid of science or any empirical inquiry. Moreover, he contends, the failure to solve these puzzles is not regarded as disconfirming the theory in question, but as identifying a "difficulty" that calls for *more* philosophical theorizing. Roth's examples of philosophical theories in the philosophy of science are the verifiability theory of meaning and the rational reconstructions sought by Carnap and others. Roth also criticizes the efforts of contemporary self-styled naturalists, such as Philip Kitcher, who he maintains attempt to water down Quine's arguments so as to arrive at some sort of "limited," as opposed to "radical," naturalism. These efforts, he maintains, misrepresent or misunderstand the implications of Quine's "Epistemology Naturalized," which are radical indeed.

Roth next turns to a detailed explication of the arguments of Quine's "Epistemology Naturalized" and what he takes its implications to be for the philosophy of science. Roth takes a primary source of Quinean naturalism to be (Quinean) holism, and holism in turn to be the obvious consequence of developments in empiricism post-Hume. To those who have taken "the holist turn," Roth argues, questions about the justification of empirical claims "must be adjudicated intra-theoretically," and "Epistemology Naturalized" explicates the consequences of doing so. Central to Roth's analysis is his argument that Quine demonstrates a parallel between the demise of foundationalist projects in mathematics and what Quine takes to be the demise of the foundationalist project to justify recognizably empirical claims. Roth maintains that Quine's arguments for this parallel, although "wholly ignored" by commentators, demonstrate that we are no worse off surrendering the epistemological burden to the sciences than we are in accepting incompleteness theorems of mathematics. Finally, in response to a common critique of Quine's arguments in "Epistemology Naturalized," Roth maintains that the issue of normativity is not "whether to be normative" but "how." If Quine's arguments are successful, as Roth maintains they are, *legitimation* projects—such as those undertaken in traditional philosophy of science *and*, according to Roth, in feminist philosophy of science—are nonstarters.

In the balance of his chapter, Roth turns to the specific implications of his analysis of Quine's arguments for feminist philosophy of science, including the work of feminists who describe themselves as naturalists. Emphasizing what he takes to be parallels with the Strong Programme in feminists' efforts to develop "social epistemologies" that can provide "causal/social constructionist" explanations of scientific practices, Roth maintains that all such efforts represent precisely the kind of philosophical theorizing Quine shows to be vacuous. The faith, reflected in both social constructionist and feminist approaches to science, that there is some underlying structure that "explains" why people (including scientists) believe what they do is, Roth maintains, philosophical baggage. For experience tells us that "whatever processes there are that lead people to associate beliefs in the way they do," they are impenetrable. Thus, in Roth's view, many engaged in feminist philosophy of science, including those who describe themselves as naturalists, are not yet engaged in a truly revolutionary project. Recognizing "the limits of reason in light of the science of the late twentieth century"—limits that Roth credits Quine with identifying and embracing—would yield (genuinely) revolutionary and constructive approaches to science in feminist philosophy of science.

In "The Last Dogma of Empiricism?" (Chapter 8), Jack Nelson addresses the general question of whether the distinction between science and values that Quine upholds can be maintained in light of Quine's own holistic view of evidence. Nelson argues that there are strong Quinean reasons for rejecting the distinction and that it is far from clear that doing so would, as Quine seems to think, vitiate the objectivity of science. Indeed, Nelson maintains that there is a compelling reason to attempt to accommodate value claims in science—"the hope of bringing something of the 'objectivity' and openness that are characteristic of science to bear on value claims."

Nelson devotes the first section of his chapter to outlining what he refers to as "some fairly noncontroversial boundary conditions" that any viable view about the relation between "facts" and "values," or about the nature of science, must work within. On the one hand, he maintains, it is an implication of holism that none of the theories we currently accept is immune to revision or possible abandonment. On the other hand, Nelson argues, no theory or thesis that *presently* challenges the basic success of science (at least large parts of it) is itself viable. "Any viable philosophy of science," he argues, "must recognize the indisputable success of science," a success that Nelson attributes to science's demand for empirical confirmation. The question raised by feminist science scholarship, Nelson suggests, is whether science's success can only be accomplished "by building and maintaining an absolute wall between science and values." Nelson proposes to explore this question within the bounds of empiricism and the views just outlined.

In the next sections of his chapter, Nelson explores Quine's reasons for upholding the science/value distinction and the tenability of that distinction given other of his positions. He considers a number of traditional views that took values and the sentences of value theory to be problematic, and argues that only one of these is a likely reason for Quine's defense of the distinction "that in [Quine's] view 'empirical controls' work only on science." Nelson next explores two themes within Quine's work that, at least on the surface, argue against "a complete science/value distinction": holism and Quine's "notion of posits and reality." Nelson argues that the implication of holism is that what counts for or against a claim or theory are two things: "how it is integrated in a larger theory or set of theories, and how well these interconnected claims and theories collectively predict, explain, and integrate the firings of our sensory receptors." Thus, on the surface, Quinean holism would seem "to invite, or at least allow," the inclusion of value-laden claims or value claims within science. So too, Nelson argues, Quine's arguments that our ontological commitments are to those things that we must posit to make the sentences of our theories come out true (in the Quinean sense of 'true') also suggest that such claims are included in the holistic web. "To the extent that we are concerned to understand us, *Homo sapiens*, our theories also posit social structures, and individual and social goods and rights," and we have collectively constructed a world "in which pain, suffering, happiness, joy, and prejudice are as real as trees, cars, political entities, and quarks."

Nelson next considers aspects of Quine's work that suggest that the holism Quine has in mind is, in fact, "far more modest" than that which Nelson earlier outlined. Analyzing Quine's discussions of holism, Nelson suggests that it is probable that Quine includes only the natural and social sciences within this network—that it does not in fact include what Nelson describes as "all of our seriously held beliefs." Nelson next asks what the consequences are of the view that "rationally based agreement is obtainable on all and only the claims of the traditional science." He argues that two are particularly untoward: first, that "we may mistake broad agreement concerning some specific belief with that belief as being part of science"; second, that we may be "too ready to tolerate divergence of belief in areas outside the traditional sciences." In light of these problems, Nelson advocates a broader holism than that which he attributes to Quine, according to which the web of interconnected theories consists of "all our seriously held beliefs, our whole world view including beliefs about values and value-laden beliefs." Including the disciplines of moral theory, political and social theory, and aesthetics, Nelson argues, amounts to admitting that we take these disciplines seriously. And, in the end, deciding whether science itself can, in principle, "be made value free" is less important than "bringing reason and evidence construed holistically to bear on value issues."

In his conclusion, Nelson explores the consequences of a science that, at a minimum, makes less of the science/value distinction. He argues that whether or not the science/value distinction is abandoned, the failure to take values seriously works against the doing of good science. Nelson has added a postscript to his chapter that reflects some changes in his views concerning what motivates Quine's skepticism about values and value-laden claims since his essay was originally published.

The projects of Richmond Campbell's "Feminist Epistemology Naturalized" (Chapter 9) are to defend feminist empiricism, to explicate the logic of feminist naturalized epistemology, and to extend some of Quine's positions so as to develop a normative realism. Although Campbell defends Quine's holism and his arguments for naturalism, the feminist naturalized epistemology he envisions differs in important respects from Quine's vision of naturalized epistemology. Campbell parts ways with Quine in terms of the viability of a fact/value distinction and in terms of the objectivity of values, and he uses Quine's own arguments for holism to counter Quine's skepticism about values. In the conclusion of his chapter, Campbell builds on these several arguments to advocate what he calls "a feminist normative realism."

Key to Campbell's argument that feminist empiricism is viable is a distinction he draws between what he calls "internal feminist empiricism" and "external feminist empiricism." Campbell maintains that arguments against feminist empiricism, in particular those of Harding's we earlier outlined, ironically *assume* the distinction between the contexts of discovery and justification they typically criticize. What critics of feminist empiricism have in mind, Campbell argues, is "external feminist empiricism," according to which feminist commitments are only brought to bear within the context of discovery (i.e., in forming a research agenda)—not in the context of justification where, as Harding and others assume, only empiricist norms function. Campbell uses Quinean holism to argue that factors in the context of discovery always carry over to the context of justification—thus, he maintains, even in what Harding calls "science as usual," it is not *only* empiricist norms that are at work. An "internal feminist empiricism," in which *both* feminist and empiricist norms function, is a more accurate understanding of feminist empiricism, and the latter is, indeed, a viable framework.

Campbell's argument that feminist empiricism should be understood as a version of naturalized epistemology proceeds in several stages. In the first, he seeks to demonstrate that naturalized epistemology is normative, even if "Quine misunderstands his own project." Campbell maintains that not only are empiricist methodological norms (such as induction) inherently normative, so too are the "end norms" that give them their purpose. Naturalized epistemology engages in research and/or makes use of scientific research to determine *whether* the methodological norms scientists and laypersons use *do result* in theories that satisfy the ends inquiry sets itself. Campbell builds from this argument to outline the logic of feminist naturalized epistemology. Feminist political commitments, he maintains, will function both as end norms and in the application of methodological norms such as explanatory power. To take a naturalistic approach to feminist epistemology, Campbell argues, is to follow the logic of naturalized epistemology so described to investigate whether specific methodological norms lead to hypotheses and theories that satisfy the "end norms" of feminist politics.

Campbell next turns to questions concerning realism and objectivity, first in terms of recognizably empirical theory (such as science), and subsequently in terms of moral theory. His account of the purpose and justification of the methodological and end norms that guide inquiry are central to his arguments for a feminist normative realism. He works first to demonstrate that the justification of methodological norms on the basis of their relationship to objectivity *requires* that we assume they are more likely than any alternatives to help us arrive at "reasonably accurate models of what the world is like." Campbell next argues that realism is required if we are to be able to make sense of the notion that the end norms guiding inquiry are *themselves* objective. Campbell introduces what he calls "fact-value holism" as a framework that allows for the evaluation of end norms, including feminist norms, on the basis of notions such as objectivity.

In a third line of argument, Campbell maintains that Quine's arguments that the empirical meaning (content) of particular sentences is largely determined by their relationships to other sentences come to the claim that the "factual and meaning components of language are inextricably intertwined." If we also grant, as Campbell earlier argues, that holism so understood extends to normative commitments, and that there are reciprocal relationships between one's acceptance of descriptive claims and one's norms, then it is clear that normative realism is as viable as empirical realism. Moral claims, Campbell maintains—such as "the suppression of women is unjust"—are like empirical claims in that both "can be true independently of their being recognized to be true."

In "Quine and Feminist Theory" (Chapter 10), Jane Duran argues that Quine's naturalism, which her analysis suggests she views to be central to but not identical with naturalized epistemology, is the most significant aspect of his work, and deeply commensurate with core feminist principles. Duran characterizes Quine's naturalism as the view that it is "futile" to attempt to "divorce our experience of the world from our theorizing about it." Quine demonstrates, she argues, that efforts to disentangle language, theorizing, sense data experience, and observation are necessarily doomed.

Duran builds from her account of Quinean naturalism to argue that there are fundamental differences between, on the one hand, Quine's positions and, on the other, logical positivism, Carnap's positions, and "the Received View" that long dominated the philosophy of science. Duran maintains that Quine's view of the relationship between language and world led to his critique of sense data as a form of experience prior to conceptualization and language, and ultimately to his arguments against foundationalism. Quine's view of the language/world relationship in turn relied on a model of language acquisition that maintains that children's sensory experiences are inseparable from their experiences of learning language. And, Duran argues, Quine takes the inseparability in the language-learning process of experience, conceptualization, and categorization as also attributable to the esoteric observations and categorizations of the sciences. The physicist encountering the world, using her senses and the categories implicit in her language, does so in ways and to ends not different in kind from the child who is learning a language.

Duran's third line of argument emphasizes Quine's rejection of the a priori and of what she terms "universalizability," positions that she maintains sharply distinguish Quine's naturalism from much Western philosophizing. Duran locates Quine "directly in a line of thinkers, beginning with James and Dewey [and including Rorty]," who have denied the possibility of "One True Account" and whose challenges to this are grounded in a rejection of the possibility of universalizability and an a priori construction of ontology. Duran takes the source both of Dewey's emphasis on the importance of experience and "the weakness of a priori theorizing" and of Quine's naturalism to be in their common view of the relationships between language and the world. Both Dewey and Quine reject the view that language has "a nonhuman, hypostatized link to the world."

In her conclusion, Duran argues that there is a deep convergence between Quine's naturalism and feminists' commitments to theorizing on the basis of the realities of "women's lived lives." Duran draws parallels between "the sense-oriented nature of a gynocentric world view" that reflects "immersion in the world of mundane particulars" and the emphasis in Quine's theorizing on sensory experience. In more general terms, Duran argues, Quinean naturalism is valuable for feminist theorizing "precisely because it takes us thoroughly out of the realm of a priori theorizing."

In "Feminist Naturalized Philosophy of Science" (Chapter 11), Lynn Hankinson Nelson explores the implications of Quine's positions and feminist science studies for the philosophy of science. Extending and revising "A Feminist Naturalized Philosophy of Science" (1995), Nelson advocates a philosophical framework for studying science that makes use of three methodological principles she argues to be commensurate with the implications of Quinean holism and of feminist science studies—a methodological approach she calls "feminist naturalized philosophy of science." Her central thesis is that an approach to science based on these principles allows for the recognition that many of the questions feminist raise about the *social processes* that characterize and influence science are simultaneously questions about *the bodies of evidence* available to and drawn upon by scientists. That is to say, the distinction between the "sociology of science" and "epistemology of science" that both traditional philosophers and sociologists of science assume is not genuine (cf. Rouse 1996).

Nelson positions her discussion in relation to recent debates in naturalized philosophy of science. She notes that three criteria for assessing methods used in the discipline have emerged in these discussions: the commensurability of the explanations such methods yield with the actual history and current practices of science; sufficient grounding in empirical research relevant to the study of the sciences; and consistency of methodological approaches, in particular, a consistent approach to episodes deemed progressive and nonprogressive. Nelson argues that the general commitment among naturalists to evaluate philosophical methods on the basis of *empirical warrant*, and the interdependence naturalists maintain between philosophical methods and a *current state* of science and science scholarship, make feminist naturalized epistemology a viable and promising methodological approach.

In the second section, Nelson introduces the three methodological principles, maintaining that they both satisfy the criteria largely accepted in naturalized philosophy of science and better satisfy them than currently available alternatives. Two principles concern the construal of evidence, and the second represents a revision of the article originally published with the same name (Nelson 1995). The first builds on what Nelson takes to be the implications of Quine's arguments for holism; it maintains that the evidence for specific hypotheses and theories is both empirical success and integration with bodies of accepted theory. She takes an implication of feminist science studies to be that holism must be construed inclusively so as to include claims and theories in which social beliefs and values are integrated.

Nelson's second methodological principle seeks to refine Quinean holism so that it reflects the substantial body of evidence indicating that the sciences are in fact less unified, and characterized by more dissent, than Quine recognizes or that she has identified in earlier publications. She adds to the principle calling for inclusive holism by building on the work of Alison Wylie and Ian Hacking to argue for a principle that emphasizes the importance of "evidential independence." She argues that the evidence for a particular hypothesis, whether in the form of empirical results or intertheoretic integration, is stronger if it enjoys some degree of independence (vertical and/or horizontal) from the research program within which the hypothesis emerged. Nelson's third methodological principle takes science communities, rather than scientists *qua* individuals, as the loci of philosophical reconstructions and explanations of scientific practice. She maintains that this focus is an implication of the holistic account of evidence she advocates.

In her conclusion, Nelson considers the question of whether feminist naturalized philosophy of science as she has outlined it is normative. She seeks to demonstrate that it is a significant implication of research in both the feminist and naturalist traditions that the methods employed in the philosophy of science carry both empirical and normative import, and can and should be pursued as carrying such import.

As we have had reason to note in several contexts, even contributors who support Quine's arguments for naturalizing the philosophy of science and holism, and who also agree that these positions are relevant to and promising for feminist theorizing about science, sometimes disagree deeply about the nature and implications of these positions. There is, to start, obvious disagreement about whether naturalized philosophy of science is justificatory. And like the disagreement we noted between Antony's analysis and L. H. Nelson's in Part I, contributors in this section differ sharply in their understandings of the implications of holism for realism, for correspondence theories, and for related notions—disagreements that, in some cases we suggest, are partly related to disagreements concerning the viability and/or implications of Quinean holism and his thesis of the indeterminacy of translation.

We conclude by noting some significant parallels and disagreements in the volume as a whole, and what we think are important and unresolved questions concerning the implications of feminist scholarship for Quine's positions and vice versa.

A number of contributors analyze and evaluate Quinean holism, and there are disagreements about its extent and implications. Linker maintains that this doctrine is inherently conservative and, as such, incompatible with feminist theorizing. Others, including Campbell, J. Nelson, L. H. Nelson, and Roth, argue that holism is an important resource for feminist theorizing, but the first three contributors seek to extend it so as to include more than science narrowly construed and, certainly, values. The second chapter by L. H. Nelson also seeks to develop a view of evidence that, although holistic, avoids the conservatism that she takes to rightly concern Linker. There are also important differences in the ways those sympathetic to Quinean holism understand this position. For example, Jack Nelson argues that holism as Quine understood and advocated it may only encompass the sciences, and identifies what he takes to be some unfortunate consequences if this is the case. Campbell, Duran, and L. H. Nelson, on the other hand, take Quine's arguments to entail a more inclusive holism, one that encompasses common-sense theory and theorizing as well as philosophy. Campbell goes even further to use what he calls Quine's "fact/meaning holism" as the basis for his own argument for "fact/value holism." In his efforts to expand Quinean holism to include values, Campbell's interest parallels that of J. Nelson, but their specific understandings of holism seem to us quite different.

Roth maintains that Quine does not draw distinctions between types of sciences, but understands science as incorporating any form of inquiry that respects the experimental method. At the same time, Roth's arguments would suggest that the ways other contributors seek to use Quinean holism and naturalism reflect a fundamental misunderstanding of Quine's arguments. The disagreements involved are significant, for they raise the question not only of what the philosophy of science postnaturalism *is* or *could be*, but also questions concerning where Quine's work is located in relationship to "analytic" philosophy and postmodernism.

At its heart, the disagreement seems to us to concern whether naturalized philosophy of science properly understood is or could be *an explanatory enterprise* or whether it is, instead, (merely) interpretive. In criticizing feminist approaches to science that retain the features he attributes to "philosophical theories," Roth focuses on Helen E. Longino's arguments for viewing science "as social knowledge" and on the guidelines she proposes for science communities to further the kind of objectivity she articulates. But Roth's arguments have much wider applicability. In this volume alone, a number of contributors identify themselves as feminists and naturalists, and suggest philosophical approaches to studying science—approaches that they, like Longino, take to be *simultaneously philosophical and empirical inquiries*. If Roth is correct, these are in fact philosophical in ways Quine that showed are untenable. What reason is there for thinking this is so?

As we read Roth, any attempt to *explain* the beliefs of individuals or of groups is a nonstarter. Feminist theorizing, then—including that self-described as naturalist—is not empirical inquiry, but philosophical theorizing of a sort Quine showed to be a dead end. This raises several questions, perhaps the most obvious being just what *is* the philosophy of science? And in what does the continuity between the sciences and the philosophy of science, a core tenet of Quine's argument for naturalization, consist? If the sciences are explanatory and the philosophy of science is limited to offering interpretations, it is not clear that any such continuity obtains. Perhaps, given that the problems with causal explanations that Roth emphasizes concern efforts to explain beliefs, he is of the view that the social sciences and the philosophy of science cannot be explanatory, but the physical and life sciences can. But again this seems challenged by Quinean holism and the breadth (which Roth himself stresses) of Quine's notion of what constitutes "empirical inquiry." Given these positions, it would seem to follow that either all empirical inquiry is interpretive, rather than explanatory, or all empirical inquiry, including some approaches taken to the philosophy of science, is explanatory.

Whatever the answers to these questions, we take these issues—at the heart of this disagreement and others we have noted concerning the implications of holism for the notions of realism and truth, explanation and interpretation, and all of these for the study of science and other knowledge-generating practices—to warrant further exploration in feminist theorizing. For they suggest that Quine's philosophy bridges the philosophies of the analytic and postmodern schools that many, including some contributors to this volume, take to be diametrically opposed.

On one level, there is apparently more consensus concerning Quine's commitment to individualism than there is concerning holism. Of those who discuss it, most see aspects of Quine's work, including his arguments in "Epistemology Naturalized," as presupposing epistemological individualism and view this position as problematic. On another level, there are differences in the weight contributors attribute to individualism as they evaluate the usefulness of naturalism to feminist theorizing. Code's and Linker's essays suggest that Quinean naturalism is inseparable from individualism. Duran, J. Nelson, and L. H. Nelson, while critical of Quine's commitment to individualism, see room for developing naturalism beyond it. And Campbell, J. Nelson, and L. H. Nelson argue that others of Quine's positions undermine any residual commitment he has to individualism. As importantly in terms of this issue, we take Rooney's analysis of research in cognitive science to raise significant questions about the distinction between the individual and the social that informs some of the other essays, and about the not uncommon assumption that research focused on the cognitive capacities of individuals cannot yield results with any relevance for feminist science studies.

A question enjoying center stage in these essays is whether naturalism and others of Quine's positions are able to yield a sufficiently normative philosophy of science. Although contributors disagree in their answers to this question, we end by noting arguments that we find common and significant.

Most contributors maintain that, by current lights, the methods employed by philosophers of science should be empirically grounded and should yield critical evaluation of the sciences, including those that naturalists seek to use. And all call for critical self-reflection on the part of philosophers—whether feminists, naturalists, rationalists, or some combination thereof—concerning the empirical warrant and the normative implications of our practices.

Notes

1. These include articles by Kathryn Pyne Addelson, Linda Martín Alcoff, Susan Babbitt, Elizabeth Potter, and Lynn Hankinson Nelson.

2. Quine's target in "Two Dogmas" is verificationism as promulgated by the members of the Vienna Circle—the view that individual sentences have empirical content and that such content is "the method of empirically confirming or infirming" them (Quine 1953, 37). Quine argues that most individual sentences have empirical meaning only to the extent that they are parts of larger theories that can be tested against experience. Verificationism works as a theory of meaning of larger linguistic units, and he argues that it also works for a special class of sentences (his account of observation sentences and observation categoricals made up of them). We outline these views in more detail below.

We also note that Quine would eventually offer a new version of the analytic/synthetic distinction, one that invokes his notion of "stimulus meanings" and applies only to his notion of observation categoricals (see, e.g., Quine 1990a, 17). As stimulus meanings are themselves construed in physicalistic terms, this redefined notion of analytic and synthetic sentences does nothing to resuscitate the traditional distinction.

3. The publication of "Two Dogmas" is sometimes seen as dating Quine's break with Carnap and the two core doctrines of the logico-empiricist tradition. But as Quine himself notes in the preface to *From a Logical Point of View,* "The critique of analyticity to which 'Two Dogmas' is in large part devoted is an outcome of informal discussions, oral and written, in which I have engaged from 1939 onward with Professors Carnap, Alonzo Church, Nelson Goodman, Alfred Tarski, and Morton White" (1953, viii). The arguments of "Two Dogmas" are also foreshadowed in Quine (1936).

4. This is not to say, although some have so argued, that Quine rejects "ideas." What he maintains is that mental objects such as ideas and beliefs are appropriate subjects of study, but lack sufficient identity criteria to function in explanations (see Quine 1966).

5. Quine does grant that there is "an extreme sort of definition which does not hark back to prior synonymies at all: namely, the explicitly conventional introduction of novel notations for the purposes of sheer abbreviation" (1953, 26). An example is when a logician introduces the expression 'iff' as an abbreviation for 'if and only if.' Although this is "a really transparent case of synonymy created by definition" (26) it is clear that such cases of synonymy cannot save the notion of analyticity. Not every analytic truth that is not a logical truth can be turned into a logical truth by appeal to an explicitly conventional introduction of a synonymous term.

6. We have omitted portions of Quine's arguments directed specifically at Carnap's defenses of the analytic/synthetic distinction. They are of some historical interest but are not central to Quine's basic argument.

7. We later outline the account of observation sentences and observation categoricals that Quine developed and advocated.

8. We speak of "phenomenological" experiences here because, as we note below, Quine worked hard to carve out a notion of "experience" defined only in physicalist terms.

9. We explicate these efforts in some detail in Nelson and Nelson (2000).

10. In *Pursuit of Truth* Quine remarks that "[w]hat the indeterminacy of translation shows is that the notion of propositions as sentence meanings is untenable" (1990a, 102). This suggests that indeterminacy of translation argues for holism. But we could as well say, for reasons earlier outlined, that the limits of verificationism (that it works only for a very limited range of sentences) itself argues for holism. This seems to be the argument of "Two Dogmas." And in the end, we have come to think that these several notions, verificationism, holism, and empirical content being specifiable on a sentence-by-sentence basis only for observation sentences and their kin, are so interrelated that one can start from any one and get to the others. The strong indeterminacy of translation follows from this cluster of concepts.

11. Quine views underdetermination as a thesis about evidence, and indeterminacy of translation as a semantic thesis (Quine 1990b). But given one of his formulations of underdetermination, that there could be two (or more) different and inconsistent *global* theories of nature equally compatible with all evidence, the distinction between evidential and semantic remains unclear to us.

12. The qualifier 'recognizably' reflects our agreement with Quine's contention that sentences of logic and mathematics *are* empirical, an obvious consequence of his arguments against the analytic/synthetic distinction.

13. We can grant that the logico-empiricist tradition in the philosophy of science was conservative in the ways Harding outlines, but take issue with the claim that the origins of empiricism and modernist epistemology were conservative. At the time they emerged, they were revolutionary in terms of their implications for cognitive authority.

14. Harding would later describe Helen E. Longino's work (1990) and that of Lynn Hankinson Nelson (1990) as "sophisticated" versions of feminist empiricism (e.g., in Harding 1991).

15. A number of influential articles and books in feminist philosophy of science and epistemology, dating back to 1987, positively engaged Quine's positions prior to 1994.

16. See Quine's interview in Borrardi (1994).

17. We are grateful to Joseph Rouse, who first suggested the difference and the implications on which we focus (personal communication).

References

Alcoff, Linda Martín. 1987. "Justifying Feminist Social Science." *Hypatia* 2(3): 107–27. Reprint, 1989. In *Feminism and Science*, ed. N. Tuana. Bloomington and Indianapolis: Indiana University Press.

Ayer, A. J. 1959. *Logical Positivism*. New York: The Free Press.

Borrardori, Giovanna. 1994. *The American Philosopher*. Chicago: University of Chicago Press.

Carnap, Rudolf. 1928. *Der Logische Aufbau der Welt*. Berlin: Felix Meiner Verlag.

Flax, Jane. 1983. "Political Philosophy and the Patriarchal Unconscious: A Psychoanalytic Perspective on Epistemology and Metaphysics." In *Discovering Reality*, ed. S. Harding and M. Hintikka.

Harding, Sandra. 1983. "The Visibility of the Sex/Gender System." In *Discovering Reality*, ed. S. Harding and M. Hintikka.

———. 1986. *The Science Question in Feminism*. Ithaca: Cornell University Press.

———. 1991. *Whose Science? Whose Knowledge?* Ithaca: Cornell University Press.

Harding, Sandra, and Merrill Hintikka, eds. 1983. *Discovering Reality*. Dordrecht: D. Reidel.

Harstock, Nancy. 1983. "The Feminist Standpoint: Developing the Ground for a Specifically Feminist Historical Materialism." In *Discovering Reality*, ed. S. Harding and M. Hintikka.

Jaggar, Alison. 1983. *Feminist Politics and Human Nature*. Totowa, N.J.: Rowman & Allenheld.

Longino, Helen E. 1987. "Beyond 'Bad Science': Skeptical Reflections on the Value Freedom of Scientific Inquiry." *Science, Technology, and Human Values* 8(1): 7–17.

———. 1990. *Science as Social Knowledge*. Princeton: Princeton University Press.

———. 1995. "Gender, Politics, and the Theoretical Virtues." *Synthese* 104(3): 383–97.

———. 1996. "Cognitive and Non-cognitive Values in Science: Rethinking the Dichotomy." In *Feminism, Science, and the Philosophy of Science*, ed. L. H. Nelson and J. Nelson. Dordrecht: Kluwer Academic Publishers.

Nelson, Lynn Hankinson. 1990. *Who Knows: From Quine to Feminist Empiricism*. Philadelphia: Temple University Press.

———. 1995. "A Feminist Naturalized Philosophy of Science." *Synthese* 104(3): 399–421.

Nelson, Lynn Hankinson, and Jack Nelson. 2000. *On Quine*. Belmont, Ca.: Wadsworth.

Potter, Elizabeth. 1988. "Modeling the Gender Politics in Science." *Hypatia* 3(1): 19–33. Reprint, 1989. In *Feminism and Science*, ed. N. Tuana. Bloomington and Indianapolis: Indiana University Press.

Quine, W. V. 1936. "Truth by Convention." In *Philosophical Essays for A. N. Whitehead*, ed. O. H. Lee. New York: Longmans. Reprint, 1966. In *The Ways of Paradox and Other Essays*.

———. 1953. "Two Dogmas of Empiricism." In *From a Logical Point of View*. Cambridge, Mass.: Harvard University Press.

———. 1960. *Word and Object*. New York: John Wiley and Sons; Cambridge, Mass.: MIT Press.

———. 1966. *The Ways of Paradox and Other Essays*. New York: Random House.

———. 1966a. "On Mental Entities." In *The Ways of Paradox and Other Essays*.

———. 1966b. "Posits and Reality." In *The Ways of Paradox and Other Essays*.

———. 1969. *Ontological Relativity and Other Essays*. New York: Columbia University Press.

———. 1969a. "Epistemology Naturalized." In *Ontological Relativity and Other Essays*.

———. 1969b. "Speaking of Objects." In *Ontological Relativity and Other Essays*.

———. 1969c. "Ontological Relativity." In *Ontological Relativity and Other Essays*.

———. 1969d. "Natural Kinds." In *Ontological Relativity and Other Essays*.

———. 1981. *Theories and Things*. Cambridge, Mass.: Harvard University Press.

———. 1981a. "Empirical Content." In *Theories and Things*.

———. 1981b. "On the Very Idea of a Third Dogma." In *Theories and Things*.

———. 1981c. "Things and Their Place in Theories." In *Theories and Things*.

———. 1987. "Response to Gibson." In *The Philosophy of W. V. Quine*, ed. E. L. Hahn and P. A. Schilpp. LaSalle, Ill.: Open Court Publishers.

———. 1990a. *Pursuit of Truth*. Cambridge, Mass.: Harvard University Press.

———. 1990b. "Three Indeterminacies." In *Perspectives on Quine*, ed. R. Barrett and R. Gibson. Cambridge, Mass.: Blackwell.

Rose, H. 1983. "Hand, Brain, and Heart: A Feminist Epistemology for the Natural Sciences." *Signs* 9(1): 73–90.

Rouse, J. 1996. "Feminism and the Social Construction of Scientific Knowledge." In *Feminism, Science, and the Philosophy of Science*, ed. L. H. Nelson and J. Nelson. Dordrecht: Kluwer Academic Publishers.

Part I

Early Feminist Analyses of Quine

1

Who Knows: From Quine to Feminist Empiricism

Lynn Hankinson Nelson

The empiricist-derived epistemology that has directed most social and natural scientific inquiry . . . explicitly holds that historical social relations can only distort our "natural," trans-historical abilities to arrive at reliable beliefs. . . . From this perspective can emerge only bizarre accounts of [feminist inquiry].

—Sandra Harding, *The Science Question in Feminism*

As a theory of evidence . . . empiricism remains with us.
—W. V. Quine, "On the Very Idea of a Third Dogma"

In 1983, I was a graduate student at Temple University, beginning work on a dissertation that focused on the disagreement between Quine and Hugues Leblanc concerning the interpretation of quantifiers. (Quine favors objectual interpretation, Leblanc, substitutional.) Leblanc was supervising my research, but I was increasingly drawn to Quine's position. As Quine's arguments for objectual interpretation are rooted in his philosophy of science, my research quickly expanded to include his broader views.[1]

During the same year, Sandra Harding visited Temple to give a paper entitled "The Science Question in Feminism." As Harding sketched the major lines of arguments against empiricism she would later offer in a book of that name, I was struck by two things. On the one hand, feminist scientists and science scholars were raising issues that seemed well beyond the scope of Quine's positions and/or that constituted significant challenges to them. There was nothing, for example, in Quine's positions to suggest that divisions in experience and cognitive authority along the lines of gender or other social relations might have a bearing on the directions or content of scientific research (at least when things were going as they should). In itself, this was not surprising. There was little by way of assumptions, categories, or emphases in empiricist philosophy of science to suggest or accommodate such divisions or consequences. (Indeed, the disavowal of empirical investigations of science in the tradition was longstanding.) But in Quine's work, the assumption of a rather seamless and monolithic epistemic community was pronounced. Quine typically speaks of one epistemic community, divided at most by expertise, which contributes to and refines one ("our") "overall theory of nature." As much to the point, the continuities reflected in his descriptions of science as "refined common sense," and the philosophy of science as "science gone self-conscious," are important aspects of some of his most significant positions, holism and naturalism among them.

On the other hand, some of the "dogmas" Harding attributed to empiricism are not attributable to Quine, at least not baldly. Consider, for example, scientism. Quine does maintain that science is "our most serious" knowledge-seeking enterprise, and this deeply shapes a number of his positions. At the same time, his arguments for underdetermination, indeterminacy of translation, and holism reflect and support a robust fallibilism. Harding also viewed the commitment to a distinction between the contexts of discovery and justification as inseparable from empiricism, and noted that this distinction would make it difficult to explain the emergence of feminist science scholarship, let alone its findings. Although heir to the tradition that maintained this distinction, Quine's arguments for holism undermined the plausibility of any such distinction. Moreover, his arguments that epistemology should be naturalized called for the kinds of empirical investigation into the context of discovery that proponents of the distinction deemed irrelevant to the philosophy of science. Finally, his argument against the analytic/synthetic distinction undermined the claim that the statements of the philosophy of science were themselves nonempirical.

Harding also maintained that empiricism's core tenet concerning sensory experience would make it impossible to accommodate another significant implication of feminist science scholarship: that *who* is theorizing matters to the content of theorizing. I earlier noted that Quine typically speaks as if there is one epistemic community, and one overall theory of nature it maintains. But again, his broad positions—including his arguments against foundationalism—attest to a thoroughgoing historicism. Complicating such historicism by engaging in an empirically adequate sociology seemed a natural step—at least for those convinced by Quine's arguments for naturalizing the philosophy of science.

I also saw substantive parallels between specific and general arguments that feminist science scholars and Quine advanced. Quine has long challenged the boundaries alleged to exist between metaphysics and science, and between "common-sense" theorizing and science. He also maintains that "the scientific system, ontology and all, is a conceptual bridge of our own making" (Quine 1981f, 2)—*and* that it is constrained by evidence. Crucial to these several positions is naturalism—a position and methodology that seemed particularly promising for feminist philosophy of science.

I was sufficiently intrigued to change the topic of my dissertation to an exploration of parallels and discontinuities between Quine's positions and the implications of feminist science scholarship. By the time I published *Who Knows* in 1990, I was as much interested in using Quine's positions to reopen or redirect a discussion of empiricism among feminists as I was interested in convincing mainstream philosophers that feminist science scholarship raises significant issues.

There have been, of course, critical developments in feminist science scholarship and naturalized philosophy of science in the intervening years. The forthcoming discussion, excerpted from *Who Knows*,[2] is dated in a number of respects, and a later chapter in this volume reflects my current interest in developing feminist naturalized philosophy of science. But I remain convinced of the general lines of argument in this essay, and it explores positions of Quine's that are not explored in other chapters in this volume. It presupposes familiarity with feminist science critiques in the 1980s and with Quine's arguments concerning empirical content. For those not familiar with the latter, Quine's arguments are outlined in the first half of the introduction to this volume.

I would also note that in this discussion, I use 'experience' in the phenomenological sense, as Quine is so using it in the passages I quote. However, as outlined in the introduction to this volume, Quine worked throughout his career to develop a nonphenomenological notion of experience, to define that notion in purely physicalistic terms. Jack Nelson and I elsewhere suggest that the association of sentences construed holophrastically with specific physical experiences is itself learned within and constrained by a body of publicly accepted theory—and is, in this respect, like phenomenological experience in its dependence on such theories and the communities who maintain them (Nelson and Nelson 2000). Thus, the arguments advanced here against individualism and foundationalism seem to me still sound.

Feminism and Empiricism: Reopening a Discussion[3]

This discussion attempts to reopen or redirect, among feminists, a discussion of empiricism, and to facilitate, among scientists and philosophers of science, a serious discussion of feminist criticisms of science. The obstacles to these discussions are several, but the largest is surely that most scientists and philosophers of science are empiricists and the issues raised in and by feminist science criticism seem, to many feminists and empiricists, to presuppose the abandonment of empiricism. One aspect of furthering these discussions is ascertaining what it is these communities actually disagree about, and to what extent (if any) they have been talking past each other. I use and build from the work of W. V. Quine to explore these issues.

To those familiar with feminist science criticism, it might seem anachronistic or reactionary to undertake a serious consideration of feminism and empiricism, and to suggest that radical alternatives to longstanding views about science might emerge through it. For the most part, recent feminist discussions of science, epistemology, and the philosophy of science have concluded or assumed that it is not possible or desirable to reconcile feminist science criticism with empiricism.

This is not surprising. At best, the frameworks criticized in recent feminist discussions as the possible bases for "feminist empiricism" have been naive, incorporating views of knowers and of science that are severely challenged by the focuses of feminist science critique—and, before this, by debates in mainstream philosophy of science and the social sciences.[4] More interestingly, the "feminist empiricism" sketched in these discussions appears self-defeating—either because it incorporates views of knowers and science that cannot accommodate the focuses of feminist and other critical science scholarship, or because, as Sandra Harding has recently argued, if feminists move beyond such views of knowers and science, their arguments "deeply subvert empiricism" (Harding 1986, 25).

But it is time to reopen, or at least to redirect, a sustained discussion of feminism and empiricism. The most pragmatic reason for doing so can be stated with the details of my larger discussion. The point of feminist science scholarship must be, in the end, to change science, and changing science requires that scientists and other science scholars be brought into the dialogue. The initial goal of this hoped-for engagement should be to gain a central place for feminist perspectives in those conversations about science that shape scientists' and science scholars' understandings of science.

The arguments I will advance for feminist empiricism are reactionary neither in rationale nor in conclusions. Though I believe that empiricism warrants more serious consideration than it is now accorded in feminist scholarship, I do not take the views underlying the feminist move away from empiricism as obstacles to be overcome in developing feminist empiricism. Rather, they are indications of what a viable empiricist philosophy of science will be like. At the same time, I will be suggesting some alternatives to what, paraphrasing Sandra Harding, might be called "the philosophy of science (or epistemology) question in feminism."

The first alternative has to do with the characterization of empiricism sometimes assumed by feminist science scholars. Contemporary empiricism represents a far more radical departure from traditional and positivist empiricism than often taken into account by feminist critics of empiricism. The task of reconciling feminist science scholarship with empiricism is very different from what it would be if we were limited to logical positivism, or its most immediate heir, the "postlogical" positivist tradition represented by Rudolf Carnap, Carl Hempel, and Ernest Nagel. But we are not so limited.

A second assumption underlying my discussion is that those insights of feminist science scholarship that have been understood to require "anti-empiricist solutions" will need to be incorporated in any viable empiricist philosophy of science. This suggests the view that anti-empiricist approaches can be avoided, and that the most valuable implications of feminist and other critical science scholarship are commensurate with empiricism.

A third alternative is also related to frameworks, such as feminist standpoint theories, that their advocates take to be "anti-empiricist" (see, e.g., Harding 1986 and Jaggar 1983). I will argue that there is no need to posit the existence of an "epistemological chasm" between feminist scientists and science scholars and their nonfeminist colleagues—i.e., no reason to assume that feminists know things that empiricists (or nonfeminists more generally) *cannot* know. I don't deny the uniqueness of the insights feminist science scholarship has provided into science, or that it may require a revolution in some standards for nonfeminists to come to know what feminists know. But the revolution need not be based on faith. Rational, critical discussion of evidence and of standards of evidence is possible.

Finally, I bring a somewhat different view of the relationships between the philosophy of science or epistemology on the one hand, and science and feminist theorizing within and about it on the other, from that presupposed in recent feminist discussions. I assume that an epistemology or philosophy of science is not foundational to—or autonomous of—the other empirical theorizing it is concerned to understand. I take Quine's arguments, the history of epistemology, and developments in the philosophy of science and feminist science scholarship to indicate that the philosophy of science is radically interdependent with the sciences proper, and with other things we know.

Naturalism distinguishes what I demand of a philosophy of science or epistemology from those who demand a noncircular relationship between these, and the theories and theorizing they seek to explain. I assume that the "justification" of theories and claims requires much more than an appeal to an epistemology or philosophy of science, although such appeals will also be made. Theories, including theories of knowledge or science, are justified (if and when they are) on the basis of their coherence with experience. In contrast, Sandra Harding maintains that "no conceptual system can provide the justificatory grounds for itself" and that to "avoid vicious circularity, justificatory grounds always must be found outside the conceptual system one is trying to justify" (Harding 1986, 49). I doubt there are such grounds. I also doubt that the circularity involved, which I have referred to as radical interdependence (Nelson 1990, 9), is in every instance vicious. To the point here, it is not vicious if we do not assume that the philosophy of science "justifies" our theories or theorizing.

I bring to this work the basic assumption that empiricism is a theory of evidence for which there is currently no viable alternative. Beyond that core (and until such time as it is necessary to abandon it), any so-called dogmas of empiricism are signs that things have gone off track.

Quine, Boundaries, and the Philosophy of Science

Traditional philosophy of science demanded rigid boundaries between epistemology, metaphysics, science, and values—including social and political values. But in the last three decades, research into the assumptions, theories, and practices of the sciences, and into the social and political contexts in which science communities are located, has demonstrated interrelationships between all of these activities, which the traditional view wanted to keep separate.

These relationships have proved to be neither unidirectional nor superficial. Social and political contexts have been found to play a significant role in shaping the directions of scientific interest and research, affecting the questions addressed, the methodologies adopted, and the hypotheses and theories accepted in a range of social and biological sciences. It has also become increasingly clear how extensively the theories, research programs, and methodologies adopted in science in turn shape so-called common-sense beliefs and practices.

The evidence for these relationships represents a devastating challenge to the view that science is a practice autonomous of other practices and systems of beliefs, and feminist science scholars have made significant contributions to it. I have chosen to reexamine Quine's philosophy of science in the light of feminist science scholarship for several reasons. Some of the more controversial aspects of Quine's work represent the logical extension of central tenets of empiricism in light of developments in science and the philosophy of science, and thus, his work is an appropriate choice for exploring questions raised by feminist science scholarship for empiricist philosophy of science.

It is, in my view, of equal significance that Quine's positions constitute a more sophisticated view of evidence, inquiry, theory formation, and testing than those associated with the tradition of Carnap, Hempel, and Nagel—at the same that they avoid the relativism alleged to follow from Thomas Kuhn's positions. As much to the point, some of Quine's positions are deeply commensurate with those emerging in feminist science scholarship. Quine has also challenged the boundaries alleged to prevail between science, common sense, metaphysics, and the philosophy of science. I exploit Quine's challenges to the proponents of clear boundaries, but also argue that the traditional boundary he upholds—that between science and (nonepistemic) values—is no more real than those he challenges. Finally, I use Quine's holism to argue against the assumption of an epistemological chasm between feminists and nonfeminists.

Two qualifications about my use of Quine's work are in order. First, I have no reason to think that Quine is a feminist (or, to put things in more Quinean terms, that Quine would assent to the sentence "I am a feminist"). But I suspect this has more to do with what Quine believes about his beliefs than it does with Quine's beliefs about science and inquiry. The second qualification is this: that we can get help from Quine is not an indication that feminist science scholarship provides no new insights into science. The views I will advocate do not everywhere coincide with Quine's. I do think his views are well worth considering, are almost never wildly wrongheaded. I will expand upon his views, in light of insights provided by feminist science scholarship, to argue that empiricism can and should be separated from its traditional commitments to epistemological individualism, and to a hard and fast boundary between "good" science and (nonepistemic) values.

Empiricism Without Foundations

In an important sense, we are all empiricists. The hypothesis that there is a world that shapes and constrains what it is reasonable to believe, and that it does so by impinging on our sensory receptors, is woven through most beliefs, theories, and practices with good reason: it makes the most sense of what we experience. Moreover, the criterion of justifying and judging claims to know by reference to experience, however loose, enables us to distinguish claims that warrant serious consideration from those that do not. Most of us (at least in our less philosophical moments) make use of and appeal to this criterion.

A second, more fundamental thesis about evidence is usually at issue when empiricism is at issue. This discussion, like most discussions of empiricism, takes philosophical empiricism to be a theory that embraces the more contentious thesis that *all* the evidence there is for science is, in the end, sensory. This thesis is the core of empiricism as I will advocate it. It marks empiricism as a theory of evidence and distinguishes it from other such theories.

Empiricism's status as a theory of evidence depends on the viability of this thesis. In the philosophy of science, it further depends on our ability to build from this theory to explanations of scientific practice commensurate with our experiences of science.[5] There have been, of course, a number of empiricist accounts of science, some better than others. But I draw attention to the distinction between empiricism as a theory of evidence and empiricist accounts of science built on this theory.

In maintaining that all evidence for science is, in the end, sensory evidence, empiricists contend they are on solid ground. Sensory receptors are our only access to the world (at least so say our current best theories). Nonetheless, this thesis is contentious. Some grant the last point, but deny that the information so provided has much to do with the stories we tell about how things are. In addition, this tenet is qualified by many contemporary empiricists, including Quine.

In a number of arguments he offered from the 1960s well into the 1980s, Quine insisted that (phenomenological) sensory experience is not, and could not be, foundational.[6] Rather, he maintained, such experiences are shaped and mediated—indeed, they are made *coherent*—by numerous specific theories that are themselves embodied in and inseparable from language.

> Impressed with the fact that we know external things only mediately through our senses, philosophers from Berkeley onward have undertaken to strip away the physicalistic conjectures and bare the sense data. Yet even as we try to recapture the data, in all their innocence of interpretation, we find ourselves depending upon sidelong glances into natural science.
>
> The trouble is that immediate experience simply will not, of itself, cohere as an autonomous domain. References to physical things are largely what hold it together. These references are not just inessential vestiges of the initially intersubjective character of language, capable of being weeded out by devising an artificially subjective language for sense data. . . . Conceptualization on any considerable scale is inseparable from language. (Quine 1960, 2)

Conceptualization is necessary for coherent sensory experience, language is necessary for conceptualization, and language, Quine argues, is necessarily public (Quine 1960, 3; cf. Gibson 1988).[7]

Thus, Quine rejects the possibility of "grounding" science in something like "sense-datum" experience (i.e., pre-theoretic or "raw" experience) in the ways that logical positivism envisioned, and the project of rationally reconstructing a sense-datum language that Carnap also envisioned. Both the grounding and the project of reconstructing it are impossible. For this and other reasons, Quine maintains that an epistemology or philosophy of science is, and could only be, continuous with science (Quine 1969).

I later consider the scope and depth of the interdependence Quine maintains between science, philosophy, and so-called common sense in some detail, and the implications of this interdependence for feminist science scholarship. Here, I note two general implications of Quine's arguments against foundationalism. First, his insistence on the role of language and bodies of theory in shaping experience is deeply commensurate with feminist arguments that experience is shaped by bodies of accepted theory. We inherit conceptual frameworks and theories, Quine maintains, that shape what it is possible to experience and to know.

Second, I suggested at the outset that a consequence of empiricism's core thesis is that we can and should distinguish between theories and beliefs on the basis of experience, and that giving content to this claim is an important task for the philosophy of science. But empiricists who no longer seek an extra-theoretic foundation face a different task from their predecessors. A coherence theory of evidence is the overarching criterion in Quine's positions and, as explicated in his work, it is a dual constraint. Theories and beliefs[8] need to cohere with experiences of the world *and* with other accepted theories.[9] Quine's understanding of each of these constraints builds on his arguments concerning empirical content, and I briefly summarize them in the next section.[10]

Holism, Empirical Content, and a Coherence Theory of Evidence

Quine describes what he calls "the two cardinal tenets of empiricism" as "[w]hatever evidence there is for science is sensory evidence" and "[a]ll inculcation of meanings of words must rest ultimately on sensory evidence"

(Quine 1969, 75). But he does not take the understandings of these tenets to be static. In "Five Milestones of Empiricism," he explores continuities and discontinuities between earlier empiricist positions and those he advocates by noting important shifts in empiricism (1981b). Four of these shifts involve empirical content—what it is by way of theories that bears a relationship to nonverbal stimuli; the fifth is the shift to naturalized epistemology. In order, the shifts in what is recognized to have empirical content are first, from ideas to words, next from words to whole sentences, then from sentences to systems of sentences, and, finally, the abandonment of the analytic/synthetic distinction for the view that all sentences share empirical content.

I focus in this section on the third advance in Quine's list, the shift from viewing individual sentences as the bearers of empirical content to recognizing systems of sentences as the bearers of such content. This shift, of course, reflects Quine's arguments against verificationism in "Two Dogmas of Empiricism" (1953b).[11] In "Two Dogmas" Quine takes the verification theory of meaning, which he describes as the view that "the meaning of a statement is the method of empirically confirming or infirming it" (37), to be very closely connected with radical reductionism, which he describes as the view that "[e]very meaningful statement . . . is translatable into a statement (true or false) about immediate experience" (38).

Quine makes a "countersuggestion" to this verification theory of meaning—that "our statements about the external world face the tribunal of sense experience not individually but only as a corporate body" (41). This is holism, the thesis that it is a substantial body of theory (and, in principle, the whole of a current theory of nature) that figures in the adjudication of any particular theory or claim. The last section of "Two Dogmas" suggests that it is an argument concerning empirical content that underlies Quine's countersuggestion. Of the "man-made fabric" that constitutes "the totality of our so-called knowledge or beliefs," Quine maintains that "no particular experiences are linked with any particular statements in the interior of the field, except indirectly though considerations of equilibrium affecting the field as a whole" (42–43; cf. Quine 1981b).

Elsewhere, the relationship between holism and a view of empirical content is clear. In "Epistemology Naturalized," for example, Quine argues that there is no determinate list of sensory stimulations from which most individual sentences are derived or derivable. Rather, which sensory stimulations or features of the world come to be associated with a specific claim (or theory) is largely determined by broad bodies of accepted theories and standards. "The typical statement about bodies has no fund of experiential implications it can call its own. A substantial mass of theory, taken together, will commonly have experiential implications; this is how we make verifiable predictions" (Quine 1969, 79). A similar argument appears earlier, in "Posits and Reality." "Statements about bodies, common-sense or recondite, commonly make little or no empirical sense except as bits of a collectively significant containing system. Various statements can surely be supplanted by their negations, without conflict with any possible sensory contingency, provided that we revise other portions of our science in compensatory ways. Science is empirically underdetermined: there is slack" (Quine 1966b, 241). Still earlier, in *Word and Object*, Quine uses an arch metaphor to emphasize the sharing of empirical content by sentences:

> Theory may be deliberate, as in a chapter on chemistry, or it may be second nature, as is the immemorial doctrine of ordinary enduring middle-sized objects. In either case, theory causes a sharing, by sentences, of sensory supports. In an arch, an overhead block is supported immediately by other overhead blocks, and ultimately by all the base blocks collectively and none individually; and so it is with sentences, when theoretically fitted.
>
> What comes of the association of sentences with sentences is a vast verbal structure which, primarily as a whole, is multifariously linked to non verbal stimulation. (Quine 1960, 11–13)

In short, it is broad bodies of theory that have empirical significance, i.e., yield observational conditionals. Moreover, at least in principle, it is "as a whole" that common-sense, scientific, and philosophical theories confront experience. At the very least, scientific theories so confront experience. "What is important," Quine argues, "is that we cease to demand or expect of a scientific sentence that it have its own separable empirical meaning" (Quine 1981b, 71). "The unit of empirical significance is the whole of science" (Quine 1953b, 42).

I earlier stated that Quine maintains a "coherence theory of evidence," and I can now give more content to this view. As an overarching standard of evidence, coherence emerges in Quine's positions as a twofold standard and an alternative to both coherence and correspondence theories of truth. Specific theories, hypotheses, or claims are to be assessed on the basis of empirical success and integration with broader bodies of accepted theory.

The first constraint reflects three positions earlier summarized: the empiricist thesis that evidence is, in the end, sensory; Quine's arguments against foundationalism outlined earlier; and the arguments, just rehearsed, that individual sentences do not have empirical content in isolation from broad bodies of theory. The "checkpoints" of science, in Quine's view, are the observational conditionals yielded by bodies of theory.

The second constraint, integration with accepted theories, is also an implication of Quine's arguments for a holistic account of empirical content, for these arguments maintain that there is a fundamental interdependence among the sentences of the theories we maintain, an interdependence reflected in Quine's use of an arch metaphor to talk about the sharing of sensory supports.

The foregoing discussion highlights some significant shifts in empiricist philosophy of science advocated by Quine, and some deep continuities between his views and earlier empiricist views. Systems of sentences, rather than ideas or individual sentences, are recognized as the bearers of empirical content, but the empiricist thesis that all evidence is, in the end, sensory remains. At the same time, Quine does not assume unmediated access to the world. We experience the world through the lens of conceptualization and accepted theories. Moreover, the empiricist thesis is itself construed naturalistically, as an implication of science. There is also the suggestion—one that the next section indicates needs to be further developed—that Quine views the "fabric of science" to be inclusive, as the passage from *Word and Object* suggests, of "everything we ever say about the world."

Science (Almost) Without Boundaries

In this section, I build on the positions just outlined to introduce Quine's challenges to several thick and interconnected boundaries: those between metaphysics and science, between common sense and science, and between theories and observation. My discussion of these boundaries will not do justice to Quine's arguments, which carry more resonance than it will be possible to convey here.

My aim is twofold: to show that Quine's general arguments against these boundaries can be useful to feminist scientists and science scholars, and that feminist science scholarship indicates the need for expansions of and revisions in Quine's positions.

Metaphysics and Science

Quine says many things about ontology, the heart of metaphysics, but the best place to begin is with a relatively early discussion in "On What There Is" (1953a). The focus of this discussion is epistemological rather than metaphysical, reflecting its fundamental argument: that it is impossible to discuss "ontology" (what there is) without discussing theory (what we say there is). Ontological questions are always relative to some theory (or "set of coordinates" or "background theory") itself taken at "face value." Moreover, ontologies are always propounded in the activity of theorizing; they are not established, discovered, or posited prior to this activity. So readers who turn to "On What There Is" to find out what there is or what Quine thinks there is will be disappointed.

The answer, Quine tells us at the outset, to the question "What is there?" is "Everything." There are two (partially) separate theses underlying Quine's answer. The first is that we cannot separate ontology from ideology. There are no bare particulars or "things in themselves." "One tends to imagine that when someone propounds a theory concerning some sort of objects, our understanding of what he is saying will have two phases: first we must understand what the objects are, and second we must understand what the theory says about them. . . . [But] our understanding of 'what the objects are' awaits the second phase. . . . We do not learn first what to talk about and then what to say about it" (Quine 1960, 16). The second thesis is that there are no "absolute" ontological decisions. The only answer to "What is there?" is what this or that theory says there is. The "there is" idiom, Quine maintains, is invoked in all theorizing about the world; the objects we are committed to are the objects our theories say there are. "We commit ourselves to an ontology containing numbers when we say there are prime numbers larger than a million; we commit ourselves to an ontology containing centaurs when we say there are centaurs; and we commit ourselves to an ontology containing Pegasus when we say Pegasus is" (1953a, 8). And, as Quine's arguments against the analytic/synthetic distinction suggest, more general statements of ontology are part of the general network of theories that collectively shape and confront experience. These are statements that reflect the commitments (for example, to "law-like" natural relationships, and to macroscopic, enduring physical objects) to which specific theories in this network commit us.[12]

I have noted that Quine maintains that the objects we are committed to are those our theories say there are. But his arguments concerning ontology also suggest that such commitments can and should be evaluated. Following Bertrand Russell, Quine maintains that we can expose the ontic commitments honored by a particular theory by rendering its sentences in first-order quantification and looking at its domain. This is not to say that, as used in this exercise, logic tells us what there is. Ontology shows itself in what we are willing to quantify over. But one aspect of *evaluating* a theory (but only one less than a global theory) is determining whether the ontic commitments it carries are congenial with other accepted theories. Current theories do, Quine argues, suggest criteria—among these, simplicity and clarity of identity criteria—that can and should be used to assess ontologies. So, for example, Quine is loath to accept a theory that commits us to propositions, or meanings, or "mental objects," on the grounds that these alleged entities have no clear identity criteria, make for a more complicated ontology, and there are insufficient counterbalancing benefits to be obtained by countenancing them.

Whether one agrees with Quine about the usefulness of the entities he views as "suspect," or about the criterion of simplicity (I will argue that the clarity of identity criterion is one we should agree with Quine about), the general consequences of the arguments just summarized are significant. One is that science is *permeated* with metaphysical commitments. These are not "hidden," as aspects of Kuhn's accounts of normal and revolutionary science would suggest; nor are they "avoidable," as Hume and some logical positivists had hoped; nor are they able to be ignored, as the emphasis on the context of justification in postlogical positivist philosophy of science would suggest.

Second, we are not free to accept a theory *and disclaim* the ontic commitments it brings with it. That is to say, we are not free to adopt or pursue a methodology, research project, or hypothesis—and simultaneously claim that we are not "really committed" to the ontological commitments it carries, that our theory should not be judged on their basis, and so forth.

Finally, science can lead to *better* metaphysics. Hypotheses, theories, categories, and assumptions should be evaluated on the basis of the ontologies to which they commit us. What supports our specific and general ontological commitments is that theories that include them help us to explain and predict some of what happens. So, insofar as a specific ontological commitment enables good explanations, and insofar as it has clear identity criteria, it is warranted. Both criteria should be used to assess ontic commitments.

I suggest that these positions can be particularly useful to feminist science scholars in framing arguments about the metaphysical commitments they have found to shape research questions, methods, and theories in a number of sciences.

Consider, for example, the behaviors and objects posited by Sociobiologists that feminists have criticized (see, e.g., Bleier 1984). The list is substantial, but representative examples include "female coyness" in worms, "bluebird adultery," the "rampant machismo" of male insects, "prostitution" among chimpanzees, and "primate harems" (see, e.g., Barash 1977, 1979). Following Quine's lead, we are warranted in maintaining that Sociobiology is committed to these objects, warranted in evaluating them, and warranted in evaluating the theory partly on their basis.

If we make use of Quine's criterion of "clarity of identity," it becomes clear that these objects are indeed problematic. What, for example, are the behavioral criteria of "coyness" such that this is appropriately attributed to female worms, nonhuman primates, and humans? What are the behavioral criteria for "adultery" such that it is appropriately attributed to bluebirds (and presumably many more species given Sociobiology's core thesis that females are "reproductive resources")? As feminists have argued, it would seem that, as used by Sociobiologists (and, arguably, by anyone), these objects have no clear identity criteria. Rather, they enjoy or carry cognitive salience because of their connections to so-called common sense—but even as they function in the latter, their identity criteria are fuzzy at best. When generalized to other species, ascertaining their identity criteria is rather like trying to hold water in one's hand.

Quine argues that dubious metaphysical commitments work against any theory, but such commitments are particularly problematic for Sociobiology. This is because the alleged universality of such objects and behaviors functions as *prima facie* evidence for Sociobiology's core hypothesis that they are genetically determined. That is to say, adaptationists can declare (by definition) any behavior to be the product of natural selection. If Sociobiology's claims are to come to more than a "just-so story," then until such time as they are able to come up with the "goods" (the evidence linking such objects to genes) we can and should assess the theory on the basis of these commitments. Using the standard of clear identity criteria, I have argued, these commitments are dubious—and thus so too is the theory. (Nor, of course, are these the only dubious metaphysical commitments that undermine Sociobiology's plausibility.)

Not all of the metaphysical commitments that feminist scientists have identified as shaping research questions, observations, and hypotheses are as obviously anthropomorphic and androcentric as those just considered, or as wholly reliant for their salience on so-called common-sense associations, or as lacking in substantive content. Feminist critiques of the attributions of gender dimorphism to nonhuman species, and to objects that are not sexed (bacteria, cells, hormones, and so forth), demonstrate that such commitments are often more subtle and more pervasive (see, e.g., Bleier 1984; Fausto-Sterling 1985; and Hubbard et al. 1982). Moreover, there are a number of cases in which, contrary to Sociobiology, it seems unlikely that scientists are aware of the relationships between the metaphysical commitments their research questions presume and so-called common-sense views. More subtle still are assumptions that natural and social relationships are linear and hierarchical, assumptions that feminists argue have unduly limited models of social dynamics, biological processes, and natural relationships more generally (see, e.g., Bleier 1984; Haraway 1978; and Keller 1983, 1985).

Again, I suggest that Quine's arguments are particularly useful. Feminist scientists may never convince their colleagues that commitments to "aggressivity" in male rodents, to "masters" and "executives" of biological processes, and to "laws of nature" that govern all that happens reflect Western political experience. More to the point, Quine's arguments suggest that such *relationships* are not the most significant problem. The significant problem, in the first case, is lack of identity criteria; in the second and third, that such commitments unduly restrict the kinds of relationship and/or distort the dynamics and relationships that obtain in the relevant domains. We are warranted in identifying these commitments and in evaluating theories that incorporate them on their basis.

I have suggested that Quine's general arguments concerning ontology can be used to support feminists' claims that metaphysical commitments have a substantial role in science and that many of them are problematic. But the critiques feminists have leveled at a number of such commitments also indicate the need for significant expansions or revisions in some of Quine's related positions. For although I have maintained that their relationships to social beliefs and values are not what make the metaphysical commitments so far considered problematic, it is likely that the acceptance and prevalence of such commitments is a function of their relationship to such beliefs and values. But relationships between the kinds of social belief and values that feminist scholarship reveals have been consistently denied or ignored by empiricists. In this regard, two of Quine's positions, his account of "common-sense theory" and his defense of a boundary between science and values, warrant critical attention.

Common Sense, Values, and Science

I have noted that Quine denies the possibility of "absolute ontological decisions," i.e., of determining what there is in isolation from what this or that theory says there is. One of his arguments for this claim is that physical object ontology is "our conceptual first" *and* theoretical. One aspect of his argument for the conceptual primacy of physical object ontology has already been noted: his claim that the project of reconstructing a sense-datum language is impossible, that "references to physical things are largely what hold [sensory experience] together." Coherent sensory experience requires conceptualization, and Quine maintains that physical objects are the basics of the conceptual scheme into which we are inculcated as we learn language. He also maintains that learning physical object *ontology* is inseparable from learning physical object *theory*.

> It is only when the child has got on to the full and proper use of individuative terms like 'apple' that he [sic] can properly be said to have taken to using terms as terms, and speaking of objects. . . . To learn 'apple' it is not sufficient to learn how much of what goes on counts as apple; we must learn how much counts as *an* apple, and how much is another. . . . Only at this stage does it begin to make sense to wonder whether the apple now in one's hand is the apple noticed yesterday. (Quine 1969b, 7–10)

The conceptual primacy Quine claims for "physical object" ontology and theory is more than temporal. Scientific ontologies, he argues, depend on physical object ontology in important ways. Such ontologies are often constructed *by analogy* to common-sense objects and their behavior. More importantly, the evidence for "unobservable" objects and events (e.g., subatomic particles, a past episode of speciation, and so forth) is constituted by its "indirect bearing on observable reality" (1966b, 235).

At the same time, Quine argues, scientific ontologies and theories systematize "common-sense" theories and experience. Thus, neither ontology is "epistemologically privileged." "The physical particles are naturally fundamental in this kind of way: laws of behavior of those particles afford, so far as we know, the simplest formulation of a general theory of what happens. Common-sense bodies . . . are conceptually fundamental: it is by reference to them that the very notions of reality and evidence are acquired, and that the concepts which have to do with physical particles or even with sense data tend to be framed and phrased" (239). Quine's view of the relationship between the notion of evidence and common-sense ontology is even clearer in the following passage from "Posits and Reality." "Having noticed that man has no evidence for the existence of bodies beyond the fact that their assumption helps him to organize experience, we should [do] well, instead of disclaiming evidence for the existence of bodies, to conclude: such, then, at bottom, is what evidence is, both for ordinary bodies and for molecules" (238). Specific and general standards of evidence, as well as the notion of evidence itself, have their roots in common-sense theorizing, which itself, for reasons earlier cited, is theoretical.

From the perspective of feminist science scholarship, Quine's arguments for fundamental relationships between common-sense theory and science constitute an obvious advance over views of science as independent of, and unshaped by, "common-sense" beliefs and practices. His argument that scientific ontologies are often analogous to common-sense objects and their behavior, and that the evidence for nonobservable objects and events is that theories that posit them more systematically explain common-sense events and objects, support feminists' arguments that there are significant relationships between beliefs and values held in the broad communities within which science is undertaken, and ontological commitments that shape methodologies, research questions, and theories in a number of sciences.

When we look somewhat closer, however, it is clear that what Quine means by "common sense" and the social beliefs and values that feminists have found to inform science are not co-extensive. Most of what Quine says about common-sense theory and theorizing is couched in terms of physical object theory. His account of common sense does not include significant aspects of everyday theory and practices, including beliefs and practices concerning gender and Western political experiences more generally.

Moreover, as it figures in Quine's arguments, physical object theory is virtually ahistorical (recall, for example, his reference to "the immemorial doctrine of physical objects"). Thus, although the interdependence Quine maintains between these levels of theorizing is promising, feminist science scholarship indicates the need to expand the view of common-sense theorizing so that it reflects many more kinds of beliefs and assumptions that can impact on scientific theorizing.

In addition, Quine's views about values would further limit the kinds of beliefs and practices that can influence or inform science. In his autobiography, Quine muses about what he calls his "disdain of conceptual [boundaries]," noting that his "love of earthly boundaries . . . stacks up oddly with [his] disdain of conceptual ones" (Quine 1985, 477). So, it is interesting that Quine's efforts to rub out the alleged boundaries so carefully forged by earlier empiricists never included a challenge to the alleged boundary between science and values. It is also surprising, given his argument that there is no "natural" boundary between common-sense theorizing and the sciences proper, or between either of these and philosophical thinking.

But Quine only incorporates within philosophy what he calls "scientific philosophy" and describes himself as engaged in those studies of moral and analytic values that are "of an analytical cast . . . and apt to offer little in the way of inspiration or consolation" (Quine 1981, 193). We have seen that his account of common-sense theory is virtually exhausted by a general, ahistorical "physical object theory." And Quine proclaims the boundary between science and values as strongly as he questions virtually every other boundary separating science from other things. "Scientific theory," he maintains, "stands proudly and notoriously aloof from value judgments" (Quine 1981e, 49).

> I think that what sets morals apart from scientific theory is a substantive point of modern scientific theory itself: a scientific doctrine as to the origins and basis of morality. Science sees the moral law no longer as coeval with the cosmos, but as the work of society. Therefore science addresses itself to the origins of the moral law, among other things, but does not incorporate its content. This divorce of science from moral values is a sophisticated

> manifestation, reflecting no significant quirk in language learning. (1981, 51–52)

But science's concerns with the *origins* of morality are by no means as innocent of values in terms of directions or implications as Quine would suggest, a point made abundantly clear by Sociobiology. Indeed, the "naturalization" of so-called common-sense beliefs about gender and other social relations via appeals to selection pressures on hominid ancestors typically results in *value judgments* on a selective and consequential set of practices and values. As importantly, our so-called common-sense dealings with the world, including those involving physical objects, are imbued with values, and feminist science scholarship indicates that many of these values, like the more narrow relationships Quine maintains between physical object theory and physics, are both reflected in and reinforced by scientific theorizing.

Several things have emerged in this discussion of ontology. One is Quine's general argument for fundamental relationships between common-sense theorizing and science. A second is Quine's view that standards of evidence emerge concomitantly with theorizing. A third is the view that, although there is no "metaphysically innocent" science, science can lead to better metaphysics. We have also explored some reasons why Quine often uses the term 'science' inclusively, to include "common sense" and philosophy as well as science "proper." Finally, I have argued that feminist science scholarship indicates that the common-sense theories that share an interdependence with science include more than physical object theorizing and that the boundary between science and values is untenable.

But this discussion of "ontology," although useful in illuminating some relationships Quine maintains, has also been somewhat strange. For reasons already considered, Quine maintains that ontology is inseparable from theory. I next turn to his views about theories, and their implications for another traditional boundary: that alleged to obtain between theories and observation statements.

Theories and Observation

In "Facts of the Matter," Quine remarks that "ontology is not what mainly matters" (1978, 64–65). Putting together various views we have so far considered, it is clearly theories that mainly matter in Quine's view.

We can say more specifically that Quine views theories as sets of sentences. His construal of theories as sets of sentences is in keeping with his emphasis on the relationship between language, conceptualization, and coherent sensory experience. It also reflects his view that the smallest "units" of empirical content are generally systems of sentences.[13]

Given the view that systems of sentences have empirical content, and that the philosophy of science is itself part of (rather than foundational to) science, how do theories face or link up with the world? Logical positivism and postlogical positivist philosophy of science used "observation sentences" to forge this link. Does holism as Quine advocates it allow for the notion of observation sentences? If not, does holism allow for the notion that theories and theorizing are constrained by experience?

Quine maintains that we can classify some sentences as "observation sentences" and that these do forge a link between experience and theories. Although single sentences do not have isolable empirical content, the stimulus conditions associated with some sentences can be, he maintains, roughly specified by reference to a community of speakers. These are occasion sentences that most members of a specific language community will assent to in the presence of rather specific circumstances, and dissent from in their absence.

> Occasion sentences whose stimulus meanings vary none under the influence of collateral information may naturally be called observation sentences, and their stimulus meanings may without fear of contradiction be said to do full justice to their meanings. The observation sentences as we have identified them are just the occasion sentences on which there is pretty sure to be firm agreement on the part of well-placed observers. Thus they are just the sentences on which a scientist will tend to fall back when pressed by doubting colleagues. (Quine 1960, 43–44)

Quine argues that the observational conditionals yielded by theories do allow for theories to be constrained by sensory experience. Testing a theory involves testing observational conditionals in relation to the stimulus conditions a community associates with them, and the link between observation statements and theories is forged by shared theoretical notions. "The problem of relating theory to sensory stimulation may now be put . . . as that of relating theory formulations to observation sentences. In this we have a head start in that we recognize the observation sentences to be theory laden. What this means is that terms embedded in observation sentences recur in the theory formulations" (Quine 1981c, 25–26). Although there is considerable disagreement concerning this point, I submit that Quine's argument does not resurrect the traditional boundary between "theoretical statements" and observation statements. The occasion sentences that Quine maintains can and do function as observation sentences are *theoretical*. Although their stimulus meanings may not vary with collateral information, these sentences do not have associations with specific stimulus conditions in isolation from a body of theory.[14]

Let me conclude this section by saying some general things about why and how Quine's account of the "link" between theories and the world differs from that maintained by Hempel and Nagel. Consider, first, the "world" side. Although we can ascertain observational conditionals yielded by a theory, we are not testing these by reference to *the world*, but by reference to *experiences of* the world. On the "theory" side, it is bodies of theory, not individual theories or hypotheses, that yield observational conditionals. Finally, it is a consequence of holism that if a prediction misfires, it will not be clear which of the sentences of the embedding theory is the problem. We can always adjust aspects of the theory in question, or others that we maintain, to accommodate the apparent mismatch.

Feminist Science Scholarship and Quine's Positions

It might seem that the extent to which observation is theory laden is one of the primary issues at stake in feminist science criticism. But the relationship between observations and theories was settled decades ago. As much to the point, feminist scientists and science scholars are not attempting to establish *that* observations are theory laden, and if they were they would not be raising new or interesting issues.

Nor, Quine's arguments suggest, are the metaphysical commitments feminists criticize problematic because science should be *free* of such commitments. Positing objects, and working within broad metaphysical assumptions concerning ontology and natural relationships that are implicit in accepted theory, are part and parcel of the doing of science. So, too, are refining ontological commitments and evaluating theories on the basis of those they carry.

Finally, Quine maintains that analogies between scientific ontologies and common-sense ontologies are to be expected—that not only are such relationships not problematic, they are, he suggests, unavoidable. Common-sense theory is our conceptual first, part of the network that collectively faces experience, and interdependent with science narrowly construed.

Notwithstanding these continuities between Quine's general positions and emphases in feminist science scholarship, the latter does suggest new lessons. In most general terms, this scholarship reveals factors having a bearing on scientific theorizing and theories that Quine fails to recognize (or, in the case of values, even to allow). It is not, as I earlier argued, only those aspects of common sense that Quine terms "physical object" theory that have an impact on theorizing and theories in many sciences. Nor is it the case that nonepistemic values have no role in "good science." Moreover, the monolithic "we" Quine speaks of and his notion that there is one overall theory of nature that "we" share, are challenged by feminist science scholarship. Currently, it makes a difference to one's observations, appraisals of ontological commitments, observations, and theories if one brings the category of gender to bear on science, and comes to recognize the role of androcentrism and implicit assumptions about gender, dominance hierarchies, and the prevalence of linear, hierarchical natural relationships throughout human and nonhuman nature. And, as I explore in my conclusion, it is equally clear that neither feminist perspectives nor the perspectives they criticize are the creation or property of individual scientists or researchers *qua* individuals.

How are the problems feminists have uncovered best characterized and explained? And how might feminists' abilities to recognize these problems be characterized and explained? I will certainly not offer an explanation of these things here. Any such explanations will need to encompass historical and contemporary social relations and practices. What I propose is a model of evidential relations, based in part on Quinean holism and in part on the implications of feminist science critique, to function as part of such explanations. I use the example of the critiques offered in the 1970s and 1980s of the "man, the hunter" theory of evolution to illustrate this model. Although the example is dated, the issues it raised continue to inform feminist science critiques and I can assume readers' familiarity with it.

One aspect of the criticism feminists offered of the "man, the hunter" theory was directed at an organizing principle that the theory incorporated:

that males are socially oriented—their activities and behaviors central to and determinative of social dynamics; and that females are biologically oriented—their activities and behaviors primarily reproductive, with reproductive activities assumed to be "natural" and unskilled, and without consequence for social dynamics or culture. As evidence of this organizing principle, feminist critics pointed out that the "man, the hunter" theory credited the evolution of *Homo sapiens* to behaviors and activities its advocates attribute to our male ancestors. According to the theory, the invention of tools and the development of social organization led to the evolution of bipedal and speaking "man," and both were the achievements of our male ancestors in order to facilitate the hunting of large animals (see, e.g., Bleier 1984; Hubbard et al. 1983).[15]

As feminist critics pointed out, this organizing principle had far-reaching consequences; in addition to shaping the general outlines of an androcentric reconstruction of human evolution, it shaped the interpretation of fossil and archeological data and underwrote arguments—by Sociobiologists, for example—that a sexual division of labor and male dominance are the products of selection pressures on our ancestors (Bleier 1984; Longino and Doell 1983).

Much of the criticism directed at the theory's organizing principle centered on questions of evidential warrant. Ruth Hubbard argued, for example, that without androcentric bias, there was no reason to assume a sexual division of labor in early hominid and human groups. In her extensive and detailed criticism of the theory, Ruth Bleier argued that it "starts with a set of assumptions concerning the eternal nature of the characteristics . . . of women and men" (Bleier 1984, 123). Other feminist critics argued similarly, citing androcentrism as both shaping the general outlines and details of the "man, the hunter" account, and wholly unwarranted.

Considered on their own terms, in isolation from other theories, both the organizing principle and the "man, the hunter" account do seem without warrant. Accordingly, Helen E. Longino and Ruth Doell argued that in the case of the "man, the hunter" theory and that of the "woman, the gatherer" theory, the gap between theory and data was filled in by "preconceived and culturally determined ideas" (Longino and Doell 1983, 175).

Few of us, I suspect, would deny that androcentrism and gynocentrism were factors, respectively, in the development and advocacy of the "man, the hunter" and "woman, the gatherer" theories, or deny that feminist criticism of the former was enabled by feminist scholarship. It seems no less clear that there was a gap between these accounts of evolution and the fossil and archeological evidence, and that problems attendant to historical explanations were at work including the role of current contexts in shaping such explanations and the relative lack of "data" and their unevenness.[16]

But construing evidential relations holistically suggests an alternative to two assumptions at least implicit in the feminist criticism I have summarized: one, that there was little or no evidential warrant for the organizing principle or "man, the hunter" theory; the other, that the *only* assumptions that mediated between each hypothesis and the data were "culturally determined beliefs."

Consider, for example, an issue of debate between advocates of the two theories: the significance of chipped stones found near fossil remains of *Homo erectus* (Longino and Doell 1983). Were they evidence that our male ancestors made tools to facilitate the hunting of large animals, as "man, the hunter" theorists assumed; evidence that females made tools related to gathering, as those advocating the "woman, the gatherer" theory argued; or evidence of some other activity that a future theory might posit (Longino and Doell 1983)? If we consider the stones and other artifacts to be the *only* available evidence, then any answer to the question of the stones' significance will be based, to use Longino's and Doell's phrase, on considerations other than "direct evidence" (175). Hence on a narrow construal of evidence, any such answer will be supplied by beliefs and assumptions that are inappropriate, that don't themselves constitute evidence.

In contrast, a holistic theory of evidence suggests that the evidence actually brought to bear—and appropriately—on the question of the significance of these stones was *vast:* that it included hypotheses and results in other fields (primate anatomy, geology, and primatology, for example) as well as theories that underwrite our assumptions about how such fields are relevant (or are not). And, in fact, feminist attention to the "man, the hunter" theory revealed a substantial feedback system supporting the theory and the organizing principle it incorporates. Far from being developed in isolation, this theory represented a *synthesis* of theories, models, and observations from a number of sciences, including primate anatomy, neurobiology, evolutionary biology, geology, paleontology, and population genetics.

Connections to other theories and research were no less apparent in terms of the organizing principle feminists have criticized. Both the theory's advocates and its feminist critics noted that in reconstructing the social dynamics of early hominid and human groups, "man, the hunter" theorists drew on accounts of behavior and social dynamics in contemporary hunter-gatherer societies, and theories and observations in primatology and biobehavioral science. And in each of these fields, feminist scientists and science critics documented *similar, androcentric methods as organizing principles that guided the interpretation of data and observations*. Finally, feminist critics of the theory noted the deep convergence between the "man, the hunter" account of early hominid social organization and behavior and contemporary Western social arrangements (at least idealized versions of them).

When we construe evidence broadly, it becomes clear that, far from being *unwarranted*, both the theory and the organizing principle enjoyed *substantial* evidential support and that the evidence for both lay in great measure in just such connections. Equally important, recognizing such evidential relations is necessary if we are to provide an accurate account of the evidence that supported feminist criticism of the "man, the hunter" theory and that supported the "woman, the gatherer" theory. In both cases, scientists and science critics synthesized research in primatology, anthropology, and the biobehavioral sciences that was *not shaped by androcentric organizing principles and assumptions*. The evidence for feminist critiques of "man, the hunter" also included knowledge of androcentrism in other sciences and of the deep relationships between gender and science that had become visible in the preceding decade.

I am not suggesting that when we construe evidence broadly, the gap between reconstructions of human evolution and evidence will be closed. That gap will always remain, a consequence of the more general underdetermination of theories, of the specific problems faced by historical reconstructions, and of the relative lack of artifacts in this particular case. My point is that individual theories neither develop nor face experience in isolation; that the evidence available, relevant, and appropriate is broader than "data"; and that this evidence is not (at least when it is interesting) arbitrary. These points are not simply implications of Quinean holism; they are also an implication of feminist science criticism, and surely of the critiques we have been considering.

Philosophical legend credits Hobbes with the line "The Inn of Evidence has no signpost." I don't know if the legend is true, but I like to cite it. Viable theories, like evidence, are not self-announcing. When we judge a theory as viable or not, when we judge a research project, a model, a methodological principle, or a theory as an example of "good" or "bad" science, when we judge a particular claim or belief as warranted or unwarranted, it can not be on the basis of some simple test or criterion. These judgments require attention to as much evidence as we can (or find it necessary to) accommodate. After such evaluation, we may find that rather than pointing to a theory like the "man, the hunter" theory as an example of "bad science," we will want to say that it was once promising in the context of then current knowledge and standards, but we are now in a position—(although certainly not ever in a position to say that all the evidence is in)—to see that it is not viable.

An additional benefit of construing evidence broadly is that this undermines the claim that cases like the one just considered involve incommensurability. Advocates of the "man, the hunter" theory and feminist critics disagreed about many things, including models and observations in sciences currently viewed as relevant to human evolution—and even whether some sciences are relevant—as well, perhaps, as so-called common-sense assumptions about gender. But they did not disagree about everything; they shared larger bodies of knowledge and standards, including the view that humans evolved and that their activities were factors in that process. Hence members of these groups were able to disagree about the significance of chipped stones without any lapse in conversation. The flip side of the point is this: although the knowledge and standards currently at issue are community specific, feminist communities and science communities overlap (consider feminist primatologists), and are themselves subcommunities of larger communities—a situation that, along with the changing social relations that made it possible, has enabled feminist science criticism and feminist knowledge more broadly.

Finally, cases such as that just considered suggest that the appropriate focuses of our analyses are communities. We cannot credit individual scientists with the assumptions, ontologies, organizing principles, and theories that constitute evidence for the "man, the hunter" theory or with synthesizing these. The assumptions and models were common to various sciences; moreover, androcentric assumptions and methodologies, like feminist assumptions and methodologies, have been generated within social experiences, relations, traditions, and historically and culturally specific ways of organizing social life. Nor, of course, can we credit any individual with the recognition that male dominance is not an inevitable feature of social groups, or that organizing principles like the one at issue in the "man, the hunter" theory distort observations and theories. The standards and knowledge that underwrite the acceptability of androcentric and feminist assumptions are communal.

It is to the implications of such cases and of some of Quine's own positions to which I next turn.

Who Knows

Acceptable answers to the question "Who knows?" include "Everyone," "All of us," "Lots of people," or "Many of us," but only very problematically "*Only* me." What I know depends inextricably on what *we* know, for some "we." My claims to know are subject to community criteria, public notions of what constitutes evidence—so that in an important sense, I *can* only know what *we* know, for some "we." In those rare cases when I claim exclusive knowledge, my claim is usually either uninteresting (others could know if they looked) or false. In those even rarer cases when I claim to know something revolutionary (for example, that Jupiter has four moons), something that does not meet community standards of evidence, *and* my claim is eventually accepted, it will have required a concomitant revolution in standards of evidence before I really know. And then, of course, *we* will know, for some "we."

These are not musings on the meaning of "knowledge" or definitions of what is to count as knowledge. We can begin to illuminate how my knowing requires our knowing by considering beliefs. Beliefs appear to be more like the "private property" of individuals. But for much the same reasons, this private ownership is mostly illusory. Beliefs, like knowledge, require public conceptual schemes for their formulation. The allegedly "unvarnished news" of sense data is not only never heard, it was never there to begin with. And although beliefs are not as closely tied to evidence as claims to know, we don't really understand someone's claim to believe what is inconsistent with obvious evidence. Nor can we ourselves succeed in believing what we also recognize to be unreasonable given the evidence. The most we will tolerate is belief in the absence of convincing counterevidence. As Quine notes, the White Queen who claims to engage in "the activity of believing" for at least half an hour a day, sometimes managing to believe as many as six impossible things before breakfast, is "atypical" on both counts (Quine 1987, 19). Beliefs are constrained by evidence.

These considerations argue for the view that it is communities or groups that acquire and possess knowledge, and that the traditional focus in epistemology and the philosophy of science on individuals *qua* individuals is inappropriate. Individuals "have" beliefs and do know, but largely derivatively. Their beliefs and knowing depend on language and the conceptual schemes it embodies, and what they know and believe is constrained by public standards of evidence. The primary epistemological agents are groups—or, more accurately, epistemological communities.

An empiricist account of science that took communities rather than individuals as its focus would not be, of course, like any contemporary empiricist approach to science. Although many of the things I have said about believing and knowing are implications of Quine's positions, his specific proposal for naturalizing epistemology suggests the view that when "we know," "we" really means "me and you and you . . . and you." The interesting questions, then, are these: When "we know" is this because "me and you and you . . . and you" each independently knows, or is the activity more communal than this? And, if the "we" of "we know" is the collective "we," is there a future for empiricism's theory of evidence?

Quine's specific proposal for how epistemology should be naturalized suggests that, at bottom, the "we" in "we know" really means "me and you and you . . . and you." In the project he envisions, explanations of how and what "we" know will be couched in terms of the connection between neurophysiological states and stimuli. But, I suggest, the project as envisioned, and Quine's own positions earlier discussed, attest to the fundamental problems of the commitment to individualism.

Quine's description of the epistemological model he envisions is very general. In "Epistemology Naturalized" he describes the experimental model this way:

> Epistemology, or something like it, simply falls into place as a chapter of psychology and hence of natural science. It studies a natural phenomenon, viz., a human subject. This human subject is accorded a certain experimentally controlled input—certain patterns of irradiation in assorted frequencies, for instance—and in the fullness of time the subject delivers as output a description of the three-dimensional external world and its history. The relation between the meager input and the torrential output is a relation that we are prompted to study for somewhat the same reasons that always prompted epistemology; namely, in order to see how

> evidence relates to theory, and in what ways one's theory of nature transcends any available evidence. (Quine 1969, 82–83)

Although Quine discusses correlating behaviors and "input" in this description, he also maintains that behaviors are not mental states (Quine 1966a, 1978). Mental states are physical states, behaviors are a way of identifying and individuating these, lacking (as we at least presently lack) specification of the physical states. Thus, Quine's experimental model suggests that an explanation of a given belief would involve correlating the physical state of my environment, the triggerings of my exteroceptors, and the neurophysiological state brought about by these things.

We are not now in a position to provide the list of correlations that would figure in explanations of how we construct theories, acquire beliefs, and so forth. Nor are we close to providing the domino-like series of causal explanations that Quine envisions, in which "causal explanations of psychology are to be sought in physiology, of physiology in biology, of biology in chemistry, and of chemistry in physics—in the elementary physical states" (Quine 1978, 167). But we could be satisfied with a promissory note if the prospects for answering epistemological questions within empirical psychology were indeed promising. The question I want to explore is whether or not the promissory note holds any promise.

There are two ways of interpreting Quine's proposal, and I will consider each briefly. The difference between the interpretations concerns *what* it is that empirical psychology (or philosophers making use of research in this discipline) might someday explain. In one interpretation of Quine's proposal, and I take it be the least likely interpretation of his proposal, empirical psychologists would attempt to explain specific beliefs. Using the "meager input" accorded in an experimental situation, and noting how the subject behaves in response to it, we would discover the relationship between the acquisition of a particular belief and current stimuli.

If this model represents the future of epistemology, then we need to assume that it reflects what occurs in actual cases of belief acquisition, that it represents how individuals come to have beliefs. Given the most ideal (but, by current lights, highly unlikely) situation—in which all the relationships assumed in the model obtain, and also lend themselves to one-to-one correlations—would we obtain useful insights into the current state of science by focusing on how individual scientists have come to have the beliefs they do? I want to make the nature of the question I am asking clear, and also make it clear that I am not being facetious about the project so envisioned. If we adopt this general model of explanation, either by actively pursuing it or by continuing to focus on scientists *qua* individuals, we risk setting aside or de-emphasizing a host of other factors, such as language, inherited conceptual schemes, and interpersonal experience, as explanatory.

That there are problems with the model so understood emerges in Quine's description of the experimental situation. This description suggests that the meager input provided to the subject produces the output (whether torrential or relatively modest). Even in the controlled experimental environment Quine outlines, it is not the stimuli provided by the psychologists that *alone* explain the output. Our subject is not a solipsist. She or he speaks a language (presumably, one the psychologist also speaks), and has a lifetime of prior experience and accepts a system, however unsystematized, of beliefs and theories. It is on the basis of these that the subject is even able to respond to the presented stimuli, and that she or he responds in certain ways. An explanation of the subject's behavior or belief on this particular occasion would be inclusive of much input, including necessarily prior interpersonal experiences and public theory. The behavior, and thus the belief, is not explained without reference to these factors. Of course, Quine might have envisioned the experiment he outlines as the following of our subject through her or his entire development, from womb to maturity. But such an experiment would not, in advance, circumscribe a range of epistemologically relevant events and variables.

I think that Quine's proposal should be interpreted differently, that he does not foresee that we will ever be involved in the project of correlating specific beliefs to specific neurophysiological states, and correlating such states to specific stimuli. He may envision the task as arriving at a general explanation of how beliefs (again understood as neurophysiological states) are caused by stimuli, and seeing what the slippage is between the meager input accorded the species (an allusion to underdetermination) and the torrential output the species produces. But, so understood, the project still assumes that answers to general epistemological questions can be found, in principle, in relationships between neurophysiological states and stimuli, and significant difficulties remain.

One of the first things a genuinely naturalized epistemology would need to take into account is that the human brain has a history. Its evolution, together with the development of language, conceptualization, the positing of objects, and so forth, would need to be included in any general theory of human theorizing. But any theory that reconstructed our evolutionary history, including our biological history, would need to recognize the fundamental role of interpersonal relationships. It would need to assume, evolutionary biologists and anthropologists tell us, that the acquisition of language was a social feat, and that among the factors that helped to propel brain evolution were human practices.

A genuinely naturalized epistemology would also need to take into account that each *adult* human brain has a history, and that postnatal development, development that results in the structural capacities for language, learning, and many kinds of perceptual experience, *requires* complex interaction with external stimuli, including interpersonal experience (see, e.g., Bleier 1984).

In short, naturalized epistemology will need to incorporate, among its most basic organizing principles, the condition that the acquisition of language and beliefs requires sociolinguistic communities. Indeed, it is a consequence of Quine's own arguments against foundationalism that we are not and could not be "knowers" without intersubjective experience, and that we do not, individually or collectively, have access to the world unmediated by the theories we inherit.

These brief considerations of two interpretations of Quine's proposal indicate that naturalized epistemology will need to look to more than empirical psychology, and that its primary focus should be on human social groups. The interesting questions involve the directions we should take in developing such an epistemology, and how the changes have come about that now prompt us to reconsider the empiricist commitment to individualism. As naturalists, I submit, answers to the latter question should affect those we give to the former; they indicate which directions are likely to be most fertile.

Notes

1. This, of course, is not surprising. In "Two Dogmas of Empiricism," Quine argued that statements of logic are empirical—part and parcel of an overall theory of nature. His argument against substitutional interpretation was based on his view that the domain of "our most serious theory of nature" is non-denumerable.

2. An exception is the article by Jack Nelson.

3. This section is largely excerpted from the introduction and chapter 1 of Nelson (1990).

4. Representative feminist discussions include Fee (1981), Harding (1983, 1986), Jaggar (1983), and Rose (1983).

5. I distinguish between epistemology, which is concerned with knowledge in general, and the philosophy of science, which takes science as its subject matter.

6. In Quine's more recent work, *Pursuit of Truth* and *From Stimulus to Science*, a commitment to foundationalism on some level is suggested by his account of observation sentences. We discuss this in the introduction to this volume. Neither work was published when I was writing *Who Knows*. See also n. 7.

7. I note the time frame of those of Quine's discussions to which I am here referring because Quine's more recent work (e.g., *Pursuit of Truth*) may reflect a shift toward granting sensory experience at the physical level something like a foundational role.

8. See, for example, "On the Very Idea of a Third Dogma" in Quine (1981), and "Two Dogmas of Empiricism" in Quine (1953).

9. See, for example, "Two Dogmas of Empiricism" in Quine (1953), especially the last section; "On the Very Idea of a Third Dogma" in Quine (1981, 38–42); and chapters 1 and 2 of Quine (1960).

10. See n. 4 of the introduction to this volume.

11. These shifts are described in more detail in our introduction to this volume.

12. These arguments are outlined in the introduction to this volume.

13. This, as I noted in the introduction to this chapter, is not accurate as stated. Quine defines "stimulus meaning" in terms of those physical processes (triggerings of exteroceptors) that would lead a person to assent or dissent from a sentence construed holophrastically. Thus, he maintains, both observation sentences, when construed holophrastically, and observation categoricals made up of them, are linked directly to sensory stimulations.

14. See n. 13.

15. Some advocates of the theory construed the implications of hunting more broadly, arguing that what they call the "hunting adaptation" underlies human psychology, biology, emotions, and divisions of labor by sex (see the discussion in Bleier 1984). Hence the implications of the theory were broader than the discussion here suggests.

16. Bleier (1984), Harding (1986), Longino and Doell (1983), and Longino (1990) include extensive consideration of these problems.

References

Barash, D. 1977. *Sociobiology and Behavior*. New York: Elsevier.

———. 1979. *The Whisperings Within*. New York: Harper & Row.

Bleier, R. 1984. *Science and Gender*. New York: Pergamon Press.

Fee, E. 1982. "A Feminist Critique of Objectivity." In *Woman's Nature: Rationalizations of Inequality*, ed. M. Lowe and R. Hubbard. New York: Pergamon Press.

Gibson, R. 1988. *Enlightened Empiricism: An Examination of W. V. Quine's Theory of Knowledge*. Tampa: University Presses of Florida.

Harding, S. 1986. *The Science Question in Feminism*. Ithaca: Cornell University Press.

Hubbard, R., M. S. Henifin, and B. Fried, eds. 1982. *Biological Woman: The Convenient Myth*. Cambridge, Mass.: Schenkman.

Jaggar, A. 1983. *Feminist Politics and Human Nature*. Totowa, N.J.: Rowman & Allenheld.

Quine, W. V. 1953. *From a Logical Point of View*. Cambridge, Mass.: Harvard University Press.

———. 1953a. "On What There Is." In *From a Logical Point of View*.

———. 1953b. "Two Dogmas of Empiricism." In *From a Logical Point of View*.

———. 1960. *Word and Object*. New York: John Wiley and Sons; Cambridge: MIT Press.

———. 1966. *The Ways of Paradox and Other Essays*. New York: Random House.

———. 1966a. "On Mental Entities." In *The Ways of Paradox and Other Essays*.

———. 1966b. "Posits and Reality." In *The Ways of Paradox and Other Essays*.

———. 1969. "Epistemology Naturalized." In *Ontological Relativity and Other Essays*. New York: Columbia University Press.
———. 1978. "Facts of the Matter." In *Essays on the Philosophy of W. V. Quine*, ed. R. Shahan and C. Swoyer. Norman: The University of Oklahoma Press
———. 1981. *Theories and Things*. Cambridge, Mass.: Harvard University Press.
———. 1981a. "On the Very Idea of a Third Dogma." In *Theories and Things*.
———. 1981b. "Five Milestones of Empiricism." In *Theories and Things*.
———. 1981c. "Empirical Content." In *Theories and Things*.
———. 1981d. "Responding to Schuldenfrei." In *Theories and Things*.
———. 1981e. "On the Nature of Moral Values." In *Theories and Things*.
———. 1981f. "Things and Their Place in Theories." In *Theories and Things*.
———. 1985. *The Time of My Life: An Autobiography*. Cambridge: MIT Press.
———. 1987. *Quiddities: An Intermittently Philosophical Dictionary*. Cambridge, Mass.: Harvard University Press.
———. 1990. *Pursuit of Truth*. Cambridge, Mass.: Harvard University Press.
Rose, H. 1983. "Hand, Brain, and Heart: A Feminist Epistemology for the Natural Sciences," *Signs* 9(1) 73–90.

2

Quine as Feminist: The Radical Import of Naturalized Epistemology

Louise M. Antony

The truth is always revolutionary.
—Antonio Gramsci

Introduction

Do we need a feminist epistemology? This is a very complicated question. Nonetheless it has a very simple answer: yes and no.

Of course, what I should say (honoring a decades-old philosophical tradition) is that a great deal depends on what we *mean* by "feminist epistemology." One easy—and therefore tempting—way to interpret the demand for a feminist epistemology is to construe it as nothing more than a call for more feminists *doing* epistemology. On this way of viewing things, calls for "feminist political science," "feminist organic chemistry," and "feminist finite mathematics" would all be on a par, and the need for any one of them would be justified in exactly the same way, viz., by arguing for the general need for an infusion of feminist consciousness into the academy.

Construed in this way, an endorsement of "feminist epistemology" is perfectly neutral with respect to the eventual content of the epistemological theories that feminists might devise. Would it turn out, for example, that feminists as a group reject individualism or foundationalism? Would they favor empiricism over rationalism? Would they endorse views that privileged intuition over reason or the subjective over the objective? We'd just have to wait and see. It must even be left open, at least at the outset, whether a feminist epistemology would be discernibly and systematically different from epistemology as it currently exists, or whether there would instead end up being exactly the same variety among feminists as there is now among epistemologists in general.

Now it might appear that the project of developing a feminist epistemology in this sense is one that we can all happily sign on to, for who could object to trying to infuse the disciplines with feminist consciousness? But now I must honor a somewhat newer philosophical tradition than the one I honored earlier, and ask, "We, who?" For though the determined neutrality of this way of conceiving feminist epistemology—let me call it "bare proceduralism"—may give it the superficial appearance of a consensus position, it is in fact quite a partisan position. Even setting aside the fact that there are many people—yes, even some philosophers—who would rather be infused with bubonic plague than with feminist consciousness, it's clear that not everyone is going to like bare proceduralism. And ironically, it is its very neutrality that makes this an unacceptable reading of many, if not most, of the theorists who are currently calling for a feminist epistemology.[1]

To see the sticking point, consider the question of whether we should, as feminists, have an obligation to support *any* project whose participants represent themselves as feminists. Should we, for example, support the development of a "feminist sociobiology" or a "feminist military science," on the grounds that it's always a good idea to infuse a discipline, or a theory, with feminist consciousness, or on the grounds that there are people who are engaged in such projects who regard themselves as feminists and therefore have a claim on our sympathies? The answer to these questions, arguably, is no. Some projects, like the rationalization of war, may simply be *incompatible* with feminist goals; and some theories, like those with biological determinist presuppositions, may be *inconsistent* with the results of feminist inquiry to date.

Bare proceduralism, with its liberal, all-purpose, surely-there's-something-we-can-all-agree-on ethos, both obscures and begs the important question against those who believe that not all epistemological frameworks cohere—or cohere equally well—with the insights and aims of feminism. Specifically, it presupposes something that many feminist philosophers are at great pains to deny, namely the *prima facie* adequacy, from a feminist point of view, of those epistemological theories currently available within mainstream Anglo-American philosophy. At the very least, one who adopts the bare proceduralist standpoint with respect to feminist epistemology is making a substantive presupposition about where we currently stand in the process of feminist theorizing. To allow even that a feminist epistemology *might* utilize certain existing epistemological frameworks is to assert that feminist theorizing has not yet issued in substantive results regarding such frameworks.[2] Such a view, if not forthrightly expressed and explicitly defended, is disrespectful to the work of those feminists who claim to have already shown that those very epistemological theories are incompatible with feminism.

So we can't simply interpret the question, "Do we need a feminist epistemology?" in the bare proceduralist way and nod an enthusiastic assent. If we do, we'll be obscuring or denying the existence of substantive disagreements among feminists about the relation between feminism and theories of knowledge. One natural alternative to the bare proceduralist interpretation would be to try to give feminist epistemology a *substantive* sense—that is, take it to refer to a particular kind of epistemology or to a particular theory within epistemology, one that is specifically feminist.

But this won't work either, for two good reasons. First, there simply is no substantive consensus position among feminists working in epistemology, so that it would be hubris for anyone to claim that his or her epistemology was *the* feminist one.[3] Second, many feminists would find the idea that there *should* be such a single "feminist" position repellent. Some would dislike the idea simply for its somewhat totalitarian, "PC" ring. (Me, I'm not bothered by that—it seems to me that one should strive to be correct in all things, including politics.) Some theorists would argue that variety in feminist philosophical positions is to be expected at this point in the development of feminist consciousness, and that various intra- and intertheoretic tensions in philosophical inquiry reflect unprocessed conflicts among deeply internalized conceptions of reality, of ourselves as human beings, and of ourselves as women.[4] Still others would see the expectation or hope that there will *ever* be a single, comprehensive, "true" feminist position as nothing but a remnant of outmoded, patriarchal ways of thinking.[5]

Thus, while individual feminist theorists may be advertising particular epistemological theories as feminist theories, general calls for the development of a feminist epistemology cannot be construed as advocacy for any particular one of these. But recognition of this fact does not throw us all the way back to the bare proceduralist notion. It simply means that in order to decide on the need for a feminist epistemology, we need to look at details—both with respect to the issues that feminism is supposed to have raised for the theory of knowledge and with respect to the specific epistemological theories that have been proffered as answering to feminist needs.

This is where the yes-and-no comes in. If we focus on the existence of what might be called a "feminist agenda" in epistemology—that is, if the question, "Do we need a feminist epistemology?" is taken to mean, "Are there specific questions or problems that arise as a result of feminist analysis, awareness, or experience that any adequate epistemology must accommodate?"—then I think the answer is clearly yes. But if, taking for granted the existence of such an agenda, the question is taken to be, "Do we need, in order to accommodate these questions, insights, and projects, a specifically feminist alternative to currently available epistemological frameworks?" then the answer, to my mind, is no.

Now it is on this point that I find myself in disagreement with many feminist philosophers. For despite the diversity of views within contemporary feminist thought, and despite the disagreements about even the desiderata for a genuinely feminist epistemology, one theoretical conclusion shared by almost all those feminists who explicitly advocate the development of a feminist epistemology is that existing epistemological paradigms—particularly those available within the framework of contemporary analytic philosophy—are fundamentally unsuited to the needs of feminist theorizing.

It is this virtual unanimity about the inadequacy of contemporary analytic epistemology that I want to challenge. There is an approach to the study of knowledge that promises enormous aid and comfort to feminists attempting to expose and dismantle the oppressive intellectual ideology of a patriarchal, racist, class-stratified society, and it is an approach that lies squarely within the analytic tradition. The theory I have in mind is Quine's "naturalized epistemology"—the view that the study of knowledge should be treated as the empirical investigation of knowers.

It's both unfortunate and ironic that Quine's work has been so uniformly neglected by feminists interested in the theory of knowledge, because although naturalized epistemology is nowadays as mainstream a theory as there is, Quine's challenges to logical positivism were radical in their time, and still retain an untapped radical potential today. His devastating critique of epistemological foundationalism bears many similarities to contemporary feminist attacks on "modernist" conceptions of objectivity and scientific rationality, and his positive views on the holistic nature of justification provide a theoretical basis for pressing the kinds of critical questions feminist critics are now raising.

Thus my primary aim in this essay is to highlight the virtues, from a feminist point of view, of naturalized epistemology. But—as is no doubt quite clear—I have a secondary, polemical aim as well. I want to confront head-on the charges that mainstream epistemology is irremediably phallocentric, and to counter the impression, widespread among progressives both within and outside of the academy, that there is some kind of natural antipathy between radicalism on the one hand and the methods and aims of analytic philosophy on the other. I believe that this impression is quite false, and its promulgation is damaging not only to individual feminists—especially women—working within the analytic tradition, but also to the prospects for an adequate feminist philosophy.

The "Bias" Paradox

I think the best way to achieve both these aims—defending the analytic framework in general and showcasing naturalized epistemology in particular—is to put the latter to work on a problem that is becoming increasingly important within feminist theory. The issue I have in mind is the problem of how properly to conceptualize *bias*. There are several things about this issue that make it particularly apt for my purposes.

In the first place, the issue provides an example of the way in which feminist analysis can generate or uncover serious epistemological questions, for the problem about bias that I want to discuss will only be recognized as a problem by individuals who are critical, for one reason or another, of one standard conception of objectivity. In the second place, because of the centrality of this problem to feminist theory, the ability of an epistemological theory to provide a solution offers one plausible desideratum of a theory's adequacy as a feminist epistemology. Last of all, because the notions of bias and partiality figure so prominently in feminist critiques of mainstream analytic epistemology, discussion of this issue will enable me to address directly some of the charges that have led some feminist theorists to reject the analytic tradition.

But what is the problem? Within certain theoretical frameworks, the analysis of the notion of "bias" is quite straightforward. In particular, strict empiricist epistemology concurs with liberal political theory in analyzing bias as the mere possession of belief or interest prior to investigation. But for anyone who wishes to criticize the liberal/empiricist ideal of an "open mind," the notion of bias is enormously problematic and threatens to become downright paradoxical.

Consider feminist theory: On the one hand, it is one of the central aims of feminist scholarship to expose the male-centered assumptions and interests—the male *biases*, in other words—underlying so much of received "wisdom." But on the other hand, there's an equally important strain of feminist theory that seeks to challenge the ideal of pure objectivity by emphasizing both the ubiquity and the value of certain kinds of partiality and interestedness. Clearly, there's a tension between those feminist critiques that accuse science or philosophy of displaying male bias and those that reject the ideal of impartiality.

The tension blossoms into paradox when critiques of the first sort are applied to the concepts of objectivity and impartiality themselves. According to many feminist philosophers, the flaw in the ideal of impartiality is supposed to be that the ideal itself is biased: Critics charge either that the concept of "objectivity" serves to articulate a masculine or patriarchal viewpoint (and possibly a pathological one),[6] or that it has the ideological function of protecting the rights of those in power, especially men.[7] But how is it possible to criticize the partiality of the concept of objectivity without presupposing the very value under attack? Put baldly: If we don't think it's good to be *im*partial, then how can we object to men's being *partial*?

The critiques of "objectivity" and "impartiality" that give rise to this paradox represent the main source of feminist dissatisfaction with existing epistemological theories. It's charged that mainstream epistemology will be forever unable to either acknowledge or account for the partiality and locatedness of knowledge, because it is wedded to precisely those ideals of objective or value-neutral inquiry that ultimately and inevitably subserve the interests of the powerful. The valorization of impartiality within mainstream epistemology is held to perform for the ruling elite the critical ideological function of *denying the existence of partiality itself*.[8]

Thus Lorraine Code, writing in the *APA Newsletter on Feminism and Philosophy*,[9] charges that mainstream epistemology (or what she has elsewhere dubbed "malestream" epistemology[10]) has "defined 'the epistemological project' so as to make it illegitimate to ask questions about the identities and specific circumstances of these knowers." It has accomplished this, she contends, by promulgating a view of knowers as essentially featureless and interchangeable, and by donning a "mask of objectivity and value-neutrality." The transformative potential of a feminist—as opposed to a malestream—epistemology lies in its ability to tear off this mask, exposing the "complex power structure of vested interest, dominance, and subjugation" that lurks behind it.

But not only is it not the case that contemporary analytic epistemology is committed to such a conception of objectivity, it was analytic epistemology that was largely responsible for initiating the critique of the empiricistic notions Code is attacking. Quine, Goodman, Hempel, Putnam, Boyd, and others within the analytic tradition have all argued that a certain received conception of objectivity is untenable as an ideal of epistemic practice. The detailed critique of orthodox empiricism that has developed within the analytic tradition is in many ways more pointed and radical that the charges that have been leveled from without.

Furthermore, these philosophers, like many feminist theorists, have emphasized not only the *ineliminability* of bias but also the *positive value* of certain forms of it. As a result, the problems that arise for a naturalized epistemology are strikingly similar to those that beset the feminist theories mentioned above: Once we've acknowledged the necessity and legitimacy of partiality, *how do we tell the good bias from the bad bias?*

What kind of epistemology is going to be able to solve a problem like this? Code asserts that the specific impact of feminism on epistemology has been "to move the question '*Whose* knowledge are we talking about?' to a central place in epistemological discussion,"[11] suggesting that the hope lies in finding an epistemological theory that assigns central importance to consideration of the nature of the subjects who actually do the knowing. I totally agree: No theory that abjures empirical study of the cognizer, or of the actual processes by which knowledge develops, is ever going to yield insight on this question.

But more is required than this. If we as feminist critics are to have any basis for distinguishing the salutary from the pernicious forms of bias, we can't rest content with a *description* of the various ways in which the identity and social location of a subject make a difference to her beliefs. We need, in addition, to be able to make *normative* distinctions among various processes of belief-fixation as well. Otherwise, we'll never escape the dilemma posed by the bias paradox: Either endorse pure impartiality or give up criticizing bias.[12]

It is here that I think feminist philosophy stands to lose the most by rejecting the analytic tradition. The dilemma will be impossible to escape, I contend, for any theory that eschews the notion of *truth*—for any theory, that is, that tries to steer some kind of middle course between absolutism and relativism. Such theories inevitably leave themselves without resources for making the needed normative distinctions, because they deprive themselves of any conceptual tools for distinguishing the grounds of a statement's truth from the explanation of a statement's acceptance.

Naturalized epistemology has the great advantage over epistemological frameworks outside the analytic tradition (I have in mind specifically standpoint and postmodern epistemologies) in that it permits an appropriately realist conception of truth, viz., one that allows a conceptual gap between epistemology and metaphysics, between the world as we see it and the world as it is.[13] Without appealing to at least this minimally realist notion of truth, I see no way to even state the distinction we ultimately must articulate and defend. Quite simply, an adequate solution to the paradox must enable us to say the following: What makes the *good* bias good is that it facilitates the search for truth, and what makes the *bad* bias bad is that it impedes it.

Now that my absolutist leanings are out in the open, let me say one more thing about truth that I hope will forestall a possible misunderstanding of my project here. I do believe in truth, and I have *never* understood why people concerned with justice have given it such a bad rap. Surely one of the goals of feminism is to *tell the truth* about women's lives and women's experience. Is institutionally supported discrimination not a *fact*? Is misogynist violence not a *fact*? And isn't the existence of ideological denial of the first two facts *itself* a fact? What in the world else could we be doing when we talk about these things, *other* than asserting that the world actually *is* a certain way?

Getting at the truth is complicated, and one of the things that complicates it considerably is that powerful people frequently have strong motives for keeping less powerful people from getting at the truth. It's one job of a critical epistemology, in my view, to expose this fact, to make the mechanisms of such distortions transparent. But if We, as critical epistemologists, lose sight of what we're after, if we concede that there's nothing at stake other than the matter of whose "version" is going to prevail, then our projects become as morally bankrupt and baldly self-interested as Theirs.

This brings me to the nature of the current discussion. I would like to be clear that in endorsing the project of finding a "feminist epistemology," I do not mean to be advocating the construction of a serviceable epistemological ideology "for our side." And when I say that I think naturalized epistemology makes a good feminist epistemology, I don't mean to be suggesting that the justification for the theory is instrumental. A good *feminist* epistemology must be, in the first place, a good epistemology, and that means being a theory that is likely to be *true*. But of course I would not think that naturalized epistemology was likely to be true unless I also thought it explained the facts. And among the facts I take to be central are the long-ignored experiences and wisdom of women.

In the next section, I will explain in more detail the nature of the charges that have been raised by feminist critics against contemporary analytic epistemology. I'll argue that the most serious of these charges are basically misguided—that they depend on a misreading of the canonical figures of the Enlightenment as well as of contemporary epistemology. In the last section, I'll return to the bias paradox and try to show why a naturalized approach to the study of knowledge offers some chance of a solution.

What Is Mainstream Epistemology and Why Is It Bad?

One difficulty that confronts anyone who wishes to assess the need for a "feminist alternative" in epistemology is the problem of finding out exactly what such an epistemology would be an alternative to. What is "mainsteam" epistemology anyway? Lorraine Code is more forthright than many in her willingness to name the enemy. According to her, "mainstream epistemology," the proper object of feminist critique, is "postpositivist empiricist epistemology: the epistemology that still dominates in Anglo-American philosophy, despite the best efforts of socialist, structuralist, hermeneuticist, and other theorists of knowledge to deconstruct or discredit it."[14]

By the "epistemology that still dominates in Anglo-American philosophy," Code would have to be referring to the set of epistemological theories that have developed within the analytic paradigm, for analytic philosophy has been, in fact, the dominant philosophical paradigm in the English-speaking academic world since the early twentieth century.[15] This means, at the very least, that the agents of sexism within academic philosophy—the individuals who have in fact been the ones to discriminate against women as students, job applicants, and colleagues—have been, for the most part, analytic philosophers, a fact that on its own makes the analytic paradigm an appropriate object for feminist scrutiny.

But this is not the main reason that Code and others seek to "deconstruct or discredit" analytic epistemology. The fact that the analytic paradigm has enjoyed such an untroubled hegemony within this country during the twentieth century—the period of the most rapid growth of American imperial power—suggests to many radical social critics that analytic philosophy fills an ideological niche. Many feminist critics see mainstream analytic philosophy as the natural metaphysical and epistemological complement to liberal political theory, which, by obscuring real power relations within the society, makes citizens acquiescent or even complicit in the growth of oppression, here and abroad.

What is it about analytic philosophy that would enable it to play this role? Some have argued that analytic or "linguistic" philosophy, together with its cognate fields (such as formal linguistics and computationalist psychology), is inherently male, "phallogocentric."[16] Others have argued that the analytic paradigm, because of its emphasis on abstraction and formalization and its valorization of elite skills, may be an instrument of cognitive control, serving to discredit the perspectives of members of nonprivileged groups.[17]

But most of the radical feminist critiques of "mainstream" epistemology (which, as I said, must denote the whole of analytic epistemology) are motivated by its presumed allegiance to the conceptual structures and theoretical commitments of the Enlightenment, which provided the general philosophical background to the development of modern industrialized "democracies."[18] By this means, "mainstream" epistemology becomes identified with "traditional" epistemology, and this traditional epistemology becomes associated with political liberalism. Feminist theorists like Alison Jaggar and Sandra Harding, who have both written extensively about the connection between feminist political analysis and theories of knowledge, have encouraged the idea that acceptance of mainstream epistemological paradigms is tantamount to endorsing liberal feminism. Jaggar contends that the connection lies in the radically individualistic conception of human nature common to both liberal political theory and Enlightenment epistemology. In a chapter entitled "Feminist Politics and Epistemology: Justifying Feminist Theory," she writes:

> Just as the individualistic conception of human nature sets the basic problems for the liberal political tradition, so it also generates the problems for the tradition in epistemology that is associated historically and conceptually with liberalism. This tradition begins in the 17th century with Descartes, and it emerges in the 20th century as the analytic tradition. Because it conceives humans as essentially separate individuals, this epistemological tradition views the attainment of knowledge as a project for each individual on her or his own. The task of epistemology, then, is to formulate rules to enable individuals to undertake this project with success.[19]

Harding, in a section of her book called "A Guide to Feminist Epistemologies," surveys what she sees as the full range of epistemological options open to feminists. She imports the essentially conservative political agenda of liberal feminism, which is focused on the elimination of formal barriers to gender equality, into mainstream epistemology, which she labels "feminist empiricism": "*Feminist empiricism* argues that sexism and androcentrism are social biases correctable by stricter adherence to the existing methodological norms of scientific inquiry."[20] Harding takes the hallmark of feminist empiricism (which on her taxonomy is the only alternative to feminist standpoint and postmodernist epistemologies) to be commitment to a particular conception of objectivity, which, again, is held to be part of the legacy of the Enlightenment. In her view, acceptance of this ideal brings with it faith in the efficacy of "existing methodological norms of science" in correcting biases and irrationalities within science, in the same way that acceptance of the liberal ideal of impartiality brings with it faith in the system to eliminate political and social injustice.

In Harding's mind, as in Jaggar's, this politically limiting conception of objectivity is one that can be traced to traditional conceptions of the knowing subject, specifically to Enlightenment conceptions of "rational man." The message, then, is that mainstream epistemology, because it still operates with this traditional conception of the self, functions to limit our understanding of the real operations of power, and of our place as women within oppressive structures. A genuine feminist transformation in our thinking therefore requires massive overhaul, if not outright repudiation, of central aspects of the tradition.

This is clearly the message that political scientist Jane Flax gleans from her reading of feminist philosophy; she argues that feminist theory ought properly to be viewed as a version of postmodern thought, since postmodern theorists and feminist theorists are so obviously engaged in a common project:

> Postmodern philosophers seek to throw into radical doubt beliefs still prevalent in (especially American) culture but derived from the Enlightenment. . . ,[21] feminist notions of the self, knowledge and truth are too contradictory to those of the Enlightenment to be contained within its categories. The way to feminist future(s) cannot lie in reviving or appropriating Enlightenment concepts of the person or knowledge.[22]

But there are at least two serious problems with this argument. The first is that the "tradition" that emerges from these critiques is a gross distortion and oversimplification of the early modern period. The critics' conglomeration of all classical and Enlightenment views into a uniform "traditional" epistemology obscures the enormous amount of controversy surrounding such notions as knowledge and the self during the seventeenth and eighteenth centuries, and encourages crude misunderstandings of some of the central theoretical claims. Specifically, this amalgamation makes all but invisible a debate that has enormous relevance to discussions of bias and objectivity, viz., the controversy between rationalists and empiricists about the extent to which the structure of the mind might constrain the development of knowledge.[23]

The second problem is that the picture of analytic epistemology that we get once it's allied with this oversimplified "traditional" epistemology is downright cartoonish. When we look at the actual content of the particular conceptions of objectivity and scientific method that the feminist critics have culled from the modern period, and which they subsequently attach to contemporary epistemology, it turns out that these conceptions are precisely the ones that have been the focus of *criticism* among American analytic philosophers from the 1950s onward. The feminist critics' depiction of "mainstream" epistemology utterly obscures this development in analytic epistemology, and in glossing over the details of the analytic critique of positivism, misses points that are of crucial relevance to any truly radical assault on the liberal ideology of objectivity.[24]

The second problem is partly a consequence of the first. The feminist critics, almost without exception, characterize mainstream epistemology as "empiricist." But one of the chief accomplishments of the analytic challenge to positivism was the demonstration that a strictly empiricistic conception of knowledge is untenable. As a result, much of analytic epistemology has taken a decidedly rationalistic turn. Neglect of the rationalist/empiricist debate and misunderstanding of rationalist tenets make the critics insensitive to these developments and blind to their implications.

But the misreading of contemporary epistemology is also partly just a matter of the critics' failure to realize the extent to which analytic philosophy represents a *break* with tradition. I do not mean to deny that there were *any* important theoretical commitments common to philosophers of the early modern period. One such commitment, shared at least by classical rationalists and empiricists, and arguably by Kant, was an epistemological meta-hypothesis called "externalism."[25] This is the view that the proper goal of epistemological theory is the rational *vindication* of human epistemic practice. But if externalism is regarded as the hallmark of "traditional epistemology," then the identification of analytic epistemology with traditional epistemology becomes all the more spurious.

It was the main burden of Quine's critique of positivism to demonstrate the impossibility of an externalist epistemology, and his suggested replacement, "naturalized epistemology," was meant to be what epistemology could be once externalist illusions were shattered. As a result of the analytic critique of externalism, the notions of objectivity and rationality available to contemporary analytic epistemologists are necessarily more complicated than the traditional conceptions they replace. This is so even for epistemologists who would not identify themselves as partisans of naturalized epistemology.

In what follows, I'll discuss in turn these two problems: first, the mischaracterization of the tradition, and then the caricature of contemporary analytic epistemology.

Rationalism v. Empiricism: The Importance of Being Partial

What I want to show first is that the "traditional epistemology" offered us by Jaggar and Flax grafts what is essentially a rationalist (and in some respects, specifically Cartesian) theory of *mind* onto what is essentially an empiricist conception of *knowledge*. This is a serious error. Although Jaggar and Flax claim that there are deep connections between the one and the other, the fact of the matter is that they are solidly opposed. The conception of objectivity that is ultimately the object of radical critique—perfect impartiality—is only supportable as an epistemic ideal on an empiricist conception of *mind*. Thus, I'll argue, the rationalistic conception of the self attacked by Jaggar and Flax as unsuitable or hostile to a feminist point of view actually provides the basis for a critique of the view of knowledge they want ultimately to discredit.

Much of what is held to be objectionable in "traditional epistemology" is supposed to derive from the tradition's emphasis on *reason*. But different traditional figures emphasized reason in different ways. Only the rationalists and Kant were committed to what I'll call "cognitive essentialism," a feature of the "traditional" conception of mind that comes in for some of the heaviest criticism. I take cognitive essentialism to be the view (1) that there are certain specific properties the possession of which is both distinctive of and universal among human beings; (2) that these properties are cognitive in nature; (3) that our possession of these properties amounts to a kind of innate knowledge; and (4) that our status as moral agents is connected to the possession of these properties. Empiricists denied all these claims—in particular, they denied that reason had anything but a purely instrumental role to play in either normative or nonnormative activity, and tended to be opposed to any form of essentialism, cognitive or otherwise.

Although the purely instrumental conception of reason is also criticized by feminist scholars, cognitive essentialism is the focus of one specific set of feminist concerns. It is held to be suspect on the grounds that such a doctrine could easily serve to legitimate the arrogant impulses of privileged Western white men: first to canonize their own culture- and time-bound speculations as revelatory of the very norms of human existence, and then simultaneously to deny the very properties deemed "universal" to the majority of human beings on the planet.

Here's how it is supposed to work: Cognitive essentialism is supposed to engender a kind of fantasy concerning actual human existence and the actual prerequisites of knowledge. Because of its emphasis on *cognitive* characteristics, it's argued, the view permits privileged individuals to ignore the fact of their embodiment, and with that, the considerable material advantages they enjoy in virtue of their class, gender, and race.[26] To the extent that the characteristics they find in themselves are the result of their particular privileges instead of a transcendent humanity, the fantasy provides a basis for viewing less-privileged people—who well may lack such characteristics—as inherently less human. But since these characteristics have been lionized as forming the essence of moral personhood, the fantasy offers a rationale for viewing any differences between themselves and others as negative deviations from a moral norm.

Recall, for example, that the particular elements of Enlightenment thought that Flax finds inimical to feminist theory and praxis are the alleged universality, transcendence, and abstractness assigned to the faculty of reason:

> The notion that reason is divorced from "merely contingent" existence still predominates in contemporary Western thought and now appears to mask the embeddedness and dependence of the self upon social relations, as well as the partiality and historical specificity of this self's existence. . . .
>
> In fact, feminists, like other postmodernists, have begun to suspect that all such transcendental claims reflect and reify the experience of a few persons—mostly White, Western males.[27]

But moreover, cognitive essentialism is supposed to lead to what Jaggar calls "individualism,"[28] the view that individual human beings are epistemically self-sufficient, that human society is unnecessary or unimportant for the development of knowledge. If the ideal "man of reason" is utterly without material, differentiating features, then the ideal knower would appear to be *pure* rationality, a mere calculating mechanism, a person who has been stripped of all those particular aspects of self that are of overwhelming human significance. Correlatively, as it is precisely the features "stripped off" the self by the Cartesian method that "traditional" epistemology denigrates as distorting influences, the ideally objective cognizer is also the man of reason. Knowledge is then achieved, it appears, not by active engagement with one's world and with the people in it, but by a pristine transcendence of the messy contingencies of the human condition.[29]

Lending support to Lorraine Code's grievance against "traditional" epistemology, Jaggar thus insists that it is this abstract and detached individualism that underwrites a solipsistic view of the construction of knowledge and precludes assigning any epistemological significance to the situation of the knower.

> Because it conceives humans as essentially separate individuals, this epistemological tradition views the attainment of knowledge as a project for each individual on his or her own. The task of epistemology, then, is to formulate rules to enable individuals to undertake this project with success.[30]

It is here that the link is supposed to be forged between the Cartesian/Kantian conception of the self and the particular conception of objectivity—objectivity as pure neutrality—that is thought to be pernicious.

But the individualism Jaggar takes to unite rationalists and empiricists is not in fact a view that *anyone* held. She derives it from a fairly common—indeed, almost canonical—misreading of the innate ideas debate. Significantly, Jaggar acknowledges the existence of disagreements within the early modern period, but avers that such issues as divided rationalists from empiricists are differences that make no difference. Both were foundationalists, she points out, and though the foundation for rationalists was self-evident truths of reason and the foundation for empiricists was reports of sensory experience, "in either case, . . . the attainment of knowledge is conceived as essentially a solitary occupation that has no necessary social preconditions."[31]

The reading, in other words, is that whereas the empiricists thought all knowledge came from experience, the rationalists thought *all knowledge came from reason*. But the second element of this interpretation is simply wrong. It was no part of *Descartes's* project (much less Kant's) to assert the self-sufficiency of reason. Note that a large part of the goal of the exercise of hyperbolic doubt in the *Meditations* was to establish the reliability of sensory experience, which Descartes took to be essential to the development of adequate knowledge of the world. And although he maintained the innateness of many ideas, including sensory ideas, he carefully and repeatedly explained that he meant by this only that human beings were built in such a way that certain experiences would trigger these ideas and no others.[32]

Furthermore, Descartes himself explicitly endorses two of the very epistemic values his position is supposed to preclude. Not only does he clearly reject the sort of epistemic individualism Jaggar deplores, but he strongly upholds the necessity of acquainting oneself with the variety of human experience in order to form a just conception of the world. Expressing his contempt for the contradictions and sophistries of his learned and cloistered teachers, he recounts how, as soon as he was old enough to "emerge from the control of [his] tutors," he "entirely quitted the study of letters."

> And resolving to seek no other science than that which could be found in myself, *or at least in the great book of the world* [my emphasis], I employed the rest of my youth in travel, in seeing courts and armies, in intercourse with men of diverse temperaments and conditions, in collecting varied experiences, in proving myself in the various predicaments in which I was placed by fortune, and under all circumstances bringing my mind to bear on the things which came before it, so that I might derive some profit from my experience.[33]

And far from recommending the divestiture of one's particular concerns as sound epistemic practice, Descartes affirms the importance of concrete engagement in finding the truth, pointing to the degradation of knowledge that can result from disinterestedness.

> For it seemed to me that I might meet with much more truth in the reasonings that each man makes on the matters that specially concern him, and the issue of which would very soon punish him if he made a wrong judgment, than in the case of those made by a man of letters in his study touching speculations which lead to no result, and which bring about no other consequences to himself excepting that he will be all the more vain the more they are removed from common sense, since in this case it proves him to have employed so much the more ingenuity and skill in trying to make them seem probable.[34]

The bottom line is that rationalists, Descartes especially, did not hold the view that experience was inessential or even that it was unimportant; nor did they hold the view that the best epistemic practice is to discount one's own interests. The misreading that saddles Descartes with such views stems from a popular misconception about the innate ideas debate.

The disagreement between rationalists and empiricists was not simply about the existence of innate ideas. Both schools were agreed that the mind was natively structured and that that structure partially determined the shape of human knowledge. What they disagreed about was the *specificity* of the constraints imposed by innate mental structure. The rationalists believed that native structure placed quite specific limitations on the kinds of concepts and hypotheses the mind could form in response to experience, so that human beings were, in effect, natively *biased* toward certain ways of conceiving the world. Empiricists, on the other hand, held that there were relatively few native constraints on how the mind could organize sensory experience, and that such constraints as did exist were *domain-general* and *content-neutral*.

According to the empiricists, the human mind was essentially a mechanism for the manipulation of sensory data. The architecture of the mechanism was supposed to ensure that the concepts and judgments constructed out of raw sense experience accorded with the rules of logic. This did amount to a minimal constraint on the possible contents of human thought—they had to be logical transforms of sensory primitives—but it was a highly general one, applying to every subject domain in precisely the same way. Thus, on this model, any one hypothesis should be as good as any other as far as the mind is concerned, as long as both hypotheses are logically consistent with the sensory evidence.[35] This strict empiricist model of mind, as it turns out, supports many of the elements of epistemology criticized by Code, Jaggar, and others (e.g., a sharp observation/theory distinction, unmediated access to a sensory "given," and an algorithmic view of justification). I'll spell this out in detail in the next section. For present purposes, however, the thing to note is that the model provides clear warrant for the particular conception of the ideal of objectivity—perfect neutrality—that is the main concern of Jaggar and the others and that is supposed to follow from cognitive essentialism. Here's how.

Because the mind itself, on the empiricist model, makes no substantive contribution to the contents of thought, knowledge on this model is *entirely* experience-driven: All concepts and judgments are held to reflect regularities in an individual's sensory experience. But one individual cannot see everything there is to see—one's experience is necessarily limited, and there's always the danger that the regularities that form the basis of one's own judgments are not general regularities, but only artifacts of one's limited sample. (There is, in other words, a massive restriction-of-range problem for empiricists.) The question then arises how one can tell whether the patterns one perceives are present in nature generally, or are just artifacts of one's idiosyncratic perspective.

The empiricists' answer to this question is that one can gauge the general validity of one's judgments by the degree to which they engender reliable expectations about sensory experience. But although this answer addresses the problem of how to tell whether one's judgments are good or bad, it doesn't address the problem of how to get good judgments in the first place. Getting good judgments means getting good data—that is, exposing oneself to patterns of sensations that are representative of the objective distribution of sensory qualities throughout nature.

This idea immediately gives rise to a certain ideal (some would say fantasy) of epistemic location—the best spot from which to make judgments would be that spot which is *least particular*. Sound epistemic practice then becomes a matter of constantly trying to maneuver oneself into such a location—trying to find a place (or at least come as close as one can) where the regularities in one's own personal experience match the regularities in the world at large. A knower who could be somehow stripped of all particularities and idiosyncrasies would be the best possible knower there is.

This is not, however, a fantasy that would hold any particular appeal for a rationalist, despite the image of detachment evoked by a cursory reading of the *Meditations*. The rationalists had contended all along that sensory experience *by itself* was insufficient to account for the richly detailed body of knowledge that human beings manifestly possessed, and thus that certain elements of human knowledge—what classical rationalists called *innate ideas*—must be natively present, a part of the human essence.

Because the rationalists denied that human knowledge was a pure function of the contingencies of experience, they didn't need to worry nearly as much as the empiricists did about epistemic location. If it is the structure of mind, rather than the accidents of experience, that largely determines the contours of human concepts, then we can relax about at least the broad parameters of our knowledge. We don't have to worry that idiosyncratic features of our epistemic positions will seriously distort our worldviews, because the development of our knowledge is not dependent upon the patterns that happen to be displayed in our particular experiential histories. The regularities we "perceive" are, in large measure, regularities that we're *built* to perceive.

"Pure" objectivity—if that means giving equal weight to every hypothesis consistent with the data, or if it means drawing no conclusions beyond what can be supported by the data—is thus a nonstarter as an epistemic norm from a rationalist's point of view. The rationalists were in effect calling attention to the *value* of a certain kind of partiality: If the mind were not natively biased—i.e., disposed to take seriously certain kinds of hypotheses and to disregard or fail to even consider others—then knowledge of the sort that human beings possess would itself be impossible. There are simply too many ways of combining ideas, too many different abstractions that could be performed, too many distinct extrapolations from the same set of facts, for a pure induction machine to make much progress in figuring out the world.

The realization that perfect neutrality was not necessarily a good thing, and that bias and partiality are potentially salutary, is thus a point that was strongly present in the early modern period, *pace* Jaggar and Flax. There was no single "traditional" model of mind; the model that can properly be said to underwrite the conceptions of rationality and objectivity that Jaggar brings under feminist attack is precisely a model to which Descartes and the other rationalists were *opposed*, and, ironically, the one that, on the face of it, assigns the most significance to experience. And although it is the cognitive essentialists who are charged with deflecting attention away from epistemically significant characteristics of the knower, it was in fact these same essentialists, in explicit opposition to the empiricists, who championed the idea that human knowledge was necessarily "partial."

Hume, Quine, and The Break with Tradition

Let me turn now to the second serious problem with the feminist criticisms of "mainstream" epistemology: To the extent that there really is a "tradition" in epistemology, it is a tradition that has been explicitly rejected by contemporary analytic philosophy.

If the rationalists solved one problem by positing innate ideas, it was at the cost of raising another. Suppose that there are, as the rationalists maintained, innate ideas that perform the salutary function of narrowing down to a manageable set the hypotheses that human minds have to consider when confronted with sensory data. That eliminates the problem faced by the empiricists of filtering out idiosyncratic "distortions." But now the question is, How can we be sure that these biases—so helpful in getting us to *a* theory of the world—are getting us to the *right* theory of the world? What guarantees that our minds are inclining us in the right direction? Innate ideas lead us somewhere, but do they take us where we want to go?

The rationalists took this problem very seriously. A large part of their project was aimed at validating the innate constraints, at showing that these mental biases did not lead us astray. Descartes's quest for "certainty" needs to be understood in this context: The method of hyperbolic doubt should be viewed not as the efforts of a paranoid to free himself forever from the insecurity of doubt, but as a theoretical exercise designed to show that the contours imposed on our theories by our own minds were proper reflections of the topography of reality itself.

It is at this point that we're in a position to see what rationalists and empiricists actually had in common—not a conception of mind, not a theory of how knowledge is constructed, but a theory of *theories* of knowledge. If there is a common thread running through Enlightenment epistemologies, it is this: a belief in the possibility of providing a *rational* justification of the processes by which human beings arrive at theories of the world. For the empiricists, the trick was to show how the content of all knowledge could be reduced to pure reports of sensory experience; for the rationalists, it was showing the indubitability of the innate notions that guided and facilitated the development of knowledge. Philosophers in neither group were really on a quest for certainty—all they wanted was a reliable map of its boundaries.

But if one of the defining themes of the modern period was the search for an externalist justification of epistemic practice, then *Hume* must be acknowledged to be the first postmodernist. Hume, an empiricist's empiricist, discovered a fatal flaw in his particular proposal for justifying human epistemic practice. He realized that belief in the principle of induction—the principle that says that the future will resemble the past or that similar things will behave similarly—could not be rationally justified. It was clearly not a truth of reason, since its denial was not self-contradictory. But neither could it be justified by experience: Any attempt to do so would be circular, because the practice of using past experience as evidence about the future is itself only warranted if one accepts the principle of induction.

Hume's "skeptical solution" to his own problem amounted to an abandonment of the externalist hopes of his time. Belief in induction, he concluded, was a *custom*, a tendency of mind ingrained by nature, one of "a species of natural instincts, which no reasoning or process of the thought and understanding is able, either to produce or to prevent."[36] For better or worse, Hume contended, we're stuck with belief in induction—we are constitutionally incapable of doubting it and conceptually barred from justifying it. The best we can do is to *explain* it.

Hume's idea was thus to offer as a replacement for the failed externalist project of rational justification of epistemic practice, the *empirical* project of characterizing the cognitive nature of creatures like ourselves, and then figuring out how such creatures, built to seek knowledge in the ways we do, could manage to survive and flourish. In this way, he anticipated to a significant degree the "postmodernist" turn taken by analytic philosophy in the twentieth century as the result of Quine's and others' critiques of externalism's last gasp—logical positivism.

Before fast-forwarding into the twentieth century, let me summarize what I take to be the real lessons of the modern period—lessons that, I've argued, have been missed by many feminist critiques of "traditional" epistemology. First, there is the essentially rationalist insight that perfect objectivity is not only impossible but undesirable, that certain kinds of "bias" or "partiality" are necessary to make our epistemic tasks tractable. Second, there is Hume's realization that externalism won't work, that we can never manage to offer a justification of epistemic norms without somehow presupposing the very norms we wish to justify. See this, if you will, as the beginning of the postmodern recognition that theory always proceeds from an "embedded" location, that there is no transcendent spot from which we can inspect our own theorizing.

The rationalist lesson was pretty much lost and the import of Hume's insight submerged by the subsequent emergence and development of neo-empiricist philosophy. This tradition, which involved primarily the British empiricists Mill and Russell, but also Wittgenstein and the Vienna Circle on the Continent, culminated in the school of thought known as logical positivism.[37] The positivists' project was, in some ways, an externalist one. They hoped to develop criteria that would enforce a principled distinction between empirically significant and empirically meaningless sentences. In the minds of some positivists (Schlick, arguably, and Ayer), this criterion would help to vindicate scientific practice by helping to distinguish science from "metaphysics," which was for positivists, a term of abuse.

The positivists were perfectly well aware of Hume's dilemma about the status of the principle of induction—similar problems about even more fundamental principles of logic and mathematics had come to light since his time. But the positivists in effect attempted to rehabilitate epistemological externalism by means of a bold move. They took all the material that was needed to legitimize scientific practice but that could not be traced directly to sensory experience, and relegated it to the *conventions* of human language. This tack had, at least *prima facie*, some advantages over Hume's nativist move: If our epistemic norms are a matter of convention, then (1) there's no longer any question of explaining how we got them—they're there because we *put* them there; and (2) there's no need to justify them because the parameter of evaluation for conventions is not truth but *utility*.

The positivists thus embarked on a program they called "rational reconstruction"—they wanted to show, in detail, how any empirically meaningful claim could be reduced, by the successive application of semantic and logical rules, to statements purely about sensory experience. If such reconstructions could be shown to be possible at least in principle, then all theoretical disagreements could be shown to be susceptible to resolution by appeal to the neutral court of empirical experience. And in all of this, the positivists were committed to basically the same series of assumptions that warranted the view of objectivity that I earlier associated with classical empiricism.

But there were two things absolutely essential to the success of this project. First, there had to be a viable distinction that could be drawn between statements whose truth depended on empirical contingencies (the contentful claims of a theory that formed the substance of the theory) and statements that were true "by convention" and thus part of the logical/semantic structure of the theory. Second, it would have to be shown that the reduction of empirically contentful statements to specific sets of claims about sensory experience could be carried out. But in the early 1950s, Quine (together with Hempel, Goodman, Putnam, and others) began producing decisive arguments against precisely these assumptions.[38] The ensuing changes in analytic epistemology were nothing short of radical.

Quine's main insight was that individual statements do not have any specific consequences for experience if taken individually—that it is only in conjunction with a variety of other claims that experiential consequences can even be derived. It follows from this that no single experience or observation can decisively refute any theoretical claim or resolve any theoretical dispute, and that all experimental tests of hypotheses are actually tests of *conjunctions* of hypotheses. The second insight—actually a corollary of the first point—was that no principled distinction can be drawn among statements on the basis of the grounds of their truth—there can be no distinction between statements made true or false by experience and those whose truth value depends entirely on semantic or logical conventions.

The implications of these two insights were far-reaching. Quine's arguments against the "two dogmas of empiricism" entailed, in the first place, that the confirmation relation could not be hierarchical, as the foundationalist picture required, but must rather be holistic. Because theories have to face "the tribunal of sensory experience as a corporate body" (to use Quine's military-industrial metaphor), there can be no evidentially foundational set of statements that asymmetrically confirm all the others—every statement in the theory is linked by some justificatory connections to every other.

It also meant that responses at the theoretical level to the acquisition of empirical data were not fully dictated by logic. If experimental tests were always tests of *groups* of statements, then if the prediction fails, logic will tell us only that *something* in the group must go, but not *what*. If logic plus data don't suffice to determine how belief is modified in the face of empirical evidence, then there must be, in addition to logic and sensory evidence, *extra-empirical* principles that partially govern theory selection. The "justification" of these principles can only be pragmatic—we are warranted in using them just to the extent that they work.[39]

But to say this is to say that epistemic norms—a category that must include any principle that in fact guides theory selection—are themselves subject to empirical disconfirmation. And indeed, Quine embraces this consequence, explicitly extending the lesson to cover not only pragmatic "rules of thumb," but to rules of logic and language as well. In short, any principle that facilitates the development of knowledge by narrowing down our theoretical options becomes itself a part of the theory, and a part that must be defended on the same basis as any other part. So much for the fact/value distinction.

The reasoning above represents another of the many routes by which Quine's attack on foundationalism can be connected with his critique of the analytic/synthetic distinction, so central to positivist projects. With the demonstration that any belief, no matter how apparently self-evident, could in principle be rejected on the basis of experience, Quine effectively destroyed the prospects for any "first philosophy"—any Archimedean fixed point from which we could inspect our own epistemic practice and pronounce it sound.

But his critique also pointed the way (as Hume's "skeptical solution" did to the problem of induction) to a different approach to the theory of knowledge. Epistemology, according to Quine, had to be "naturalized," transformed into the empirical study of the actual processes—not "rational reconstructions" of those processes—by which human cognizers achieve knowledge.[40] If we accept this approach, several consequences follow for our understanding of knowledge and of the norms that properly govern its pursuit.

The first lesson is one that I believe may be part of what the feminist critics are themselves pointing to in their emphasis on the essential locatedness of all knowledge claims. The lesson is that all theorizing *takes some knowledge for granted.* Theorizing about theorizing is no exception. The decision to treat epistemology as the empirical study of the knower requires us to presume that we can, at least for a class of clear cases, distinguish epistemic success from epistemic failure. The impossibility of the externalist project shows us that we cannot expect to learn *from our philosophy* what counts as knowledge and how much of it we have; rather, we must begin with the assumption that we know certain things and figure out how that happened.

This immediately entails a second lesson. A naturalized approach to knowledge requires us to give up the idea that our own epistemic practice is transparent to us—that we can come to understand how knowledge is obtained either by a priori philosophizing or by casual introspection. It requires us to be open to the possibility that the processes that we actually rely on to obtain and process information about the world are significantly different from the ones our philosophy told us had to be the right ones.

Let me digress to point out a tremendous irony here, much remarked upon in the literature on Quine's epistemology and philosophy of mind. Despite his being the chief evangelist of the gospel that everything is empirical, Quine's own philosophy is distorted by his a prioristic commitment to a radically empiricistic, instrumentalist theory of psychology, namely psychological behaviorism. Quine's commitment to this theory—which holds that human behavior can be adequately explained without any reference to mental states or processes intervening between environmental stimuli and the organism's response—is largely the result of his philosophical antipathy to intentional objects, together with a residual sympathy for the foundationalist empiricism that he himself was largely responsible for dismantling.

Chomsky, of course, was the person most responsible for pointing out the in-principle limitations of behaviorism, by showing in compelling detail the empirical inadequacies of behaviorist accounts of the acquisition of language.[41] Chomsky also emphasized the indefensibility of the a prioristic methodological constraints that defined empiricistic accounts of the mind, appealing to considerations that Quine himself marshaled in his own attacks on instrumentalism in nonpsychological domains.[42]

Chomsky's own theory of language acquisition did not differ from the behaviorist account only, or even primarily, in its mentalism. It was also rationalistic: Chomsky quite self-consciously appealed to classical rationalistic forms of argument about the necessity of mental partiality in establishing the empirical case for his strong nativism. Looking at the actual circumstances of language acquisition, and then at the character of the knowledge obtained in those circumstances, Chomsky argued that the best explanation of the whole process is one that attributes to human beings a set of innate biases limiting the kinds of linguistic hypotheses available for their consideration as they respond to the welter of data confronting them.[43]

Chomsky can thus be viewed, and is viewed by many, as a naturalized epistemologist *par excellence*. What his work shows is that a naturalized approach to epistemology—in this case, the epistemology of language—yields an *empirical* vindication of rationalism. Since Chomsky's pathbreaking critique of psychological behaviorism, and the empiricist conception of mind that underlies it, nativism in psychology has flourished, and a significant degree of rationalism has been imported into contemporary epistemology.

A casual student of the analytic scene who has read only Quine could, of course, be forgiven for failing to notice this, given Quine's adamant commitment to an empiricist conception of mind; this may explain why so many of the feminist critics of contemporary epistemology seem to identify analytic epistemology with empiricism and to ignore the more rationalistic alternatives that have developed out of the naturalized approach. But I think, too, that the original insensitivity to the details of the original rationalist/empiricist controversy plays a role. Anyone who properly appreciates the import of the rationalist defense of the value of partiality will, I think, see where Quine's rejection of externalism is bound to lead.

So let's do it. I turn now to the feminist critique of objectivity and the bias paradox.

Quine as Feminist: What Naturalized Epistemology Can Tell Us About Bias

I've argued that much of the feminist criticism of "mainstream" epistemology depends on a misreading of both contemporary analytic philosophy, and of the tradition from which it derives. But it's one thing to show that contemporary analytic philosophy is not what the feminist critics think it is, and quite another to show that the contemporary analytic scene contains an epistemology that can serve as an adequate *feminist* epistemology. To do this, we must return to the epistemological issues presented to us by feminist theory and see how naturalized epistemology fares with respect to them. I want eventually to show how a commitment to a naturalized epistemology provides some purchase on the problem of conceptualizing bias, but in order to do that, we must look in some detail at those feminist arguments directed against the notion of objectivity.

Capitalist Science and the Ideal of Objectivity

As we've seen, one of the most prominent themes in feminist epistemology and feminist philosophy of science concerns the alleged ideological function of a certain conception of objectivity. Many feminist critics see a connection between radical (i.e., nonliberal) critiques of science and feminist critiques of "received" epistemology. Such critics take as their starting point the observation that science, as it has developed within industrialized capitalist societies like the United States, is very much an instrument of oppression: Rather than fulfilling its Enlightenment promise as a liberatory and progressive force, institutionalized science serves in fact to sustain and even to enhance existing structures of inequality and domination.[44]

Although all feminists agree that part of the explanation of this fact must be that modern science has been distorted by the sexist, racist, and classist biases it inherits from the society in which it exists, feminist theorists divide on the issue of whether some "deeper" explanation is required. Alison Jaggar's "liberal feminists" and Sandra Harding's "feminist empiricists" hold that society and science are both potentially self-correcting—that more equitable arrangements of power and more scrupulous enforcement of the rules of fairness would turn science back to its natural progressive course.

But Harding and Jaggar, together with Lorraine Code and Evelyn Fox Keller, disagree with this liberal analysis. They contend that the modern scientific establishment has not simply inherited its oppressive features from the inequitable society that conditions it. Rather, they claim, a large part of the responsibility for societal injustices lies deep within science itself, in the conception of knowledge and knowers that underlies "scientific method." These critics charge that the very ideals to which Western science has traditionally aspired—particularly rationality and objectivity—serve to sanction and promote a form of institutionalized inquiry uniquely suited to the needs of patriarchy. Thus, it's argued, feminist critique must not stop at exposing cases in which science has broken its own rules; it must press on to expose the androcentric bias inherent in the rules themselves.

Thus Evelyn Fox Keller claims that any critique that does not extend to the rules of scientific method allies itself with political liberalism in virtue of its epistemology. Any such critique, she argues, "can still be accommodated within the traditional framework by the simple argument that the critiques, if justified, merely reflect the fact that [science] is not sufficiently scientific." In contrast, there is "the truly radical critique that attempts to locate androcentric bias . . . in scientific ideology itself. The range of criticism takes us out of the liberal domain and requires us to question the very assumptions of rationality that underlie the scientific enterprise."[45]

All this seems to set a clear agenda for feminist philosophers who wish to be part of the struggle for a genuinely radical social transformation: If one is going to go deeper politically and criticize the presuppositions of liberal political theory, then one must coordinately go deeper *conceptually* and criticize the presuppositions of the epistemology and metaphysics that underwrite the politics.

But does this argument work? I think that it doesn't. To see why, we need to look more closely at the epistemological position that the feminist critics take to be allied with liberalism and look in more detail at the argument that is supposed to show that such a view of knowledge is oppressive.

The "traditional" epistemology pictured in the work of Flax, Code, and Jaggar, I've argued, is an unvigorous hybrid of rationalist and empiricist elements, but the features that are supposed to limit it from the point of view of feminist critique of science all derive from the empiricist strain. Specifically, the view of knowledge in question contains roughly the following elements:

1. It is strongly foundationalist: It is committed to the view that there is a set of epistemically privileged beliefs, from which all knowledge is in principle derivable.
2. It takes the foundational level to be constituted by reports of sensory experience, and views the mind as a mere calculating device, containing no substantive contents other than what results from experience.
3. As a result of its foundationalism and its empiricism, it is committed to a variety of sharp distinctions: observation/theory, fact/value, context of discovery/context of justification.

This epistemological theory comes very close to what Hempel has termed "narrow inductivism,"[46] but I'm just going to call it the "Dragnet" theory of knowledge. To assess the "ideological potential" of the Dragnet theory, let's look first at some of the epistemic values and attitudes the theory supports.

To being with, because of its empiricistic foundationalism, the view stigmatizes both inference and theory. In this view, beliefs whose confirmation depends upon logical relations to other beliefs bear a less direct, less "objective" connection to the world than reports of observations, which are supposed to provide us transparent access to the world. To "actually see" or "directly observe" is better, in this conception, than to infer, and an invidious distinction is drawn between the "data" or "facts" (which are incontrovertible) on the one hand and "theories" and "hypotheses" (unproven conjectures) on the other.

Second, the view supports the idea that any sound system of beliefs can, in principle, be rationally reconstructed. That is, a belief worth having is either itself a fact or can be assigned a position within a clearly articulated confirmational hierarchy erected on fact. With this view comes a denigration of the epistemic role of hunches and intuitions. Such acts of cognitive impulse can be difficult to defend "rationally" if the standards of defense are set by a foundationalist ideal. When a hunch can't be defended, but the individual persists in believing it anyway, that's *ipso facto* evidence of irresponsibility or incompetence. Hunches that happen to pay off are relegated to the context of discovery and are viewed as inessential to the justification of the ensuing belief. The distinction between context of discovery and context of justification itself follows from foundationalism: As long as it's possible to provide a rational defense of a belief *ex post facto* by demonstrating that it bears the proper inferential relation to established facts, we needn't give any thought to the circumstances that actually gave rise to that belief. Epistemic location becomes, to that extent, evidentially irrelevant.

Finally, the Dragnet theory is going to lead to a certain conception of how systematic inquiry ought to work. It suggests that good scientific practice is relatively mechanical: that data gathering is more or less passive and random, that theory construction emerges from the data in a relatively automatic way, and that theory testing is a matter of mechanically deriving predictions and then subjecting them to decisive experimental tests. Science (and knowledge-seeking generally) will be good *to the extent that* its practitioners conform to the ideal of objectivity.

This ideal of objective method requires a good researcher, therefore, to put aside all prior beliefs about the outcome of the investigation, and to develop a willingness to be carried wherever the facts may lead. But other kinds of discipline are necessary, too. Values are different in kind from facts, on this view, and so are not part of the confirmational hierarchy. Values (together with the emotions and desires connected with them) become, at best, epistemically irrelevant and, at worst, disturbances or distortions. Best to put them aside, and try to go about one's epistemic business in as calm and disinterested a way as possible.

In sum, the conception of ideal epistemic practice yielded by the Dragnet theory is precisely the conception that the feminist critics disdain. Objectivity, on this view (I'll refer to it from now on as "Dragnet objectivity"), is the result of complete divestiture—divestiture of theoretical commitments, of personal goals, of moral values, of hunches and intuitions. We'll get to the truth, sure as taxes, provided everyone's willing to be rational and to play by the (epistemically relevant) rules. Got an especially knotty problem to solve? Just the facts, ma'am.

Now let's see how the Dragnet theory of knowledge, together with the ideal of objectivity it supports, might play a role in the preservation of oppressive structures.

Suppose for the sake of argument that the empirical claims of the radical critics are largely correct. Suppose, that is, that in contemporary U.S. society institutionalized inquiry does function to serve the specialized needs of a powerful ruling elite (with trickle-down social goods permitted insofar as they generate profits or at least don't impede the fulfillment of ruling-class objectives). Imagine also that such inquiry is very costly, and that the ruling elite strives to socialize those costs as much as possible.

In such a society, there will be a great need to obscure this arrangement. The successful pursuit of the agendas of the ruling elite will require a quiescent—or, as it's usually termed, "stable"—society, which would surely be threatened if the facts were known. Also required is the acquiescence of the scientists and scholars, who would like to view themselves as autonomous investigators serving no masters but the truth and who would deeply resent the suggestion (as anyone with any self-respect would) that their honest intellectual efforts subserve any baser purpose.

How can the obfuscation be accomplished? One possibility would be to promote the idea that science is organized for the sake of *public* rather than *private* interests. But the noble lie that science is meant to make the world a better place is a risky one. It makes the public's support for science contingent upon science's producing tangible and visible public benefits (which may not be forthcoming) and generates expectations of publicity and accountability that might lead to embarrassing questions down the road.

An altogether more satisfactory strategy is to promote the idea that science is *value-neutral*—that it's organized for the sake of *no* particular interests at all! Telling people that science serves only the truth is safer than telling people that science serves *them*, because it not only hides the truth about who benefits, but deflects public attention away from the whole question. Belief in the value-neutrality of science can thus serve the conservative function of securing *unconditional* public support for what are in fact ruling-class initiatives. Any research agenda whatsoever—no matter how pernicious—can be readily legitimated on the grounds that it is the natural result of the self-justifying pursuit of truth, the more or less inevitable upshot of a careful look at the facts.

It will enhance the lie that science is objective to augment it with the lie that scientists as individuals are especially "objective," either by nature or by dint of their scientific training. If laypersons can be brought to believe this, then the lie that scientific practice can transcend its compromised setting becomes somewhat easier to swallow. And if *scientists* can be brought to embrace this gratifying self-image, then the probability of *their* acquiescence in the existing system will be increased. Scientists will find little cause for critical reflection on their own potential biases (since they will believe that they are more able than others to put aside their own interests and background beliefs in the pursuit of knowledge), and no particular incentive to ponder the larger question of who actually is benefiting from their research.[47]

Now in such a society, the widespread acceptance of a theory of knowledge like the Dragnet theory would clearly be a good thing from the point of view of the ruling elite. By fostering the epistemic attitudes it fosters, the Dragnet theory helps confer special authority and status on science and its practitioners and deflects critical attention away from the material conditions in which science is conducted. Furthermore, by supporting Dragnet objectivity as an epistemic ideal, the theory prepares the ground for reception of the ideology of the objectivity of science.

In a society in which people have a reason to believe that science is successful in yielding knowledge, the Dragnet theory and the ideology of objectivity will in fact be mutually reinforcing. If one believes that science must be objective to be good, then if one independently believes that science is good, one must also believe that science *is objective*! The Dragnet theory, taken together with propagandistic claims that science is value-neutral, etc., offers an *explanation* of the fact that science leads to knowledge. Against the background belief that knowledge is actually structured the way the Dragnet theory says it is, the *success* of science seems to confirm the ideology.

We can conclude from all this that the Dragnet theory, along with the ideal of objectivity it sanctions, has clear ideological value, in the sense that acceptance of the theory may play a causal role in people's acceptance of the ideology of scientific objectivity.

But we cannot infer from this fact either that the Dragnet theory is false or that its ideals are flawed. Such an inference depends on conflating what are essentially *prescriptive* claims (claims about how science ought to be conducted) with *descriptive* claims (claims about how science is in fact conducted). It's one thing to embrace some particular ideal of scientific method and quite another to accept ideologically useful assumptions about the satisfaction of that ideal within existing institutions.[48]

Note that in a society such as the one I've described, the ideological value of the Dragnet theory depends crucially on how successfully it can be promulgated *as a factual characterization* of the workings of the intellectual establishment. It's no use to get everyone to believe simply that it would be a good thing if scientists *could* put aside their prior beliefs and their personal interests; people must be brought to believe that scientists largely *succeed* in such divestitures. The ideological cloud of Dragnet objectivity thus comes not so much from the belief that science *ought* to be value-free, as from the belief that it *is* value-free. And of course it's precisely the fact that science is *not* value-free in the way it's proclaimed to be that makes the ideological ploy necessary in the first place.

If science as an institution fails to live up to its own ideal of objectivity, then the character of existing science entails nothing about the value of the ideal, nor about the character of some imagined science which *did* live up to it. In fact, notice that the more we can show that compromised science is *bad* science (in the sense of leading to false results), the less necessary we make it to challenge the Dragnet theory itself. A good part of the radical case, after all, is made by demonstrating the ways in which scientific research has been *distorted* by some of the very factors a Dragnet epistemologist would cite as inhibitors of epistemic progress: prejudiced beliefs, undefended hunches, material desires, ideological commitments.

There's no reason, in short, why a Dragnet theorist couldn't come to be convinced of the radical analysis of the material basis of science. Such a person might even be expected to experience a special kind of outrage at discovering the way in which the idea of objectivity is ideologically exploited in the service of special interests, much the way many peace activists felt when they first learned of some of the realities masked by U.S. officials' pious avowals of their commitment to "human rights" and "democracy."

A materialist analysis of institutionalized science leads to awareness of such phenomena as the commoditization of knowledge, the "rationalization" of scientific research, and the proletarianization of scientists. Such phenomena make the limits of liberal reformism perfectly clear: Not even the most scrupulous adherence to prescribed method on the part of individual scientists could by itself effect the necessary transformations. But it's possible for even a Dragnet theorist to acknowledge these limits, and to do so without giving up the ideal of neutral objectivity.

I began by considering the claim, defended by several feminist theorists, that "traditional" epistemology limits the possibilities for exposing the machinations of the elite because it endorses the rules of the elite's game. On the contrary, I've argued; since a big part of the lie that needs exposing is the fact that capitalist science *doesn't follow* its own rules, the task of exposing the ideology of scientific objectivity needn't change the rules. A radical critique of science and society, *even if* it implicates certain ideals, *does not require repudiation of those ideals.*

Naturalized Epistemology and the Bias Paradox

What I think I've shown so far is that if our only desideratum on an adequate critical epistemology is that it permits us to expose the real workings of capitalist patriarchy, then the Dragnet theory will do just fine, *pace* its feminist critics. But I certainly do not want to defend that theory; nor do I want to defend as an epistemic ideal the conception of objectivity as neutrality. In fact, I want to join feminist critics in rejecting this ideal. But I want to be clear about the proper basis for criticizing it.

There are, in general, two strategies that one can find in the epistemological literature for challenging the ideal of objectivity as impartiality. (I leave aside for the moment the question of why one might want to challenge an epistemic ideal, though this question will figure importantly in what follows.) The first strategy is to prove the *impossibility* of satisfying the ideal—this involves pointing to the *ubiquity* of bias. The second strategy is to try to demonstrate the *undesirability* of satisfying the ideal—this involves showing the *utility* of bias. The second strategy is employed by some feminist critics, but often the first strategy is thought to be sufficient, particularly when it's pursued together with the kind of radical critique of institutionalized science discussed above. Thus Jaggar, Code, and others emphasize the essential locatedness of every individual knower, arguing that if all knowledge proceeds from some particular perspective, then the transcendent standpoint suggested by the ideology of objectivity is unattainable. All knowledge is conditioned by the knower's location, it is claimed; if we acknowledge that, then we cannot possibly believe that anyone is "objective" in the requisite sense.

But the appeal to the *de facto* partiality of all knowledge is simply not going to justify rejecting the ideal of objectivity, for three reasons. In the first place, the wanted intermediate conclusion—that Dragnet objectivity is impossible—does not follow from the truism that all knowers are located. The Dragnet conception of impartiality is perfectly compatible with the fact that all knowers start from some particular place. The

Dragnet theory, like all empiricist theories, holds that knowledge is a strict function of the contingencies of experience. It therefore entails that differences in empirical situation will lead to differences in belief, and to that extent validates the intuition that all knowledge is partial.[49] Thus the neutrality recommended by the Dragnet theory does not enjoin cognizers to abjure the particularities of their own experience, only to honor certain strictures in drawing conclusions from that experience. Impartiality is not a matter of where you are, but rather how well you do from where you sit.

In the second place, even if it could be shown to be impossible for human beings to achieve perfect impartiality, that fact in itself would not speak against Dragnet objectivity *as an ideal.* Many ideals—particularly moral ones—are unattainable, but that does not make them useless, or reveal them to be inadequate as ideals.[50] The fact—and I have no doubt that it is a fact—that no one can fully rid oneself of prejudices, neurotic impulses, selfish desires, and other psychological detritus, does not impugn the moral or the cognitive value of attempting to do so. Similarly, the fact that no one can fully abide by the cognitive strictures imposed by the standards of strict impartiality doesn't entail that one oughtn't to try. The real test of the adequacy of a norm is not whether it can be realized, but (arguably) whether we get closer to what we want if we try to realize it.

But the third and most serious problem with this tack is that it is precisely the one that is going to engender the bias paradox. Notice that the feminist goal of exposing the structures of interestedness that constitute patriarchy and other forms of oppression requires doing more than just demonstrating that particular interests are being served. It requires criticizing that fact, showing that there's something wrong with a society in which science selectively serves the interests of one dominant group. And it's awfully hard to see how such a critical stand can be sustained without some appeal to the value of impartiality.

A similar problem afflicts the variation on this strategy that attempts to base a critique of the norm of objectivity on the androcentric features of its *source.* Even if it could be established that received epistemic norms originated in the androcentric fantasies of European white males (and I meant to give some reason to question this in the second section), how is that fact supposed to be elaborated into a *critique* of those norms? All knowledge is partial—let it be so. How then does the particular partiality of received conceptions of objectivity diminish their worth?

The question that must be confronted by anyone pursuing this strategy is basically this: If bias is ubiquitous and ineliminable, then what's the good of exposing it? It seems to me that the whole thrust of feminist scholarship in this area has been to demonstrate that androcentric biases have distorted science and, indeed, distorted the search for knowledge generally. But if biases are distorting, and if we're all biased in one way or another, then it seems there could be no such thing as an *undistorted* search for knowledge. So what are we complaining about? Is it just that we want it to be distorted in *our* favor, rather than in theirs? We must say something about the badness of the biases we expose or our critique will carry no normative import at all.

We still have to look at the second of the two strategies for criticizing the ideal of objectivity, but this is a good place to pick up the question I bracketed earlier on: *Why* might one want to challenge an epistemic ideal? If my arguments have been correct up to this point, then I have shown that many of the arguments made against objectivity are not only unsound but ultimately self-defeating. But by now the reader must surely be wondering why we need *any* critique of the notion of objectivity as neutrality. If radical critiques of the ideology of scientific objectivity are consistent with respect for this ideal, and if we need some notion of objectivity anyway, why not this one?

The short answer is this: because the best empirical theories of knowledge and mind do not sanction pure neutrality as sound epistemic policy.

The fact is that the Dragnet theory is *wrong*. We know this for two reasons: First, the failure of externalism tells us that its foundationalist underpinnings are rotten, and second, current work in empirical psychology tells us that its empiricist conception of the mind is radically incorrect. But if the Dragnet theory is wrong about the structure of knowledge and the nature of the mind, then the main source of warrant for the ideal of epistemic neutrality is removed. It becomes an open question whether divestiture of emotions, prior beliefs, and moral commitments hinders, or aids, the development of knowledge.

The fact that we find ourselves wondering about the value of a proposed epistemic ideal is itself a consequence of the turn to a naturalized epistemology. As I explained in the second section, Quine's critique of externalism entailed that epistemic norms themselves were among the presuppositions being subjected to empirical test in the ongoing process of theory confirmation. This in itself authorizes the project of *criticizing* norms—it makes coherent and gives point to a project which could be nothing but an exercise in skepticism, to an externalist's way of thinking.

Naturalized epistemology tells us that there is no presuppositionless position from which to assess epistemic practice, that we must take some knowledge for granted. The only thing to do, then, is to begin with whatever it is we think we know, and try to figure out how we came to know it: Study knowledge by studying the knower. Now if, in the course of such study, we discover that much of human knowledge is possible only because our knowledge seeking does not conform to the Dragnet model, then we will have good empirical grounds for rejecting perfect objectivity as an epistemic ideal. And so we come back to the second of the two strategies I outlined for challenging the ideal of objectivity. Is there a case to be made against the desirability of epistemic neutrality? Indeed there is, on the grounds that a genuinely open mind, far from leading us closer to the truth, would lead to epistemic chaos.

As I said in the second section, empirical work in linguistics and cognitive science is making it increasingly clear how seriously mistaken the empiricist view of the mind actually is. From Chomsky's groundbreaking research on the acquisition of language, through David Marr's theory of the computational basis of vision, to the work of Susan Carey, Elizabeth Spelke, Barbara Landau, Lila Gleitman, and others in developmental psychology, the evidence is mounting that inborn conceptual structure is a crucial factor in the development of human knowledge.[51]

Far from being the streamlined, uncluttered logic machine of classical empiricism, the mind now appears to be much more like a bundle of highly specialized modules, each natively fitted for the analysis and manipulation of a particular body of sensory data. General learning strategies of the sort imagined by classical empiricists, if they are employed by the mind at all, can apply to but a small portion of the cognitive tasks that confront us. Rationalism is vindicated.

But if the rationalists have turned out to be right about the structure of the mind, it is because they appreciated something that the empiricists missed—the value of partiality for human knowers. Whatever might work for an ideal mind, operating without constraints of time or space, it's clear by now that complete neutrality of the sort empiricists envisioned would not suit human minds in human environments. A completely "open mind," confronting the sensory evidence we confront, could never manage to construct the rich systems of knowledge we construct in the short time we take to construct them. From the point of view of an *unbiased* mind, the human sensory flow contains both too much information and too little: too much for the mind to generate *all* the logical possibilities, and too little for it to decide among even the relatively few that *are* generated.

The problem of paring down the alternatives is the defining feature of the human epistemic condition. The problem is partly solved, I've been arguing, by one form of "bias"—native conceptual structure. But it's important to realize that this problem is absolutely endemic to human knowledge seeking, whether we're talking about the subconscious processes by which we acquire language and compute sensory information, or the more consciously accessible processes by which we explicitly decide what to believe. The everyday process of forming an opinion would be grossly hampered if we were really to consider matters with anything even close to an "open mind."

This point is one that Quine has emphasized over and over in his discussions of the underdetermination of theory by data. If we had to rely on nothing but logic and the contingencies of sensory experience, we could never get anywhere in the process of forming an opinion, because we would have *too many choices*. There are an infinite number of distinct and incompatible hypotheses consistent with any body of data, never mind that there are always more data just around the corner, and never mind that we're logically free to reinterpret the "data" to save our hypotheses. If we really had to approach data gathering and theory building with a perfectly open mind, we wouldn't get anywhere.

This insight is also borne out by the history of science. As Thomas Kuhn has pointed out, science is at its least successful during the periods in its history when it most closely resembles the popular models of scientific objectivity. During a discipline's "pre-paradigm" phase, when there is no consensus about fundamental principles, nor even about what to count as the central phenomena, research is anarchic and unproductive. But progress accelerates dramatically when a discipline enters its mature period, marked by the emergence of a theory—a paradigm—capable of organizing the phenomena in a compelling enough way that it commands near-universal acceptance.

Kuhn emphasizes that one of the chief benefits a paradigm brings with it is a degree of closure about foundational issues, instilling in members of the community a principled and highly functional unwillingness to reconsider basic assumptions. The paradigm not only settles important empirical controversies, but also decides more methodological matters—

what are the acceptable forms of evidence, what is the right vocabulary for discussing things, what are the proper standings for judging research. The fact is that all of these matters are disputable in principle—but a paradigm relieves its adherents of the considerable burden of having constantly to dispute them.

But what this means is that the practice and attitudes of scientists working within a paradigm will systematically deviate from the popular ideal of scientific objectivity: They will approach their research with definite preconceptions, and they will be reluctant to entertain hypotheses that conflict with their own convictions. Kuhn's point, however, is that the existence of such closed-mindedness among working scientists—what he calls "the dogmatism of mature science"—is not to be regretted; that it is actually beneficial to the course of scientific development: "Though preconception and resistance to innovation could very easily choke off scientific progress, their omnipresence is nonetheless symptomatic of characteristics upon which the continuing vitality of research depends."[52]

Once we appreciate these aspects of mature science, we can explain a great deal about how a fantasy of the pure objectivity of science can take hold independently of any ideological purposes such a fantasy might serve. (This is important if we want a serious, nuanced story about how ideologies work.) The fact that certain tenets of theory are, for all practical purposes, closed to debate can render invisible their actual status as hypotheses. Deeply entrenched theoretical principles, like the laws of thermodynamics or the principle of natural selection, become established "facts."[53] Similarly, the high degree of theoretical background required to translate various numbers and images into observations or data is forgotten by people accustomed to performing the requisite inferences on a daily basis.

Consensus and uniformity thus translate into objectivity. The more homogeneous an epistemic community, the more objective it is likely to regard itself, and, if its inquiries are relatively self-contained, the more likely it is to be viewed as objective by those outside the community. This suggests one fairly obvious explanation for the general perception that the physical sciences are more objective than the social sciences: Sociology, political science, economics, and psychology are disciplines that still lack paradigms in Kuhn's technical sense. Because there is still public debate in these fields about basic theoretical and methodological issues, there can be no credible pretense by any partisan of having hold of the unvarnished truth.

The kind of bias that Kuhn is here identifying is, of course, different in several important respects from the kinds of biases that classical rationalists and contemporary cognitive psychologists are concerned with. For one thing, the biases that come with belief in a paradigm are acquired rather than innate; for another, there is an important social component in one case but not in the other. The lesson, however, is still the same: Human beings would know less, not more, if they were to actualize the Dragnet ideal.

What all this means is that a naturalized approach to knowledge provides us with *empirical* grounds for rejecting pure neutrality as an epistemic ideal, and for valuing those kinds of "biases" that serve to trim our epistemic jobs to manageable proportions. But it also seems to mean that we have a new route to the bias paradox—if biases are now not simply ineliminable, but downright *good*, how is it that *some* biases are *bad*?

I'm going to answer this question, honest, but first let me show how bad things really are. It's possible to see significant analogies between the function of a paradigm within a scientific community, and what is sometimes called a "worldview" within other sorts of human communities. Worldviews confer some of the same cognitive benefits as paradigms, simplifying routine epistemic tasks, establishing an informal methodology of inquiry, etc., and they also offer significant social benefits, providing a common sense of reality and fostering a functional sense of normalcy among members of the community.

But what about those outside the community? A shared language, a set of traditions and mores, a common sense of what's valuable and why—the very things that bind some human beings together in morally valuable ways—function simultaneously to exclude those who do not share them. Moreover, human communities are not homogeneous. In a stratified community, where one group of people dominates others, the worldview of the dominant group can become a powerful tool for keeping those in the subordinate groups in their places.

The real problem with the liberal conceptions of objectivity and neutrality begins with the fact that while they are unrealizable, it's possible for those resting comfortably in the center of a consensus to find that fact invisible. Members of the dominant group are given no reason to question their own assumptions: Their worldview acquires, in their minds, the status of established fact. Their opinions are transformed into what "everybody" knows.[54] Furthermore, these privileged individuals have the power to promote and elaborate their own worldview in public forums while excluding all others, tacitly setting limits to the range of "reasonable" opinion.[55]

Because of the familiarity of its content, the "objectivity" of such reportage is never challenged. If it were, it would be found woefully lacking *by liberal standards*. That's because the liberal ideal of objectivity is an *unreasonable* one; it is not just unattainable, but unattainable by a long measure. But because the challenge is *only* mounted against views that are aberrant, it is *only* such views that will ever be demonstrated to be "non-objective," and thus *only* marginal figures that will ever be charged with bias.[56]

Lorraine Code makes a similar point about the unrealistic stringency of announced standards for knowledge.[57] She rightly points out that most of what we ordinarily count as knowledge wouldn't qualify as such by many proposed criteria. I would go further and say that as with all unrealistically high standards, they tend to support the status quo—in this case, received opinion—by virtue of the fact that they will only be invoked in "controversial" cases, i.e., in case of challenge to familiar or received or "expert" opinion. Since the standards are unreasonably high, the views tested against them will invariably be found wanting; since the only views so tested will be unpopular ones, their failure to pass muster serves to add additional warrant to prevailing prejudices, as well as a patina of moral vindication to the holders of those prejudices, who can self-righteously claim to have given "due consideration" to the "other side."

But what are we anti-externalist, naturalized epistemologists to say about this? We can't simply condemn the members of the dominant class for their "bias," for their lack of "open-mindedness" about our point of view. To object to the hegemony of ruling-class opinion on this basis would be to tacitly endorse the discredited norm of neutral objectivity. "Biased" they are, but then, in a very deep sense, so are we. The problem with ruling-class "prejudices" cannot be the fact that they are deeply-held beliefs, or beliefs acquired "in advance" of the facts—for the necessity of such *kinds* of belief is part of the human epistemic condition.

The real problem with the ruling-class worldview is not that it is biased; it's that it is false. The epistemic problem with ruling-class people is not that they are closed-minded; it's that they hold too much power. The recipe for radical epistemological action then becomes simple: Tell the truth and get enough power so that people have to listen. Part of telling the truth, remember, is telling the truth about how knowledge is actually constructed—advocates of feminist epistemology are absolutely correct about that. We do need to dislodge those attitudes about knowledge that give unearned credibility to elements of the ruling-class worldview, and this means dislodging the hold of the Dragnet theory of knowledge. But we must be clear: The Dragnet theory is not false because it's pernicious; it's pernicious because it is false.

Whether we are talking in general about the ideology of scientific objectivity, or about particular sexist and racist theories, we must be willing to talk about truth and falsity. If we criticize such theories primarily on the basis of their ideological function, we risk falling prey to the very illusions about objectivity that we are trying to expose. I think this has happened to some extent within feminist epistemology. Because so much of feminist criticism has been oblivious to the rationalistic case that can be made against the empiricistic conception of mind at work in the Dragnet theory, empiricistic assumptions continue to linger in the work of even the most radical feminist epistemologists. This accounts, I believe, for much of the ambivalence about Dragnet objectivity expressed even by those feminist critics who argue most adamantly for its rejection.

This ambivalence surfaces, not surprisingly, in discussions about what to do about bad biases, where positive recommendations tend to fall perfectly in line with the program of liberal reformism. Lorraine Code's discussion of stereotypical thinking provides a case in point.[58] Code emphasizes, quite correctly, the degree to which stereotypical assumptions shape the interpretation of experience, both in science and in everyday life. But despite her recognition of the "unlikelihood of pure objectivity,"[59] the "unattainability of pure theory-neutrality,"[60] and her acknowledgment of the necessary role of background theory *in science*, her recommendations for reforming everyday epistemic practice are very much in the spirit of liberal exhortations to open-mindedness. She sees a difference between a scientist's reliance on his or her paradigm, and ordinary dependence on stereotypes:

> It is not possible for practitioners to engage in normal science without paradigms to guide their recognition of problems, and their problem-solving endeavours. Stereotype-governed thinking is different in this respect, for it is both possible and indeed desirable to think and to know in a manner *not* governed by stereotypes.[61]

But it's by no means clear that it *is* possible. I sense that Code has not appreciated the depth of human reliance on theories that cannot be shown to be "derived from the facts alone." In characterizing certain kinds of background belief and certain forms of "hasty generalization" *as stereotypes*, she is presupposing a solution to the very problem that must be solved: viz., telling which of the background theories that we routinely bring to bear on experience are *reliable* and which ones are not.

The liberal epistemological fantasy, still somewhat at work here, is that there will be formal marks that distinguish good theories from bad. The empiricist version of this fantasy is that the formal mark consists in a proper relation between theory and "fact." In this case, the good theories are supposed to be the ones that derive in the proper way from the data, whereas the bad ones—the biases, the prejudices, the stereotypes—are the ones that antedate the data. But once we realize that theory infects observation and that confirmation is a multidirectional relation, we must also give up on the idea that the good theories are going to look different from the bad theories. They can't be distinguished on the basis of their formal relation to the "facts," because (1) there are no "facts" in the requisite sense; and (2) there are too many good biases whose relation to the data will appear as tenuous as those of the bad ones.

But what's the alternative?

A naturalized approach to knowledge, because it requires us to give up *neutrality* as an epistemic ideal, also requires us to take a different attitude toward bias. We know that human knowledge requires biases; we also know that we have no possibility of getting a priori guarantees that our biases incline us in the right direction. What all this means is that the "biasedness" of biases drops out as a parameter of epistemic evaluation. There's only one thing to do, and it's the course always counseled by a naturalized approach: *We must treat the goodness or badness of particular biases as an empirical question.*

A naturalistic study of knowledge tells us biases are good when and to the extent that they facilitate the gathering of *knowledge*—that is, when they lead us to the truth. Biases are bad when they lead us *away* from the truth. One important strategy for telling the difference between good and bad biases is thus to evaluate the overall theories in which the biases figure. This one point has important implications for feminist theory in general and for feminist attitudes about universalist or essentialist theories of human nature in particular.

As we saw in section two, much of the feminist criticism raised against cognitive essentialism focused on the fact that rationalist and Kantian theories of the human essence were all devised by men, and based, allegedly, on exclusively male experience. Be that so—it would still follow from a naturalized approach to the theory of knowledge that it is an *empirical* question whether or not "androcentrism" of that sort leads to bad theories. Partiality does not in general compromise theories; as we feminists ourselves have been insisting, all theorizing proceeds from *some* location or other. We must therefore learn to be cautious of claims to the effect that particular forms of partiality will inevitably and systematically influence the outcome of an investigation. Such claims must be treated as empirical hypotheses, subject to investigation and challenge, rather than as enshrined first principles.

So what about universalist or essentialist claims concerning human nature? I have argued that there really are no grounds for regarding such claims as antipathetic to feminist aspirations or even to feminist insights regarding the importance of embodiment or the value of human difference. Suggestions that essentialist theories reify aspects of specifically male experience, I argued, involve a serious misunderstanding of the rationalist strategy. But notice that even if such charges were true, the real problem with such theories should be their *falseness*, rather than their androcentrism. A theory that purports to say what human beings are like essentially must apply to *all human beings*; if it does not, it is wrong, whatever its origins.

In fact, I think there is excellent evidence for the existence of a substantial human nature and virtually no evidence for the alternative, the view that there is no human essence. But what's really important is to recognize that the latter view is as much a substantive empirical thesis as the Cartesian claim that we are essentially rational language-users. We need to ask ourselves *why* we ought to believe that human selves are, at the deepest level, "socially constructed"—the output of a confluence of contingent factors.[62]

Another thing that a naturalized approach to knowledge offers us is the possibility of *an empirical theory of biases*. As we've already seen, there are different kinds of biases—some are natively present, some are acquired. An empirical study of biases can refine the taxonomy and possibly tell us something about the reliability and the corrigibility of biases of various sorts. It may turn out that we can on this basis get something like a principled sorting of biases into good ones and bad ones, although it will be more likely that we'll learn that even a "good" bias can lead us astray in certain circumstances.[63]

One likely upshot of an empirical investigation of bias is a better understanding of the processes by which human beings design research programs. What we decide to study and how we decide to study it are matters in which unconscious biases—tendencies to see certain patterns rather than others, to attend to certain factors rather than others, to act in accordance with certain interests rather than others—play a crucial role. We can't eliminate the biases—we shouldn't want to, for we'd have no research programs left if we did—but we can identify the particular empirical presuppositions that lie behind a particular program of research so that we can subject them, if necessary, to empirical critique.

One important issue is the *saliency* of certain properties. Every time a study is designed, a decision is made, tacitly or explicitly, to pay attention to some factors and to ignore others. These "decisions" represent tacit or explicit hypotheses about the likely connection between various aspects of the phenomena under study, hypotheses that can be subjected to empirical scrutiny.

Imagine a study purporting to investigate the development of human language by examining a sample of two hundred preschoolers. Must the sample, to be a valid basis for extrapolation, contain boys and girls? Must it be racially mixed? How one answers this question will depend on the empirical assumptions one makes about the likely connection between parameters like gender and race, on the one hand, and the language faculty on the other. To think that gender or race must be controlled for in such studies is to make a substantive empirical conjecture—in this case, it is to deny the rationalistic hypothesis that human beings' biological endowment includes a brain structured in a characteristic way, and to make instead the assumption that cognitive development is sensitive to the kinds of differences that we *socially* encode as gender and race.

Such an assumption, laid out this baldly, seems pretty dubious. Indeed, it's hard to see what such an assumption is doing other than reflecting sexist, racist, and classist beliefs to the effect that social groupings are determined by biological groupings. Realizing this is a necessary first step to countering the genuinely pernicious "essentialist" theories of Jensen, Herrnstein, and the human sociobiologists and to exposing the racism and sexism inherent in their programs of "research." Such "research" is precisely at odds with rationalist methodology, which only invokes human essences as a way of explaining human *commonalities*—and then, only when such commonalities cannot plausibly be explained by regularities in the environment.

Consider, for example, the claims that blacks are "innately" less intelligent than whites.[64] In the first place, we must point out, as we do, that race is not a biological kind, but rather a *social* kind. That is to say that while there may be a biological explanation for the presence of each of the characteristics that constitute racial criteria—skin color, hair texture, and the like—the *selection of those characteristics as criteria* of membership in some category is *conventionally* determined. Here is where the empiricist notion of "nominal essence" has some work to do: Race, in contrast to some other categories, *is* socially constructed.

The second step is to point out that if such classifications as race fail to reflect deep regularities in human biology, and reflect instead only historically and culturally specific interests, then there is no reason, *apart from racist ones*, to investigate the relation between race and some presumably biological feature of human beings. Again, it takes an extreme form of empiricism to believe that brute correlations between one arbitrarily selected characteristic and another constitutes *science*—but even from such a perspective it must be an arbitrary choice to investigate one set of such correlations rather than another. Why intelligence and *race*? Why not intelligence and number of hair follicles?

It is this point that really gives the lie to Herrnstein's repugnant invocation of "scientific objectivity" in defense of his racist undertakings.[65] The fact that there is no empirical grounding for the selection of race as a theoretical parameter in the study of intelligence utterly defeats the disingenuous defense that such "science" as Herrnstein is engaged in is simply detached fact gathering—callin' 'em like he sees 'em. The decision to use race as an analytical category betrays a host of substantive assumptions that would be exceedingly hard to defend once made explicit. How could one defend the proposition that race and intelligence are connected without confronting the embarrassing fact that there's no biologically defensible definition of "race"? And how could one defend the proposition that human "mating strategies" will receive their explanation at the biological level, without having to explicitly argue against the wealth of competing explanations available at the social and personal/intentional levels?[66]

In sum, a naturalized approach to knowledge requires us, as feminists and progressives, to be critical of the saliency such categories as gender and race have *for us*. The fact that such parameters have been egregiously overlooked in cases where they are demonstrably relevant shouldn't make us think automatically that they are always theoretically significant. The recognition that selection of analytical categories is an empirical matter, governed by both background theory and consideration of the facts, is in itself part of the solution to the paradox of partiality.

The naturalized approach proceeds by showing the empirical inadequacy of the theory of mind and knowledge that makes perfect neutrality seem like a good thing. But at the same time that it removes the warrant for one epistemic ideal, it gives support for new norms, ones that will enable us to criticize some biases without presupposing the badness of bias in general. The naturalized approach can therefore vindicate all of the insights feminist theory has produced regarding the ideological functions of the concept of objectivity without undercutting the critical purpose of exposing androcentric and other objectionable forms of bias, when they produce oppressive falsehoods.

The End

I began this essay by asking whether we need a "feminist" epistemology, and I answered that we did, as long as we understood that need to be the need for an epistemology informed by feminist insight, and responsive to the moral imperatives entailed by feminist commitments. But I've argued that we do not necessarily need a conceptual transformation of epistemological theory in order to get a feminist epistemology in this sense. We need, in the first instance, a *political* transformation of the society in which theorizing about knowledge takes place. We've got to stop the oppression of women, eliminate racism, redistribute wealth, and *then* see what happens to our collective understanding of knowledge.

My bet? That some of the very same questions that are stimulating inquiry among privileged white men, right now in these sexist, racist, capitalist-imperialist times, are *still* going to be exercising the intellects and challenging the imaginations of women of color, gay men, physically handicapped high school students, etc.

I'm not saying that we should stop doing epistemology until after the revolution. That would of course be stupid, life being short. What I am saying is that those of us who think we know what feminism is, must guard constantly against the presumptuousness we condemn in others, of claiming as Feminist the particular bit of ground upon which we happen to be standing. We need to remember that part of what unites philosophers who choose to characterize their own work as "feminist" is the conviction that philosophy ought to matter—that it should make a positive contribution to the construction of a more just, humane, and nurturing world than the one we currently inhabit.

I have argued that contemporary analytic philosophy is capable of making such a contribution and that it is thus undeserving of the stigma "malestream" philosophy. But there's more at stake here than the abstract issue of mischaracterization. Attacks on the analytic tradition as "androcentric," "phallogocentric," or "male-identified" are simultaneously attacks on the feminist credentials of those who work within the analytic tradition. And the stereotyping of contemporary analytic philosophy—the tendency to link it with views (like the Dragnet theory) to which it is in fact antipathetic—has turned feminists away from fruitful philosophical work, limiting our collective capacity to imagine genuinely novel and transformative philosophical strategies.

I acknowledge both the difficulty and the necessity of clarifying the implications of feminist theory for other kinds of endeavors. It's important, therefore, for feminist theorists to continue to raise critical challenges to particular theories and concepts. But surely this can be done without the caricature, without the throwaway refutations, in a way that is more respectful of philosophical differences.

Let's continue to argue with each other by all means. But let's stop arguing about which view is more feminist, and argue instead about which view is more likely to be true. Surely we can trust the dialectical process of feminists discussing these things with other feminists to yield whatever "feminist epistemology" we need.[67]

Notes

1. A possible exception may be Jean Grimshaw, who comes closer than any other thinker I've encountered to endorsing what I'm calling a "bare proceduralist" conception of feminist philosophy: "There is no particular view, or example, of autonomy, of morality, of self, no one characterisation of women's activities which can be appealed to in any clear way as the woman's (or feminist) view. But I think nevertheless that feminism makes a difference to philosophy. The difference it makes is that women, in doing philosophy, have often raised new problems, problematised issues in new ways and moved to the centre questions which have been marginalised or seen as unimportant or at the periphery." From Grimshaw, *Philosophy and Feminist Thinking* (Minneapolis: University of Minnesota Press, 1986), 260.

2. Naomi Scheman made this point in a letter to members of the Committee on the Status of Women of the American Philosophical Association in 1988, when she and I were serving on the

committee. Her letter was partly a response to a letter of mine raising questions about whether our charge as a committee should include the promotion of "feminist philosophy."

3. For discussions of epistemological frameworks available to feminists, see Sandra Harding, *The Science Question in Feminism* (Ithaca: Cornell University Press, 1986), especially 24–29; Mary Hawkesworth, "Feminist Epistemology: A Survey of the Field," *Women and Politics* 7 (1987): 112–24; and Hilary Rose, "Hand, Brain, and Heart: A Feminist Epistemology for the Natural Sciences," *Signs* 9, 11 (1983): 73–90.

4. See Mary E. Hawkesworth, "Knowers, Knowing, Known: Feminist Theory and Claims of Truth," *Signs* 14, 3 (1989): 533–57.

5. See, for example, Sandra Harding: "I have been arguing for open acknowledgment, even enthusiastic appreciation, of certain tensions that appear in the feminist critiques. I have been suggesting that these reflect valuable alternative social projects which are in opposition to the coerciveness and regressiveness of modern science. . . . [S]table and coherent theories are not always the ones to be most highly desired; there are important understandings to be gained in seeking the social origins of instabilities and incoherences in our thoughts and practices—understandings that we cannot arrive at if we repress recognition of instabilities and tensions in our thought" (*Science Question in Feminism*, 243–44).

6. See Naomi Scheman, "Othello's Doubt/Desdemona's Death: The Engendering of Skepticism," in *Power, Gender, Values*, ed. Judith Genova (Edmonton, Alberta: Academic Printing and Publishing, 1987); and Scheman, "Though This Be Theory, Yet There Is Madness in It," in *A Mind of One's Own: Feminist Essays on Reason and Objectivity*, ed. L. Antony and C. Witt (Boulder, Colo.: Westview, 1993). See also Evelyn Fox Keller, "Cognitive Repression in Physics," *American Journal of Physics* 47 (1979): 718–21; and "Feminism and Science," in *Sex and Scientific Inquiry*, ed. S. Harding and J. O'Barr (Chicago: University of Chicago Press, 1987), 233–46, reprinted in *The Philosophy of Science*, ed. Richard Boyd, Philip Gaspar, and John Trout (Cambridge: MIT Press, 1991).

7. For example, see Catharine A. MacKinnon, *Towards a Feminist Theory of the State* (Cambridge, Mass.: Harvard University Press, 1989).

8. This is not quite right—the ideology of "objectivity" is perfectly capable of charging those *outside* the inner circle with partiality, and indeed, such charges are also crucial to the preservation of the status quo. More on this below.

9. Lorraine Code, "The Impact of Feminism on Epistemology," *APA Newsletter on Feminism and Philosophy* 88, 2 (March 1989): 25–29.

10. Lorraine Code, "Experience, Knowledge, and Responsibility," in *Feminist Perspectives in Philosophy*, ed. Morwenna Griffiths and Margaret Whitford (Bloomington: Indiana University Press, 1988), 189ff.

11. Code, "Impact of Feminism on Epistemology," 25.

12. It might be objected that there is a third option—that we could criticize those biases that are biases against our interests and valorize those that promote our interests. But if we are in fact left with only this option, then we are giving up on the possibility of any medium of social change other than power politics. This is bad for two reasons: (1) As moral and political theory, egoism should be repugnant to any person ostensibly concerned with justice and human well-being; and (2) as tactics, given current distributions of power, it's really stupid.

13. I have defended a kind of non-realist conception of truth, but one that maintains this gap. See my "Can Verificationists Make Mistakes?" *American Philosophical Quarterly* 24, 3 (July 1987): 225–36. For a defense of a more robustly realist conception of truth, see Michael Devitt, *Realism and Truth* (Princeton: Princeton University Press, 1984).

14. Code, "Impact of Feminism on Epistemology," 25.

15. Significantly, these theories are not all empiricist, and the theories that are most "post-positivist" are the least empiricist of all. I'll have much more to say about this in what follows.

16. See, e.g., Hélène Cixous, "The Laugh of the Medusa," trans. Keith Cohen and Paula Cohen, *Signs* 1, 4 (1976): 875–93; Luce Irigaray, "Is the Subject of Science Sexed?" trans. Carol Mastrangelo Bove, *Hypatia* 2, 3 (Fall 1987): 65–87; and Andrea Nye, "The Inequalities of Semantic Structure: Linguistics and Feminist Philosophy," *Metaphilosophy* 18, 3–4 (July–October 1987): 222–40. I must say that for the sweepingness of Nye's claims regarding "linguistics" and "semantic theory," her survey of work in these fields is, to say the least, narrow and out-of-date.

17. See, e.g., Ruth Ginzberg, "Feminism, Rationality, and Logic" and "Teaching Feminist Logic," *APA Newsletter on Feminism and Philosophy* 88, 2 (March 1989): 34–42, 58–65.

18. Note that the term "Enlightenment" itself does not have any single, precise meaning, referring in some contexts to only the philosophers (and *philosophes*) of eighteenth-century France, in other contexts to any philosopher lying on the trajectory of natural-rights theory in politics, from Hobbes and Locke through Rousseau, and in still other contexts to all the canonical philosophical works of the seventeenth and eighteenth centuries, up to and including Kant. I shall try to use the term "early modern philosophy" to denote seventeenth-century rationalism and empiricism, but I may slip up.

19. In Alison Jaggar, *Feminist Politics and Human Nature* (Totowa, N.J.: Rowman and Allenheld, 1983), 355.

20. In Harding, *Science Question in Feminism*, 24.

21. Jane Flax, "Postmodernism and Gender Relations in Feminist Theory," *Signs* 12, 4 (Summer 1987); 624.

22. Ibid., 627.

23. Never mind Kant, who, apart from this note, I'm going to pretty much ignore. Virtually nothing that Flax cites as constitutive of the Enlightenment legacy can be easily found in Kant. He was not a dualist, at least not a Cartesian dualist; his opinions regarding the possible existence of a mind-independent reality were complicated (to say the least), but he clearly thought that it would be impossible for human beings to gain knowledge of such a world if it *did* exist; and the reading of the categorical imperative—how does it go? "Treat others as ends-in-themselves, never merely as means"?—that has Kant coming out as ignorant or neglectful of human difference seems to me to be positively Orwellian.

24. Harding is an exception, since she acknowledges Quine, though nothing after Quine. Code does allude to there being some changes in mainstream epistemology since the heyday of positivism, but she says that the changes are not of the right nature to license the questions she thinks are central to feminist epistemology.

25. Since I wrote this essay, the term "externalism" has acquired a very different meaning from the one I give it here. Now the term, together with its partner "internalism," is used to designate different positions on the question of whether the factors necessary for a subject's being *justified* in believing something are all internal to the subject or not. The naturalized epistemological position that I am defending in this essay might well count as "externalist" in this sense, because it replaces the traditional a prioristic conditions for justification with reliabilist conditions, the satisfaction of which depends only on facts about the relationship between the subject and her environment independently of what the subject knows or believes about that relationship.

"Externalism" and "internalism" have yet another, slightly different, meaning in the context of the debate about reasons in ethics. Jaggar, too, acknowledges that positivism has lost favor, but says nothing about the shape of the theories that have succeeded it. See Jaggar, *Feminist Politics*.

26. Cognitive essentialism generally gets associated with another thesis singled out for criticism—namely, dualism, the view that the mind is separate from the body and that the self is to be identified with the mind. Although dualism is not exclusively a rationalist view (Locke is standardly classified as a dualist), it is most closely associated with Descartes, and it is Descartes's *a priori* argument for dualism in the *Meditations* that seems to draw the most fire. Cartesian dualism is seen as providing a metaphysical rationale for dismissing the relevance of material contingencies to the

assessment of knowledge claims, because it separates the knowing subject from the physical body, and because it seems to assert the sufficiency of disembodied reason for the attainment of knowledge.

In fact, dualism is a red herring. It's an uncommon view in the history of philosophy. Many people classically characterized as dualists, like Plato, were surely not Cartesian dualists. And on top of that, the dualism does no work. Being a dualist is neither necessary nor sufficient for believing that the human essence is composed of cognitive properties.

27. Flax, "Postmodernism," 626.

28. "Individualism" as Jaggar uses it is rather a term of art. It has a variety of meanings within philosophical discourse, but I don't know of any standard use within epistemology that matches Jaggar's. In the philosophy of mind, the term denotes the view that psychological states can be individuated for purposes of scientific psychology, without reference to objects or states outside the individual. This use of the term has *nothing* to do with debates in political theory about such issues as individual rights or individual autonomy. A liberal view of the moral/political individual can work just as well (or as poorly) on an anti-individualist psychology (such as Hilary Putnam's or Tyler Burge's) as on an individualist view like Jerry Fodor's.

29. See also Scheman (1993).

30. Jaggar, "Postmodernism," 355.

31. Ibid.

32. See, for example, the excerpts from *Notes Directed against a Certain Program*, in Margaret Wilson, ed., *The Essential Descartes* (New York: Mentor Press, 1969).

33. Ibid., 112.

34. Ibid. One passage from one work should, of course, not be enough to convince anyone, and Descartes is clearly fictionalizing his own history to some extent (like who doesn't?). I do not have the space here to provide a full defense of my interpretation, but I invite you to read the *Discourse* on your own.

35. A little qualification is necessary here: The empiricist's requirement that all concepts be reducible to sensory simples does count as a substantive restriction on the possible contents of thought, but it's one which is vitiated by the reductionist semantic theory favored by empiricists, which denies the meaningfulness of any term which cannot be defined in terms of sensory primitives. See the discussion of this point in Jerry Fodor, *Modularity of Mind: An Essay on Faculty Psychology* (Cambridge: MIT Press, 1983).

Also, the empiricists did allow a kind of "bias" in the form of innate standards of similarity, which would permit the mind to see certain ideas as inherently resembling certain others. This innate similarity metric was needed to facilitate the operation of *association*, which was the mechanism for generating more complex and more abstract ideas out of the sensory simples. But the effects of a bias such as this were vitiated by the fact that associations could also be forged by the contiguity of ideas in experience, with the result once more that no effective, substantive limits were placed on the ways in which human beings could analyze the data presented them by sensory experience.

36. David Hume, *An Enquiry Concerning Human Understanding* (Indianapolis: Hackett, 1977), 30. For a different assessment of Hume's potential contributions to a feminist epistemology.

37. I have been much chastised by serious scholars of early-twentieth-century analytic philosophy (specifically Warren Goldfarb, Neil Tennant, and Philip Kitcher) for here reinforcing the myth that logical positivism was a uniform "school of thought." I guess I should thank them. The view that I am labeling "positivism" is the usual received view of the movement, but it may have belonged to only some of the more flatfooted and marginal members of the group (like A. J. Ayer) and certainly was not the view of the most important philosopher in the movement, Rudolf Carnap.

Still, the version of positivism I am outlining is the version that Quine attributed to his predecessors, and the version that he was reacting against. Moreover, even if Carnap was not an externalist in the sense of seeking a metaphysical vindication of scientific practice (as Michael Friedman argues in "The Re-evaluation of Logical Positivism," *Journal of Philosophy* 88, 10 [October 1991]:

505–19), he still was committed to a sharp separation between contentful and merely analytic statements, which is enough to generate the kinds of difficulties that I'm claiming beset positivism generally. My thanks to Marcia Homiak for calling my attention to the Friedman article.

38. Here are some of the most important works: W. V. Quine, "Two Dogmas of Empiricism," reprinted in Quine, *From a Logical Point of View* (Cambridge, Mass.: Harvard University Press, 1953); Carl G. Hempel, "Problems and Changes in the Empiricist Criterion of Meaning," *Revue Internationale de Philosophie* 11 (1950): 41–63, and "Empiricist Criteria of Cognitive Significance: Problems and Changes," in Hempel, *Aspects of Scientific Explanation and Other Essays in the Philosophy of Science* (New York: Free Press, 1965); Nelson Goodman, *Fact, Fiction, and Forecast* (Cambridge, Mass.: Harvard University Press, 1955); and Hilary Putnam, "What Theories Are Not," reprinted in Putnam, *Mathematics, Matter, and Method: Philosophical Papers, Vol. I* (Cambridge: Cambridge University Press, 1975).

39. Quine and J. S. Ullian catalog these principles—which they refer to as the "virtues" of hypotheses—in an epistemological primer called *The Web of Belief* (New York: Random House, 1970). Quine and Ullian employ a strikingly Humean strategy in trying to explain the epistemological value of the virtues.

40. W. V. Quine, "Epistemology Naturalized," in Quine, *Ontological Relativity and Other Essays* (New York: Columbia University Press, 1969), 69–90.

41. See Noam Chomsky, "Review of B. F. Skinner's *Verbal Behavior*," *Language*, 35 (1): 53–68 (1959).

42. See Noam Chomsky, "Quine's Empirical Assumptions," in *Words and Objections: Essays on the Work of W. V. Quine*, ed. D. Davidson and J. Hintikka (Dordrecht: D. Reidel, 1969). See also Quine's response to Chomsky in the same volume.

I discuss the inconsistency between Quine's commitment to naturalism and his *a prioristic* rejection of mentalism and nativism in linguistics in "Naturalized Epistemology and the Study of Language," in *Naturalistic Epistemology: A Symposium of Two Decades*, ed. Abner Shimony and Debra Nails (Dordrecht: D. Reidel, 1987), 235–57.

43. For an extremely helpful account of the Chomskian approach to the study of language, see David Lightfoot's *The Language Lottery: Toward a Biology of Grammars* (Cambridge: MIT Press, 1984).

44. I take this to be an established fact. There's a mountainous body of scholarship on this issue, much of it the result of feminist concerns about specific ways in which women have been excluded from and damaged by institutionalized science. The whole area of biological determinist theorists provides an excellent case study of the ways in which science both supports and is distorted by social stratification. *Genes and Gender II*, ed. Ruth Hubbard and Marian Lowe (New York: Gordion Press, 1979), is a collection of now classic articles critically examining alleged biological and ethological evidence for the genetic basis of gender differences. For a more current analysis of similar research in neurophysiology and endocrinology, see Helen Longino, *Science as Social Knowledge* (Princeton: Princeton University Press, 1990), chap. 6. Two excellent general discussions of the interactions among politics, economics, ideology, and science as exemplified by the growth of biological determinist theories are Stephen Jay Gould, *The Mismeasure of Man* (New York: W. W. Norton, 1981); and R. C. Lewontin, Steven Rose, and Leon J. Kamin, *Not in Our Genes* (New York: Pantheon Books, 1984).

45. Evelyn Fox Keller, "Feminism and Science," in Boyd, Gaspar, and Trout, eds., *Philosophy of Science*, 281. In this passage, Keller is also remarking on the tendency of (what she views as) the liberal critiques to focus on the "softer" biological and social sciences, and to leave alone the "harder" sciences of math and physics.

46. Carl R. Hempel, *Philosophy of Natural Science* (Englewood Cliffs, N.J.: Prentice-Hall, 1966). See especially 10–18.

47. There's a good case to be made that scientists actually have *disincentives* to ponder such questions. The structure of incentives in academia necessitates rapid generation and publication of

research, and research requires securing long-term funding, usually from a government agency or a private corporate foundation. Scientific research is thus heavily compromised at the outset, whatever the ideals and values of the individual scientist. For a detailed discussion of the ways in which academic and economic pressures systematically erode "objectivity" in science, see William Broad and Nicholas Wade, *Betrayers of the Truth: Fraud and Deceit in the Halls of Science* (New York: Simon and Schuster, 1982).

48. This follows from a general point emphasized by Georges Rey in personal conversation: It's important in general to distinguish people's theories of human institutions from the actual character of these institutions.

49. This despite the fact that the Dragnet theory supports a strong context of discovery/context of justification distinction. On empiricist theories, the justification of an individual's belief is ultimately a relation between the belief and the sensory experience of that individual. Location matters, then, because the same belief could be justified for one individual and unjustified for another, precisely because of the differences in their experiences.

50. This is not to say that there are no puzzling issues about moral ideals that are in some sense humanly unattainable. One such issue arises with respect to the ideals of altruism and supererogation, ideals which it would be, arguably, *unhealthy* for human beings to fully realize. See Larry Blum, Marcia Homiak, Judy Housman, and Naomi Scheman, "Altruism and Women's Oppression," in *Women and Philosophy*, ed. Carol C. Gould and Marx W. Wartofsky (New York: G. P. Putnam, 1980), 222–47. On the question of whether it would be good for human beings to fully realize *any* moral ideal, see Susan Wolf, "Moral Saints," *The Journal of Philosophy* 79, 8 (August 1982): 419–39.

51. Jerry Fodor, *Modularity of Mind* (Cambridge: MIT Press, 1983); Noam Chomsky, *Reflections on Language* (New York: Random House, 1975); David Marr, *Vision: A Computational Investigation Into the Human Representation and Processing of Visual Information* (San Francisco: W. H. Freeman, 1982); Susan Carey, *Conceptual Change in Childhood* (Cambridge: MIT Press, 1985); Elizabeth Spelke, "Perceptual Knowledge of Objects in Infancy," in J. Mehler, E. C. T. Walker, and M. Garrett, eds., *Perspectives on Mental Respresentations* (Hilldale, N.Y.: Erlbaum, 1982); Barbara Landau and Lila Gleitman, *Language and Experience: Evidence from the Blind Child* (Cambridge, Mass.: Harvard University Press, 1985); Steven Pinker, *Learnability and Cognition: The Acquisition of Argument Structure* (Cambridge: MIT Press, 1989).

52. Thomas S. Kuhn, "The Function of Dogma in Scientific Research," (1963), reprinted in Janet A. Kourany, *Scientific Knowledge* (Belmont, Calif.: Wadsworth, 1987), 253–65. Quotation is from 254.

53. This phenomenon affects even as sensitive and sophisticated a critic of science as Stephen Jay Gould. Responding to creationist charges that evolution is "just a theory," Gould insists: "Well, evolution *is* a theory. It is also a fact. And facts and theories are different things, not rungs in a hierarchy of increasing certainty. Facts are the world's data. Theories are structures of ideas that explain and interpret facts. Facts do not go away while scientists debate rival theories for explaining them. . . . [H]uman beings evolved from apelike ancestors whether they did so by Darwin's proposed mechanism or by some other, yet to be discovered." Stephen Jay Gould, "Evolution as Fact and Theory," *Hen's Teeth and Horse's Toes* (New York: W. W. Norton, 1980), 253–62. Quotation from 254.

Gould's point, I believe, is that the world is as it is independently of our ability to understand it—a position I share. But if facts are part of the mind-independent world, they cannot also be "the world's data." "*Data*" is the name we give to that *part* of our theory about which we can achieve a high degree of interpersonal and intertheoretic agreement; however, there can be as much contention about "the data" as about "the theory." Gould concedes as much in the next paragraph when he writes: "Moreover, 'fact' does not mean 'absolute certainty.' . . . In science, 'fact' can only mean 'confirmed to such a degree that it would be perverse to withhold provisional assent.'" If *that's* what "facts" are, then they can and do sometimes "go away while scientists debate rival theories for explaining them." Ibid., 255.

54. Notice that we don't have to assume here that anyone is knowingly telling lies. Clearly, in the real world, members of the ruling elite *do* consciously lie, and they do it a lot. But here I'm trying to point out that some of the mechanisms that can perpetuate oppressive structures are epistemically legitimate.

55. See Edward Herman and Noam Chomsky, *Manufacturing Consent* (New York: Pantheon, 1988); Noam Choimsky, *Necessary Illusions: Thought Control in Democratic Society* (Boston: South End Press, 1989), esp. chap. 3 ("The Bounds of the Expressible"); and Martin A. Lee and Norman Solomon, *Unreliable Sources: A Guide to Detecting Bias in News Media* (New York: Carol Publishing Group, 1990).

56. This explains some of what's going on in the so-called "debate" about so-called "political correctness." Most of what's going on involves pure dishonesty and malice, but to the extent that there are some intelligent and relatively fair-minded people who find themselves worrying about such issues as the "politicization" of the classroom, or about "ideological biases" among college professors, these people are reacting to the *unfamiliarity* of progressive perspectives. Those foundational beliefs that are very common within the academy—belief in a (Christian) god, in the benignity of American institutions, in the viability of capitalism—generally go without saying and are thus invisible. *Our* worldviews are unfamiliar, and so must be articulated and acknowledged. Precisely because we are willing and able to do that, while our National Academy of Scholars colleagues are not, we become open to the charge of being "ideological."

It's the very fact that there are so *few* leftist, African-American, Hispanic, openly gay, feminist, female persons in positions of academic authority that accounts for all this slavish nonsense about our "taking over."

57. Lorraine Code, "Credibility: A Double Standard," in *Feminist Perspectives*, ed. Code, Mullett, and Overall, 65–66.

58. Ibid.

59. Ibid., 71.

60. Ibid., 73.

61. Ibid., 72.

62. Ironically, the preference among many feminist theorists for "thin" theories of the self, like postmodernist constructivist theories, is itself a vestige of an incompletely exorcised empiricism in contemporary feminist thought. It is a specifically empiricist position that the groupings of objects into kinds effected by human cognition are not keyed to "real essences," but are rather reflections of superficial regularities in experience that persist only because of their pragmatic utility.

63. We know, for example, that some of the built-in rules that make it possible for the human visual system to pick out objects from their backgrounds—so-called structure from motion rules—also make us subject to certain specific kinds of visual illusions. See A. L. Yuille and S. Ullman, "Computational Theories of Low-Level Vision," in *Visual Cognition and Action*, ed. Daniel N. Osherson, Stephen M. Kosslyn, and John M. Hollerbach, vol. 2 of *An Invitation to Cognitive Science*, ed. Daniel N. Osherson (Cambridge: MIT Press, 1990), 5–39.

64. I am here reiterating the arguments Chomsky mounted against Herrnstein's apologia for Jensen's theory of race and intelligence. See Noam Chomsky, "Psychology and Ideology," reprinted in Chomsky, *For Reasons of State* (New York: Random House, 1973), 318–69; excerpted and reprinted as "The Fallacy of Richard Herrnstein's IQ," in *The IQ Controversy*, ed. Ned Block and Gerald Dworkin (New York: Random House, 1976), 285–98.

65. See Herrnstein's reply to Chomsky, "Whatever Happened to Vaudeville?" in Block and Dworkin, eds., *IQ Controversy*, esp. 307–9.

66. These considerations also help defeat the charge, hurled against critics of biological determinist theories, that we progressives are the ones guilty of "politicizing" the debate about nature and nurture. The Herrnsteins and E. O. Wilsons of this world like to finesse the meticulously arrayed empirical criticisms of their work by accusing their critics of the most pathetic kind of

wishful thinking—"Sorry if you don't *like* what my utterly objective and bias-free research has proven beyond a shadow of a doubt. You must try to be big boys and girls and learn to cope with the unpleasant truth." For examples, see Herrnstein, "Whatever Happened to Vaudeville?" in Block and Dworkin, eds., *IQ Controversy*; and E. O. Wilson, "Academic Vigilantism and the Political Significance of Sociobiology," reprinted in *The Sociobiology Debate*, ed. Arthur L. Caplan (New York: Harper and Row, 1978), 291–303.

67. Much of the preliminary work for this essay was done during a fellowship year at the National Humanities Center, and I wish to thank both the center and the Andrew J. Mellon Foundation for their support. The essay is based on a presentation I gave at the Scripps College Humanities Institute Conference, "Thinking Women: Feminist Scholarship in the Humanities," in March 1990. I want to thank the institute, especially Norton Batkin, for the invitation to think about these issues. I also want to thank my co-participants at the conference, especially Naomi Scheman, to whom I owe a special debt. I have enjoyed an enormous amount of stimulating and challenging conversation and correspondence with Naomi about all the issues in this essay. It's a tribute to her sense of intellectual fairness and her commitment to feminist praxis that she and I have managed to conduct such an extended dialogue about these issues, given the intensity of our disagreements. I also want to make it clear that while I had the benefit of reading Naomi's essay before completing my own, I did not finish mine in time for her to react to any of the points I raise here.

Many other people have helped me with this essay. I want to thank Judith Ferster, Suzanne Graver, Charlotte Gross, Sally Haslanger, Barbara Metcalf, and Andy Reath for hours of valuable conversation. Marcia Homiak, Alice Kaplan, and Georges Rey supplied extremely useful comments on earlier drafts; David Auerbach did all that *and* extricated me from an eleventh-hour computer crisis, and I thank them heartily. Very special thanks to Charlotte Witt, for her excellent philosophical and editorial advice and for her abundant patience and good sense. I cannot fully express my thanks to Joe Levine for all he's done, intellectually and personally, to help me complete this project. Thanks as well to my children, Paul and Rachel, for their patience during all the times I was out consorting with my muse.

Part II

Is Quine's "Naturalized Philosophy of Science" Philosophy of Science Enough?

3

A Case for a Responsibly Rationalized Feminist Epistemology

Maureen Linker

An emerging criticism from scholarship in feminist epistemology draws attention to the traditional focus on the individual in philosophical analyses of science and knowledge. This criticism, coupled with the dawning realization in analytic philosophy that theories of language, mind, reason, and rationality will not progress if there is a continued neglect of social and political factors,[1] has resulted in a renewed attention to naturalized models of epistemology. In particular, Quine's holist view of naturalized epistemology has recently been advocated by several feminist philosophers. As Linda Alcoff has suggested, for some feminist scholars Quine's epistemology provides an appealing alternative as compared with social constructivist models,[2] since some version of positivism and sensory experience is integral to the holist's naturalized account. The holist can maintain that the "web of beliefs" that constitutes our conceptual scheme corresponds with physical reality even if all our beliefs are in principle revisable, and even if we can't say exactly which beliefs are correspondingly true. Despite these limitations, holists are still in a better position than most for avoiding the threat of radical relativism.

The charge of radical relativism is a significant concern for feminist epistemologists because philosophical feminism strives to identify and condemn epistemic and moral wrongs. Feminists working in philosophy have provided arguments to show that while epistemology has traditionally advocated impartiality and objectivity, the tradition and the research it has produced has been exclusive and has favored particularly white, Western, male virtues. To criticize this tradition from a nonrelativistic standpoint would mean that feminism could be a corrective offering a more complete account of knowledge as compared with the "mainstreams" of philosophy.

This potentially promising route is the one that Lynn Hankinson Nelson takes in her book *Who Knows: From Quine to a Feminist Empiricism.*[3] Nelson draws upon Quine's work to show how feminist empiricism provides the next step in the development of naturalized epistemology. Though Nelson argues that Quine's view cannot be relied upon as a starting point without some refinements, she still regards the general model as one that can further feminist accounts of science and knowledge.

Yet, even given the refinements that Nelson proposes, I will argue that a reliance on Quine to underwrite feminist epistemology inherits some of the problems that Quine's model falls prey to. Specifically, the minimally realist account of meaning and truth that Quine's model offers is, in my view, not adequate to handle the normative force behind feminist criticisms of science and knowledge. Therefore, I suggest a reconsideration of a more *rationalized* epistemology for feminism despite the current interest in naturalism.

I. Quine and Nelson

Epistemological accounts concerning the role of social factors in the acquisition of knowledge have generally challenged traditional epistemology and have been included under naturalized epistemology. In Quine's formulation, naturalized epistemology would ideally be a branch of psychology. Feminist epistemology, a particular offshoot of the more socially motivated epistemologies, has as a goal the analysis of categories like "gender" and "group membership" using naturalized models ranging from postmodern critiques of reason to more empiricist philosophy of science. From within these empiricist accounts, there are those views in particular that draw upon the resources of the Anglo-American tradition and attempt to transform the apolitical discourse into one that is capable of accounting for gender bias and power relations within systems of knowledge. Nelson's use of Quine falls into this latter category.

Naturalized epistemology involves a commitment to the evaluation of beliefs and the related notions of evidence and justification according to relevant psychological and sociological factors as well as sensory experience. Advocates of naturalized epistemology agree that the measure of a belief's warrantability is related to the question of how that belief was caused as well as to the factors that link the believer to a position within the wider social matrix. Moreover, within the naturalized framework the question of when to revise beliefs is answered not by an appeal to rationalized procedures for obtaining transcendent truth, but instead is evaluated in light of the "web" of interdependent beliefs and/or biases already held. The principles guiding inquiry are modest and amount to a general principle of noncontradiction, along with the pragmatic principle of keeping revisions to a minimum. In Quine's naturalized model there are no hard and fast boundaries between epistemology and metaphysics, epistemology and science, and epistemology and psychology.

Quine's attempt to "rub out" the boundaries of the past, thereby integrating the theory of knowledge with publicly institutionalized pursuits of knowledge, provides a starting point for Nelson's rereading of Quine. However, Nelson argues that we must move a step beyond the naturalized picture Quine presents to "overthrow a remaining boundary" (Nelson 1990, 134). The particular view of naturalism Nelson envisages is implied in Quine's work, even if it is not outright stated. For Nelson, the last boundary remaining in Quine's account is the boundary between science and social, moral, and political values

While Quine maintains that our theories are generally without boundaries, he does not, as Nelson points out, address the question of how issues in the larger social community might have an effect on the development and acceptance of scientific theories. For Quine, the network of our going theories is structured in such a way that scientific theories are more "embedded" and more "centralized" than theories that systematize social and political values. Thus, they are protected from the influence of the less orderly data that arise in those areas. Yet, as Nelson says, this implicit hierarchy should not follow on an epistemological model that interweaves common sense, science, and philosophy as all theoretical, mutually dependent, and continually evolving. Nelson disagrees with Quine that there is nothing "objective" about values, and questions whether the monolithic "we" that Quine uses really means everyone when he claims that "there is no clash of interests as *we* pursue our separate ways. Our scales of values blend in social harmony" (132).

Quine serves as a springboard for Nelson in her advocacy of holism and naturalized epistemology. The fact that Quine's epistemology does not recognize categories like race, gender, or social location is, for Nelson, a fundamental inadequacy. Thus, integrating feminism with holism and naturalized epistemology requires that Nelson revise some aspects of Quine's views and abandon others. Specifically, Quine's empiricist commitment to "individualism" in the sense that the ontological status of knowledge acquirers must be in terms of individuals, is, for Nelson, artificial and ultimately untenable. Alternatively, Nelson proposes an analysis from the perspective of the community of interdependent knowers. She writes: "The critical self-reflection warranted by the collapse of these traditional boundaries is not a matter of working to erase an individual's signature from the content of science. . . . [I]f we recognize that individuals are only knowers in a derivative sense, then 'self'-reflection can be seen to be, at bottom, something a community needs to undertake" (314).

In addition to the collapse of the boundary between epistemology and science, Quine blurs the boundaries between the positivist distinction of a context of discovery and a context of justification. "Discovery" traditionally referred to an individual's history as well as their system of beliefs. Justification involved valid, formal rules of inference and was, for positivists, the only legitimate domain for philosophical and scientific theorizing. Quine collapses this alleged boundary between psychology and logic and argues first, that all beliefs including our confidence in the laws of logic are in principle revisable; and second, such a view does not lead to radical relativism. This feature of Quine's model has the advantages described earlier. An avoidance of radical relativism can ground the critique of practices that are exclusionary, sexist, or oppressive. For Nelson, it is not the mere shift of power relations that should guide our revision of theories, but instead, the community-wide unearthing and evaluating of beliefs and values that have unreflectively been incorporated into our descriptions of reality.

This brief sketch of some of the critical points of intersection and disjunction between Quine and Nelson will frame my discussion of the use of Quine's work and naturalized epistemology for feminism. The objections I will raise against this reliance on Quine stem from what I see as an incompatibility between the goals of feminist epistemology and Quine's efforts to collapse the relevant traditional boundaries. Nelson's goal is to formulate a working model that can, on the one hand, explain how social and cultural values are incorporated into science and knowledge, and on the other hand, avoid a relativistic account of truth. While I am quite sympathetic with this effort, I do not see Quine's holism and naturalized epistemology as providing the best starting point for reaching these ends.

The acceptance of both Quine's attack on the analytic/synthetic distinction and his proposal for a naturalized epistemology have been enormously influential in a variety of philosophical circles. However, I want to argue that the use of Quine's work for feminist analyses of language and knowledge undermines the strong normative and corrective potential of feminist theory. Both in late twentieth century philosophy traditionally and in more recent socially influenced epistemologies, realism and philosophical rationalism have taken a back seat. Alternatively, I would like to propose a reconsideration of these less popular approaches and argue for why they may be more consistent with the normative goals of feminist theory.

I will begin by outlining a view of language derived from the work of J. J. Katz to show that Quine has not given a knockdown argument against the distinction between analytic and synthetic propositions. Secondly, I will discuss what I see as internal inconsistencies in Quine's view of the embeddedness of logic and mathematics. This internal inconsistency, along with unconvincing arguments for the collapse of the analytic/synthetic distinction, shows that naturalized epistemology and holism, as they are developed by Quine, are too weak normatively to meet the goals of feminist epistemology. If the possibility remains for a certain class of propositions to be a priori and analytic, then the evaluation of beliefs and standards can rest on more than organizing contingent, a posteriori propositions. My conclusion will be that feminist philosophers who are seeking a viable model of theory choice should forego the adoption and expansion of naturalized epistemology and reconsider a revised rationalized approach to knowledge that makes room for social responsibility.

II. Revisiting the Analytic/Synthetic Distinction

I begin with a return to Quine's arguments against the analytic/synthetic distinction. Quine's move to collapse traditional boundaries began with his attack on the distinction between statements the truth of which depended upon empirically contingent matters of fact and statements that were true by "convention" and dependent upon the logical and semantic structures of a theory. In Quine's view this proposed distinction between synthetic sentences and analytic sentences is an illusion. Quine's claim rests on two related arguments: first, that there are no "things" that are meanings; and second, that translation is indeterminate.

The first argument appears in "Two Dogmas of Empiricism" (Quine 1963, 20–46). Here, Quine maintains that the traditional notion of analyticity rests on a notion of synonymy, and in his view it is not possible to make objective sense out of the concept of synonymy. As a result there are ultimately no meanings. Quine explains that in science, one cannot claim that an object of study exists without having conditions for type identifying such objects. By "type identifying" Quine means that theorists must be able to describe the properties and conditions for the existence of the object. With regard to meaning, the identity condition assumed has been the notion of synonymy or sameness of meaning. So, if there are meanings, there must be a clear and objective notion of synonymy. Quine examines three possibilities in which a clear notion of synonymy might be found. He shows how each possibility in turn begs the question and therefore fails to provide type-identifying conditions for meaning.

However, Quine takes these three possibilities as the *only* possibilities for what meaning could be. If there is another account of meaning not considered by Quine, then his arguments show only that the available evidence underdetermines theories of meaning, not that meaning are indeterminate and nonobjective.

The indeterminacy thesis arises from Quine's recognition that the identity of meaning would have to be determined on the basis of verbal behavior. And verbal behavior would provide an "indeterminate" translation in the sense that "manuals for translating one language into another can be set up in divergent ways, all compatible with the totality of speech dispositions, yet incompatible with one another. In countless places they will diverge in giving, as their respective translations of a sentence of one language, sentences of the other language which stand to each other in no plausible sort of equivalence however loose" (Quine 1960, 27). Quine's conclusion that the totality of linguistic evidence cannot eliminate incompatible translations is developed in the situation he calls "radical translation" (28). From these arguments Quine advanced the view that all sentences involve the contingent organization and content of empirical data. The collapse of the analytic/synthetic distinction means that all sentences, even the seeming necessary truths of logic and mathematics, possess some empirical content and are therefore subject to revision.

However, in Quine's view, not all sentences are equally likely to be revised. Some sentences in the network of our going theories are less likely to be revised because they are more "embedded," as is the case with logical and mathematical truths. As Nelson points out, there are two aspects to Quine's notion of embeddedness. Logical and mathematical truths are embedded in one sense in that the probability is low that they will be challenged by any of our experiences. This is for the reason that they are far from sensory experiences, and don't really have any specific sensory experiences associated with them. Secondly, these sentences play a role throughout all our theories and serve as a structural feature upon which these theories are built (Nelson 1990, 91–92).

The embeddedness of logical and mathematical statements gives them a unique, though not nonempirical, status. Revising these statements would result in the upset of all theories throughout our going network. Since it is Quine's belief that we, for pragmatic reasons, seek to revise our theories in only modest increments, his conclusion is that we will most likely never come to the point of revising these central statements.

The pragmatism behind Quine's notions of revisability and embeddedness does not entail a skeptical or relativistic conception of truth, according to Nelson. Rather, since we cannot speculate or evaluate except from already within a theory, the kinds of doubts we could raise must be limited to "localized" areas. This approach requires that we remain confident in some of the sentences we believe to be true, even if we can't say at any given time exactly which sentences are in fact true.

Given the above outline of Quine's views, a model of holistic theory-choice emerges. In this model theories are viewed as sets of sentences, the component features of which include sensory experience as well as judgments with regard to the coherency of the experience in light of other beliefs. The model is, in principle, not hierarchical in the sense that we cannot mandate what a theory must cohere to other than to distinguish the more central from the more peripheral parts of our web of beliefs. As was stated earlier, the more central or embedded beliefs are the ones we are least likely to revise in the face of disconfirming experiences, as they would require radical readjustment throughout our entire system of beliefs. So, adopting a particular conclusion amounts to making it cohere with currently held beliefs.

III. Another Possibility for Meaning

If we accept Quine's conclusion that actual translation is indeterminate, that is, that there is in principle nothing that allows for objective translation, then we are committed to a metaphysical result. The result is metaphysical because Quine contends that there is no fact of the matter with regard to what theories of translation are about. This is for the reason that there are no meanings a theory of translation could take as its object of investigation. I want to suggest that this metaphysical claim is not backed up by the epistemological arguments provided by Quine in *Word and Object*. The arguments offered there prove that we do not have sufficient evidence to know the properties of meanings; but this only indicates that the available evidence underdetermines theories of meaning. And underdetermination is not a special problem for theories of meaning. Rather, it is a problem for all scientific theories. Thus, as far as Quine's arguments go, theories of meaning are on a par with scientific theories generally.

What needs to be shown is that Quine's arguments do not rule out meaning in general, only meaning as construed by the three possibilities considered in "Two Dogma's of Empiricism." J. J. Katz, in his work, offers such an argument (Katz 1990). I will outline the structure of Katz's view and offer it as an alternative not considered by Quine and Quine's supporters. Since the purpose of this chapter is not to offer a detailed defense of Katz's semantic theory, but instead to explore what possibilities arise for feminism if the analytic/synthetic distinction is not collapsed, I will *describe* some of the ingredients of a realist meaning theory. In addition, I will show the relationship such a meaning theory could have to feminist epistemology.

Katz begins with Quine's assumption that the method of substitution criterion is the proper method of defining concepts in the theory of meaning. This method holds that some feature, like truth, of the context in which substitutions are made, remains invariant, and this feature must not be intensional, otherwise the account is circular. Yet Katz argues that there is a better method of defining concepts in the theory of meaning. This better method entails defining concepts on the basis of axiomatic specification of the relations between concepts, much in the same way that concepts are defined in logic or mathematics. This is the notion of theoretical definition. In Katz's view, there is a fundamental pool of semantic primitives that have necessary connections and relations. What justifies this model for Katz is that by assuming such an "axiomatic" system, we can deduce a consistent system of meaning relations whereby the facts of our language are explained. These facts include properties like infinite expressibility, contradiction, literalness, meaningfulness, and redundancy.

In the *realist* view of meaning, language is understood as a set of abstract objects epistemologically accessed through our linguistic *intuition*. Unlike Gottlob Frege's more conceptual account, the linguistic realist supports a view of intuition as "a mental act, but its object is not, for that reason, something psychological" (160). By not theorizing the objects of intuition to be psychological objects, the realist bypasses some of the more substantial arguments by Wittgenstein and other naturalists on rule following.[4] For the realist, apprehension by our conscious intuition of abstract objects is not a report of concrete subjective psychological states. For this reason, intuition provides knowledge of a general kind, as opposed to particularized knowledge that one may access through psychological introspection. The realist's reliance on intuition as opposed to introspection parallels the logician's model of generalized knowledge through intuition. My intuition of "If *p* then *q*; and *p*, therefore *q*" validates the general truth that all instances of *modus ponens* are valid. Similarly, the linguistic intuition that the sentence type "Promising entails intending to do" validates for us the general truth that all literal tokens of the type are analytic.

Just as the realist accepts psychological or conceptual analyses of meaning, she or he recognizes a distinction between "knowledge" of a language and the language itself. What this distinction amounts to for the realist is that the set of abstract objects that makes up the language has an ontological status independent of a speaker's knowledge of the set.

The language itself consists of a set of abstract objects that include infinitely many senses and sentence types. Generally most linguists as well as most speakers of a language agree that there are an infinite number of possible grammatical sentences that could be constructed in any natural language. For example, when I parse the sentence "My mother's mother is female," there is a syntactic and semantic structure that constitutes my literal understanding of the sentence. From this understanding of the literal sense I can generate novel sentences of the same form with some variability in reference: "My mother's mother's mother was female." Clearly this could go on ad infinitum, whereby each new sentence followed the form of a grammatical, meaningful sentence of English. After a few multiple embeddings of "mother" my cognitive capacities might reach their limits; however, this empirical fact does not falsify the grammaticality of the admittedly long and complex sentences. In other words, there is a form or structure to the language itself—and as speakers of the language we rely upon this literal form as the basis for meaningful communication in our use of language. Our actual utterances do not exhaust the number of possible grammatical sentences that could be generated within our language, nor does literal meaning constitute the totality of our speech dispositions. We can speak figuratively, metaphorically, literally, ironically—depending on the contextual and pragmatic factors that make up our "utterance environment." Thus, data from linguistics show that there is a need to account for (1) the infinite expressibility of the syntactic and semantic components of language; (2) literal meaning; and (3) the relationship of literal meaning to pragmatic meaning contexts.

The realist interprets this set of factors as data that can be explained by postulating a theory of mind-independent sentences, senses, and sense relationships. Our particular utterance of a sentence in English, for example, is an instance of a *token* sentence that corresponds to a sentence *type*. A token utterance gets its meaning in virtue of the sense of the sentence type. The sense of the sentence type arises as a result of the compositional relationship of the senses of the word types. This relationship of word types constitutes the *literal* meaning of the sentence token, along with various pragmatic factors about the context of the utterance environment.

Thus, for the realist, there is an objective source underlying behavior, use, or mere convention to set the semantic norms guiding a speaker's grasp of the sense of sentences in her language. Moreover, some sense relations are understood to be unrevisable and *analytic*. For example, the propositions "Squares are four-sided figures" or "Promising entails accepting an obligation" or "Murder implies killing" are instances of necessary sense relations that yield contradictions if conceived differently. These are compared with *contingent* sense relations such as "The square is my favorite shape" or "I make promises often" or "The murder took place in August," in which the sentences are meaningful but the sense relations could intuitively be related in a different fashion. Our ability to grasp the necessity and contingency of these sense relations is understood, in the realist account, as resulting from the combined use of both our rational and linguistic faculties. Thus, unlike naturalists who view our language faculty as being the result of contingent elements in our social experience and psychology, realists view our knowledge of the language as corresponding with an objective realm of types and senses akin to metaphysical realism in logic and mathematics. What warrants the postulation of objective, necessary senses for the realist is the theoretical explanation they provide for a subset of propositions. It was Noam Chomsky's work on generative grammar coupled with the necessity of logical, linguistic, and mathematical truths that led Katz to follow out the progression from linguistic rationalism to metaphysical realism.

Returning to Quine's arguments, they could be construed, according to Katz, as a reductio of the idea that the identity conditions for a theory of meaning should be defined by way of substitution criteria. For Katz, the only legitimate charge that Quine can make against meaning theories is that they are undetermined but not indeterminate. Quine has not shown that the objects of linguistic investigation do not exist.

Katz's arguments provide a way of overcoming Quine's skepticism about meaning and analyticity. Yet, thus far, in employing these arguments, linguistics is merely on a par with other sciences in Quine's framework. And while Quine is clearly skeptical of the existence of "meanings," he is not an obvious realist with regard to the existence of the objects of natural science. For Quine, there are no "absolute" ontological decisions. We do not, in his view, discover objects and then theorize about them. Ontologies are proposed and evaluated within theories. Hence even if we can show that analytic propositions "exist" in the same way that the objects of natural science exist, this does not confer upon them a necessity or unrevisablity. In Quine's epistemological view, no statement is immune from revision. This includes logical and mathematical truths as well as statements closest to the "periphery" of sensory stimulation that we are less likely to get wrong. So their centrality or "embeddedness" can still explain the "absolute" character of analytic, logical, and mathematical statements.

Yet how viable are the dual notions of "embeddedness" and "revisablity?" Do they provide a clear explanation of the role of analytic, logical, and mathematical truths within our theories? Along with Katz's argument for the possibility of meaning, I want to argue further that there are also reasons to question Quine's centrality and revisablity thesis.

In *From A Logical Point of View* Quine writes: "[N]o statement is immune to revision. Revision even of the logical law of the excluded middle has been proposed as a means of simplifying quantum mechanics" (Quine 1963, 43). However, Quine also explains that it is rational to keep revisions in our body of knowledge to a minimum. To revise or abandon central logical principles would have consequences we can hardly begin to envisage. In *Methods of Logic* he writes:

> Our system of statements has such a thick cushion of indeterminacy, in relation to experience, that vast domains of law can easily be held immune to revision in principle. We can always turn to other quarters of the system when revisions are called for by unexpected experiences. Mathematics and logic, central as they are to our conceptual scheme, tend to be accorded such immunity, in view of our conservative preference for revisions which disturb the system least. (Quine 1972, xiii)

Quine seems to hold both a radical and conservative interpretation of revisability. On the one hand, he argues that there are many statements of logic and mathematics for which we feel certain, and quite reasonably, that their truth value will never come into question. This is not because our knowledge of them has a special source that guarantees their truth. Rather, the source of our certainty is explained by the systematic role that such statements have within the body of our beliefs. These statements are in some sense "remote" from experience, but they are not totally immune from future experiential evidence.

On the other hand, Quine also explains that it is pragmatic to keep revisions in our body of knowledge to a minimum. To revise or abandon central logical principles would have consequences we can hardly begin to envisage. While Quine argues for epistemological holism, he is not prevented from seeing how mathematics and logic differ from other sciences. It may be possible to conceive of states of affairs that contravene the laws of physics or psychology, but the laws of logic seem to be operative in all states of affairs. The necessity we intuit in mathematics and logic is explained by the fact that they are so deeply embedded in our framework of beliefs. Hence it is unlikely that any evidence could force us to undertake the enormous revisions that would be required if we were to abandon one of them. It follows that it may be absolutely rational to hold these principles immune from falsification in the light of *any* new evidence.

Consequently, wholesale revisability is in principle a possibility. However, no foreseeable circumstances would ever arise that might lead us to revise the embedded statements of logic and mathematics. Thus, there is a justification for believing that the only rationally admissible conceptual schemes are those that do not falsify the central laws of logic and mathematics. So what does "in principle revisable" amount to for logic, mathematics, and the analytic propositions described above? Given what has been said so far, the answer seems to be "Not much." Why hold onto a tenet of revisability and centrality that can never in principle be employed? If we join the arguments for meaning with the view that what is central to our system of knowledge is a set of foundational a priori beliefs, then we can begin to see the structure emerge for a rationalized epistemology.

IV. Implications of Realism and Rationalism for Feminism

So far, I have tried to argue that it is possible to reintroduce a science of meaning into a holist account that is as "objective" as the other sciences and yet is not entirely empirical. However, I have gone on to say that some of the sense relationships within the science of meaning have the property of being analytic and necessarily true, thereby occupying a central place, along with logic and mathematics, within our web of beliefs. However, for naturalized epistemologists, even these central beliefs are empirical and in principle revisable. If we accept this conclusion then we fail to capture the apparent necessity of embedded beliefs. My conclusion is that the very notions of revisability and embeddedness are not as viable as they might at first appear. This because there is no model for a conceptual scheme that falsifies the apparent necessity of logical, mathematical, and (I want to add) linguistic propositions. While we may revise *our* understanding of these properties and relationships, we are revising in light of some goal. The procedures involved for devising proofs and uncovering structures and formal relationships in mathematics, logic, and linguistics are procedures aimed at *discovering* properties and relationships. The nature of investigation in these areas is neither pure social construction nor straightforward descriptive reporting. Rather, the investigation requires conceptual analysis, reconstruction, the input of a variety of rational and linguistic perspectives, and the continual refinement of sense properties and relationships.

Rationalism and metaphysical realism provide the opportunity for feminist philosophers to evaluate beliefs in relation to inferences that are necessary and, therefore, more *truth productive*. This is significantly different from the naturalist's focus on psychology and sociology as the source for our commitment to the truth of various propositions. Nelson wants to add social, political, and moral beliefs to Quine's framework and argues that what grounds feminist condemnation of particular beliefs is their inconsistency within a coherent system of truth. But a fundamental reliance on consistency and coherence can only provide a strong program of rational censure if these principles are grounded in more than psychology or sociology. After all, history has demonstrated that social groups can manage to work out a psychological system of belief that is more or less consistent and severely oppressive. By making readjustments throughout segments in their collective belief system, many white men were able to justify the belief that women and African Americans were not full-fledged human beings in terms of their rights. Feminist condemnation of such a way of thinking requires a standard of evaluation that transcends the psychology of individuals or groups. Metaphysical realism and a socially informed rationalism can provide such a model by attending to the overall logic of such a justification and the methods used to justify the belief. By focusing on the logic of justification rather than the psychological states of believers, rationalists offer the possibility of real revisability guided by more than pragmatic considerations. It is this possibility of revisability in light of the goal of *truth* that more adequately meets the feminist goal of offering a corrective analysis.

The normative role of necessity in linguistics, including the necessity of certain ethical propositions, does not restrict the occurrence of acts that are inconsistent with their necessity. Rather, the realist argues that truths in these areas restrict the logical possibilities in specifying the actual, the possible, and the impossible (Katz 1990, 289). The truths of mathematics and logic carve away the impossible from the meaningfully expressible. The necessary truths of language carve away the meaningless and contradictory from the meaningful. The truths of morality carve away the ethically impossible from the ethically meaningful. For example, the necessity of the proposition "The conscious exclusion of a social group from access to opportunity and power, on the basis of that group's gender, race, class, or sexual orientation, is wrong" does not prevent such an act from occurring. What a realist evaluation shows, however, is that such an act could never be a *morally justifiable* act.

Thus, once we arrive at a necessary property or relationship, we have arrived at a proposition that, though it may be misapplied or misused, is nevertheless a guide for truth-productive investigation. Such unrevisable relationships are typified in propositions like "Squares are four-sided figures," "If *p* then *q*; and *p*, therefore *q*," and "'Sincerely promises to do *x*' entails 'intends to do *x*.'" Feminists have rightly pointed out the paltry nature of such propositions and formal analyses for explaining the complex social components of knowledge. Yet what I want to suggest is that if realists and epistemic rationalists have left out the social, political, and moral dimensions in their analysis of knowledge and language, then what might be needed is a revised *rationalism* informed by social responsibility, as opposed to a naturalized epistemology. Through a realist investigation of excluded or marginalized perspectives we could begin to flesh out a revised rationalism guided by the collective weighing of a variety of intuitions, evidence, and arguments. What makes such a proposal different from the naturalized model is that the evaluation and revision of beliefs would not be guided by psychology, standpoint, or social location, but rather by the most intuitively defensible forms of reasoning aimed at distinguishing necessary from contingent truth.

Realism also has the advantage of shifting the focus away from empirical knowledge to more generalized, abstract knowledge. For Nelson, holism and underdetermination lead to the end of rigid divides between a priori, necessary truths and contingent matters of fact. Since for the naturalized epistemologist there is no way to distinguish on purely conceptual grounds "good" values from "bad," we must rely on pragmatic, empirical, social, and political criteria. By prioritizing the coherence of the physicalistic conceptual scheme over all others, "objective" knowledge is contingent and revisable. Therefore, the naturalized model directs feminist research toward better empirical knowledge and to the use of empirical methods to show how bias and exclusivity have compromised knowledge.

Nelson offers examples of this kind of procedure in her descriptions of competing paradigms (Nelson 1990, 208–12). In anthropology, feminist critics who uncovered the androcentric assumptions unexplored in the background of these long accepted models challenged "hunter/gatherer" theories. In biology, "master molecule" theories were challenged by feminists who advanced the view that the genetic determination of traits could be understood more effectively in terms of protein synthesis. For Nelson, it was only because there was a shared point of reference for things like molecules, macroscopic objects, continents, societies, and so on that feminists could raise the criticisms of science and show other scientists that bias was operative. In this way, Nelson recognizes the inclusion of social and political values within science but does not see these as leading to the kind of "epistemological chasms" that historicist philosophers of science like Kuhn advance. That is to say, while Nelson is sympathetic to Kuhn's historical analysis of science, she rejects his advocacy of the "incommensurability" thesis. It is not the case for Nelson that two groups share nothing that can be brought to bear as evidence regarding those things about which they disagree. In the situation between the feminist and nonfeminist, there remain a large number of beliefs and theories, particularly in physical object theory, that are not in question and that can settle the matter in the case of empirical disputes.

Yet Nelson is also committed to the idea that what guides research has to do with our social and political values. Like Quine, she rejects the positivist distinction between pure observation and confirmation and instead sees the two as essentially integrated. But is the objectivity derived from empirical methods sufficient to support feminist theory and practice? The objectivity required must ground theories and social arrangements that call for a change to unfair and exclusive social practices. This requirement separates Nelson from more mainstream naturalized epistemologists in the business of merely describing the subject who, in Quine's words, "delivers as output a description of the three-dimensional external world and its history" (Quine 1969, 82–83). Instead, Nelson is concerned with defending alternative theories and practices that seek an end to unjust arrangements. But if Nelson preserves Quine's collapse of necessity into contingency, including social, political, and moral propositions into empiricism, then what justifies the corrective lens of feminism? Surely it cannot be just that it will produce a more complete report of physical reality since feminists have shown that scientific investigation incorporates and relies upon values as well as empirical descriptions. The questions researchers ask, the methods they use in gathering their data, the ability to see the relation of their work to economic and political circumstances, and the correctives offered by social and moral analyses of these practices involve complex considerations that can not be settled on purely empirical, contingent grounds. While we can agree with Quine and Nelson that the observation and confirmation of our theories most likely occurs from within a holistic, naturalized context we can still withhold our confidence that such a context justifies our belief in the principles guiding the revision of our moral, social, and political beliefs.

If, as I have suggested above, Quine has not done away with the notion of meaning and necessity, then a new alternative to a pure empiricist epistemology emerges. By separating out empirical issues of confirmation holism from a realist theory of necessary, formal truth, we can begin to develop a model for explaining the practice of empirical correctives by feminists as one that is consistent with, but not identical to, the normativity of feminists' moral and political correctives.

My view is that Quine's naturalized epistemology entails a conflation of confirmation with meaning, since empirical content is what constitutes meaning. This conflation of confirmation holism with meaning holism is carried over to Nelson's account, and runs at odds with feminism's corrective potential. Thus, marking out a distinction between empiricist confirmation holism and a realist theory of necessity will allow for a coherence theory of empirical truth and a correspondence theory of logical, linguistic, and moral truth. With this more rationalized account feminist philosophers may address the threat of radical relativism. That is, not only can feminist research be seen as offering empirical correctives but, in addition, feminist research provides the much needed rational corrective for accounts of knowledge that failed to live up to their own standards of reasonableness.

V. Conclusion

Throughout this chapter I have tried to justify the separation of matters of causal, historical, empirical fact from matters of normative, objective, truth-productive procedure. Yet in suggesting this I am not relying on all elements in the tradition of rationalism and metaphysical realism. Like Nelson, I agree that the standard account of knowledge as analyzed from the perspective of the individual is theoretically limited. The rationalized account that I have proposed is not inconsistent with the view that the locus of epistemology should be sought in a community of interdependent knowers. "Rational equilibrium" can be reached from the sensitivity to evidence that a variety of political positions and social locations bring about. My view is that a more social epistemology does not have to lead to a naturalized epistemology. Rather, standards and principles of reason and fairness can be construed in a rationalized way, and whether or not these ideals are being implemented correctly could be decided through the interaction among social groups who each occupy different evidential perspectives, thereby offering more varied intuitions.

The version of rationalism that I have proposed can reduce the threat of radical relativism always lurking behind naturalized models committed to coherence and consensus. This separation of justification, necessary truth, and standards of reason from the limiting features of *any* social position is based on a view of language and logic in which meanings, properties, and forms of inference are construed as real, formal entities underlying reason and language, discoverable through conceptual investigation. Yet, as feminist critics of science and knowledge have shown, investigations of reality can be, and have been, obscured by the limited perspective of social position and power. By making our methods of justification more inclusive, it becomes possible for us to eradicate the limitations of social location and not forsake the goal of objective truth seeking. A strong program of rationalized epistemology, as I have suggested, does not have to be blind to the embodied experiences of social groups. The development of procedures to prevent false conclusions is one of the hallmarks of rational methodology. The significance of the contributions of feminist philosophers of knowledge can be found in the critical stance taken toward existing paradigms and in the novel and informative reinterpretation of data. Nelson has provided some important examples in her work of the ways in which the interpretation of data in science has been very much affected by social, political, and cultural bias. However, these contributions do not offer new reasons to accept naturalized epistemology. Instead, Nelson analyzes these contributions through the lens of an assumed model. My concerns are that Nelson has not shown that the ideals of reason have been compromised as a result of her research nor has she given new reasons to think that Quine's skepticism about meaning or his thesis of revisability are correct. What she and other feminist epistemologists and philosophers of science have shown is that to realize the ideals of reason more completely, we cannot continue to ignore the significance of social, political, and moral experience.

Finally, I want to add that what has been argued for thus far is limited to *propositional* knowledge and meaning. My case for a more responsible rationalized epistemology has as its focus the relationships inherent in the syntactic and semantic components of senses and word and sentence types. However, there have been recent attempts to systematize the nonpropositional aspects of knowledge and meaning by feminist epistemologists and philosophers of science.[5] These accounts share a commitment to the embodied nature of knowledge, and to the knowing "how" that is different from the knowing "that." Thus, my proposal should be read as a way of overcoming the far too limited versions of rationalism and linguistic realism regarding the propositional nature of knowledge. This suggestion is not an attempt to exclude the nonpropositional components of knowing and understanding that are emerging in other feminist work.

Notes

1. See, for example, Schmitt (1995) for some recent work in analytic philosophy devoted to "excavating" some of the social factors left unexplored in more traditional accounts of knowledge. See also C. A. J. Coady (1992) for an account of a knower's reliance on others for the justification of her or his knowledge.
2. Alcoff in Tuana (1989, 85–103).
3. Nelson (1990).
4. For an interesting discussion of this material see chapter 3 in Katz (1990).
5. I have in mind here people like Nancy Tuana, Lorraine Code, and Linda Alcoff.

References

Alcoff, Linda Martín. 1989. "Justifying Feminist Social Science." In *Feminism and Science*, ed. N. Tuana. Bloomington and Indianapolis: Indiana University Press.

Coady, C. A. J. 1992. *Testimony*. Oxford: Oxford University Press.

Katz, J. J. 1990. *The Metaphysics of Meaning*. Cambridge: MIT Press.

Nelson, Lynn Hankinson. 1990. *Who Knows: From Quine to a Feminist Empiricism*. Philadelphia: Temple University Press.

Quine, W. V. 1960. *Word and Object*. Cambridge: MIT Press.

———. 1961. *From a Logicial Point of View*. Cambridge, Mass: Harvard University Press.

———. 1969. "Epistemology Naturalized." In *Ontological Relativity and Other Essays*. New York: Columbia University Press.

———. 1972. *Methods of Logic*. 3d ed. New York: Holt, Rinehart and Winston

Schmitt, Frederick. 1995. *Socializing Epistemology*. Lanham, Mass.: Rowman & Littlefield.

4

What Is Natural About Epistemology Naturalized?

Lorraine Code

Naturalistic Promise, Emancipatory Hopes

Naturalized epistemologies open up an impressive range of resources and possibilities to participants in successor epistemology projects. The new naturalisms promise to dissolve many of the prohibitions and exclusions that have held the principal Anglo-American epistemologies of the twentieth century at a distance from the very knowledge they claim to explicate. They shift epistemology away from idealized abstraction to establish connections with epistemic practice that could enable theories of knowledge to engage constructively and critically with everyday cognitive activities. Neither committed to analyzing what ideal knowers ought to do nor constrained to devoting their best efforts to silencing the skeptic, naturalists assume that knowledge is possible and seek to understand its real-world (natural) conditions. They abandon any quest for a priori, necessary, and sufficient conditions for knowledge in general, to examine how epistemic agents actually produce knowledge, variously, within the scope and limits of human cognitive powers as these powers are revealed in the same projects of inquiry. In this essay I ask how epistemologists working, specifically, from a feminist agenda might best draw on these resources.[1]

According to Sabina Lovibond, feminists have good reasons to participate in a naturalistic revival. Feminist theory, she contends, is

> indebted to the efforts of philosophy over the last century and more to "naturalize" epistemology . . . to represent the activity we call "enquiry" as part of the natural history of human beings. For naturalist or materialist analyses of the institutions of knowledge-production—schools, universities, the wider "republic of letters"—have made it possible to expose the unequal part played by different social groups in determining standards of judgement. . . . They have revealed the ideological character of value-systems which have passed as objective or universally valid.[2]

Feminists are engaged, albeit from diverse theoretical positions, in demonstrating how epistemologies—often tacitly—carry within them a potential either to sustain a social-political status quo or to promote emancipatory ends. Tracing the effects of theories of knowledge in the world where knowledge is sought and made, feminist and other critiques of epistemology have demonstrated that epistemic agendas and social-political commitments are inextricably intertwined and mutually constitutive.[3]

Naturalistic analyses of institutions and processes of knowledge-production contribute invaluably to projects of explicating the repressive and/or potentially transformative consequences of epistemic assumptions in their trickle-down effects in everyday knowledge making.[4] Although investigations of the emancipatory potential of theories of knowledge have not been much in fashion or favor in the heyday of twentieth century preoccupations with determining necessary and sufficient conditions for knowledge in general, it is worth recalling that, historically, such investigations commanded wider respect. For example, Plato's quest for principles of certain knowledge was animated by his need to ensure that the guardians in the Republic would exercise knowledgeable authority; and Bacon believed scientific inquiry would contribute to securing the best life for humanity.[5] Marxist commitments to developing emancipatory epistemologies that could shatter the naturalistic illusions of the capitalist social order are well known.[6] And the early positivists proclaimed the benefits of scientific knowledge for liberating humanity from thralldom to religious or metaphysical excesses by enhancing standards of "clarity and responsibility."[7] It is this kind of interest that the new naturalists might be able to reanimate.

In this essay, then, I endorse Lovibond's hopes for a naturalistic engagement with questions about knowledge when the aspirations of "the epistemological project" are under strain from postmodern, postcolonial, and postpatriarchal critiques. I offer some suggestions about how feminists can make the most of the rich possibilities a well conceived (natural historical) naturalism has to offer. Yet I engage critically with naturalism's most successful North American version—the line that claims an originary debt to the work of W. V. Quine—regarding features that, in my reading, limit its promise. My contention will be that the transformative potential of this strand of naturalism is thwarted in three principal ways which are interconnected, mutually informative, and yet separable. First, naturalistic venerations of physical science as the only "institution of knowledge-production" worthy of analysis tend to generate an excessive and reductive scientism. Second, Quinean naturalists' consequent reliance on scientific psychology and cognitive science as uncontested sources of exemplary knowledge of human cognitive functioning begs the question about the epistemic status of psychology itself. Third, naturalism works with contestable representations of "nature," both physical and human. I elaborate the first and second set of issues in the next section of this essay, and the third in section three. In section four I sketch out a version of naturalism that could enable feminists to reclaim the promise that I, with Lovibond, see in epistemology naturalized.

Natural Science, Human Subjects

It is impossible in one essay to address the whole vast naturalistic project, whose literature is proliferating more rapidly than even the most assiduous scholar could read it.[8] Hence I am restricting my analysis to the line of inquiry that derives from Quine's now-landmark claim that "epistemology, or something like it, simply falls into place as a chapter of psychology and hence of natural science. It studies a natural phenomenon, viz., a physical human subject."[9] I pick up the Quinean thread where Hilary Kornblith picks it up in his 1991 essay "The Naturalistic Project in Epistemology: A Progress Report," to identify its two principal questions as "What is the world that we may know it? And what are we that we may know the world?"[10] Answers to these questions are to be sought at the places where the best current theories of the nature of the world and the best current psychological theories dovetail. For knowledge about the world, state-of-the-art science may include chemistry, biology, physics, and other laboratory sciences. For the knowledge about "us" that it gleans from scientific psychology, it relies upon a rejuvenated doctrine of "natural kinds" and assumes that these "kinds" are not denatured when they are studied in a laboratory setting and so still count as "natural."[11] It studies "how we are adapted to the structure of the world around us"[12] so that it makes sense for us to rely on the information we acquire through our perceptual apparatus and on the conclusions of our inductive inferences. Science need not exclude mental states and processes from its ontology, but it tends to assume that they are physically constituted. In psychological as in physical inquiry, it grants pride of place to prediction, (causal) explanation, and technological application as knowledge-attesting activities.[13]

Guided by their commitment to deriving normative recommendations from the demonstrated scope and limits of human cognition, naturalists study psychological experiments that show how people justify their beliefs, generalize to new conclusions, correct perceptual errors, conserve information in memory, assimilate testimony, and accommodate or resist novelty, to cite just a few examples.[14] Taking the findings of such research seriously enables epistemologists to tailor their normative demands to what people *can* achieve epistemically, to how they tend to process evidence and respond to incongruities. Thus, for example, exhortations about how knowers should go about justifying their probabilistic conclusions that extend beyond available evidence may be tempered by readings of Kahneman and Tversky's experiments that show, repeatedly, how "people regularly violate [a] basic tenet of probabilistic reasoning."[15] The aim is not for naturalists to learn to tolerate this violation, thus turning the "is" into an "ought." It is, rather, to enable them to offer manageable guidelines within which to urge improvement, or to be well placed to assess the extent of epistemic culpability, say, when a subject fails "to recover or activate something from long-term memory."[16] This, then, is the physical human subject who becomes the new epistemic subject; the human being as processor of knowledge as information, whose experiential input is quite inadequate to account for the "torrential output" that emerges in its knowledge of "the three-dimensional external world and its history."[17] Because people can survive only to the extent that they can process the information available from their environments, understanding their information processing capacities should yield an epistemology more adequate to human purposes than one that directs its recommendations toward an ideal of epistemic perfection that no human knower could achieve. And naturalism's commitment to studying how real people perform in experimental situations prompts Alvin Goldman to commend it for maintaining contact with "epistemic folkways."[18]

Naturalists show, then, that epistemic injunctions are worthless if they require people to perform cognitive tasks that their intellectual or perceptual capacities do not permit. (Hence it would be ludicrous to require people to learn to distinguish between ultraviolet intensities with the unaided eye.) As Goldman puts the point, given that "epistemology is in the business of saying what psychological states a cognizer *should* be in in various circumstances, or what states it would be *rational* or *intelligent* for him [or her?] to be in, we need as good a specification as possible of the range of cognitive states open to him."[19] Yet naturalists are not thus advocating a static, purely descriptive—thence non-normative—epistemology. They are insisting that normativity is as much a practical as a purely logical concern, that epistemic imperatives acquire their force from a demonstrable congruence between their urgings and the possibilities human cognitive equipment affords. Naturalism will transform epistemology's justificatory strategies just as radically as it will restructure its evidence-gathering procedures.[20]

I discuss Quine-derived naturalism here not just because of its professional success in English-language philosophy, but because, in following this line, feminist epistemologists have produced some of their most innovative work. Lynn Nelson has developed subtle readings of Quine as a proto-feminist, as the articulator of a version of empiricism that can be critically elaborated to serve feminist ends; and Jane Duran sees in naturalism a valuable resource for developing a feminist epistemology.[21] Essays by Susan Babbitt, Elizabeth Potter, and Kathryn Addelson in the 1993 collection *Feminist Epistemologies*[22] all (albeit variously) claim a debt to naturalistic epistemology. Yet none of these philosophers adopts naturalism's aims and ideals uncontested and whole; to varying degrees, they work, at once, in and out of naturalized epistemology, drawing on its resources even as they criticize its reductive and exclusionary features. Their principal challenges to naturalistic orthodoxy are directed at its scientistic excesses, which I discuss here, and its epistemic individualism, which figures centrally in the next section of this essay.[23]

The Quinean naturalists have an impressive record of scientific and technological successes to cite as evidence when they represent natural science as the best knowledge of how the *physical* world works that human beings have produced and when they read this record of success to show that scientific method is pretty much in order as it stands. Kornblith—I think rightly—asserts that philosophy "does not have the credentials . . . to dictate how science itself should be carried out."[24] But neither does science have the credentials to dictate how philosophy—and hence epistemology—should be carried out. I am suggesting that naturalism escalates into an uncritical *scientism* when it ignores this cautionary point.[25] Arthur Danto's definition underscores my claim. Naturalism, he says, is "a species of philosophical monism according to which whatever exists or happens is *natural* in the sense of being susceptible to explanation through methods which, although paradigmatically exemplified in the natural sciences, are continuous from domain to domain of objects and events. . . ." For naturalists, there neither exist nor could exist "any entities or events which lie, in principle, beyond the scope of scientific explanation."[26] It is the "monism" that gives pause, with its echoes of the old, reductive "unity of science" credo. Thus, although naturalism's focus on human cognitive activity indeed counts as a radical departure from older commitments to a decontextualized a prioricity, its affirmations of the scientificity of all knowledge yield a new a priori that exerts an equivalently restrictive, reductive pressure.

There is, moreover, a troubling circularity in the assumption, central to Quinean naturalism, that scientific psychology can yield definite explanations of natural human knowledge-making.[27] At issue in this inquiry are, precisely, the scope and limits of scientific explanation: its capacity to yield these very conclusions. Nor has the debate between cognitive science and folk psychology been won, despite the rhetorical strategy cognitive scientists deploy in labelling the opposition with so trivializing a name that it cannot expect a serious hearing. While the scientific and epistemic status of scientific psychology remains within the debate, it cannot, without begging the question, be enlisted whole to establish conclusions that serve, rather, to contest its own epistemic warrant.

Feminist and other postcolonial hopes for Quinean naturalism and its progeny are tempered, then, by their claims to re-colonize the territory, to have at their command all of the best, and indeed the only, reliable means of regulating and judging beliefs and knowledge-claims. They are tempered further by naturalistic denigrations of the "native" practices of the colony with such derogatory labels as "folkways" and "folk psychology," the latter, as Jerome Bruner observes, "*coined in derision* by the new cognitive scientists for its hospitality toward such intentional states as beliefs, desires, and meanings . . ."[28] Even psychology's impressive successes in showing how people go about knowing do not show that epistemology and psychology converge to the extent that epistemology *reduces to* psychology. There are too many left-overs.

The temporal and local contingency of its own hegemony makes it still more difficult for science to justify arrogating to itself dominion over the whole natural history of human beings. Joseph Rouse, for example, notes that although philosophy has "made common cause with the sciences" within the English-speaking world, "relations between philosophy and the sciences have been rather different in much of Continental Europe . . . [where] the concern has been to situate the sciences with respect to other social interests and practices."[29] And ongoing post-Wittgensteinian challenges in Anglo-American philosophy to the global pretensions of "scientific" social science attest further to the local contingency of the status of natural science as the paradigmatic institution of knowledge production.[30] In short, Quinean naturalism keeps too many positivist-empiricist presuppositions intact, especially the presuppositions that scientific knowledge alone merits epistemological attention and that it alone can provide truly explanatory accounts.

Designating physical and psychological science as the places where natural knowledge-making occurs ignores, and hence effectively denaturalizes (both normatively and descriptively), the practices and wisdoms of extra-scientific, non-mainstream, marginalized people, practices whose effectiveness is often empirically demonstrable. Naturopathic medicine, women's traditional healing practices, Native medicine, the myriad knowledgeable dimensions of *allgemeine Alltäglichkeit*, the much-maligned "folk psychology," and the narrative knowledge and meaning-making practices that shape and inform human lives, unfettered by the stringent dictates of scientific-instrumental rationality are all excluded from critical evaluation. Withholding the (honorific) label "knowledge," a priori, from the workable deliverances of such practices reaffirms the hegemony of a narrowly conceived science as the arbiter of what counts as knowledge and of its practitioners as paradigmatically worthy knowers. Such exclusions relieve scientific knowers from any need to reconsider the theoretical underpinnings of their projects or to engage seriously with knowledge-producing institutions beyond a narrowly, demarcated subset, thus truncating the promise that many feminists, and other Others, have held out for a naturalistic revival. Because its construction of "the natural" denigrates the credibility of knowledge made in places other than the laboratory and equally integral to responsible epistemic conduct, Quinean naturalism neither exposes what Lovibond calls "the unequal part played by different social groups in determining standards of judgement" nor does it engage with reason "in all its historical and cultural particularity."

Tom Sorell proposes a corrective that is consonant with the reservations I have been voicing about the exclusiveness of Quinean commitments to a particular kind of scientific discipline, informed by a monistically conceived set of theoretical assumptions out of which "science" itself also emerges as a natural kind. Theorists of knowledge, he suggests, could actively acknowledge the mutual influence of epistemology and psychology, so that epistemology would be transformed, even radically, by joining forces with scientific psychology, for it would abandon its commitment to a prioricity. Yet its practitioners would acknowledge the limits of psychological explanation, and would therefore refrain from pushing the reductive claim.[31] The appeal of this deflationary position would be that experimental psychology, judiciously interpreted, would restrain philosophy's speculative excesses, yet philosophy would maintain vigilance for scientistic excesses, and naturalism would not need to denature itself in the process.

Many of the experiments to which the Quine-line naturalists appeal have what I am calling a "denaturing" effect in consequence of their implicit adherence to a latter-day methodological solipsism, translated into self-contained, isolated moments of the one-on-one, observer-observed laboratory experiments. Such experiments preserve a commitment to the purity of a statistical formalism that glosses over differences and specificities within the very natural kinds that are its subjects of study. Here the presumed homogeneity of human beings as members of a natural kind, manifested in Quine's observation that "the uniformity of people's quality spaces virtually assures that similar presentations will elicit similar verdicts,"[32] erases any possibility of factoring "historical and cultural particularity" into investigations of reason's natural operations. Hence what are at first glance the most promising aspects of the naturalistic program in the end invite an interpretive wariness, a hermeneutic of suspicion, even as they bring reason down from its sublime purity to engage in producing a "natural history of human beings."

What Is Natural?

In a 1994 essay, Sabina Lovibond reaffirms her enthusiasm for naturalism, declaring it "indispensable" to twentieth-century epistemology, which

> works with a conception of reason that has been "irrevocably desublimated" . . . revealed . . . in all its historical and cultural particularity. Human reason is now understood not as the sign of our participation in something that goes *beyond* our merely natural existence . . . but as one expression of our identity as a natural species whose members are exposed to an enormous variety of environmental and social conditions.[33]

Yet I am suggesting that even when reason and knowledge-production come under discussion as expressions of our identity as a natural species, there are choices at work determining what counts as "our" natural identity and which of its expressions merit analysis. The very idea of producing a "natural history" of human knowledge-seeking is hampered by our remarkable ignorance, still, of what "we" naturally are: of where nature begins and where cultural or other "artificial" accretions end.

Constrained, perhaps, by these imponderables, epistemology, like philosophy in general, has been in the business of naturalizing as it goes. Theories of knowledge, like metaphysical and moral theories, have claimed to derive from and pertain to what human nature is and can permit. Yet their effects have often been to naturalize the very attributes and actions they purport to discover and thence to recommend. Thus women's rational inferiority has been naturalized in representations of female nature as more emotional than rational, or less rational than male nature;

and hierarchical social arrangements have been naturalized in similar assumptions about some people's—blacks', women's, slaves'—incapacity for rational self-governance. (Aristotle, whom one could name as the first naturalist, was notorious in these respects.)

Quine-derived naturalized epistemology claims to have a rather different agenda. No longer will it tacitly naturalize as a by-product of its theoretical hypotheses; rather, it will base its conclusions on the nature of human cognitive capacities as these are empirically revealed in the findings of scientific psychology. Yet feminist and non-white, non-affluent philosophers who endorse the hopes that I, with Lovibond, have been voicing will observe that the laboratory, which naturalists who follow the Quine-line choose as the place where knowledge is naturally made, has been designed and usually occupied by affluent white men, with women and other Others rarely gaining ready access. The laboratory's accredited occupants have produced much of the knowledge that naturalizes women's irrationality along with the cognitive inferiority and diminished epistemic authority of other non-standard knowers.

Even as some critics worry, then, that naturalism eschews normativity, the rhetoric of "the natural" claims a proximity to "the real" that exercises a normative persuasion of a different ilk, dismissing the practices of its interrogators as unnatural, supernatural, "unreal"—as its patronizing references to "the folk" amply show.[34] In their packaging within the language of naturalism, these projects locate themselves within a discursive, rhetorical space that commands immediate late-twentieth-century (postmodern) attention. Within this space, "returns to nature" claim to strip away the cultural, theoretical, and political accretions that have impeded philosophical progress, to return to "the things themselves," with the aid of the most sophisticated methods of inquiry that humankind has ever known: the exact and esoteric techniques of physical science and scientific psychology. Hence "the naturalistic turn" acquires the aura of a turning away from rarefied abstractions and toward demonstrations, at last, of how things really are; and the language of "naturalism" implies that no stipulating has occurred, that philosophers are merely observing what naturally reveals itself. In fact, however, rather than returning to nature, as the rhetoric of its presentation implies, naturalism participates in constructing both its subject and its object. And although any self-declared naturalism has to begin by choosing what it will count as natural—for "nature" is not simply self-announcing—stipulations in philosophy are rarely innocent or neutral. The presuppositions and principles of the stipulative choices on which everything that follows depends have to be examined for the inclusions and exclusions they effect. These, in Quine-derived naturalized epistemology, have sociopolitical consequences that invite critical reevaluation; for the "naturalistic" terminology produces many of the problems I shall address, even as it generates the enthusiasms Lovibond rightly articulates.

Designating its object of study as "a natural phenomenon . . . a physical human subject," whose performance in experimental situations shows that its informational output vastly exceeds its available input, attests to naturalism's ingrained presuppositions about the kinds of knowledge that count as revealing what this "natural phenomenon" can do. The designation generates a further set of assumptions about who or what this creature is. But how, one wonders, can naturalists justify delimiting conceptions of knowledge and subjectivity as they do? Why would anyone think that this kind of knowledge shows what human cognizers are, erasing so many equally plausible options?

Human beings are more—and other—than information processors and problem-solvers; nor can all of their natural epistemic practices be adequately understood as multiples and/or elaborations of these activities. Arguments to the effect that human survival attests to the reliability of "our" perceptual-inferential processes can count at best as the first word, certainly not the last.[35] As long as survival, both qualitative and quantitative, varies so widely across the human species, and as long as possibilities of claiming epistemic authority on the basis of information processed and inductions successfully performed are so unevenly distributed, there is more to be told about who "we" are. Hence I am suggesting that naturalism cannot deliver on its promise to relinquish a prioricity in favor of a return to natural cognitive activity if it grants uncontested pride of place, in its study of natural knowledge, to behaviors studied in the laboratory. For, although human beings could not survive were they unable to process information competently, were this all that they could do, the quality of their survival would at best be dubious.

When naturalism represents human subjects as essentially solitary, even if reliable, processors of information, the contestability of its constructs is especially apparent. For in individual isolation human survival would *not* be possible. The abstract individual who figures, implicitly, as the knower is one such construct, a faceless, dispassionate, infinitely replicable "individual" who *knows* only when he is successful in suppressing interdependence, affect, and meaning, and indeed all aspects of his individuality.[36]

It is neither ideology nor fancy that prompts natural historians (in Lovibond's sense) to emphasize the fundamental interdependence of human existence, but reasonably invariant features of the *biology* of human procreation and maturation. Hence individualism sits uneasily with naturalism. Now, naturalists might maintain that human maturation follows a natural trajectory away from interdependence, toward autonomy, self-sufficiency, and a fully realized individualism of the sort that feminist and other postmodern thinkers have discerned in the man of reason whose works Western philosophy has principally studied.[37] But such a vision is plausible only if one overlooks the cognitive interdependence that is an inescapable feature of being born a human infant and living in a culture or social group without which an individual, strictly defined, would be unable even as an adult to know enough to survive. A project of studying natural knowledge-making has, from the outset, to guard against foreclosing on equally natural sources and resources that could enhance its explanatory potential. There are ways of naturalizing with effects less unnatural than those that Quine-derived naturalism yields.

Prompting feminist critiques of naturalism's individualist assumptions is a conviction that adequate successor epistemologies must be able, non-imperialistically, to address issues of individual and local specificity, socio-culturally realized and situated, a possibility that abstract individualism disallows.[38] Nor do such specificities amount merely to interchangeable identities into which anyone could fit at will. The problem with individualism for emancipatory projects is that it cannot account for how "individual" options, whether cognitive or other, are systematically thwarted or enhanced in their constitution within diverse, power-infused social-material situations. Moreover, an individualist ontology implicitly underwrites a methodological solipsism for which knowers are, can, and should be wholly self-reliant in their information-gathering and corroborating activities.[39] Hence individualists can simply assume that all evidence is equally available to any self-sufficient observer and any observer who fails to take it into account is epistemically culpable. This too-simple example shows how individualism fosters epistemic assumptions whose (probably unintended) effects come out as sexist, racist, or otherwise obstructive of the very self-realization that individualists advocate. Indeed, the "individual" of individualism is a mythic construct, a product of the very discourse that relies upon and seeks to defend it.[40]

There is, moreover, a curious tension in (Quinean) naturalists' identifying individuals as *biological* creatures whose innate "spacing of qualities," or innate linguistic readiness, demonstrates the universality of rational processes;[41] for the "individuals" that populate these theories are rarely embodied, except accidentally and inconveniently. That same biology is subsequently read out of the picture in justificatory strategies designed to legitimate universal, global conclusions that obliterate differences consequent upon embodiment in variously gendered, aged, colored, or abled bodies. Paradoxically, then, individualism in its empiricist/scientific psychology forms fails, indeed refuses, to individuate. Rather, it reduces and assimilates differences, both "natural" and sociopolitical, under its universality and objectivity requirements; and in so doing it denatures the very natural kinds to which its best intuitions appeal.

Outlining a "naturalist view of persons" quite different from Quine-line naturalism's solitary information-processor, Annette Baier observes:

> A naturalist . . . takes it as obvious that a person is, as Montaigne put it, "marvellously corporeal" . . . and that a person's ability to think is affected by genetic inheritance from parents and is vitally dependent upon the sort of care received in childhood, for example in being introduced into a language community.[42]

Baier shows throughout her work how the same tradition that gives rise to (Quinean) naturalism *reads past* human interdependence to establish its conclusions.[43] Her naturalistic view, which "emphasize[s] the interdependence of persons,"[44] shows that individualism is an incongruous ontology for naturalists, unless they mean to work with so abstracted a view of persons as to render dubious its claims to be natural.

An ontology like Baier's need not eschew possibilities of drawing upon the best psychology can offer, for there are distinguished voices in professional psychology that accord well with hers. To cite just two, Couze Venn protests against conceiving of psychology as the science of the individual: the science whose subject is "the 'rational man' with no past"; "the 'individual subject' minus everything that pins down its identity and its lived experience of social relations."[45] And Jerome Bruner puts the point more forcefully: "It is man's participation *in* culture and the realization of his mental powers *through* culture that make it impossible to construct a human psychology on the basis of the individual alone."[46]

Addressing the individualist implications of many cognitive science programs and of Chomskyian theses about the universality of innate language-readiness, Bruner cites primate studies to show that it is "sensitivity to the requirements of living in groups that provides the criterion for evolutionary selection in high primates."[47] His purpose is neither to discredit Chomskyian linguistics nor to minimize its value as a resource for understanding the deep structures that enable human language development. Yet he adduces compelling evidence to show that the "triggering" of an innate mechanism manifests a complexity of an order quite different from the process Chomsky and his followers represent, for it depends

> not only upon . . . appropriate exemplars in the linguistic environment of the child but also upon the child's "context sensitivity" that can come only from . . . participation in language as an instrument of communication . . . triggered by the acts and expressions of others and by certain basic social contexts in which human beings interact.[48]

Studying how sociality makes individuality possible opens up ways of addressing the unevenness of survival with which a natural history must engage. For it is in radically diverse social-material circumstances that such inequities are produced and manifested.

Bruner, in effect, reclaims a revivified "folk psychology" from cognitive scientific dismissals, establishing a place for it within an elaborated "cultural psychology." He does this not out of nostalgia for a more romantic conception of human nature, but because he believes cultural psychology can avoid some of the most egregious denaturings on which a naturalism that attributes explanatory power only to cognitive science depends. Nor does Bruner make monistic, reductive claims for interpretive-cultural analyses that explicate and situate information processing. His is, rather, a plea for analyzing context and content together, recognizing that scientific psychology produces remarkably informative content, yet that its offerings neither arise without context nor speak for themselves. The cultural psychology he advocates is

> an interpretive psychology, in much the sense that history and anthropology and linguistics are interpretive disciplines. But that does not mean that it need be unprincipled or without methods, even hard-nosed ones. It seeks out the rules that human beings bring to bear in creating meanings in cultural contexts.[49]

Meaning-making practices, the narratives in which information is embedded, the stories in which people locate and explicate their experiences, are integral to any adequately naturalized account of cognition. Those stories will be peopled by human actors as fully as by medium-sized information-generating objects and perceptual-memory stimulants. And, for Bruner, it is only within communicable narratives exposed to critical and self-critical discussion that people can negotiate the circumstances that make laboratory experiments worth doing and accord their results a cultural-social significance.

Psychologists such as Bruner and Venn explicitly resist framing the options available to professional psychologists as a forced choice between (hard, scientific) experimentation and (soft, folksy) narrative; nor do they advocate supplanting the former with the latter. The debate is rather between those who believe that what happens in a laboratory is self-justifying, that its genesis within scientific psychology provides its warrant, and those who, to borrow a phrase from Steve Fuller, see in naturalism "a call to self-reflection, or reflexivity"[50] on the part of knowledge producers, who refuse to exempt any location or institution of knowledge-production from the need to account for itself. The reflexivity requirement does not amount to a naive refusal to acknowledge the power of experimentation in going beyond a merely conservative naturalism and in revealing where the naturalist's "ought" really does imply "can" (one of naturalism's most significant contributions to "desublimating" reason). But in its best late-twentieth-century forms the reflexivity requirement enlists genealogical techniques to address critically the manifestations of power that shape both experimental and narrative knowledge-making. It insists that the significance of experimental findings beyond the narrow confines of the laboratory is rarely self-announcing; that even within the laboratory, findings can be as much a product of the contrived situation out of which they emerge, as indicative of how things "naturally" are; and that even the most "sincere" narratives are contestable, open to critical scrutiny.[51] It is to untangle issues such as these that interpretation enters the inquiry.

In a cultural climate where reason is "irrevocably desublimated," it is puzzling that "the naturalistic turn" and "the interpretive turn"[52] should amount to turnings away from one another, usually in antagonism. Collaboratively, combining their resources, they could issue in impressively re-skilled, re-sensitized ways of understanding and evaluating knowledge production. Cultural narrative and interpretation invite scorn from many science-oriented naturalists, for they admit of no definitive causal or predictive explanations and hence, the charge is, they yield merely subjective conclusions. Yet interpretation is as "natural" and as evidence-reliant as the other activities naturalists study; and it is just as essential to survival. The fact that people are radically, ineluctably "located," that they cannot achieve perfect understanding, makes of every inquiry, whether scientific or secular, a reading "from somewhere" whose circumstances of origin and production are constitutive of its presuppositions and conclusions. The interpretations that "naturalize" laboratory life have to be as closely interrogated as the circumstances that restrict the populations within laboratories to a chosen few. Interpretation thus construed is a powerful critical tool, an instrument for change, which uncovers and reveals the contingency of motivations, power structures, and extrascientific assumptions that are often so embedded in experimental design and in narrative structures as to seem merely a matter of course.[53]

To return to the area of inquiry of most interest to Quinean naturalists, establishing a commonality of purposes between naturalized epistemology and feminist/postcolonial analyses of "desublimated" reason in action requires strategies for working past psychology's complicity in the tacitly productive, politically implicated naturalizing that erases human differences even as it casts the object of inquiry in its own image. Critical interpretation uncovers this complicity and opens spaces for countering it. Examples are too numerous to detail here, but the very title of Naomi Weisstein's now-classic article "Psychology Constructs the Female" heralds her demonstration that natural (female) human "kinds" are as artefactual as they are factual.[54] In developmental psychology, Carol Gilligan's work engages critically with Lawrence Kohlberg's precisely at the place where its effect is to naturalize female moral immaturity because of women's tendency to score lower than men on the Kohlberg test.[55] And critical readings show that the connections Philippe Rushton draws between genital and brain size work effectively to *produce* "natural" differences in black, Oriental and white intelligence, at least as persuasively as they record them.[56] In these diverse studies, "nature" emerges as, partially at least, a product of experimental design, suggesting that, when it notices them, psychology tends to construct—not find—the female, the Black, or the other Other, as a natural kind. More commonly, it does not notice them, for the "individual" subjects in most academic psychology are gender-, class-, race-, and ethnicity-neutral, surely an odd way of viewing a species so (naturally) diverse as the human species.

Psychology is not the only scientific discipline that studies the physical human subject as a natural species. Biology has at least as strong a claim to this description, and hence to inclusion among inquiries that contribute to the production of a natural history of human beings. Yet feminist critiques have shown that biology is no more innocent than psychology of the charge that it constructs and thus denatures subjects who are the objects of its inquiry.[57] Biologist Karen Messing's studies of women's occupational health provide instructive examples. Her work reveals a persistent (establishment) preference for "controlled studies . . . in situations which bear little resemblance to real life;"[58] for studies of nonhuman cells or cells in culture, rather than of live human subjects; and for laboratory rather than field (i.e., workplace) studies. Messing and her associates have discerned patterns familiar to feminist and other post-colonial science critics: women's dizziness, nausea, and headaches after prolonged exposure to toxic solvents or pesticides represented as "mass psychogenic illness;" restrictive, "universal" definitions of occupational impacts on health that read past effects specific to female workers, such as menstrual abnormalities and pregnancy-associated problems; statistical procedures that conceal class- or sex-biased assumptions "which increase the suffering of workers;" sampling procedures that eliminate women "to make samples uniform;"[59] and techniques and presuppositions that sustain representations of women as "physically, mentally and emotionally 'the weaker sex.'"[60] Messing shows how company interests in denigrating worker credibility have generated an "image of workers as lazy malingerers coddled by their colluding physicians [that is] cited to block compensation to injured workers who stay out 'too long.'"[61] Add a refusal to accept self-reported experiences of workplace events as evidence, and the capacity of (Quine's) innate "standard of similarity" to underwrite the explanatory force of natural kinds is revealed as highly dubious.[62] "Objective" science often masks pertinent variations within natural kinds, fails to address human suffering, and ignores the systemic effects of the social-institutional power structures that provide its own warrant.

These examples from psychology and biology, areas that have especially interested (Quinean) naturalists, count as minimal illustrations of the denaturing that naturalism accomplishes. Feminists have examined and detailed other denaturings too numerous to list,[63] presenting incontestable reminders that the procedural rationality that naturalism analyzes is—to recall Lovibond—just *one* "expression of our identity." Helen Verran's detailed documentation of the logic in Australian Aboriginal mappings of the world that contests the hegemony of Western presuppositions about the natural order of things is but one example from a long line of anthropological research that exposes Western knowledge as just one expression of the "cultural particularity" of natural reason.[64] Amy Mullin's study of feminist art and aesthetics as culturally unsettling, yet indisputably *cognitive*, engagements with the world underscores my claim that other kinds of knowledge-making are just as natural, hence that science has to make good its claim to count as *the* natural site.[65] Theorists need interpretive-genealogical, natural-historical analyses if they are to achieve a just evaluation of the place—and the naturalness—of naturalism.

In summary, then, in its scientistic manifestations, naturalism denatures itself in locating itself within a laboratory, assuming that knowledge-making activities there are paradigmatic of natural knowledge-making; in working with an abstract individualism that blocks its engagement with human differences, both diachronic and synchronic; in restricting itself to one kind of knowledge, thus distancing itself from the meaning-making and interpretive activities that are just as natural as information-processing; and in separating "the natural" from Nature, both in the subject and in the object of knowledge. In the next section I propose a different regional mapping, where Quine-line naturalism will occupy *a*, but not *the*, central place; and where it is as important for a naturalist to understand that place and its surroundings as to develop a picture of what goes on within it.

Nature Reclaimed: Ecology and Epistemology

In the revisioned naturalism I am advocating, the guiding model of epistemic normativity is an ecological model of reciprocally sustaining and critically interrogating practices of engaged inquiry. In this model, relationships within and among institutions of knowledge production—their effects within social-political structures and the effects of sociopolitical structures within them, their interworkings, their negotiated, dialogical character, and their socioenvironmental implications—have to be analyzed as meticulously as their separate self-consistency and internal coherence. Unlike the individual subject whose epistemic processes are flattened in a mechanical, input-output modeling, the ecological subject is—like Baier's—"marvellously corporeal" and fundamentally interdependent, active, resistant and reactive, accountable; created out of sociality and itself creative of the forms of sociality in which it participates.

Sociality is the (mutable) frame within which seemingly isolated experiences and experimental performances contribute to the ongoing realization (or deterioration) of subjectivities.[66]

An ecological model for explicating knowledge and subjectivity builds on the mutual relations of organisms with one another. Moreover, their environment is conceived not merely as the physical environment, nor just the present one, but as the complex network of relations within which an organism strives to realize its potential, be those relations social, historical, material, geographical, cultural, racial, institutional, or other. An organism at any moment in its natural history exhibits its state of accommodation both of, and to, such relations; yet not passively, for ecology emphasizes the participation of organisms, whose choices are relationally structured, and who themselves shape socioenvironmental relations. The agency of ecological subjects figures centrally in evaluations of their epistemic activities, as do the developmental processes that foster or circumscribe agency. Ecological analyses examine the implications, for organisms, of living in certain environments, and work to develop strategies for producing environments that are exploitative neither of the habitat nor other inhabitants.

An ecologically modeled epistemology will evaluate the potential of cognitive practices for creating environments where people can live well. It works with a conception of materially situated subjectivity, for which embodied locatedness and interdependence are integral to the very possibility of knowledge and action.[67] Picking up a Piagetian line that is fruitfully pursued in Bruner's work, an ecological naturalism learns equally from developmental studies of human cognition and from its adult manifestations. The persistent individualism even of such projects as Goldman's, with its later evolution into a social theory, is sustained by its concentration on experiments whose subjects are adult, hence seemingly well individuated, human beings.[68] (They are also presumptively male, and members of the dominant, "normal," social group.) Critical developmental analyses sensitive to how individuality is variously and unevenly fostered and/or thwarted in diverse social arrangements promise results more cognizant of the interplay between independence and interdependence in the production of cognitive agency. Refusing to treat knowledge as information gained in isolation and articulated in monologic statements, an ecological model takes its point of departure from the (natural) dependence of knowledge production upon human interaction, as much in adult lives as in infancy and childhood.[69]

This model is by no means antiscientific, for it must draw on the best available scientific and social scientific evidence to determine how survival can be ensured and enhanced, not just quantitatively, but qualitatively; not by requiring epistemology to "fall into place as a chapter" of ecological science, but by learning, analogically, from the science of ecology. It establishes its (contestable) conception of "best available" evidence in self-critical reflexivity, through which locally, environmentally informed studies of disciplines, their subject matters, and their interdisciplinary relations with one another and within "the world" generate an ongoing skeptical suspicion of presumptions to theoretical hegemony. Although this version of naturalism counts state-of-the-art natural and psychological science among its principal resources, it rejects their claims to joint occupancy of the position of master metanarrative. It is less sanguine than many Quinean naturalists about the before-the-fact reliability of "our" capacities to generalize the relevant features of natural kinds "against the background of the environments in which they operate."[70] For it is wary of the power-infused tendencies of racial/gender/class stereotypes and of essentialized conceptions of "science" and "nature" to take on self-fulfilling, self-perpetuating qualities.

Ecology (literally) succeeds only if it is well informed by state-of-the-art natural science; yet it fails if it assumes that state-of-the-art science merits uncontested licence to intervene in nature wherever it pleases. Ecology (metaphorically) draws disciplinary conclusions together, maps their interrelations, their impoverishing and mutually sustaining effects within established and putative locations of knowledge-production, and in the social-political-natural world where the effects of institutional knowledge are enacted—for better or worse. The ecological human subject is made by and makes its relations in reciprocity with other subjects and with its (multiple, diverse) environments. Yet this model is not self-evidently benign in the sense of generating a natural, unimpeded unfolding of fully realizable epistemic potential. For ecosystems are as often competitive and as unsentimentally destructive of their less viable members as they are cooperative and mutually sustaining. So if work within the model is to avoid replicating the exclusions endemic to traditional epistemologies, its adherents will have to derive moral-political-epistemological guidelines for regulating and adjudicating competing claims for cognitive and epistemic authority.

The most delicate tasks in making such a model epistemologically workable are, first, that of achieving an appropriate balance between literal and metaphorical readings of the governing concept—ecology—so as to benefit from ecological science without running aground on details of analogy/disanalogy with specific ecological events; and second, that of developing an adequate moral epistemology within which to address conflicts between mutually inconsistent survival and flourishing claims. I cannot engage in either task adequately in the space available here, but some preliminary observations will clarify the issues.

Ecology talk has an immediate late-twentieth-century appeal in an era where "right-thinking people" are horrified by the destruction of natural and social environments and repelled by the imperialism, both local and global, that accompanies and/or promotes it. The protective, nurturant aspects of ecology seem to promise a better future. Yet that very appeal is often counteracted by ecology's cloying aura, its coziness, its flavor of too-goodness, its sometime rhetoric of unremitting sentimentality, of a naive, depoliticized, even narcissistic closeness to nature, and of forced identifications of women and nature.[71] Thus its potential has to be elaborated with care. Nonetheless, I am claiming that an ecologically modeled naturalism can offer a better mapping of the epistemic terrain than the scientism into which other versions of naturalism risk solidifying: nor can I think of a model better suited to address the complex interrelations that characterize the late-twentieth-century world. I am not, however, just recommending a different, aesthetically more pleasing vocabulary: a way of talking about "the same things," with a grammar and semantics that are perfectly in order as they stand. Ecological thinking will not yield what Robyn Ferrell has aptly called a "poet's utopia," such as Richard Rorty's free-play of the ironic, liberal imagination promises.[72] Ecosystems—both metaphorical and literal—are as cruel as they are kind; as unpredictable and overwhelming as they are orderly and nurturant. Epistemologically, their transformative, emancipatory potential can be realized only by active participants within them who are prepared to take on the burdens as well as the blessings of place, materiality, and history; and to work within the locational possibilities, both found and made, of their being in the world.

The ecological subject, who is but a distant relative of the abstract liberal individual, denies that a view from nowhere is desirable or possible. She is self-critically cognizant of being part of the world, both social and natural, in which her knowings, feelings, and actings always produce effects, be they positive, negative, or indifferent. For this subject, human and social-natural interdependence are given, to be cultivated, elaborated, evaluated; their joys to be celebrated, their sorrows and errors to be acknowledged. They are neither to be repudiated nor transcended in illusory gestures of an impossible self-sufficiency, nor elaborated into a romanticized immersion of self in nature or in Others. Acknowledging the partiality of their knowings and self-knowings, and their potential effects (however small, however local), ecological subjects are well placed to "own" their activities and to be responsible for them.[73]

The normative possibilities of this model are instrumental, deriving as they do from a hypothetical imperative to the effect that epistemic activity be appraised—in its form and content—according to its success in promoting ecologically sustaining communities, committed to fostering ecological viability within the "natural" world.[74] Appraisals of ecological goals and of epistemologies that can promote them and are modeled upon them will proceed in concert, dialectically, integrating epistemology with moral-political-historical-anthropological debate.[75] Yet even crossing these boundaries does not turn epistemology into a chapter of ecological science; and single observational *S*-knows-that-*p* claims may be neutral in this regard, with no immediate ecological import either way.

Consider Ursula Franklin's "impact studies."[76] During their summer jobs, however menial, however "non-scientific," engineering students were to record the impact of their work on the immediate environment, an exercise designed to teach them that whatever they did, from house painting, to child minding, to table serving, would produce effects they would not have thought to notice. At issue were not simple empirical claims of the *S*-knows-that-*p* variety: Sara knows that paint is messy, that children need good food, that coffee must be served hot. Hence the point is not that such claims take on direct ecological significance. But only by discerning their impact, which extends well beyond one's first imaginings, can evaluations within a larger ecological network be conducted. Franklin's purpose was to show that there is no knowledge, and no knowledge-informed practice, that is without consequences, and hence none that should escape critical scrutiny.

Bioregional narratives, introduced into environmental ethics by Jim Cheney, afford a point of entry into ecological thinking. They capture the import of Franklin's studies, catch something of the cultural-narrative recommendations that Bruner advances, and resonate with a critique of "monoculture" that is pivotal to the ecofeminist work of Vandana Shiva. In developing an ethics of accountability, Cheney suggests, "narrative is the key . . . but it is narrative grounded in geography rather than in a linear, essentialized narrative self."[77] A bioregional narrative maps local ecological relations to set out the conditions for mutually sustaining lives within a specific locality—be it an institution, a geographical region, an urban environment, a community, society, state, or the interrelations among them, separately traced and characterized. Appropriately elaborated, it can become a chapter in the "natural history of human beings" that Lovibond advocates. Its strength is in the detail of its contextual sensitivity: its capacity to offer genealogical (i.e., power-focused) analyses of local knowledge-making and knowledge-circulating conditions. Its weakness is in its propensity to remain only locally pertinent; to represent a regional ecosystem as closed, harmonized, static. Hence it cannot be justified merely internally, but will have to address its interconnections with the power-saturated systems of the wider world.

Shiva produces one such narrative in her analysis of the impact on rural Indian agriculture of Western-style "development." *Monocultural* agriculture operates from the principle that land is most productive when it is cultivated to produce only one large crop. According to the rhetoric of development, Shiva observes, "natural forests remain unproductive till they are developed into monoculture plantations of commercial species."[78] Yet a genealogical charting of the interconnections of ideology, people, political power structures, and land management reveals that monoculture operates reductively, coercively, as a leveler that depletes the land's resources and its inhabitants' self-reliance at one stroke. Possibilities of local and diverse production are erased as populations producing a single crop are forced to rely on other monocultural populations, often located at a distance, for all other nutritional needs. Shiva details the achievements of women's cultures in India in contesting the dominance of monocultural practices by reclaiming the potential of agricultural diversity to foster self-sustaining communities.

Now critics might object that Shiva's is just that romanticized yearning, against which I have cautioned, for practices that are no longer viable in late-twentieth-century mass societies. Although I disagree, my purpose is not to argue the point but to propose an analogy with the ecological model of knowledge I have been gesturing toward. My contention is that the dominant epistemological model, drawn from the successes of physical and psychological science, produces an *epistemological monoculture* in Anglo-American philosophy—and in judgments about knowledge in everyday life—whose consequences are to suppress and denigrate ways of knowing that depart from the stringent dictates of scientific knowledge-making. By contrast, contextual, multifaceted analyses of knowledge production and circulation within social (i.e., regional) contexts, tracing the interests and power structures they enlist and address, should be able to produce ecological mappings within which to articulate nuanced appraisals of the myriad human and (other) environmental implications of all knowledge-gathering. Bioregional narratives would map these enhancing and impeding activities, critically, to derive normative conclusions that can translate from one region to another, in discussion and negotiation, not without remainder, but as instructively in their disanalogies as in the analogies they successfully establish. Michel Foucault's analyses of "local knowledges" fit this description in some respects.[79] Patricia Williams's separate yet interconnected mappings of the effects of systemic racism produce another narrative of this sort: specific to the (regional) experiences of a professional black woman in the United States, yet translatable by analogy to racism and democratic accountability in ever-widening circles of relevance.[80] Bruno Latour also speaks in favor of just such narratives (borrowing an ecological metaphor from Michel Serres): "the only way to respect the heterogeneity and the locality is . . . to do *a lot* of philosophy. But philosophy is not unifying factors . . . [it] is a *protection* against the hegemony of the present sciences."[81] In bioregional narratives, epistemic issues intersect with issues of responsibility and agency, with the uneven distribution of cognitive resources in late-twentieth-century societies, and with the moral-political effects of institutional knowledge-production. A bioregional narrative refuses the reductivism of global, totalizing theory while producing moral-epistemic analyses of specific, local epistemic resources.

The aim of this naturalism will be, amid the instabilities of the postmodern world, to articulate guidelines for adjudicating responsibility claims. Its analyses will focus as closely on how people know one another—both in everyday and in social scientific contexts—as on how they know "facts" about the natural world.[82] It will examine social structures of expertise and authority, and intersubjective negotiations that assume—and often presume—to know other persons. Such interactions make knowledge possible; yet they are primary sites of empowerment and disempowerment in patriarchal, racist, and other hierarchically ordered societies. And the knowledge they assume as their starting point is often obscured by stereotyped social identities posing as accurate knowledge of human natural kinds.

With its recognition of the inherent sociality of human life, and thus of knowledge construction, as well as its recognition of the constitutive effects of material, social, cognitive, and political circumstances in realizations of subjectivity, an ecological model opens up rhetorical/discursive spaces from which theorists can engage with social and global issues as fully as with questions about the "nature" of knowledge. With its emphasis on the implicit and explicit workings of power within institutions of knowledge-production, the model contests assumptions of pure rationality and the "natural" emergence of truth to work toward understanding the "artefactual" dimensions of reason, knowledge, subjectivity, and nature. Conceived as interactive, finely differentiated, interpretive analyses in which no one can take on all of the pertinent issues, these projects could issue in collaborative enterprises where philosophers would work together, and in concert with other inquirers, for more equitably achieved human survival.

The question remains, can naturalism proceed, normatively, and not merely descriptively, as some critics allege? I have two responses. First, even if it does come out, for now, as primarily descriptive, it will not be *purely* descriptive, if my arguments have any cogency. For descriptions are always value-laden. They are products of location and choice; they begin (and end) within theoretical presuppositions and background assumptions that are always contestable, even though they may afford nodal points at which action is possible. It is not as though good descriptions are easily achieved, nor are they final. Articulating good, plausible descriptions and circulating them well are among the most difficult tasks, and once inserted into the public domain they become catalysts of ongoing deliberation. If it should turn out that epistemology has systematically misdescribed all but a select part of cognitive activity, then better descriptions are crucial to ongoing survival. A second, related, response centers on an ambiguity in the sense of "description" that evidently prompts worries about naturalism's "mere descriptiveness"; worries that naturalists violate prohibitions against deriving *is* from *ought*. Such pitfalls need to be distinguished from the working hypotheticals that naturalists establish, appealing to consequential patterns in the natural (and human-natural) world: "If you want to succeed in doing X, then you [had] best do Y."[83] For Bruner, narrative descriptions are always normative; it is impossible to "argue any of these interpretations without taking a moral stance and a rhetorical posture."[84] An ecology-modeled epistemology brings such a moral stance directly into its epistemic deliberations, insisting on the obligation to answer for oneself, to maintain skepticism about overweening authority, and to work toward better ways of establishing community.

Part of the answer to my question "what is natural about epistemology naturalized?" can be found, then, in ecological thinking. Naturalistic projects can contribute to emancipatory epistemological agendas to the extent that they are prepared to examine the constructed dimensions both of nature and of scientific knowledge, and to assess the ecological effects of those constructs. Hence they need to engage questions of historical, cultural, gendered epistemic specificity as constitutive features of "science as an institution or process in the world."[85] Naturalized epistemology is natural in its positioning as one episode—albeit a major one—in a natural history of human beings. Its provenance and effects are as significant as its remarkable predictive and explanatory powers, powers whose pretensions to global dominance need to be curbed in the interests of respectful coexistence.[86]

Notes

1. Representative examples of feminist work in epistemology are Linda Alcoff and Elizabeth Pottery, eds., *Feminist Epistemologies* (New York: Routledge, 1993); Louise Antony and Charlotte Witts, eds., *A Mind of One's Own: Feminist Essays on Reason and Objectivity* (Boulder, Colo.: Westview Press, 1993); and Kathleen Lennon and Margaret Whitford, eds., *Knowing the Difference: Feminist Perspectives in Epistemology* (London: Routledge, 1994).

2. Sabina Lovibond, "Feminism and Postmodernism," in the *New Left Review*, 178. November–December 1989 (5–28), 12–13.

3. A now-classic elaboration of such alignments is Alision Jaggar, *Feminist Politics and Human Nature* (Totowa, N.J.: Rowman & Allenheld, 1983).

4. The work of Michel Foucault is especially pertinent in this regard. See especially his *Power/Knowledge: Selected Interviews and Other Writings, 1972–1977* (New York: Pantheon Books, 1980). Ed. Colin Gordon. Trans. by Colin Gordon, Leo Marshall, John Mepham, and Kate Soper.

5. Mary Tiles and Jim Tiles argue that it is only at certain periods, hence only as a matter of historical contingency, that theoretical separations have been maintained between knowledge and social-political-moral concerns. See their *An Introduction to Historical Epistemology: The Authority of Knowledge* (Oxford: Basil Blackwell, 1993).

6. For a reading of the feminist potential of Marxist theory, see Nancy Hartsock, "The Feminist Standpoint: Developing the Ground for a Specifically Feminist Historical Materialism," in Sandra Harding and Merrill Hintikka, eds., *Discovering Reality* (Dordrecht: Reidel, 1983).

7. Rudolph Carnap, "Autobiography," in P. Schilpp, *The Philosophy of Rudolph Carnap* (LaSalle, Ill.: Open Court, 1963), 21; quoted in Tom Sorell, *Scientism: Philosophy and the Infatuation With Science* (London: Routledge, 1991), 8. Sorell discusses how this interest in the beneficial character of science evolved into a less desirable "scientism."

8. See for example the extensive bibliographies in the 2d. Ed. of Hilary Kornblith, ed., *Naturalizing Epistemology* (Cambridge: MIT Press, 1994); and in Werner Callebaut, *Taking the Naturalistic Turn, or How Real Philosophy of Science Is Done* (Chicago: University of Chicago Press, 1993).

9. W. V. O. Quine, "Epistemology Naturalized." (Reprinted from W. V. O. Quine, *Ontological Relativity and Other Essays* (New York: Columbia University Press, 1969). In Kornblith, *Naturalizing Epistemology*, 25.

10. Hilary Kornblith, "The Naturalistic Project in Epistemology: A Progress Report," APA Pacific Division paper, Los Angeles, May 1990. Kornblith poses the questions differently in his Introduction to *Naturalizing Epistemology*. There he asks: "1. How ought we to arrive at our beliefs? 2. How do we arrive at our beliefs? 3. Are the processes by which we do arrive at our beliefs the ones by which we ought to arrive at our beliefs?" (1). And he states the tasks of naturalized epistemology rather differently in his "Naturalism: Both Metaphysical and Epistemological," in Peter French, Theodore E. Uehling, and Howard K. Wettstein, eds., *Midwest Studies in Philosophy, Volume 19, Philosophical Naturalism* (Notre Dame: University of Notre Dame Press, 1994). He writes: "We must now try to explain how creatures with the faculties cognitive science tells us we have could come to understand the kind of world which the sciences generally tell us that we inhabit" (43). I opt for the 1990 formulation in appreciation of its more secular tone.

11. Quine observes: "For surely there is nothing more basic to thought and language than our sense of similarity; our sorting of things into kinds" (W. V. O. Quine, "Natural Kinds," in Kornblith, ed., *Naturalizing Epistemology*, 58).

12. Kornblith, "The Naturalistic Project in Epistemology," 15.

13. Other versions of naturalism grant to other sciences the privileged place that Quineans accord to scientific psychology. Evolutionary biology, neuroscience, cognitive sociology, genetic epistemology, history of science, and ethnomethodology are the most prominent contenders. See in this regard James Maffie, "Recent Work On Naturalized Epistemology," *American Philosophical Quarterly*, 27 (1990). Here I draw on 290 n. 7.

14. These examples come from articles in Kornblith, *Naturalizing Epistemology*, from Alvin Goldman, *Epistemology and Cognition* (Cambridge: Harvard University Press, 1986); and from Callebaut, *The Naturalistic Turn*.

15. The Kahneman and Tversky studies figure prominently in Hilary Kornblith's essays, "The Laws of Thought," *Philosophy and Phenomenological Research* 52 (1992); and "Naturalism: Both Metaphysical and Epistemological"; and in Alvin Goldman's "Epistemic Folkways and Scientific Epistemology"; and Stephen Stich's "Could Man Be an Irrational Animal? Some Notes on the Epistemology of Rationality," both in Kornblith, ed., *Naturalizing Epistemology*.

16. Alvin Goldman cites experiments that reveal the workings of long-term memory in his "Epistemic Folkways and Scientific Epistemology," in Kornblith, ed., *Naturalizing Epistemology*, 310.

17. Quine, "Epistemology Naturalized," 75.

18. Alvin Goldman "Epistemic Folkways and Scientific Epistemology," in Kornblith, ed., *Naturalizing Epistemology*.

19. Alvin Goldman, "Epistemology and the Psychology of Belief." *The Monist* 61 (1978), 525, italics in original.

20. Jaegwon Kim charges Quinean naturalists with setting aside "the entire framework of justification-centered epistemology . . . to put in its place a purely descriptive, causal-nomological science of human cognition" (Jaegwon Kim, "What Is 'Naturalized Epistemology'?," in Kornblith, ed., *Naturalizing Epistemology*, 40). In my reading, by contrast, naturalism secularizes justification with reference, also, to its pragmatic dimensions; it does not eschew it.

21. In Lynn Hankinson Nelson, *Who Knows: From Quine to a Feminist Empiricism* (Philadelphia: Temple University Press, 1990); and "Epistemological Communities," in Alcoff and Potter, eds. *Feminist Epistemologies*. I discuss Nelson's rereading of Quinean naturalism in "Critiques of Pure Reason," in my *Rhetorical Spaces: Essays on (Gendered) Locations* (New York: Routledge, 1995). See also Jane Duran, *Toward a Feminist Epistemology* (Savage, Md.: Rowman & Littlefield, 1990).

22. See Elizabeth Potter, "Gender and Epistemic Negotiation;" Susan Babbitt, "Feminism and Objective Interests: The Role of Transformation Experiences in Rational Deliberation;" and Kathryn

Pyne Addelson, "Knowers/Doers and Their Moral Problems," in Alcoff and Potter, eds., *Feminist Epistemologies*.

23. Louise Antony also affirms the radical feminist import of Quinean naturalism; but she is committed to an epistemological individualism and a degree of scientism that separate her analysis from those I mention here. See Louise Antony, "Quine As Feminist: The Radical Import of Naturalized Epistemology," in Antony and Witt, eds., *A Mind of One's Own*; and "Individualism, Ideology, and the Nature of Feminist Epistemology," APA Central Division paper, Kansas City, May 1994.

24. Kornblith, "Naturalism: Both Metaphysical and Epistemological," ms. 50. Indeed, most philosophers—and I among them—do not have the credentials even to endorse Kornblith's statement with much confidence.

25. Tom Sorell characterizes "scientism" as "the belief that science, especially natural science, is much the most valuable part of human learning . . . because it is much the most authoritative, or serious, or beneficial" and that "science is the *only* valuable part of human learning , or . . . that it is always good for subjects that do not belong to science to be placed on a scientific footing." Tom Sorell, *Scientism: Philosophy and the Infatuation with Science* (London: Routledge, 1991), 1, emphasis in original.

26. See Arthur Danto, "Naturalism," in Paul Edwards, ed., *The Encyclopedia of Philosophy* (New York: Macmillan, 1967), 5:448. Cited in Werner Callebaut, *Taking the Naturalistic Turn*, 1–2.

27. Michael Friedman, for example, takes note of this circularity, yet he writes: "although the justification we obtain by deriving the reliability of scientific method from general facts about the actual world is undoubtedly circular, it is not necessarily *viciously* circular." Michael Friedman, "Truth and Confirmation," in Kornblith, ed., *Naturalizing Epistemology*, 177. Vicious or not, its circularity obliges it to offer extra-epistemological reasons why epistemologists might claim the convergence with psychology that naturalists require.

28. Jerome Bruner, *Acts of Meaning* (Cambridge, Mass.: Harvard University Press, 1990), 36, my emphasis.

29. Joseph Rouse, *Knowledge and Power: Toward a Political Philosophy of Science* (Ithaca: Cornell University Press, 1987), viii–ix. And see also Tiles and Tiles, *An Introduction to Historical Epistemology*.

30. The outlines of these debates are set out in Bryan Wilson., ed., *Rationality* (Oxford: Basil Blackwell, 1970) and Martin Hollis and Steven Lukes, eds., *Rationality and Relativism* (Cambridge: MIT Press, 1982). For more recent contributions, see Paul Rabinow and William M. Sullivan, eds., *Interpretive Social Science: A Second Look* (Berkeley and Los Angeles: University of California Press, 1987); and David R. Hiley, James F. Bohman and Richard Shusterman, eds., *The Interpretive Turn: Philosophy, Science, Culture* (Ithaca: Cornell University Press, 1992).

31. Sorell's view entails that "epistemology and empirical psychology can influence one another, but it stops short of implying that epistemology contains or is contained by empirical psychology, and carries no suggestion that work on any unresolved issue from traditional epistemology should be stopped," *Scientism*, 139.

32. Quine, "Natural Kinds," 65.

33. Sabina Lovibond, "The End of Morality?," in Lennon and Whitford, eds., *Knowing the Difference*, 72.

34. Tiles and Tiles observe that "Science disputes the cognitive credentials of its critics, encouraging skepticism with respect to their methods and claims. Environmentalists, humanists and feminists seek to limit the scope of the authority of science, examining its methods and arguing that it really cannot claim decisive authority in matters social and environmental." *An Introduction to Historical Epistemology*, 206.

35. I refer to Quine's pronouncement: "Creatures inveterately wrong in their inductions have a pathetic but praiseworthy tendency to die before reproducing their kind" (Quine, "Natural Kinds," in Kornblith, ed., *Naturalizing Epistemology*, 66).

36. My point is not to ignore recent departures from individualism in "socialized" theories,

particularly in naturalized philosophy of science. See, for example, Stephen Downes, "Socializing Naturalized Philosophy of Science," *Philosophy of Science*, 60 (1993); Lynn Hankinson Nelson, "A Feminist Naturalized Philosophy of Science," *Synthese*, 104 (1995); Miriam Solomon, "Social Empiricism" (*Nous* 28 (1994); and David Stump, "Naturalized Philosophy of Science with a Plurality of Methods," *Philosophy of Science*, 59 (1992). My concern is with naturalism's individualist articulations, apparent in the essays in *Naturalizing Epistemology*, and in Alvin Goldman's claims that "individual" epistemology "needs help from the cognitive sciences," in *Epistemology and Cognition* (Cambridge, Mass.: Harvard University Press, 1986), and his assertion that knowledge "is the property of individual minds" (1). Although Goldman's 1986 book is presented as part of a project that will go on to "socialize" epistemology, the assumption that individuals are prior to sociality, to which this ordering attests, implies an ontology of separate individuals who are only derivatively social.

37. The now-classic text on this subject is Genevieve Lloyd's *The Man of Reason: "Male" and "Female" in Western Philosophy*, 2d. ed. (London: Routledge, 1993).

38. Linda Alcoff and Elizabeth Potter observe: "The authors in this collection who agree that epistemology should be naturalized disagree with malestream naturalization programs in two important ways. Nelson, Addleson, and Potter reject the assumption of epistemological individualism that the individual is the primary epistemic agent of knowledge. It follows that the use of sciences such as neurophysiology to study individual human brains or evolutionary biology to study the evolution of human individuals puts the epistemological cart before the horse." (The second disagreement is with the reduction of epistemology to science.) "Introduction: When Feminisms Intersect Epistemology," in Alcoff and Potter, eds., *Feminist Epistemologies*, 10–11.

39. James Maffie observes that both Goldman and J. Angelo Corlett "favor an information-processing approach to human cognition which is solipsistic, i.e., which seeks to understand cognition without reference to states external to the mind-brain of the cognizer." James Maffie, "What is Social About Social Epistemics?," in *Social Epistemology*, 5 (1991), 106. *Contra* this approach, Maffie argues, convincingly, that "the native vs. acquired distinction lacks both epistemic significance and conceptual precision" (101).

40. In his provocative reading of the features—both positive and negative—of psychology experiments, Steve Fuller remarks that "the institution of experiments in psychology . . . exaggerated the foregrounding effects of ordinary vision by physically isolating the organism in the artificially sparse setting of the laboratory." In his "Epistemology Radically Naturalized: Recovering the Normative, the Experimental, and the Social," in Ronald N. Giere, ed., *Cognitive Models of Science* (Minneapolis: University of Minnesota Press, 1992), 436. Analytic epistemologists, Fuller notes, "form a close-knit subculture who, through frequent written and oral rehearsals of the test cases for knowledge, prime each other's intuitions into mutual conformity" (441).

41. Quine refers to an "innate spacing of qualities" in "Natural Kinds" (64–67), claiming that "A standard of similarity is in some sense innate" (63). The theory of innate linguistic readiness is due to Noam Chomsky. See his *Cartesian Linguistics* (New York: Harper & Row, 1966) and *Aspects of the Theory of Syntax* (Cambridge: MIT Press, 1965). (Stephen Stich, it should be noted, parts company with other naturalists on this issue, arguing that it is "extremely plausible that there are substantial individual differences in cognitive competence." "Could Man Be an Irrational Animal?" in Kornblith, ed., *Naturalizing Epistemology*, 353).

42. Annette Baier, "A Naturalist View of Persons," *Proceedings and Addresses of the American Philosophical Association*, 65:3 (November 1991), 7.

43. See especially Annette Baier, "Cartesian Persons," in her *Postures of the Mind: Essays on Mind and Morals* (Minneapolis: University of Minnesota Press, 1985).

44. "A Naturalist View . . ." 5.

45. Couze Venn, "The Subject of Psychology," in Julian Henriques, Wendy Hollway, Cathy Urwin, Couze Venn, and Valerie Walkerdine, *Changing the Subject: Psychology, Social Regulation, and*

Subjectivity. (London: Methuen, 1984, 140–41.) See also Wendy Hollway, *Subjectivity and Method in Psychology: Gender, Meaning and Science* (London: Sage Publications, 1989).

46. Jerome Bruner, *Acts of Meaning*, 12. The extensive bibliographical references in Bruner's text and in the *Changing the Subject* collaboration dispel any suspicions that these are isolated voices speaking out against the hegemony of cognitive science.

47. Jerome Bruner, *Acts of Meaning*, 73. Bruner cites Roger Lewin, *In the Age of Mankind* (Washington, D.C., Smithsonian Books, 1988) in support of this suggestion.

48. Bruner, ibid., 73.

49. Bruner, *Acts of Meaning*, 118.

50. Fuller, "Epistemology Radically Naturalized," 431.

51. See in this regard my "Incredulity, Experientialism and the Politics of Knowledge," in *Rhetorical Spaces*.

52. I refer here to the title of Hiley, Bohman, and Shusterman, eds., *The Interpretive Turn: Philosophy, Science, Culture*.

53. The genealogically-informed interpretation I am advocating has its source in the work of Michel Foucault. See especially his "Nietzsche, Genealogy, History" in Donald F. Bouchard, ed., *Language, Counter-Memory, Practice: Selected Essays and Interviews by Michel Foucault* (Ithaca: Cornell University Press, 1977). Trans. by Donald Bouchard and Sherry Simon.

54. Naomi Weisstein, "Psychology Constructs the Female," in Vivian Gornick and Barbara K. Moran, eds., *Woman in Sexist Society* (New York: Basic Books, 1971). See M. Crawford and J. Marecek, "Psychology Reconstructs the Female: 1968–1988," *Psychology of Women Quarterly* 13, 147–65, for the ongoing state of these debates.

55. See Carol Gilligan, *In a Different Voice: Psychological Theory and Women's Development* (Cambridge, Mass.: Harvard University Press, 1982).

56. I offer one such reading in my *Taking Subjectivity Into Account*, in Alcoff and Potter, eds., *Feminist Epistemologies*, 27–32.

57. A minimal sampling of such critiques would include Ruth Hubbard, Mary Sue Henifin, and Barbara Fried, eds., *Biological Woman: The Convenient Myth* (Cambridge, Mass.: Schenkman, 1982); Janet Sayers, *Biological Politics* (London: Tavistock, 1982); Lynda Birke, *Women, Feminism, and Biology* (Brighton: Harvester Press, 1986); Anne Fausto-Sterling, *Myths of Gender: Biological Theories About Women and Men* (New York: Basic Books, 1985); Ruth Hubbard, *The Politics of Women's Biology* (New Brunswick: Rutgers University Press, 1990); and Donna Haraway, *Primate Visions: Gender, Race, and Nature in the World of Modern Science* (New York: Routledge, 1989).

58. Karen Messing, "Don't Use a Wrench to Peel Potatoes: Biological Science Constructed on Male Model Systems is a Risk to Women Workers' Health," in Sandra Burt and Lorraine Code, eds., *Changing Methods: Feminists Transforming Practice* (Peterborough, Ontario, and Orchard Park, N.Y.: Broadview Press, 1995), 219.

59. Messing, ibid., 230.

60. Ibid., 233.

61. Ibid., 242.

62. Consider Quine: "A standard of similarity is in some sense innate. This point is not against empiricism; it is a commonplace of behavioral psychology." "Natural Kinds," in Kornblith, ed., *Naturalizing Epistemology*, 63.

63. See Alison Wylie, Kathleen Okruhlik, Leslie Thielen-Wilson, and Sandra Morton, "Philosophical Feminism: A Bibliographic Guide to Critiques of Science," *Resources for Feminist Research* 19 (1990), 2–36.

64. Helen Watson-Verran, "Contemporary Aboriginal Life and Some Foundations in Reasoning," Department of History and Philosophy of Science, University of Melbourne, 1994. See also her earlier essay on a related topic in Helen Watson, "Investigating the Social Foundations of Mathematics: Natural Number in Culturally Diverse Forms of Life," *Social Studies of Science* 20 (1990).

65. Amy Mullin, "Art, Politics, and Knowledge: Feminism, Modernity, and the Separation of Spheres." CPA Paper, Calgary, June 1994.

66. Ecology-talk is not foreign to more standard forms of naturalism, though it does not function as a guiding, regulative concept. Ronald Giere notes that for Michael Gorman: "A claim is *externally valid* if it generalizes well to other well-controlled, idealized conditions. A claim is *ecologically valid* if it generalizes well to natural settings, for example, to the reasoning of scientists in their laboratories." (Ronald N. Giere, "Introduction: Cognitive Models of Science," in *Cognitive Models of Science*, xxvi). My resistance to designating the laboratory a natural setting will be clear from what I have said so far. For Steve Fuller, questions of ecological validity arise, rather, with reference to how the "contrived situations" analytic epistemologist study bear upon the "conditions under which people try to make sense of the world" ("Epistemology Radically Naturalized," 442), questions that also arise within the model I am seeking to develop. Although he does not use the language of ecology, Giere's discussion of naturalized philosophy of science in Ronald N. Giere, *Explaining Science: A Cognitive Approach* (Chicago: University of Chicago Press, 1988), esp. 9–18, resonates with the analysis of knowledge I favor, as does James Maffie's position in "Towards an Anthropology of Epistemology," *The Philosophical Forum* 26 (1995). Framing the issues ecologically permits integrating political and epistemological concerns in ways that depart both from Giere's and from Maffie's analyses.

67. I begin to elaborate such a conception of subjectivity in chap. 3, "Second Persons" of my *What Can She Know? Feminist Theory and the Construction of Knowledge* (Ithaca: Cornell University Press, 1991).

68. Noteworthy exceptions to this concentration on adult behavior are Kornblith's appeal to developmental psychology in his 1990 symposium paper; Ellen Markman's "Natural Kinds," in Kornblith, ed., *Naturalizing Epistemology*; and Susan Carey, "The Origin and Evolution of Everyday Concepts," in Giere, ed., *Cognitive Models of Science*.

69. In this sketch of the model I am quoting, with modifications, from my *What Can She Know?*, 269–70.

70. I quote Kornblith's *Midwest Studies* paper (16) where he notes the necessity of evaluating "our inductive inferential habits . . . against the background of the environments in which they operate . . . which are populated by natural kinds."

71. For a provocative discussion of some of these issues, see Michael E. Zimmerman, *Contesting Earth's Future: Radical Ecology and Postmodernity* (Berkeley and Los Angeles: University of California Press, 1994). Feminist engagement with ecology is often framed within ecofeminist debates. See for example Val Plumwood, *Feminism and the Mastery of Nature* (London: Routledge, 1993); and Karen J. Warren, ed., *Ecological Feminism* (London and New York: Routledge, 1994).

72. Robyn Ferrell, "Richard Rorty and the Poet's Utopia," in Rosalyn Diprose and Robin Ferrell, eds., *Cartographies: Poststructuralism and the Mapping of Bodies and Spaces* (Sydney: Allen & Unwin, 1991).

73. This description of the ecological subject has affinities with the *ethology* that, for Gilles Deleuze, informs Spinoza's *Ethics*. Ethology, Deleuze says, studies "the capacities for affecting and being affected that characterize each thing." It studies "the compositions of relations or capacities between different things . . . It is . . . a matter of sociabilities and communities." In Gilles Deleuze, *Spinoza: Practical Philosophy* (San Francisco: City Lights Books, 1988), 125, 126. Genevieve Lloyd drew my attention to this discussion.

74. Kornblith observes that epistemic norms that derive from a theory of epistemic virtue or responsibility (he cites my 1987 book) require an instrumental account of epistemic value. In "Epistemic Normativity," 375 n. 11. He is not "convinced that it is possible to give an account of epistemic norms which provides more than this." (359).

75. Writing of a balance that moral-epistemological debates must achieve between "reverence" and "suspicion," Lovibond observes: "the appropriate relation between these two attitudes will be a

mutually correcting or 'dialectical' one; and the balance between them at any given moment will be the outcome of this continual process of mutual correction," "The End of Morality?," 75.

76. Ursula Franklin, who was University Professor of Geology at the University of Toronto, is now professor emerita. I draw this example from her lecture at the University of Guelph in February, 1986.

77. Jim Cheney, "Postmodern Environmental Ethics. Ethics as Bioregional Narrative," in *Environmental Ethics* 11 (1989), 126.

78. Vandana Shiva, *Staying Alive: Women, Ecology, and Development* (London: Zed Books, 1989), 4.

79. See Michel Foucault, "Two Lectures," in Colin Gordon, ed., *Power/Knowledge: Selected Interviews and Other Writings 1972–1977* (New York: Pantheon, 1980).

80. See Patricia J. Williams, *The Alchemy of Race and Rights: Diary of a Law Professor* (Cambridge, Mass.: Harvard University Press, 1991).

81. Bruno Latour, in section 5.4.2, *Irreduction*, of Werner Callebaut, *Taking the Naturalistic Turn*, 218. In the conversation cited here, Callebaut is Latour's interlocutor, and it is he who describes the metaphor as ecological.

82. I elaborate the exemplary character of knowing other people in chapter four of *What Can She Know?*, and in "Taking Subjectivity Into Account," in Alcoff and Potter, eds., *Feminist Epistemologies*.

83. I owe this formulation to David Hull in his allusion to this ambiguity in section 3.5.2, *How to Get Beyond the Purely Descriptive*, in Callebaut, ed., *Taking the Naturalistic Turn*, 99.

84. Bruner, *Acts of Meaning*, 60.

85. Quine, "Epistemology Naturalized," 26.

86. For extensive and helpful comments on earlier versions of this paper I am grateful to Murray Code, Carmel Forde, Genevieve Lloyd, Lynn Hankinson Nelson, Richard Schmitt, James Wong, and an anonymous referee for the *American Philosophical Quarterly*. Audiences at the Chapel Hill Colloquium, The American Philosophical Association Central Division (1995), McMaster University, the University of Trondheim, the University of New South Wales, and Macquarie University, and members of the Nordiskt Natverk for Feministisk Epistemologi och Vetenskapsteori offered valuable criticism and suggestions.

5

Feminist Epistemology and Naturalized Epistemology: An Uneasy Alliance

Phyllis Rooney

I. Critical Connections and Differences

While engaging specific questions about gender and cognition, I found myself involved in an epistemological project that might well be described as both feminist and naturalistic. My larger project involves examining the ways in which traditional assumptions about gender differences in reasoning capacities have worked their way into philosophical and scientific conceptions of rationality and cognition (Rooney 1994, 1995a). This has involved, in part, exploring recent feminist critiques of scientific studies on gender and cognition (Rooney 1995b).

This project seemed to be a naturalistic one according to some basic descriptions of naturalized epistemology. James Maffie has characterized "naturalists" in epistemology as those who are "united by a shared commitment to the continuity of epistemology and science . . . [even though] they differ among themselves over what form this continuity should take" (Maffie 1990, 281). Naturalists, at the very least, advocate the development of conversations between epistemology and science, including cognitive science, and, in particular, they think that such a conversation will enhance epistemology. Yet despite my project, I had difficulty readily identifying myself as a "naturalist epistemologist." This is partly due to the fact that, unlike "naturalized epistemology," the term is relatively unfamiliar. It is one of a variety of terms used to pick out particular epistemologists—other terms include "naturalists in epistemology," "naturalistic epistemologists," or "those advocating naturalized epistemology," and, on occasion, "naturalized epistemologists" (though this could also refer to epistemologists who have been naturalized into citizenship!).

The term "naturalist epistemologist" is also confusing for what is surely a related reason. It is unclear *who* exactly the term refers to. Maffie's naturalists have a "commitment" to naturalized epistemology as a project or program, but—not unlike the way people can advocate regular exercise without actually doing it themselves—they need not be engaged in *doing* naturalized epistemology, and, in fact, usually are not. An examination of the writings in naturalized epistemology highlights this problem. Most of these writings have bibliographies with references mainly or exclusively to other philosophers published in philosophy journals and anthologies, not to scientists and their studies. These naturalists seem quite comfortable maintaining some distance from the actual work of building specific conversations and continuities between epistemology and science. There are a few exceptions, that is, epistemologists who make reference to empirical studies in cognitive science in their projects; however, even here we don't get a strong sense of what a two-way conversation with scientists would look like.[1]

These difficulties with the term "naturalist epistemologist" were also highlighted for me because of telling differences with my ease in using the term "feminist epistemologist." Because of my interest in challenging sexist assumptions in the development of conceptions of cognition and rationality, I can quite readily identify myself as a feminist epistemologist, according to a basic descriptive sense of that term. Feminist epistemologists are regularly self-identifying. The appellation normally picks out those who engage and advance particular kinds of feminism-inspired questions in epistemology, even though they may differ in the answers to, or in the methods of answering, those questions. With feminists there is often less detachment, less distance between the advocating and the doing than is typically the case with naturalists—those, that is, who are not feminists. My main goal in this chapter is to uncover this and other differences between feminist epistemology and naturalized epistemology (while not denying important continuities), and to do so in a way that helps illuminate both. In particular, I will argue that in some important senses of the designation "naturalistic," feminist epistemology exhibits more naturalistic tendencies than "regular" naturalized epistemology does.

Feminist epistemologists are often more readily identifiable because feminist epistemology more clearly subscribes to what I call a *verb-sense* of epistemology, a sense of *doing* epistemology, of *reflecting* in a systematic way on knowledge and knowing while drawing ongoing critical attention to particular kinds of motivating concerns, questions, and methods in the way one does epistemology. Feminist epistemologists are motivated by questions like the following: Has the relatively persistent traditional philosophical denigration of women as reasoners and knowers had effects on the constitution of traditional epistemological concepts and questions—including concepts like knowledge, justification, reason, and objectivity? How does the overall feminist goal of making visible the multiple constructions and influences of gender and other power-inflected social systems have an impact on thinking about knowledge, science, and epistemology? How can epistemologists develop systematic reflection on the ways in which various forms of gendering influence the kinds of knowledge people normally attain, and on the ways this might then inform greater understandings of epistemic dimensions of individual and social realities so as to enable effective change in those realities? Do we need to significantly reframe the terrain of epistemology to address these questions and these aspects of knowledge, and if so, to what extent? Feminists may well assign different levels of importance and interest to these and similar questions, yet one can usually distinguish feminist from not-specifically-feminist epistemologists by their willingness to engage and promote these kinds of questions as important in epistemology, and to resist the professional pressure (still) to dismiss them as of little or no significance to "real epistemology."[2]

A verb-sense of epistemology can be usefully contrasted with what I call a *noun-sense* of epistemology. This contrast will also help illuminate differences between feminist epistemology and naturalized epistemology—

this latter, I will argue, still subscribes to a noun-sense of epistemology. A noun-sense of epistemology (as, for instance, suggested in wording like "a foundationalist epistemology" or "a coherentist epistemology") subscribes more to the goal of arriving at a fixed theory of knowledge that is projected as including specific "final" answers to questions about the nature and limits of knowledge. Such questions and proposed answers typically stand as the primary focal points for debate in epistemology. For example, the claim that indeed there is knowledge that survives the skeptic, or the claim that knowledge is justified true belief (or that it is definitely not), are among the most visible examples of such focal points. Such a noun-sense of epistemology typically projects (in a philosophical future, if not a historical one!) "final" definitions, distinctions, claims, and theories about knowledge as the primary or only goal of epistemology, and normally subscribes to a reasonably well-defined set of philosophical methods to address these questions.

I want to stress that I am not presenting these two senses as entirely distinct or oppositional ways of doing epistemology. The possibility of arriving eventually at definite claims is not precluded by a verb-sense of epistemology: rather, it doesn't require setting out with the goal of arriving at such final claims—already earmarked in its starting questions—as the *sine qua non* of "epistemology." Yet these two senses represent a telling difference in emphasis and method that is borne out in the contrasts I will draw between feminist epistemology and naturalized epistemology. Some consequences of this, I will maintain, are—even granting the diversity of views about *naturalizing* epistemology—that theorists in this area still largely subscribe to a noun-sense of epistemology (which also helps to explain the comfortable distance from actually *doing* naturalized epistemology), that they do so in a way that is fundamentally at odds with what I maintain are some of the significant impulses underlying the whole effort to naturalize epistemology, and that in many respects—including *actual* engagement with science—naturalists who are not already engaged in feminist projects have much to learn from feminist epistemologists. I now draw upon some examples from the literature in feminist epistemology to expand on this notion of a verb-sense of epistemology and to illustrate how I think it especially distinguishes feminist epistemology.

In their edited collection titled *Feminist Epistemologies*, Linda Alcoff and Elizabeth Potter note that their selection of the plural term in their title "is meant to indicate that the term ['feminist epistemology'] does not have a single referent." They suggest that the singular term, as it is regularly used in epistemology "proper," leaves "unchallenged the premise that a general account of knowledge, one that uncovers justificatory standards a priori, is *possible*" (Alcoff and Potter 1993, 1). I take their wariness here about a general account of knowledge to involve, in part, wariness about a noun-sense of epistemology that takes such a final account as its primary goal.[3] Such a sense of epistemology includes not just the purely normative endeavors of much non-naturalized epistemology, but also (as I will argue in the second section) a significant measure of theorizing in naturalized epistemology that also projects such a universal account of the nature and limits of knowledge, albeit one that is now to incorporate findings from science.

In her paper "In Search of Feminist Epistemology," Helen Longino argues that instead of talking about "a feminist epistemology" we really need to turn our attention to the notion of "do[ing] epistemology as a feminist," which is "to engage the questions of epistemology with an awareness of . . . [among other things] the ways in which epistemological concepts like rationality and objectivity have been defined using notions of masculinity (and vice-versa), of the ways in which women have been derided as knowers, and of the need for alternative theoretical approaches to satisfy feminist cognitive goals" (Longino 1994, 475). She suggests that we understand feminist epistemology *as practice* rather than content, which draws critical attention to ongoing motivations, questions, and methods in doing epistemology, and thus subscribes to the kinds of considerations I stress with my verb-sense of epistemology. An emphasis on practice also connects with more general feminist engagement with practice, political and otherwise, and with feminist reservations about theoretical constructions that have little or no relevance for reflections on practical change.

In the final chapter of her book, *What Can She Know?*, Lorraine Code is also hesitant about whether "a feminist epistemology" is possible or desirable. She claims that the investigations of her book cannot unequivocally be called "a feminist epistemology," at least in the sense of epistemology as "the postpositivist, empiricist project of determining necessary and sufficient conditions for knowledge and devising strategies to refute skepticism" (Code 1991, 314). Her claim here, I maintain, supports this distinction between a noun-sense of epistemology (with the primary focus on arriving at such a reasonably well-circumscribed final set of conditions, definitions, and strategies) and a verb-sense of epistemology, particularly with feminist epistemology, since her book *exemplifies* feminist epistemology in this latter sense.

One of the most significant discussions in feminist epistemology and feminist philosophy of science has centered on a debate about the differences among feminist empiricism, standpoint epistemology, and feminist postmodernism as feminist epistemological positions. This debate developed largely out of Sandra Harding's work (Harding 1986). Harding's distinction among these has, I think, been regularly misread in terms of a debate among competing "final" positions or takes on feminist epistemology, each of which, in turn, is taken to involve something like final claims about women, gender, knowledge, science, and epistemology. Emphasizing a verb-sense of epistemology captures better, I think, Harding's intent of presenting these as different (and not necessarily always conflicting) methodological strategies or analyses that can be used to address different issues of feminist epistemological concern, especially in science. Because of the many contexts and purposes of justification in science, Harding claims, "feminists cannot afford to give up any of the quite different projects to which these [three] analyses respond" (1989, 200). They are the malleable critical tools that are designed to address many dimensions of science, and thus to enable many different projects, both "reformist and revolutionary," that feminists seek to advance in science (1986, 1991).

In addition to drawing on this difference between a verb-sense and a noun-sense of epistemology in my account of an uneasy alliance between feminist and (not-specifically-feminist) naturalistic projects, I also want to situate my argument within an ongoing discussion about the possibilities of such an alliance. Initially, such an alliance looks quite promising. As Code notes, both feminist and naturalized epistemologies have common cause in their claim to be successor epistemologies to "traditional" epistemology, especially the principal Anglo-American epistemologies of the twentieth century (Code 1996, 1). However, this, in itself, is not a very robust starting point of commonality, since what it is, exactly, that is being succeeded is a point of uniform agreement neither among naturalists (as I will discuss in the second section) nor among feminists, much less across these two groupings. On the more affirmative side, a starting point is suggested in something of a consensus about the importance of paying closer attention to a fuller range of knowledge practices and products in their "natural" developments and expressions, and to the study of such epistemic practices emerging from science and elsewhere; or, as Code puts it, in a consensus about "enabling theories of knowledge to engage constructively and critically with everyday cognitive activities" (1996, 1).

Those who have argued for this proposed alliance have different views concerning the most promising points of connection and commonality. Lynn Hankinson Nelson (1990) has developed in some detail both the possibilities and the limitations of Quine's naturalistic approach for feminist empiricism, focusing much of her discussion on developments in feminist science studies. Both Louise Antony (1993) and Richmond Campbell (1994, 1998) have argued that feminist epistemological projects framed by a rejection of positivist empiricism have much in common with critiques of positivism developed in "mainstream" epistemology and philosophy of science, critiques informed by naturalistic approaches particularly. Antony takes this a step further and argues that the concerns and problems raised in feminist epistemology—as she sees this field—can be addressed within the conceptual framework of contemporary analytic epistemology, especially naturalized epistemology, and that, therefore, we do not need "a specifically feminist alternative to currently available epistemological frameworks . . . to accommodate [the] questions, insights, and projects . . . that arise as a result of feminist analysis, awareness, or experience" (Antony 1993, 187). However, her argument is confined to a somewhat constricted view of feminist epistemology that is construed largely in a negative vein, that is, in terms of a rejection of the abstract individualism that is thought to typify traditional epistemology, and in terms of being stuck somewhat in a "bias paradox" resulting from (feminist) critiques of traditional ideals of objectivity and impartiality coupled with critiques of sexist and racist science as biased/partial science. She argues that feminist epistemologists need to pay attention to Quine's naturalized epistemology as an "approach to the study of knowledge that promises enormous aid and comfort to feminists" (187), since it promotes the kinds of empirical investigation of knowers that feminists seek. Since she doesn't include a discussion of feminist epistemology / philosophy of science projects where such an approach had already been seriously considered or developed, her argument is less effective than it might be. Specifically, Helen Longino (1990), Nelson (1990, with her specific focus on Quine), and Jane Duran (1991) had already engaged projects that are both naturalistic and feminist. Duran's main focus is somewhat different from that of Nelson or Longino: Duran draws more directly from ongoing work in naturalized epistemology, while Nelson and Longino (in the works noted) focus attention more on feminist *science*, and hence their projects connect more closely with naturalized philosophy of science.

We thus begin to see emerging here a range of positions about the degrees of ease or unease that characterize proposed connections between feminist epistemology and naturalized epistemology. This can be explained, in part, by the different ways theorists construe both feminist and naturalized epistemologies, since both lend themselves to broader or narrower characterizations. While Antony argues for a relatively easy alliance (though largely by subsuming feminist epistemology under naturalized epistemology), Code argues for a more uneasy one. Code perceives problems—and not just for feminists—in "Quine-derived naturalism," particularly its scientism (its "veneration of physical science as the only 'institution of knowledge-production' that is worthy of analysis"), its "reliance on scientific psychology and cognitive science as uncontested sources of exemplary knowledge of human cognitive functioning," and its contestable representations of physical and human nature (Code 1996, 2). She is not rejecting naturalism. She argues for a revisioned naturalism that draws on an *ecological* model that can sustain a better understanding of the ways in which interdependencies among embodied knowers are essential to knowledge and action, a model that can also engage commitments to "fostering ecological viability within the 'natural' world" (12, 14). Code's discussion is informed by her feminist work in epistemology, which, among other things, is evidenced by her attention to the embodied locatedness of knowers (a recurring idea in feminist epistemology) and the ways in which this attention promotes enhanced understandings of what she calls "materially situated subjectivity." Her feminist work also informs her concern about how "nature" and "natural" have traditionally been theorized: at the very least, as Antony observes elsewhere, feminists have had good reason to question what has traditionally been assigned to women "by nature" (Antony 1998).

In choosing a location for this proposed alliance (between feminist and naturalized epistemologies) on a continuum of ease to unease, I tend to place it, like Code, more on the uneasy side, though for reasons that are, in some places, different from hers. However, attempting to mark out definite locations on such a continuum belies the fact that both feminist and naturalized epistemologies are developing, not sharply defined, programs or projects in epistemology. It is for this reason especially that I disagree with Antony's suggestion about subsuming feminist epistemology under naturalized epistemology, and particularly when I compare her position with that of Mary Hesse, who argues that feminist epistemology (and philosophy of science) can be subsumed under postmodern epistemology. Hesse writes, "I do not think any new *philosophical* approaches have been added by feminism that are not generally available in the postmodern literature" (Hesse 1994, 459). In order to make such claims, both Hesse and Antony presume to have some kind of complete picture of feminist epistemology though, interestingly, they seem to have quite different pictures of it. What tweaks my feminist sensibilities here also is the intimation that feminist epistemology needs to "legitimate" itself by aligning itself with a supposedly more legitimated epistemology. (I cannot help but be reminded here of a traditional gender norm—still in effect in many contexts—that a woman best "legitimate" herself by aligning herself with the "right" well-appointed man!) I suggest, on the other hand, that we keep an open mind to the possibility that these other (naturalized and postmodern) approaches in epistemology might have much to gain from feminist epistemology, and that *their* legitimacy might be challenged in places where they are unable to systematically address questions about knowledge and epistemology that are emerging in feminist epistemology.

Drawing on my distinction between a noun- and a verb-sense of epistemology (as one that is noticeably informed by what I take to be especially illuminating in a verb-sense of feminist epistemology) I will, in the second section, elucidate what I think is problematic—from a *naturalistic* perspective—in the noun-sense of epistemology regularly in circulation in discussions about naturalized epistemology. In the third section, I will turn my attention to epistemological issues arising out of feminist work in cognitive psychology, work that I think advances important understandings of what is involved in actually *doing* naturalized epistemology generally, not just feminist naturalized epistemology specifically. I will draw upon recent scientific work on gender and cognition to reconsider, among other things, the individual/social distinction as it has been used in discussions in both feminist and naturalized epistemologies. My considerations will elicit cautions for proposals to the effect that a naturalistic approach that draws significantly on the "social" sciences (sociology, social psychology, anthropology, communication studies, sociolinguistics, and history), instead of primarily from the "individual" cognitive sciences (cognitive psychology, neurophysiology, artificial intelligence, linguistics, and perhaps evolutionary biology), is somehow adequate for feminist epistemology. I will argue that the issue here, for both feminists and naturalists, is less about which cognitive sciences epistemologists appeal to than it is about the kinds of critical attention those epistemologists need to entertain in their engagement with any such science.

I will maintain that not-specifically-feminist naturalists have much to learn from the kinds of deliberations that feminists (as knowers, as scientists, as theorists of science, and as epistemologists) are bringing to the sciences. Drawing on my point above about directions of legitimation, I would summarize my position on the proposed alliance by arguing that we take the direction of influence in the direction opposite that which Antony submits. Where she argues that "naturalized epistemology makes a good feminist epistemology," that naturalized epistemology promises "aid and comfort to feminists," (Antony 1993, 190, 187), I argue that, instead, significant parts of feminist epistemology (those, in particular, that deal with scientific knowledge) make a good naturalized epistemology, and that naturalists, many still stranded between prescriptions (about what epistemologists *ought* to do) and descriptions (of how they would *actually do* it), might seek aid and comfort from feminists.

II. Non-Naturalistic Dimensions of Naturalized Epistemology[4]

I suggested above that we seek to identify more precisely what naturalized epistemology is by asking *who* is identified or projected as actually doing naturalized epistemology and not just advocating it. Barry Stroud characterizes naturalized epistemology as "the scientific study of perception, learning, thought, language-acquisition, and the transmission and historical development of human knowledge—everything we can find out scientifically about how we come to know what we know" (Stroud 1985, 71). This, however, picks out scientists as those engaged in naturalized epistemology, not philosophers who are not scientists, a grouping that includes the vast majority of philosophers. In fact, this stipulation accords with Quine's original well-known assertion about naturalized epistemology (generally known as the *eliminativist* position), that "[e]pistemology, or something like it, simply falls into place as a chapter of psychology and hence of natural science" (Quine 1969, 82). Yet, this presumably excludes Quine himself from the ranks of those who do naturalized epistemology.

But perhaps this seems like quibbling. The findings of the cognitive sciences are just that, one might argue, whether apprehended by the scientists producing them, or by philosophers attending carefully to the scientists' reports and incorporating them into epistemological endeavors that, for non-eliminativist naturalists, still retain something of the traditional normative project in epistemology. However, apart from the non-trivial reminder that the "findings" of the sciences are not necessarily unambiguously self-announcing (that is, beyond different scientific and philosophical interpretations and appropriations), other critical questions can be raised at this point. Of the potentially innumerable findings produced by all of the various cognitive sciences, how are epistemologists to select those that they will find significant in developing an epistemology that is to be a part of, or closely allied with, science? What exactly are they to do with these findings once they get them? What I am pressing here are questions that I think are in an important sense prior to, or at least fundamentally bound up with, questions about the justification of these scientific findings and whether or not there could be a noncircular justification of naturalized epistemology—questions that have garnered significant attention in the naturalized epistemology debate that arose subsequent to Quine's original paper (Stroud 1985; Quine 1981; Kornblith 1985, 1994; Amundson 1983; Kim 1988; Almeder 1990; Maffie 1990). When we pursue these kinds of "prior" questions we are led to a reexamination of fundamental assumptions about epistemology, science, and scientific findings that makes it difficult, I will argue, to clearly demarcate naturalized epistemology, much less naturalist epistemologists. We need to be on the lookout especially for assumptions at work in discussions supportive of naturalized epistemology (linked, I maintain, to a noun-sense of epistemology) that are somewhat at odds with what we might reasonably argue are significant impulses motivating the whole project to naturalize epistemology, assumptions that might thus be termed "non-naturalistic."

Hilary Kornblith stipulates that "the naturalistic approach to epistemology [consists] in this: question 1 [how ought we to arrive at our beliefs?] cannot be answered independently of question 2 [how do we arrive at our beliefs?]. . . . [D]escriptive questions about belief acquisition have an important bearing on normative questions about belief acquisition" (Kornblith 1994, 3). Kornblith then proceeds to discuss the "different camps within the naturalistic approach," which include different views on "how direct a bearing psychology has on epistemology." His move here reflects a fairly common assumption among naturalist epistemologists that psychology (or cognitive science more generally) gives an accurate representation of how "we" (presumably regular folk in our regular activities) actually arrive at our beliefs. Allied with this is the additional assumption that scientific descriptions of cognition form (or will form) a relatively coherent uniform account, converging on, or reducible to, psychology or neuroscience (or perhaps a new favorite) as the foundational cognitive science. I also want to draw attention to a third assumption that emerges out of Kornblith's articulation: that knowledge and knowing (and hence epistemology) are paradigmatically about acquiring beliefs, and specifically beliefs held by individuals. Many epistemologists might suggest that this is less an assumption than something set by accepted definitions or general understandings of "knowledge" and "epistemology." However, such a (philosophical) stipulation is problematic for a naturalist, since it sets a prior constraint on what will be counted as epistemologically relevant information about knowing and knowledge drawn from the sciences. This is, in effect, a stipulation that simply begs the question against more robust forms of naturalizing epistemology where questions about the cognitive demarcation and delineation of beliefs are open to deliberation.

Additional assumptions emerge when we note that a significant part of the discussion in naturalized epistemology draws attention primarily or exclusively to scientific knowledge and what scientists themselves do in their epistemic practices in science (in cognitive and noncognitive science), which is not necessarily the same as what "we" do in our nonscientific endeavors, or what cognitive science says "we" do. As was clearly present in Quine's original formulation of naturalized epistemology, there is the regular assumption that scientific knowledge is like knowledge generally, only better—the best we have—and thus merits the status of paradigmatic knowledge. This draws partly on the view that scientific knowledge is more systematic, regulated, and documented, and thus more readily lends itself to naturalistic scientific study. Yet, even though the discussions about scientific knowledge now involve a distinct set of issues in *naturalized philosophy of science*, they are regularly conflated with issues about naturalized epistemology more generally. What Code calls the *scientism* problem rests significantly on this conflation.

If we focus on naturalized *philosophy of science* specifically, concerns similar to those mentioned above emerge. Scientific knowledge is often portrayed as having some kind of uniformity and generality in its methods and epistemic practices, within a given science and even across different sciences; and, again, cognitive science is portrayed such that it can or will present us with an accurate and uniform description of scientific knowledge and knowing. In reflecting on the use of cognitive science in the epistemological study of the methods and practices of science, Ron

Giere notes that there are at least "three disciplinary clusters" that naturalist philosophers of science appeal to: "(1) artificial intelligence (itself a branch of computer science), (2) cognitive psychology, and (3) cognitive neuroscience" (Giere 1992, xvi). However, Giere also remarks that some question the emphasis solely on these three clusters, noting that, as Giere articulates it, "the cognitive activities of scientists are embedded in a social fabric whose contribution to the course of scientific development may be as great as that of the cognitive interactions between scientists and the natural world" (xxv–xxvi). Thus, many argue, disciplines like sociology, anthropology, social psychology, and history (of science especially) also need to be included among the (cognitive) sciences that naturalist philosophers of science appeal to in their naturalistic accounts of scientific knowledge.[5]

In summary (and still setting aside the question about what epistemologists are to *do with* scientific accounts of knowing and knowledge), there are at least four things that naturalist epistemologists (variously) are claiming we epistemologists should take into account as a significant part of our philosophical theorizing about knowledge: (1) what and how "we" actually know (and specifically acquire and justify beliefs); (2) what cognitive science tells us about how we know; (3) scientific knowledge and knowing; and (4) what cognitive science tells us about scientific knowledge and knowing. We need to be more aware of the background assumptions about knowledge, epistemology, and science that are at work when various combinations of these—sometimes all four—are collapsed together. In addition, there are assumptions that they individually admit: (1) and often (3) assume that knowledge is paradigmatically about beliefs held by individuals, and that general universal accounts of individual knowing and/or scientific knowledge can or ought to be made (or that nothing else belongs in epistemology proper); (2) and (4) typically presuppose that the cognitive sciences (or even a specific cognitive science) present or will eventually present a coherent uniform description of "regular" knowledge and/or scientific knowledge.[6]

I maintain that these kinds of assumptions, regularly in circulation in philosophical discussions *about* naturalized epistemology, and especially by those advocating it, are non-naturalistic in that they rest largely on understandings of knowledge and science that are problematic, not because they pay too much attention to science, but because they pay too little. For example, the view that knowledge and science (and hence epistemology) are about beliefs held by *individuals* precludes naturalistic arguments like those by Nelson (1990, 1993). She examines particular episodes in science to argue that epistemologists and philosophers of science overlook important dimensions of science by not taking into account the ways in which communities (rather than individuals) are significant generators and subjects (knowers) of scientific knowledge. In the next section, I will argue that understandings of epistemic realities are limited when one attends primarily to beliefs that are always taken to be clearly distinguishable from other cognitive entities like attitudes and affects, emergent opinions, and such. (Perhaps this clear distinguishability is the case only with the standard—but relatively uninteresting—exemplars that epistemologists typically like to use, beliefs like "Jane Doe believes that the cat is on the mat," or "Smith believes that Jones owns a Ford.") Furthermore, even if cognitive scientists agree about the distinguishing markers of beliefs, one cannot assume that they will present a uniform coherent general account of their development—which is not to say that the accounts they give will be uninteresting to epistemologists.

The work to date in *naturalized philosophy of science* (which differs somewhat from work in naturalized epistemology) tends to draw on a more naturalistic understanding of science. This is largely due to the move in the last few decades to incorporate sociological and historical studies of science into the philosophy of science. Yet, even here, one still finds projections of science that rely more on non-naturalistic portrayals of ideal science than they do on actual studies of the diversity of epistemic practices and methods and subject areas in science—a diversity that does not, and need not, promise eventual convergence and uniformity. Science is nothing if not open-ended: it is not just the future that is open-ended, but so also is natural human ingenuity and creativity and human difference, not to mention the kinds of empirical investigations and new scientific disciplines that open-ended technological development enables. Indeed, it could be argued that the dynamic development of science *requires* such open-endedness, and also *requires* the differing views among scientists (necessary to the push to further investigation) that regularly circulate in particular areas of science—even during times of what Thomas Kuhn has called "normal science."

The question then for naturalists is how to engage *now* with these real (sometimes "messy") sciences, cognitive or otherwise. At the very least, I maintain, naturalists should adopt a verb-sense of naturalized epistemology (including naturalized philosophy of science) that can adapt itself to what I am essentially presenting here as a verb-sense of science—that is, science as a diversity of dynamic disciplines, the concepts, questions, and methods of which respond to changing conditions, including the changing conditions of empirical investigation and the changing social and political worlds within which such investigations are situated. Naturalists need to achieve a more critical and reflexive understanding of the assumptions and questions *they* bring to science, and a better understanding of the ways in which some of the "prior" questions and expectations, many rooted in the epistemological tradition, might be ill-adapted to the very fields of science from which they now seek input. As argued above, we tend to get, instead, debates about naturalized epistemology that are framed largely by static "final" conceptions (or projected "final" conceptions) of belief, knowledge, science, and epistemology that are characteristic of a noun-sense of epistemology. This is evident, perhaps most prominently, in the signature debate about what precise form(s) of continuity and connection between epistemology and science naturalists can eventually hope to attain. Such debates have the sense of seeking to settle *now* where naturalized epistemology's final resting place will be in relation to science, given that epistemology has been unsettled (for naturalists at least) from its former "pre-naturalist" resting place. Epistemology's projected location is still marked by final questions and claims—prominently, still, about the justification of beliefs—to which science will contribute its apportioned part of the final answers.

In pushing for a verb-sense of naturalizing epistemology, I am not claiming that naturalists cannot start out with definite questions and projects. Epistemology, like any other inquiry, cannot get going without some questions. However, instead of claims and questions that seem to have arisen in a vacuum (or in the epistemology wing of a specific place of philosophical inquiry, or even "in our tradition," which can be just as vague), I suggest we start with questions that are better identified and situated in terms of their traditional provenance (or lack of it) and their inherent assumptions. For example, the question "what is knowledge?" is meaningful if we understand knowledge to be the kind of thing that is expected to yield a certain kind of philosophical definition, or, among eliminativist naturalists, a philosophy-replacing scientific one. Similarly, a question like "what does science tell us about how beliefs are acquired or justified?" invites further questions about why one should assume that scientists agree on the defining characteristics of belief, and if they do, that they, in their many cognitive sciences or even within a given science, can be expected to arrive at some consensus about the acquisition and justification of beliefs. Such questions are more properly situated within the tradition of epistemology (the very thing naturalists say they want to go beyond) than they are within an open and inviting engagement with actual science. Epistemological questions—broadly, questions relating to knowledge (granting that there may be more than one sense of that term), to various knowing processes and methods of inquiry, to different contexts of knowledge—can be brought to science, and, of course, can emerge from science and can engage well with science, and those questions can shift and change as a result of that engagement. These questions need to be better identified in terms of their normative and descriptive genealogies, and they need to be directed to actual science in its rich diversity of disciplinary and subdisciplinary projects. We may well arrive at certain kinds of "final" claims and answers as a result of such questions and such engagement, but they too will be as situated as those questions and the particular forms of engagement with science that they elicit. I fail to see that such answers cannot be of interest to epistemologists, even if they are not the kinds of final answers epistemologists have long sought.

Despite differences among naturalists, it is regularly understood that they are at least in agreement on particular characterizations of naturalized epistemology: that is, that it is no longer "first philosophy," that it is not "transcendental" or "traditional" epistemology, that it no longer subscribes to developing a priori norms of reasoning and justification independently of naturalistic attention to cognition and knowledge in practice. (It is not clear, of course, that these characterizations amount to the same thing.) Any one of these, it might be argued, is not a characterization endorsing a noun-sense of "final" philosophizing. However, it has been argued that such characterizations rest on unfair and perhaps overly simplistic views of "traditional" epistemology. Harvey Siegel has recently argued, for example, that the rejection of traditional epistemology, as pushed by Quine and Gibson in particular, rests on a straw version of traditional epistemology, and thus that it is unclear what the dispute between it and naturalized epistemology really is (Siegel 1995, 49). If this dispute is somewhat murky, then so is any characterization of naturalized philosophy that relies on it. What I have been arguing is that a much more useful characterization of naturalized epistemology, one that sincerely promotes an alliance with science, ought to be articulated instead as a rejection of "final philosophy" as that concept is specifically countenanced by a noun-sense of epistemology. That is, it is the rejection of the project of starting out with questions that project final claims about knowledge and belief, to which (a final) science is expected to accommodate by providing its specified parts of the final answers. (Perhaps non-naturalist epistemologists will still want to argue for a noun-sense of epistemology. I have been arguing that there are problems for naturalists in doing so.) With these suggestions for naturalists in mind, I now turn to examine some ways in which these naturalists might draw inspiration from feminist epistemology. I will focus on specific examples that help to illustrate and expand on specific points and arguments presented above.

III. When Feminist Epistemology Makes a Good Naturalized Epistemology

According to at least one clear descriptive sense of the term, feminist epistemology has had some definite *naturalistic* foundations. Among the important early works in the field one can include Bleier (1984), Fausto-Sterling (1992), Keller (1985), and Harding (1986), all of which are directly concerned with science; and together they have significantly influenced the strong links that continue between feminist science, feminist epistemology, feminist philosophy of science, and other feminist studies of science. Furthermore, among notable theorists in feminist epistemology and philosophy of science there are scholars who have, or have had, primary disciplinary backgrounds in one of the sciences: these include Ruth Hubbard, Evelyn Fox Keller, Ruth Bleier, Donna Haraway, Anne Fausto-Sterling, Ruth Doell, and Karen Barad. In my explorations of work in feminist psychology (which I examine below) I have been struck by the relatively frequent references to the literature in feminist epistemology / philosophy of science. All of this can be contrasted with the situation with "mainstream" epistemology, philosophy of science, and various sciences. These mainstream projects have, historically, developed relatively independent projects and disciplines, and this has clearly contributed to the problems with naturalized epistemology that I addressed above. In effect, while many naturalist-inclined epistemologists are still discussing (among themselves mostly) whether or not and how they might develop continuity and conversation with science, feminist epistemologists/philosophers of science are already significantly engaged in such conversations. There is an important caveat to note, however, about these strong naturalistic foundations in feminist epistemology. *Not all* feminist epistemology is concerned principally with scientific knowledge. In addition, some, like Code, argue that feminist epistemologists must also question the regular identification of scientific knowledge(s) as the primary areas of knowledge worthy of philosophical analysis. The fact that women were regularly excluded or discouraged from acknowledged scientific arenas has, many maintain, something to do with this identification.

Feminist reflections in science, in philosophy of science, and in other studies of science have been many and varied. Some theorists deliberate about particular areas in science—endocrinology and sex differences research, for instance—and some draw from this or other areas of science to reflect on more general epistemological and scientific concepts—objectivity or evidential warrant, for instance. This diversity challenges any attempt at a hasty description of a "feminist position" in relation to science. As in feminist epistemology more generally, theorists come to science not with foregone conclusions, but with critical questions about the many ways in which sex, gender, and science(s) have interacted and may continue to interact. All of this applies no less to feminist empirical psychology, including feminist cognitive psychology, which will be my main focus in this section. This field lends itself particularly well to further consideration (including *naturalistic* consideration) of the topics and concerns relating to knowledge, science, epistemology, and, particularly, naturalized epistemology, that I raised above. My intention below is not to give a comprehensive account of all the issues involved in this area (that would clearly take many papers), but to draw out those that I think speak quite directly to the specific concerns I raised above, especially in the second section.

For a start, it is important to approach this particular area of science research with *two* naturalistic projects in mind, relating to two parts of the naturalized epistemology program noted in the previous section. On the one hand, when we focus on this particular field of ongoing research in science, we are made aware of the various conceptual, empirical, methodological, social, and political factors that are regularly a matter of discussion and debate in active projects in science. Research in this field proves to be a good case study to motivate further critical reflection on the assumptions about uniformity and convergence in science that, I argued above, too often characterize discussions in naturalized epistemology. Among scientists working on gender and cognition, differences emerge, for instance, concerning psychologists' understandings of the concept of *gender*, and this has an impact on the interpretation and significance of results. As we will see, questions about the role of social and political values in science, questions that have been central to many debates in the philosophy of science, are given concrete illustration here. All of this illustrates a verb-sense of doing naturalized feminist epistemology, of bringing feminism-inspired epistemological questions to science, which is seen less as a fixed given than as a dynamic, changing enterprise that is influenced by such questions, and, in turn, affects and modifies the initial questions.

On the other hand, since many of the studies in this area of psychology deal specifically with gender and *cognition*, they also speak to another important part of the naturalizing epistemology project, specifically, what the cognitive sciences tell us about cognition and knowledge. As we will see, these studies provoke reflections on various topics related to cognition, including beliefs, situated cognition, and the individual/social division that has informed much scientific and philosophical thinking about cognition—not least through the disciplinary divisions between the "individual" and "social" cognitive sciences. Clearly these two parts of the naturalizing epistemology project are related: an appreciation of the debates among scientists concerning results counsels care in articulating specific results in cognitive psychology (as elsewhere), and counsels care also in articulating the epistemological import(s) of these particular findings about cognition.

Feminists in science or feminist epistemologists and others theorizing about science have good reason to question what have at times been presented as "accepted" scientific findings and theories—about sex or race differences, for instance. This helps to explain why they tend to bring to science projects a greater range of critical assessments than many not-specifically-feminist naturalist epistemologists, who, as we noted earlier, are inclined to project somewhat idealistic and quite general claims about science, its findings, and its success. With respect to feminist psychology, in particular, the March 1995 issue of the *American Psychologist*, which was primarily devoted to "the science and politics of comparing women and men," provides a good illustration also of different feminist reactions to critical assessments. Differences concerning the significance of findings, and their relevance to various feminist research programs, emerge. There is some debate, for example, about what the quantitative meta-analytic techniques (which synthesize results from many different studies) say about the size of psychological sex differences (Eagly 1995, Hyde and Plant 1995). Alice Eagly notes: "Even though quantitative synthesis is a rule-bound activity, it entails many subjective decisions, for example, in the selection of criteria for including and excluding studies from the sample and in the subsequent implementation of these criteria" (1995, 146). Such decisions can depend, for example, on whether one is developing an explanatory framework that addresses possible differences in biology or in early development, or in more proximal factors like status, social roles, or gender-based expectancies, or various combinations of these. There isn't uniform agreement among feminists that research programs that exhibit beta bias (a preference to minimize differences) provide insights into the effects of gendering and further the goals of feminism more effectively than those that exhibit alpha bias (a preference to exaggerate differences). This discussion reveals, among other things, the way in which different understandings of the social and political values involved in undertaking specific research projects can result in different assessments of the conceptual and methodological frameworks underpinning the research. As feminist epistemologists and feminist philosophers of science continue to show, these kinds of insights, though provoked in many cases by specific feminist questions, can be extended to other areas of science, including those not directly concerned with sex/gender differences.

One concept that has garnered significant attention in feminist discussions is the concept of *gender*. This has resulted, in part, from the fact that many studies on sex/gender differences have effected a challenge to the traditional way of understanding gender. This is the case not just in feminist psychology, but in other areas too—feminist sociology and anthropology, for example. The more traditional view of gender takes it to be a relatively unproblematic *individual subject variable* that attaches—to individuals in specific social or cultural contexts—particular sets of relatively stable intrapsychic gender-marked psychological and behavioral traits and abilities. Such gender-marked traits and abilities might include, for example, aggression and visual-spatial abilities, which have been thought to be somewhat more male-inflected, and verbal ability, thought to be more female-inflected.[7] Where sex differences in traits and abilities are noted, they are typically understood to be the result of "distal" factors of biology (neonatal hormone levels, for example) and/or early and long-term socialization. The nature/nurture debate, for instance, fits *within* this more traditional model of gender: where significant and stable sex differences in psychosocial behavior are suggested from studies in a particular cultural context, that debate has then been about the relative weights that might be assigned to biological factors, on the one hand, and long-term socialization factors, on the other, in explanations of the causes of such differences.

Two important (and clearly related) critical projects resulted from further feminist examinations of these studies on sex differences and from new studies: first, questions about the "significance" of difference findings were brought into sharper focus, and second, additional studies prompted other ways of thinking about gender, suggesting, in particular, something like a *situational* view of gender. As regards the first project, theorists noted that positive findings (of "significant" sex differences) were typically given much more exposure than findings reporting no significant differences. With the aid of more sophisticated methods of meta-analysis, researchers further noted that even with the positive findings, sex accounted for less than 5 percent of the total population variance (Deaux 1984, 107; Henley 1985, 107). In addition, "significance" was also enhanced by psychologists' tendency to place greater emphasis on the difference in means between the sexes (even when that was small) than on variance—this latter measure uncovers the often sizeable distribution in the results for each sex and the significant overlap of the sexes. For many feminists, all of this raises questions about the supposed explanatory value of sex as a "main effect variable" in scientific studies of social, psychological, and cognitive behavior. The traditional appropriation of "gender" as an unproblematic individual/psychological variable, measured in terms of stable traits, Jeanne Marecek argues, reinforces the status quo view of "man" and "woman" as self-evident and unequivocal "natural" categories, not just as natural *biological* categories, but also as natural *psychological* ones (Marecek 1995). Psychologist Rhoda Unger states: "Although no adequate theoretical justification for what determines a relevant or irrelevant psychological category has ever been formulated, biological sex has long been an unquestioned psychological variable" (Unger 1990, 110).

As regards the second critical project, theorists began paying attention to studies that suggested that many of the "stable" gender-marked traits are sensitive to situation changes, and many of these theorists encouraged a shift toward what one might call a *situational view of gender*. It is helpful to consider the kinds of empirical results that prompted this move toward considering alternative frameworks for the study of *gender*, especially since these results show up too in gender and cognition studies. By using various stimulus materials, test items, and/or different measuring instruments, or by making other alterations in experimental settings, theorists began to uncover interesting findings concerning the "stability" of sex differences (even within a given social and cultural context). Among such findings are the following: gender differences in public settings often do not hold up in private settings (generally supported by data that suggest people tend to conform more to gender roles and stereotypes in public settings); instructional formats that seem to draw differentially upon gender stereotypes and expectations yield varying results with respect to sex differences; results differ depending on the sex of the experimenter; gender interacts with other power and status differentials linked to the local salience of factors like race and class (or even specific status relations like that of employer/employee) as revealed in settings where group behavior and interaction were examined (Deaux 1984; Deaux and Major 1987; Hare-Mustin and Marecek 1990). This latter finding in particular supports important refinements in the last two decades of feminist theorizing more generally, specifically, refinements of the concept of "gender" that respond to insights into the way gender is inextricably linked with other social and cultural categories like race and class.

These studies suggested that it is important, in assessments of gender differences, to take account of various "proximal" factors in the situations where traits and behaviors are exhibited and measured. Attention is then drawn to the ways in which various aspects of gender and gendering are socially encouraged and constructed in an ongoing manner by gender-schematic situations (that is, situations that, subtly or otherwise, encourage different roles or behavior in males and females), by power and status relations, and by other social structures and relations that effectively regulate and maintain norms of gender behavior and differentiation. With this shift toward taking account of its situational salience, gender emerges as significantly situational and interactive, as dynamic and performative; it involves a dynamic that depends on the many ongoing situationally reinforced practices and institutions of gendering that can differ somewhat in different social and cultural contexts. Marecek describes many of these studies exploring "alternative meanings of gender" as encouraging psychologists to "shift the focus of analysis away from matters internal to the individual to the interpersonal and institutional areas . . . [where gender is seen] as neither stable, unitary, nor universal, but rather in flux, multiple, possibly fragmented, and local (i.e., defined in particular situations)" (Marecek 1995, 162).

It would be a mistake to read this "stable versus situational" question in terms of two quite distinct, mutually exclusive approaches to the study of gender. For example, citing extensive work from social psychology, Kay Deaux and Brenda Major (1987) have developed a sophisticated experimental model that is designed to direct further study of "the degree to which gender-related behavior is variable, proximally caused, and context dependent"—though it is a model that is presented as a "supplement to existent models of sex differences" (Deaux and Major 1987, 369). In addition, noting that variability across studies is a typical feature of psychological research, and that sex differences may not be unusually inconsistent across studies, Eagly (1995) warns against a too-hasty reading of gender differences as simply situational. Furthermore, it should not be assumed that "stable" and "situational" are clearly demarcated ways of appropriating gender. Marecek lists among alternative (nonstable) conceptions of gender the following: gender as a cultural accomplishment produced by a complex of social processes, as a complex set of principles that organize male-female relations, or as a marker of hierarchy that determines relations of power, or, perhaps, various combinations of these (Marecek 1995, 162).

What emerges, in effect, out of all this work on sex/gender differences is *not* some kind of "final" account of the nature and causes of sex/gender differences, especially since the "significance" of such differences is itself a matter of debate. Instead, this work presents a clear example of the ways in which basic concepts and methodologies frame different research programs, and the ways in which such programs reflect what the researchers understand as the importance of the research—an importance that is, in no small way, bound up with specific social and cultural values. (Some also question whether gender differences research has *any* value, other than reinforcing gender dimorphism by giving the impression that there are deep, hidden, essential gender differences that science has yet to fully uncover.) That is, the value that different theorists place on different methodologies in the study of gender reflects, in no small part, differences concerning the social value of gender differences research. The issue for many feminist psychologists is not simply about initiating different research programs inspired by different (presumably feminist) values; it is, quite significantly, about providing insights into the ways in which *any* such research program reflects a particular set of social values and social agendas. Such insights also provide a critical challenge to those who think (still) that feminists exploring alternative frameworks of research are imposing values from "outside" science into fields where they do not belong—*and*, supposedly, didn't formerly operate. "The agenda of preserving the status quo is as political and at least as formidable as the agenda of changing it" (Marecek 1995, 163). These kinds of insights, amplified by feminist work in other areas of scientific research, inform significant developments in thinking about science that continue to emerge out of feminist epistemology and feminist philosophy of science.

Many of the studies noted above that suggest new, and specifically situational, ways of thinking about gender deal with gender and *cognition*. But then the question naturally arises: Do these same studies also prompt us to think in new ways about cognition? If the results concerning gender and cognition vary according to situation (captured, for instance, in instructional and other situational changes in test items and experimental protocols), doesn't this say that cognitive capacities and abilities are also, in some sense, situation sensitive? The situational salience of gender does seem to apply quite directly to contexts where *social* behavior and cognition are involved, and especially to what social psychologists call "gender-schematic contexts" where gender roles and expectations are noticeably functioning. Yet we should note that, even when the focus is on social behavior, "individual" cognition is involved at every turn—in the ways individual people perceive, reflect, and modify beliefs and attitudes about themselves and others, and in the ways they can be said to know situations, themselves, and others. In addition, as we will see, some of these studies do apply to situations that might be more readily identified as individual cognition situations. Furthermore, as I will proceed to argue, this work challenges the individual/social division itself, as it has been used in discussions about cognition.

One particular area that has garnered much attention is the study of gender and moral reasoning. This type of reasoning negotiates the individual/social divide in an interesting way. While attention is paid to the ways in which individuals perceive, structure, deliberate on, and reason about moral situations, those situations are in important ways quite social, since the potential to help or harm others is typically what marks them as moral. Some recent studies on moral reasoning challenge interpretations of Carol Gilligan's work (1982) that seek to explain purported gender differences in moral deliberation largely in terms of relatively stable "inner" dispositions and traits: women are more caring and relational, men are more autonomous and principles-governed. The critique arises especially when those explanations leave unexamined the role of gender-schematic practices, institutions, and situations in providing the ongoing contexts for the proximal realization and interpretation of these "dispositions." Nancy Clopton and Gwendolyn Sorell have taken up the "stable versus situational" question in relation to the debate about gender and moral reasoning. Their specific study supported their concern that "Gilligan's theory may derive from a bias that exaggerates differences in disposition between women and men and overlooks differences in social structure, such as power differentials, that press for different behavior in the two sexes" (Clopton and Sorell 1993, 86). These researchers found that when moral dilemmas were restricted to specific situations and to people with similar relationships to those situations (in particular, female and male parents of both handicapped and nonhandicapped children), no significant gender differences were found in "moral reasoning orientation scores." When moral dilemmas are not so restricted, however, they argue that purported gender differences must take account of situational effects in terms of differences in women's and men's daily lives, and not simply rest with explanations that rely on differences in stable intrapsychic characteristics (99–100). Situational effects, then, need not refer just to the immediate situations and contexts of specific reasoning tasks, but also to what we might call "life situations" more broadly.[8]

When we think about the empirical psychological study of individual cognition, we typically visualize what I call IISAP cognition situations, that is, isolated-individual-solving-a-puzzle cognition. The abilities we suppose are measured in these kinds of situations are abilities such as spatial ability, mathematical ability, verbal ability, or even, more broadly, intelligence and rationality; we think of them as somehow distinct, isolable, relatively well-circumscribed intrapsychic abilities or traits that cognitive science can somehow pick out and measure. Psychology's long historical association with philosophy has strongly influenced the favoring of the IISAP model of individual cognition in psychology. This model of cognition has been the standard or favored model in epistemology in projections of normative reasoning; social cognition is then, at best, reduced to a series of instances of such individual cognition. This connection has also informed the relatively stubborn disciplinary division that still holds between (individual) psychology and social psychology—for example, practitioners typically identify themselves clearly in one or the other discipline. It is helpful at this point to remind ourselves of one of the recurring questions about specific delineations of naturalized epistemology that project the philosopher-epistemologist entertaining scientific findings as empirical givens, which, in particular, have not already incorporated earlier norms of epistemology. Ron Amundson's question I think applies to this larger discipline-specific question: "each theory [within the cognitive sciences] was generated, confirmed, and defended in association with specific methodological and epistemological commitments . . . how can [the epistemologist] be sure that she is not simply gazing on the reflected face of the cognitive theory's ancestor epistemology?" (Amundson 1983, 335).

Experimental models that examine the situational effect of gender have also been extended to IISAP-type cognition situations. Studies by Matthew Sharps and colleagues on gender and spatial cognition were specifically designed to test the way in which "contextual variables" may influence performance on spatial tasks (Sharps et al. 1993, 1994). These studies examined the impact of specific changes in test formats in mental image rotation and spatial memory tasks—in particular, changes that seemed to trigger, or alternatively not trigger, gender expectations and stereotypes. In one experiment, the women performed as well as the men when the spatial character of the task was de-emphasized in the initial instructions, but the "pure cognitive construct" of the task remained the same. The authors of these studies concluded that experiments that indicate that men do better than women at spatial tasks need to be rethought in terms of the possible operation of contextual variables like the diminished motivational capacity of women in contexts where they are subject to "implicit sociocultural stereotyping" that can promote "[t]he negative feelings of women toward spatial cognitive capacities that may violate culturally mediated feminine self-concepts" (1994, 414). Where sex differences were present within the experimental frameworks they employed, they were, they noted, "derived from the interaction of gender with specific experimental task conditions" (1993, 79).

While the authors of these studies seem to distinguish between contextual factors (taken as "noncognitive factors" that can influence performance on a given task) and what they call "the pure cognitive construct alone," they also seem to waver in their projection of a pure core of cognition that can be realistically or theoretically distinguished from the "noncognitive" factors. They suggest that a relatively recent development in cognitive psychology, the notion of "situated cognition," might be useful in the interpretation of their results. They add: "This viewpoint [stressed with situated cognition] holds that cognitive processes are not reifiable, disembodied functional entities operating in isolation. . . . The processes involved in spatial cognition do not operate in isolation, but instead function interactively with other situational and organismic variables, in attempts by individuals to solve problems posed by given situations or environments" (1993, 79; 1994, 422). The philosophical implications of these and similar studies, and particularly further examinations of the idea of "situated cognition," have not been seriously explored (except, somewhat, in pragmatist epistemology), but clearly they call out for further epistemological examination.

It is useful at this point to draw together some considerations about how this excursion into work in psychology and social psychology speaks to the problematic projections of cognition that naturalist epistemologists still regularly circulate, which I discussed in the previous section. I will follow that with some considerations about the implications for feminist epistemology.

As just noted, the development of the notion of situated cognition challenges the simplicity of philosophical and earlier scientific models of cognition that posit and presume to measure distinct, isolable "inner" entities, capacities, traits, and processes (beliefs, perceptions, spatial ability, verbal ability, processes of justification, and so on); that is, "inner" traits and capacities that are theoretically distinguishable from the situational tasks that grant them meaning and measurement. Epistemologists, for example, with their focus on *beliefs*, tend to present them as distinct (typically expressed by distinct propositions), and as clearly distinguishable from other "inner" entities like hunches, affects, emergent opinions, or attitudes. Perhaps this is indeed the case with the standard (though uninteresting) beliefs epistemologists tend to grapple with, like "Jones is in Barcelona" or "there is a book on my desk." However, when psychologists study the kinds of perceptions, beliefs, and attitudes that people regularly live with and work with in negotiating networks of status in their social worlds and elsewhere, the picture that emerges is not so neat. In their recent collection of articles on work in the social psychology of interpersonal discrimination, Bernice Lott and Diane Maluso examine studies of sexism, racism, heterosexism, classism, and ageism, and they emphasize the "revealing commonalities in the ways that we tend to treat outgroup members—not just in extreme, destructive actions, but also in everyday, unnoticed patterns of distancing and avoidance" (Lott and Maluso 1995, xii). These studies highlight the interrelationships among beliefs, attitudes, affects, and behaviors (distancing behaviors, for example) that sustain these kinds of discrimination. However, these studies also draw particular attention to the difficulty of clearly demarcating and assessing beliefs, feelings, and actions, specifically in the definition of an attitude: "[T]he investigation of relationships between attitude and behavior, or between attitude and affect, or between attitude and beliefs, becomes problematic because of the difficulty of assessing an attitude independently of its presumed components" (21). Feminists and others concerned with social change regarding gender, race, and other social or status divisions have long known about the ways in which behavior and attitudes can belie beliefs—even honestly stated and reasonably justified beliefs. Any epistemology (and not just a feminist and/or naturalist one) that hopes to sustain reflection on the *epistemic* dimensions of our actual individual and social worlds as they involve a complex range of "live" beliefs must surely take account of these facts. Requiring that beliefs be apprehended in terms of their interconnections with attendant attitudes and behaviors, and that beliefs be justified not just by coherence with or foundational inference from other beliefs, but also by consistency with those attendant attitudes and behaviors, might be a good place to start.

This excursion also clearly elicits cautions about non-naturalist epistemological understandings of the nature of empirical studies and their findings. Empirical studies in psychology tend to be much more modest—and situated—in their claims than naturalist epistemologists regularly imagine. For example, no study that I know of claims to measure "spatial ability" as such. Instead, good methodology requires clear descriptions of the particular test items that are used to measure "mental image rotation," "spatial memory," or any others in a whole range of "spatial" tasks. In addition, one encounters methodological norms that require specific information about the individual subjects tested—sex, age, race, class, occupation, and so on (not necessarily all of these in all studies). It is also very common for authors, in the concluding "Discussion" sections of papers, to warn against generalizing beyond these specifics. The overall explanatory and interpretive frameworks suggested to explain and interpret specific findings are usually presented with qualifying remarks, and they are regularly a matter of difference and debate among scientists working in the specific topic area. As noted earlier with specific attention to feminist debates, fundamental conceptual and methodological criteria are continually being reassessed, discussed, and modified by experimenters working with similar—but not necessarily identical—understandings of their particular field of study and what they are hoping to achieve. This does not render these findings insignificant for epistemology: on the contrary, I would argue, this is precisely the interesting site of naturalist epistemological attention, particularly when such a naturalist has embraced a verb-sense of epistemology in engaging such a (more accurate) verb-sense of science.

Many of these points speak directly to some of Code's problems with what she calls "Quine-derived naturalism." She is doubtful about what scientists and epistemologists can glean from studies in artificial laboratory settings: they assume, for instance, that the "natural kinds" (including presumably people) are not denatured in important ways in such settings. This form of naturalism, she argues, "represents human subjects as essentially solitary," a representation that is clearly at odds with important feminist and other theoretical perspectives on subjectivity (Code 1996, 7). However, given my examinations above, the problem that Code addresses here rests, I think, more with the way naturalist epistemologists theorize "the natural" than it does with the way psychologists regularly present their results—they are clearly quite cautious about generalizing to "natural kinds" from the stated specifics and conditions of their studies. Or at least this is the case with empirical work that is informed by important feminism-inspired questions. Furthermore, this work is addressing some of the concerns Code notes: it is showing that even in "essentially solitary" lab settings people still manifest and engage with their ongoing social and situational connections.

Many of these reflections about rethinking and renegotiating the individual/social division (particularly as it applies to cognition) elicit cautions also for work in feminist epistemology. It is sometimes suggested that what distinguishes feminist epistemology is its propensity to take account of the social contexts of knowing and knowledge; to, for example, incorporate work from the sociology of knowledge into epistemology. This is true to some extent, but, given what I have argued above, I think care is needed in the way this aspect of feminist epistemology is articulated and developed, especially if such articulations take the individual/social division itself as an unproblematic given. Alcoff and Potter, in their introduction to *Feminist Epistemologies*, remark that "many feminist epistemologists [are skeptical] about the possibility of a general or universal account of the nature and limits of knowledge, an account that ignores the social context and status of knowers" (Alcoff and Potter 1993, 1). They seem to suggest here that an account that attends to social context and status could not (also) be a general or universal one. But, as I argued in the first section, the general problem that many feminist epistemologists have with what I call a noun-sense of epistemology is not the same as the problem of excluding the social. Indeed, including the social could be quite consistent with projecting a "final" account of the nature and limits of knowledge: one would just presume that there is some kind of "final" account, also, of the role of social context in knowing and knowledge. Indeed, this is what some naturalist epistemologists who "take account of the social" seem to suggest.

There are now a number of naturalist-inclined epistemologists who argue for "socializing epistemology," for taking account of what the "social" cognitive sciences say about knowledge and cognition.[9] Some of these projects meet with some of the same objections and problems that I raised above in connection with the more "individual" cognitive sciences. Again, some of these programs project models of social-naturalized epistemology that anticipate entertaining "final" claims from the social sciences: they typically do not pay enough attention to the actual open-ended development of the social cognitive sciences, which may not be able to present convergent findings in the way that epistemologists ideally hope to entertain them. In addition, as Giere's remarks (noted in the second section) suggest, there is often a sense that the "social" can be added on as something like a supplement to understandings of knowledge and cognition provided by the individual cognitive sciences. My discussions above about the individual/social division, as those discussions were informed by scientific studies in particular, belie such an easy addition.

Furthermore, and related to these other problems, one often encounters conceptions of social cognition in this work that are not informed by work in feminist epistemology, but could clearly benefit from such a connection. In his argument in "What is Social about Social Epistemics?" Maffie takes Alvin Goldman to task for his somewhat limited conception of social cognition, and he adds: "Class, race and gender affect cognitive performance in ways not fully captured in terms of information-based transactions between individuals" (Maffie 1991, 107). His particular critique of the distinction between social and nonsocial cognition, as that distinction is deployed by Goldman and others, clearly draws from work in feminist epistemology. Nelson's particular proposals for "a further naturalization of the philosophy of science" involve specific principles that, she argues, emerge quite clearly from feminist science scholarship (Nelson, 1995). Joseph Rouse, drawing from Nelson's work, among others, examines some of the differences between feminist and sociological studies of science in a way that also clearly challenges proposed alliances that subsume the former under the latter. His argument goes further than noting the paucity of adequate attention to gender in sociological studies of science. He argues that sociologists of science still rely on a conception of *knowledge* as a relatively well-circumscribed totality, and seek totalizing descriptions and explanations of science that involve a kind of theoretical detachment that feminists do not seek and often renounce. Feminist approaches provide models of science studies that, Rouse maintains, promote "engaged and self-critical participation in the making and remaking of scientific knowledges of the world we live in" (Rouse 1997, 211). The conception of knowledge as a relatively well-circumscribed totality that sociologists of science still appeal to, Rouse argues, is something that is to be rejected in what he submits as a "*post-epistemological* conception of science and scientific knowledge." Though with a somewhat similar assessment of science as that which is revealed particularly in feminist work, I argue that we not go in the direction of "post epistemology," but that we simply replace a noun-sense of epistemology with a verb-sense.

After all of this talk about tensions, divisions, and uneasy alliances, it seems quite appropriate to end on a happier note of connection, though we need to go to a meta-epistemological level to appreciate it. Both Quine and feminist epistemology have shaken up epistemology in some good ways. Quine shook it up by, in a sense, denying its right to existence—as a separable normative philosophical enterprise, that is. Feminist epistemology has shaken it up by having some not engaged in feminist epistemology deny *its* existence (because it incorporates "the political" it cannot be "epistemology" proper, and so on). But, in the end, these kinds of existence and nonexistence claims come back to haunt everybody, including the naysayers. They at least make everybody sit up and think again about what they are doing when they say they are doing epistemology. Epistemology, especially an ongoing, self-critical, and reflexive verb-sense of it, comes out the winner out of all of this. Both Quine-inspired epistemology and feminist epistemology—even with their uneasy alliance—are to be thanked for this.[10]

Notes

1. In his 1986 work, Alvin Goldman draws from empirical studies in cognitive psychology, and his bibliography (especially in part II) contains several references to journals like *Psychological Review* and *Cognitive Psychology*. Stephen Stich (1990) engages empirical studies of human reasoning strategies in his reflections on rationality. Miriam Solomon (1992) refers to studies on the psychology of

belief change and applies them to a particular episode in scientific reasoning—the development and reception of continental drift theory. In his 1993 work on inductive inference, Hilary Kornblith draws from studies on conceptual development in children and from empirical studies of patterns of inference among "ordinary folk."

2. I use the term "not-specifically-feminist" instead of "non-feminist" or "anti-feminist" because these latter terms suggest more of a division or conflict between (what is sometimes called) "mainstream" epistemology and feminist epistemology than I want to assume at this point. Feminists have used concepts, distinctions, and arguments from traditional epistemology to advance their concerns and questions in epistemology; however, many feminists think that such distinctions and arguments also need to be significantly modified or augmented to fully address the range of feminist issues.

3. In this particular context Alcoff and Potter seem to contrast such a general or universal account of knowledge with an account that addresses the social context and status of knowers. However, as I will elucidate later in this chapter, I would include in my noun-sense of epistemology some programs that start out projecting "final" answers to questions about the epistemological import of social context.

4. This section is reprinted (with minor changes) from my essay "Putting Naturalized Epistemology to Work," in *Epistemology: The Big Questions*, ed. Linda Martín Alcoff (Oxford: Blackwell, 1998), 288–93. It is reproduced here by permission of the publisher.

5. For more on these arguments about the importance of the social cognitive sciences in naturalizing philosophy of science, see Downes (1993), Fuller (1988), and Solomon (1992, 1994). Also see Hankinson Nelson (1995) for a discussion of the significance of these debates for the development of a feminist naturalized philosophy of science. As Nelson effectively shows with specific case studies, feminists are clearly interested in the communal and social aspects of scientific knowledge-making, especially when they help to illuminate the sociopolitical dimensions of the background context that, it is argued by many feminists (see also Longino 1990 and Rooney 1992), informs the "internal" constitutive values, methods, and substantive claims of science.

6. In his 1993 work Kornblith describes Quinean epistemology as he understands it two and a half decades after the publication of Quine's "Epistemology Naturalized." He characterizes it thus: "as addressed to two questions: (1) What is the world that we may know it?; and (2) What are we that we may know the world? As science has progressed, it has offered an increasingly detailed account of the world around us, as well as an increasingly detailed account of what we ourselves are like. Moreover, the very success of the scientific enterprise entails that these two accounts must dovetail in important ways" (1993, 2). While Kornblith starts out with these distinct questions, some of the assumptions I note here are involved in his supposition about the entailed dovetailing. Science is perceived as something like a uniform given. The "success of science" is also assumed, though what constitutes the success of science is an ongoing question for both scientists and those theorizing about science. As I proceed to argue, I think that the dovetailing of accounts that Kornblith suggests is entailed as much by non-naturalistic assumptions by epistemologists (and some philosophers of science) as it is by actual studies of the ongoing practices and methods of the many sciences.

7. See, for example, Eleanor Maccoby and Carol Jacklin's 1974 work, *The Psychology of Sex Differences*, in which they presented a comprehensive examination of over 1,400 studies on sex differences. They reported that studies (to that date) supported only four clear differences between males and females: with respect to cognition, male superiority was reported in mathematical and visual-spatial abilities and female superiority in verbal ability; as regards social behavior, males were reported to be more aggressive. As I proceed to discuss, some of these claims have since been questioned and modified.

8. I have examined this and similar studies on gender and moral reasoning and what I think are their implications for feminist ethics debates in Rooney (2001).

9. Among these we might note Alvin Goldman's "social epistemics" (1986), Hilary Kornblith's attention to "some social features of cognition" (1987), Steve Fuller's "social epistemology" (1988),

Frederick Schmitt's "socializing epistemology" (in his edited collection with that title [1994]) and Miriam Solomon's development of "a more social epistemology" (1994). In addition, some projects in naturalized philosophy of science draw significantly from the sociology of knowledge.

10. For their thoughtful and encouraging comments on earlier drafts of this paper I want to thank Elizabeth Anderson, Richmond Campbell, Lorraine Code, Sally Haslanger, James Maffie, Lynn Hankinson Nelson, Jack Nelson, Joseph Rouse, and Charlene Haddock Seigfried. Also, much of my thinking about feminist epistemology was inspired by discussions at the 1996 NEH summer seminar *Feminist Epistemologies* at the University of Oregon, with the specific support of Nancy Tuana, its director.

References

Alcoff, Linda Martín. 1996. *Real Knowing: New Versions of the Coherence Theory*. Ithaca: Cornell University Press.

Alcoff, Linda Martín, and Elizabeth Potter. 1993. *Feminist Epistemologies*. New York: Routledge.

Almeder, Robert. 1990. "On Naturalizing Epistemology." *American Philosophical Quarterly* 27(4): 263–79.

Antony, Louise M. 1993. "Quine as Feminist: The Radical Import of Naturalized Epistemology." In *A Mind of One's Own: Feminist Essays on Reason and Objectivity*, ed. L. Antony and C. Witt. Boulder, Colo.: Westview Press.

———. 1998. "'Human Nature' and its Role in Feminist Theory." In *Philosophy in a Feminist Voice: Critiques and Reconstructions*, ed. J. Kourany. Princeton: Princeton University Press.

Amundson, Ron. 1983. "The Epistemological Status of a Naturalized Epistemology." *Inquiry* (26): 333–44.

Bleier, Ruth. 1984. *Science and Gender: A Critique of Biology and its Theories on Women*. Oxford: Pergamon Press.

Campbell, Richmond. 1994. "The Virtues of Feminist Empiricism." *Hypatia* 9(1): 90–115.

———. 1998. *Illusions of Paradox: A Feminist Epistemology Naturalized*. Lanham, Md.: Rowman & Littlefield.

Clopton, Nancy A., and Gwendolyn Sorell. 1993. "Gender Differences in Moral Reasoning: Stable or Situational?" *Psychology of Women Quarterly* 17: 85–101.

Code, Lorraine. 1991. *What Can She Know?: Feminist Theory and the Construction of Knowledge*. Ithaca: Cornell University Press.

———. 1996. "What is Natural about Epistemology Naturalized?" *American Philosophical Quarterly* 33(1): 1–22.

Deaux, Kay. 1984. "From Individual Differences to Social Categories: Analysis of a Decade's Research on Gender." *American Psychologist* 39(2): 105–16.

Deaux, Kay, and Brenda Major. 1987. "Putting Gender into Context: An Interactive Model of Gender-Related Behavior." *Psychological Review* 94(3): 369–89.

Downes, Stephen M. 1993. "Socializing Naturalized Philosophy of Science." *Philosophy of Science* 60: 452–68.

Duran, Jane. 1991. *Toward a Feminist Epistemology*. Savage, Md.: Rowman & Littlefield.

Eagly, Alice H. 1995. "The Science and Politics of Comparing Women and Men." *American Psychologist* 50(3): 145–58.

Fausto-Sterling, Anne. 1992 (1985). *Myths of Gender: Biological Theories About Women and Men*. Rev. ed. New York: Basic Books.

Fuller, Steve. 1988. *Social Epistemology*. Bloomington: Indiana University Press.

Giere, Ronald N. 1992. "Introduction: Cognitive Models of Science." In *Cognitive Models of Science*,

Minnesota Studies in the Philosophy of Science, Volume 25, ed. R. Giere. Minneapolis: University of Minnesota Press.

Gilligan, Carol. 1982. *In a Different Voice: Psychological Theory and Women's Development*. Cambridge, Mass.: Harvard University Press.

Goldman, Alvin. 1986. *Epistemology and Cognition*. Cambridge, Mass.: Harvard University Press.

Harding, Sandra. 1986. *The Science Question in Feminism*. Ithaca: Cornell University Press.

———. 1989. "Feminist Justificatory Strategies." In *Women, Knowledge, and Reality: Explorations in Feminist Philosophy*, ed. A. Garry and M. Pearsall. Boston : Unwin Hyman.

———. 1991. *Whose Science? Whose Knowledge?: Thinking from Women's Lives*. Ithaca: Cornell University Press.

Hare-Mustin, Rachel T., and Jeanne Marecek, eds. 1990. *Making A Difference: Psychology and the Construction of Gender*. New Haven: Yale University Press.

Henley, Nancy M. 1985. "Psychology and Gender." *Signs* 11(1): 101–19.

Hesse, Mary. 1994. "How to Be Postmodern Without Being a Feminist." *The Monist* 77(4): 445–61.

Hyde, Janet Shibley, and Elizabeth Ashby Plant. 1995. "Magnitude of Psychological Gender Differences: Another Side to the Story." *American Psychologist* 50(3): 159–61.

Keller, Evelyn Fox. 1985. *Reflections on Gender and Science*. New Haven: Yale University Press.

———. 1992. *Secrets of Life, Secrets of Death: Essays on Language, Gender, and Science*. New York: Routledge.

Kim, Jaegwon. 1988. "What is 'Naturalized Epistemology'?" In *Philosophical Perspectives*. Vol. 2: *Epistemology*, ed. J. Tomberlin. Atascadero, Calif.: Ridgeview.

Kornblith, Hilary. 1987. "Some Social Features of Cognition." *Synthese* 73: 27–42.

———. 1993. *Inductive Inference and Its Natural Ground: An Essay in Naturalistic Epistemology*. Cambridge: MIT Press.

———, ed. 1985. *Naturalizing Epistemology*. Cambridge: MIT Press.

———, ed. 1994. *Naturalizing Epistemology*. 2d. ed. Cambridge: MIT Press.

Longino, Helen. 1990. *Science as Social Knowledge: Values and Objectivity in Scientific Inquiry*. Princeton: Princeton University Press.

———. 1994. "In Search of Feminist Epistemology." *The Monist* 77(4): 472–85.

Lott, Bernice, and Diane Maluso, eds. 1995. *The Social Psychology of Interpersonal Discrimination*. New York: Guilford Press.

Maccoby, E., and C. Jacklin. 1974. *The Psychology of Sex Differences*. Stanford: Stanford University Press.

Maffie, James. 1990. "Recent Work on Naturalized Epistemology." *American Philosophical Quarterly* 27(4): 281–93.

———. 1991. "What is Social about Social Epistemics?" *Social Epistemology* 5(2): 101–10.

Marecek, Jeanne. 1995. "Gender, Politics, and Psychology's Ways of Knowing." *American Psychologist* 50(3): 162–63.

Nelson, Lynn Hankinson. 1990. *Who Knows: From Quine to a Feminist Empiricism*. Philadelphia: Temple University Press.

———. 1993. "Epistemological Communities." In *Feminist Epistemologies*, ed. L. Alcoff and E. Potter. New York: Routledge.

———. 1995. "A Feminist Naturalized Philosophy of Science." *Synthese* (104): 399–421.

Nelson, Jack, and Lynn Hankinson Nelson. 1994. "No Rush to Judgment." *The Monist*, 77(4): 486–508.

Nelson, Lynn Hankinson, and Jack Nelson, eds. 1997. *Feminism, Science, and the Philosophy of Science*. Dordrecht: Kluwer Academic Publishers.

Parlee, Mary Brown. 1979. "Psychology and Women." *Signs* 5(1) 121–33.

Quine, W. V. 1969. "Epistemology Naturalized." In *Ontological Relativity and Other Essays*. New York: Columbia University Press.

———. 1981. "Reply to Stroud." In *Midwest Studies in Philosophy*, Vol. 6, ed. P. French, E. Uehling, and H. Wettstein. Minneapolis: University of Minnesota Press.

Rooney, Phyllis. 1992. "On Values in Science: Is the Epistemic/Non-Epistemic Distinction Useful?" In *Proceedings of the 1992 Meeting of the Philosophy of Science Association*, Vol. 1, ed. D. Hull, M. Forbes, and K. Okruhlik, 13–22. East Lansing, Mich.: Philosophy of Science Association.

———. 1994. "Recent Work in Feminist Discussions of Reason." *American Philosophical Quarterly* 31(1): 1–21.

———. 1995a. "Rationality and the Politics of Gender Difference." *Metaphilosophy* 26(1 & 2): 22–45.

———. 1995b. "Methodological Issues in the Construction of Gender as a Meaningful Variable in Scientific Studies of Cognition." In *Proceedings of the 1994 Meeting of the Philosophy of Science Association*, Vol. 2, ed. D. Hull, M. Forbes, and R. M. Burian, 109–19. East Lansing, Mich.: Philosophy of Science Association.

———. 2001. "Gender and Moral Reasoning Revisited: Reengaging Feminist Psychology." In *Feminists Doing Ethics*, ed. P. DesAutels and J. Waugh. Lanham, Md.: Rowman & Littlefield.

Rouse, Joseph. 1997. "Feminism and the Social Construction of Scientific Knowledge." In *Feminism, Science, and the Philosophy of Science*, ed. L. H. Nelson and J. Nelson Dordrecht: Kluwer Academic Publishers.

Schmitt, Frederick F., ed. 1994. *Socializing Epistemology: The Social Dimensions of Knowledge*. Lanham, Md.: Rowman & Littlefield.

Sharps, Matthew J., Angela L. Welton, and Jana L. Price. 1993. "Gender and Task in the Determination of Spatial Cognitive Performance." *Psychology of Women Quarterly* 17: 71–83.

Sharps, Matthew J., Jana L. Price, and John K. Williams, 1994. "Spatial Cognition and Gender: Instructional and Stimulus Influences on Mental Image Rotation Performance." *Psychology of Women Quarterly* 18: 413–25.

Siegel, Harvey. 1995. "Naturalized Epistemology and 'First Philosophy.'" *Metaphilosophy* 26 (1 & 2): 46–62.

Solomon, Miriam. 1992. "Scientific Rationality and Human Reasoning." *Philosophy of Science* (59): 439–55.

———. 1994. "A More Social Epistemology." In *Socializing Epistemology: The Social Dimensions of Knowledge*, ed. F. Schmitt.

Stich, Stephen. 1990. *The Fragmentation of Reason: Preface to a Pragmatic Theory of Cognitive Evaluation*. Cambridge: MIT Press.

Stroud, Barry. 1985. "The Significance of Naturalized Epistemology." In *Naturalizing Epistemology*, ed. H. Kornblith. Cambridge: MIT Press.

Unger, Rhoda. 1990. "Imperfect Reflections of Reality: Psychology Constructs Gender." In *Making A Difference: Psychology and the Construction of Gender*, ed. R. Hare-Mustin and J. Marecek. New Haven: Yale University Press.

6

Naturalizing Quine

Kathryn Pyne Addelson

It is within science itself, not in some prior philosophy, that reality is to be identified and described.

—Quine, *Theories and Things*

All really good philosophical work is Janus-faced, and the work of W. V. Quine is no exception. Quine carried forward the philosophical ideas of his intellectual heritage at the same time that he opened new vistas. He strengthened the tradition of the earlier logical empiricists by displaying its faults and offering new and radical solutions for his own time—and in doing so, he laid the groundwork for an intellectual heritage that is still

I presented an earlier version of this paper at the University of Melbourne in the summer of 1993, and at the University of Brisbane. Nalini Bhushan and Jay Garfield gave me valuable comments on that version, and Jay commented on this version in the summer of 2000.

alive and developing. It is a heritage that carried its own faults, of course, and ridding it of the faults requires more radical solutions than Quine proposed.

Quine forged a new path by clearing away some of the debris of dogma and dualism that had accumulated from the work of his empiricist forebears. Those who took his path have had to clear away debris that Quine left untouched. Lynn Hankinson Nelson, for example, opened a view of a feminist empiricism in part by showing that Quine's reliance on a fact-value distinction did not jibe with his coherence approach to evidence. On a positive note, Nelson rejected Quine's dogmatic individualism in favor of the proposal that it is communities that know, while individuals know only in a secondary and derivative sense. The path she opened led to accepting feminist criticism as part of science(Nelson 1990). It also opened the possibility of a change in the practice of science—and in the understanding of Quine's naturalized epistemology.

Quine's Janus looked back on the modern philosophy of logical empiricism and forward to the postmodern intellectual world. To carry on his mission is to continue to use the best knowledge of the day to continue clearing dogmatic debris, for Quine is committed to a reflective and self-critical epistemology and science. Epistemology involves analyzing relations between knower and known. Quine's naturalized epistemology assigns the responsibility for analyzing the relation to science. He takes knowledge to be represented in a network of sentences and theories, saying that scientists (and others) distributed and redistributed truth values to the sentences, at least in part on the basis of experience. Through the network, scientists (and others) sketch out the nature of reality by *positing* its components—physical objects, people, quarks, are all posits. There are several questions I want to address concerning this very interesting, Quinean view of the world.

The first question concerns Quine's assumption that knowledge of nature and "reality" is embodied in language, and particularly that knowledge of nature (and human nature) is given in the discursive, representational use of language. This is an assumption that privileges a certain picture of science and devalues other ways of knowing. It has social and political implications that need to be investigated. I'll argue this by giving a story of the classic Kongo "cosmovision," which presents a different view of language and knowledge.

The second question concerns the nature of Quine's "posits." According to his metaphor of the network of sentences and theories, "what there is" can't be given in some metaphysical specification of the basic constituents of reality, or determined by some firm link with experience. It depends on the distribution of truth values to the sentences, particularly those that indicate existence, and that introduces a significant, "pragmatic" element. "To be is to be the value of a bound variable" was Quine's slogan. That is an explanation in epistemology, narrowly construed—we find out what we are committed to saying exists by seeing what we quantify over. But what does the commitment amount to, not in the abstract but in life? What is it for these posits to exist in the worlds we live in? Paying attention to the question fleshes out Quine's naturalized epistemology, and it may make some accommodation to Donald Davidson's third dogma of empiricism, the dualism of conceptual scheme and experience. I'll investigate the question by considering how individuals are constructed in the classic Kongo cosmovision, in contrast to the modern Western construction.

A third question reaches to the root of Quine's proposal that science is the authority on the nature of reality and the relation of knower to known. As Quine himself proposes it, science is not a network of sentences, but a practice, a human activity. The scientists are embodied. They work in particular cultures in politically developed institutions, and their cognitive authority is legitimated within those institutions. Unfortunately, the ideology that supports their cognitive authority includes some of the dogmas Quine debunked. That ideology may be incompatible with his "pragmatism"—that truth values are redistributed in light of experience, in accord with pragmatic considerations.

In Part One of this chapter, I'll go over Quine's position in light of the debris he cleared and the dogmatic debris he left to clutter his own route. In Part Two, I'll present the story of the classic Kongo cosmovision, then go on to use it in Part Three to argue that a respectful and self-corrective naturalized epistemology cannot restrict knowledge to sets of sentences used in the discursive, representational mode. This case offers a positive account of knowing, philosophically understood in terms of Susan K. Langer's discussion of "presentational symbolism" (Langer 1942). In Part Four, I'll turn to the issue of posits by examining how individuals are constructed in life as it might have been lived under the Kongo cosmovision. My point here is to bring Quine's "pragmatism" closer to lived practice, and to understand that the social legitimation and practices of cognitive authority are essential to understand the relation between knower and known.

In conclusion, I'll make a suggestion as to how science might take a step toward accommodating Quine's pragmatism in practice—that scientific language should be understood in terms of "sensitizing concepts," making it clear that knowers and known, experience and theory, must be understood in terms of socially, culturally, and politically embodied beings. This move gives support to the feminist insistence that the issue of "who knows" is at the core of scientific knowledge, and all knowledge.

Quine and the Dogmas

Quine framed some of his most cogent criticisms of the older empiricism in terms of "dogmas"—the dualism of the analytic and the synthetic, the dogma of reductionism. His particular quarrel was with presuppositions about meaning and reference in analyses of the discursive language of science, the claim that analytic sentences are true by meaning, while the truth of synthetic sentences lies in their connection with observable states of the world. The alternative image he proposed was that of a connected network of sentences that faced experience as a whole. Truth values could be changed (or "redistributed), even for analytic sentences that are "true come what may." His paper "Two Dogmas of Empiricism" closed with these words:

> Carnap, Lewis, and others take a pragmatic stand on the question of choosing between language forms, scientific frameworks; but their pragmatism leaves off at the imagined boundary between the analytic and the synthetic. In repudiating such a boundary, I espouse a more thorough pragmatism. Each man is given a scientific heritage plus a continuing barrage of sensory stimulation and the considerations which guide him in warping his scientific heritage to fit his continuing sensory promptings are, where rational, pragmatic. (Quine 1963, 174)

With the rejection of the dogmas, a new sort of epistemology joined the scene. Quine himself called it "naturalized epistemology." He understood epistemology to be concerned with the foundations of science, and he understood science to have to do with "natural knowledge" or "knowledge of the truths of nature." In the old sense, epistemology was a normative enterprise, and epistemologists claimed to offer the rational means for justifying scientific belief. Naturalized epistemology was not normative in this sense, for empirical science was to provide the foundations for epistemology.

There were philosophers who argued that naturalized epistemology wasn't epistemology at all. For example, Jaegwon Kim insisted that it is incontrovertible that "epistemology is a normative inquiry whose principal aim is a systematic study of the conditions of justified belief" (Kim 1994, 35). He calls this the "classic" association of epistemology with belief, justification, and truth, and claimed, quite rightly, that in Quine's account, trying to analyze normative conditions of justified belief is a mistaken effort. Kim took that to mean that Quine's naturalized epistemology was not about knowledge at all. But it may be that Quine should be seen as simply dissenting from that age-worn epistemology, for cogent reasons. Kim's epistemology defines the relations between knower and known. Quine approaches the question of the relation of knower and known in terms of the relation of sensory evidence to belief—or experience to "theory"—and he argues that it is science that we should rely on to explain that relation, not some dogmatic, "classic" philosophy.

One additional dogma of empiricism is the dualism of conceptual scheme and experience—the issue raised by Donald Davidson (1974). The dogma here lies in supposing that conceptual schemes can be specified independently of the experiences that they organize for their holders—put another way, it is the supposition that systems of concepts can be specified independent of beliefs. Given Quine's own suspicion of beliefs, I would parse it in this way: it is the supposition that conceptual schemes can be specified independent of the practices of those who use them. This locates knowledge, conceptual scheme, and experience in socially embodied knowers. I'll use this understanding to extend Quine's path.

Quine's position underlies his well-known "net metaphor":

> The totality of our so-called knowledge or beliefs, from the most casual matters of geography and history to the profoundest laws of atomic physics or even of pure mathematics and logic, is a man-made fabric which impinges on experience only along the edges. Or to change the figure, total science is like a field of force whose boundary conditions are experience. A conflict with experience

> at the periphery occasions readjustments in the interior of the field. Truth values have to be redistributed over some of our statements. . . .
>
> If this view is right, it is misleading to speak of the empirical content of an individual statement. . . . Any statement can be held true come what may, if we make drastic enough adjustments elsewhere in the system. (Quine 1963, 172–73)

This is Quine's pragmatism—the identity of the conceptual scheme at any moment consists in connections among sentences. Those connections change when their users distribute and redistribute truth values in light of their scientific heritage and their ongoing experience. What is it to "redistribute truth values"? I'll take it to mean the conceptual scheme changes with the practices of its users and can't be specified independently. This "pragmatism" must be taken seriously if the goal of Quine's naturalized epistemology is to investigate the relation of experience to theory—or to offer an explanation of "how we go about theorizing," as Lynn Hankinson Nelson argues (1990, 117).

One route to Quine's pragmatism is through notion of "posits." Posits order the experiences that impinge on the net. Posits are what we are committed to recognizing as existing. What there is depends on the distribution of truth values in the network—for to be is to be the value of a bound variable within one of the component sets of sentences. To be is to be a posit of the network of sentences, not an element of ultimate reality. Epistemology is joined to ontology. Physical objects are important posits. Presumably nature itself is a posit, at least as the totality of what scientists investigate. Presumably knowers are posits. And presumably the relation between knower and known is a posit. In Quine's naturalized epistemology, science explains this relationship.

If we care about a self-corrective and respectful science, there are questions that must be raised about Quine's epistemology, particularly about interpreting science as a network of sentences. Quine didn't share the logical positivist obsession with separating meaningless metaphysics from meaningful science—he erased that boundary. But he does share its commitment to the primacy of discursive, representational use of language in the relation of knower to known. The networks of sentences Quine concerns himself with are, as a totality, used in a literal, not a metaphorical or poetic or even ethical, sense.

The sciences that are the foundation of naturalized epistemology, the sciences that are to tell us what there is, carry their own dogmas. Some of those dogmas are not compatible with Quine's pragmatism. The crux of the matter is that the scientists of naturalized epistemology are flesh and blood professionals acting in a world in which they exercise cognitive authority over the nature of nature and knowledge. The cognitive authority, in the natural sciences at least, is legitimated by the assumption that there is one reality and science tells us what it is.[1] This epistemological-metaphysical thesis supports Western science as the route to genuine knowledge, which in turn supports scientific solutions for political and social problems in communities across the globe. It also raises philosophical questions about Quine's posits. What if, in some communities, the posits of everyday life include souls, ghosts, gods, underworlds, reincarnations, or transubstantiations, for example? Is science to legislate on the cogency of these posits, and so on the legitimacy of the social and moral practices that presuppose them?

There are other assumptions that Quine seems to share that may hide dogmas. One is Robert K. Merton's "norm of universalism in science" (Merton 1949). This norm claims that no one has special access to scientific truth. Given the proper training, any individual, whatever his or her gender, race, status, nation, or culture, can produce or reproduce (or comprehend) the knowledge produced in science. The assumption is that all human individuals are epistemically alike. Merton's claim is about scientific rationality and method. Quine's claim is about the universal relationship of knower to known, the one that science analyzes in naturalized epistemology.

A root problem here is that the sciences of Quine's naturalized epistemology operate under an ideology of science that shares much with the empiricism Quine criticized. In practice, they act under presuppositions about objective knowledge that are produced by individual knowers (or aggregates thereof), and they assume that reality is described in the language and theories of their own discourse (subject always to correction, of course, but offering the best knowledge of the day). But is this compatible with Quine's pragmatism?

Does Quine's naturalized epistemology require a more participatory analysis of the knower-known relationship? One in which reality (or world), knowledge, and knower are made and changed together? Quine's metaphors of posits and redistributing truth values seem to lead in that direction. But how does this jibe with the presumptions about knowledge in the sciences that are the foundation of naturalized epistemology? How does Quine's pragmatism suit the practice (and the dogmas) of the sciences he prefers?

These are philosophical questions, but I want to approach them out of the story of the Kongo cosmovision, which offers clues to an amplified approach to knowledge, language, and the relation of knower to world.

The Classic Kongo World Picture

The Kongo kingdom emerged in the thirteenth century and occupied an area including the present northern Angola, the Angolan enclave of Cabinda, the southwestern part of Zaire, and the southern part of the People's Republic of Congo.[2] The kingdom was organized through a system of tributes in which state officials took the surplus production from villages (though unlike the capitalist mode, the exploitation wasn't integrated into the process of production). The Portuguese and Christian missionaries arrived toward the end of the fifteenth century. The monarch was converted, and for some years there was cooperation in trade, exchange of ambassadors, and so on. However, as the Portuguese slave trade became more vicious, and as Lisbon and even the Pope ignored Kongo pleas, the cooperation deteriorated. There was full-scale war in 1660, much to the detriment of the Kongo kingdom. By the end of the eighteenth century, the kingdom was without power—and Christianity was dead among the native peoples.

Ernest Wamba-dia-Wamba explains the classic Kongo cosmology through the teachings of the four schools of higher learning in the Kongo kingdom. Wamba-dia-Wamba speaks of "epistemic structures organized through a cosmology" in this system. In the origin story of the cosmology, Kalunga had a firestorm, out of which all things came to be. So Kalunga is not only the original, self-generating force, but also the mode of existence of all things—rocks, plants, animals, communities.

Because Kalunga is a force in motion, earth and everything on it is in perpetual motion. All things are inspired with life-ness, not only animals and plants but stones and the earth itself as well. According to Wamba-dia-Wamba, this means that there is no separate "nature," set apart from

Man for human use and scientific study. There is no nature made up of material phenomena that are described as conforming to law-like regularities that allow us to predict and plan the future. The world does not conform to law in that sense, and spirit and matter are not separated in the modern Western way. All things participate in the dynamic process that is the world.

Classically, Western scientists expect conformity of nature to law, and they look for regularities that might allow prediction of one sort or another. Scientific laws are said to be descriptive rather than normative, claiming to describe the way things do behave rather than the way they ought to behave. There is reason to believe that this legislated difference between the descriptive and normative, and the insistence on prediction, is a rather late artifact of the development of Western science. At any rate, I believe that these distinctions were not made in the classic Kongo worldview (nor in earlier Western worldviews). However, in the classic Kongo perspective, there were what Wamba-dia-Wamba calls principles. Kalunga is not only the force in motion but also the *principle of change*. This principle involves transformations of rising, maturing, declining, dying (or changing form), maturing in new form, and rising again—setting afire, rising up, coming down, and cooling. This is the principle of dingo-dingo-dia-lunga, and (in Western terms) I would say it is both descriptive and normative. Or one might say that the distinction was not made and would make no sense in that dynamic, living world—provided this doesn't mean simply that their concepts were different from ours.

The world floats in Kalunga—Kalunga here taken to be endless water. Half the world is terrestrial and above the water, half is submerged below, both as the submarine and the spiritual (or ancestral) world. In this sense, Kalunga as endless water is both a doorway and a dividing wall between the two life processes, the daily life and the nightly life. In conjunction with the principle of rising and setting, the division of above and below makes a quadranodal process.

In the Kongo kingdom, there was no systematic writing. Instead, the Kongo people used a graphic system of symbols composed of colors (black, red, white, yellow), drawings, and analogies. So the Kongo graphic system is quite different from the one we use, and so I am distorting it even as I give Wamba-dia-Wamba's explanation. But as a pedagogical device, I think the symbols can be helpful. I won't do those for Kalunga's storm etc., only but for the "afterstorm" and the "dingo-dingo-dia-lunga" principle.

1. Nseluka, symbol of the sun rising. *Emergence*.

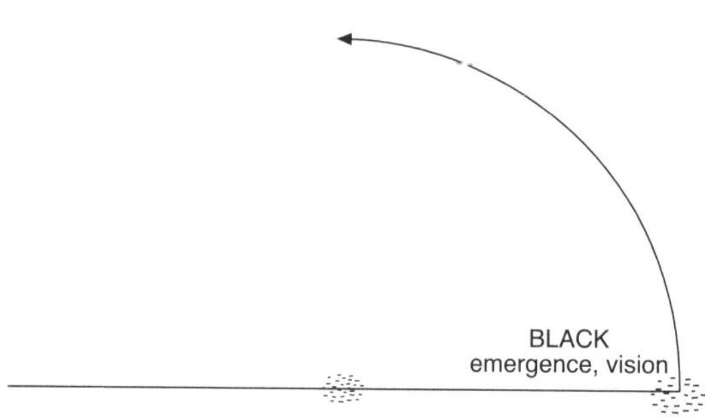

The line is the division between upper and lower world, and the entrance and exit. This is the emergence of life, and it is associated with the color black. Wamba-dia-Wamba says the symbol was also used to resolve conflicts in the community. The specialists associated with black and emergence are the visionaries or prophets, the bearers of knowledge relating to the forces present in this process.

2. Kula, symbol of the process of *growth and maturation*.

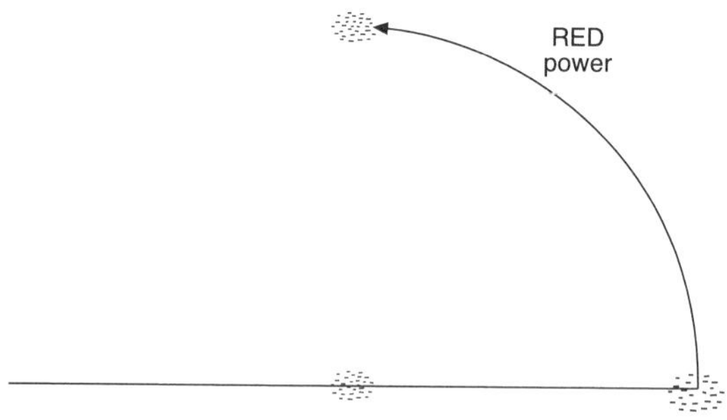

In the human life course, this symbol presents developing (making one's history) until one reaches a position of strength and maturity in the collective life of the community. It reminds me a little of the course of Aristotle's man of practical wisdom. The high point of maturation was associated with the highest position of authority and power, the king's place. The color is red, associated with mature leadership within the community, which is also leadership over collective growth and development of the community, so the specialists are the "politicians" or community leaders and elders of various sorts. The symbol also presents the growth of community as well as other processes of maturation.

3. The setting of life.

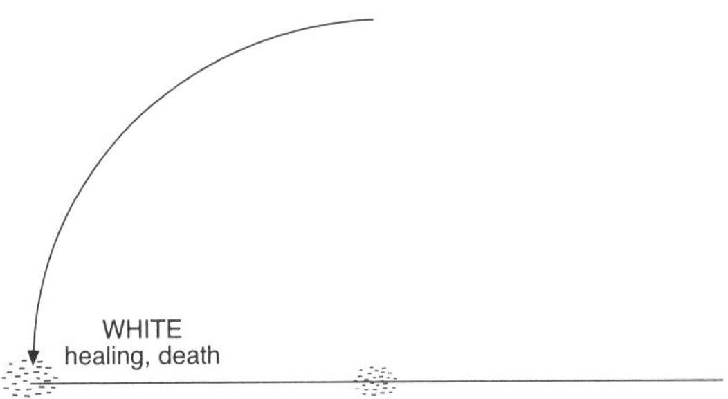

This presents a decline, marked by negative accumulation during the maturation process. It's color is white chalk. The specialists are the herbalists or healers.

And this is Makuku matatu, symbol of the upper world, which joins the above three:

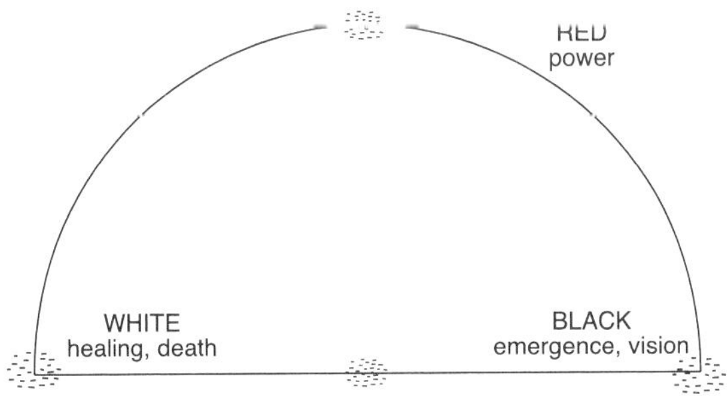

In this upper world, several elements are important for the life process: what is emerging (youth); what is ripe in the capacities of the present leaders; and the knowledge of the specialists.

But there is also the underworld.

4. The maturation process in the underworld.

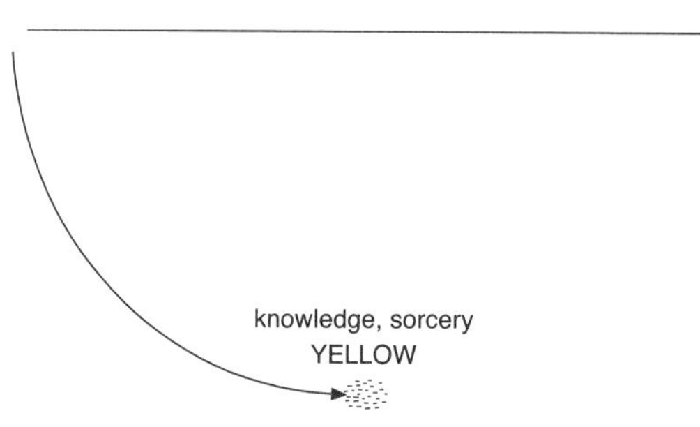

In the underworld, the body is transformed so that one becomes a true knower of what is marked on one's own minded body. One knows the higher level principles and systems. The associated color is yellow, the color for knowledge. The specialists are the sorcerers. Sorcerers can use their knowledge to help the healers, but also to do special things—like fly. In doing so, they dip into the underworld knowledge.

It's important to bear in mind that the line between upper and lower world is a doorway, and one that is not simply used at death. The ancestors who dwell in the underworld also use that doorway, offering their wisdom and guidance to those living in the upper world, and at times appearing to their kin or, in the case of evil spirits, causing trouble.

5. The decline toward the upper world (see page 253, top).

This is a negative direction as one moves to reenter the upper world. The underworld body must be transformed (or "die") to enter. Wamba-dia-Wamba says: "All that exists now, existed in one or another form in the past and can reappear in some other form in the future." This is a "theory" of reincarnation in which one may be reincarnated as a person but also as other sorts of beings, for example, a tree.

6. This is the picture of the whole, the quadernity (see page 253, bottom).

Wamba-dia-Wamba says that "a human being is a being of continuous motion" through the four stages of the quadranodal process.

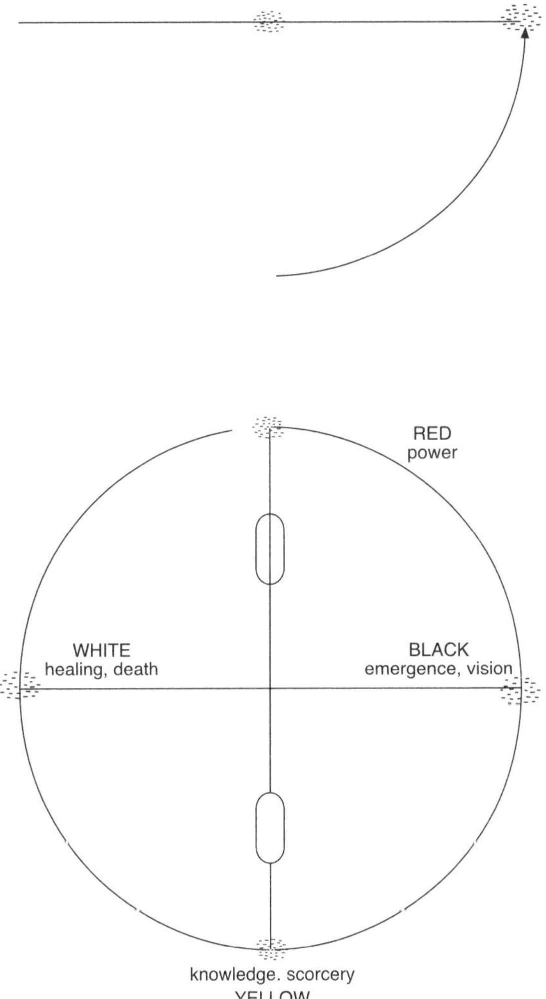

The charts and the colors are integrated with many other parts of life. For example, there are four principle hours corresponding to the four colors (compare our morning, afternoon, evening, and night), and four secondary hours. The Kongo week has four days, corresponding to the four points, with each day having the name of one of the four markets.

The clan and family relations are also organized according to a quadranodal diagram, as is the political system (local, regional, etc.). There is also an analogy with the rising and setting of the sun, the cycle of light and darkness, and so on.

At this point, I want to begin considering the dogma of individualism, by trying to understand whether the people of the classic Kongo picture can reasonably be parsed as individuals in our sense.

Speaking of Nature

In the first part of this chapter, I asked whether Quine's pragmatism could be accommodated in a naturalized epistemology that relies on a science practiced under some of the dogmas and presuppositions that he rejects. Some dogmas he seems to accept tacitly, carrying on the tradition of the logical empiricists he criticizes. These include the assumption that knowledge must be represented in language as a discursive, representational symbolism. The idea of such a symbolism singles out ideal types in a way—in actual language use, boundaries between metaphoric, emotive, and literal usage are blurred. In sketching the differences, I'll follow Susan K. Langer's discussion (1942).

Vocabulary and syntax comprise language as a discursive, representational symbolism, and in their literal use, the words have relatively fixed meanings that can be captured in dictionaries. Translations can be made using the dictionaries, even if the translations are indeterminate. Quine's dictionaries are peculiar things made up of correlated sentences, but this makes no essential difference. The world and its objects are represented in the vast network of sentences that dip into "experience" at the edges, and translation involves constructing a dictionary. The net metaphor allows Quine to say that to be is to be the value of a bound variable, or that reference is underdetermined, and takes these slogans to indicate something deeply important about knowledge and life. In this approach, knowledge has to do with the cognitive content of sets of sentences, with "cognitive content" narrowly construed.

The Kongo symbolism I described above is an example of what Langer called "presentational symbolism" (Langer 1942). The symbols present many meanings, but they are not to be clarified by disambiguation or by making a more precise dictionary. The movement in presentational symbolism is not toward precise definition. Rather, the symbolic movement is toward *amplification and association*—integrating colors, life cycles, rising and setting of sun and stars, divisions of the day and segments of the week, and so on. This use of symbolism is central in the meaning of self, myth, history, fiction, poetry, and religion. It is the use of symbols in our very dreams.[3]

Quine writes of mystical experience that "it is without content and so resists literal communication, but one may still try to *induce the feeling* in others by skillful metaphor" (Quine 1981, 188, my italics). Forty years earlier, Langer criticized Quine's elders among the philosophers of language—Russell and Carnap among them—for just such a narrow conception. Quine appears to share the two basic assumptions that Langer criticized: that literal representation is the only means of articulating thought, and that everything that is not so representable is feeling. (Langer 1942, 87–89). In short, it is the dogma that discursive, representational symbolism is the only bearer of knowledge and the only yardstick for determining reality and what there is.

In a presentational symbolism—Langer gives the example of a picture—elements are not units with independent meanings, and they have no significance by themselves. There is no vocabulary, thus no dictionary or translation. Let me give Langer's own words:

> Language in the strict sense is essentially discursive; it has permanent units of meaning which are combinable into larger units; it has fixed equivalences that make definition and translation possible; its connotations are general so that it requires nonverbal acts, like pointing, looking, or emphatic voice inflections, to assign specific denotations to its terms. In all these salient characters it differs from wordless symbolism, which is nondiscursive and untranslatable, does not allow of definitions within its own system, and cannot directly convey generalities. The meanings given through language are successively understood, and gathered into a whole by the process called discourse; the meanings of all other symbolic elements that compose a larger, articulate symbol are understood only through the meaning of the whole, through their relations within the total structure. Their very functioning as symbols depends on the fact that they are involved in a simultaneous, integral presentation. This kind of semantic may be called "presentational symbolism," to characterize its essential

distinction from discursive symbolism or "language" proper. (Langer 1942, 96–97)

She goes on to write that rationality is the essence of mind, and that it is a fundamental error to recognize it only in systematic, explicit, language-bound reasoning (99). There is nondiscursive knowledge. There is cognitive content even in music—Langer devoted a full chapter to the topic.[4] But we should extend Langer's talk of presentational symbolism to include the use of language in poetry, ritual, and so on. These are other cases of language use with cognitive content.

When I relayed Wamba-dia-Wamba's discussion of the Kongo system, it had already undergone a transformation, of course, since he (and I) had to use discursive language, given our medium and audiences. But the original symbolism presented a world and a foundation for knowledge within that world according to one's place in it, whether as ancestor in the underworld, healer or politician in the upper world, or as ordinary mother, father, child, elder, or what have you. The meaning had to be amplified collectively in life. The meaning was presented for collective living, not for mental contemplation or written representation. How might we understand Quine's posits in such a world?—remembering always that it may also be our own world, only seen from a different perspective.

Positing Individuals

The notion of posits is important to Quine's philosophy for many reasons. For one, it accommodates the indeterminacy of reference from an ontological perspective, supplementing the epistemological perspective represented in his discussions of networks of sentences. Because his remarks on posits seem tied to the discursive use of language, do we need some broader interpretation that might accommodate the presentational use of symbol in the classic Kongo cosmovision? I'll approach the question by considering human individuals as posits—Quine, after all, takes the "observable" things of everyday experience to be posits. Human individuals are posited differently in Kongo and "classic" Western worldviews. They are also central to Quine's naturalized epistemology, both in its philosophy and in the science it relies on.

The Kongo cosmovision does not posit individuals in "our" sense, but it is not primarily because of differences in the "conceptual nets" attributed to the United States and the classic Kongo. Perhaps Quine would agree, given Davidson's criticism of the dogma of the dualism of conceptual scheme and experience. But it would be a hopeless distortion of the presentational symbolism of the Kongo cosmovision to reduce it to a discursive representation, then "translate" it into some language that allows us only to ask questions like whether reincarnation is a fact, or whether the ancestors in truth stand by to advise those in the upper world. Such an investigation might be interesting if one hoped to support scientific methods over others, but it would deny the importance of other methods to life. It might be analogous to insisting that we translate poetry, art, movies, or music into the discursive language of science. It would also sacrifice Quine's ontological notion of posits to an epistemology tied to discursive, representational symbols and various remaining dogmas.[5]

Wamba-dia-Wamba says that the men and women of the Kongo were in perpetual motion, "like a living sun which rises and sets," going around a path in the upper and lower world. People in the Kongo scheme were not identical with their present incarnations—that is, people were not individual, *biological* organisms. This isn't simply a *belief* endorsed by the cosmovision, nor can it be explained in terms of a distribution of truth values. It is the way people would have been constituted in collective life. For example, a person would have been identified in terms of his or her place in a kinship line, and the place of that line relative to others. This wasn't a line of presently living relatives, nor a chart of biological progenitors (in the Western sense). It was an ancestral chart that also traced the person's previous lives. I believe it marked the responsibilities of people, not only to kin and community in the upper world, but to those of the underworld, and even to their own underworld lives to come. It gave a basis to morality as well as to knowledge of the cosmos.

Wamba-dia-Wamba gave some examples that indicate to me that we are not dealing with individuals in the sense that Quine takes them. For example, if an ancestor was too troublesome, the group might have declared the person who is that ancestor's present incarnation to be dead. They wouldn't have killed him—killing someone in this Kongo world didn't result in absolute death. Absolute death meant no reincarnation, no transformation in the underworld, no exit and no reentry, absolute death to the rising and setting of that being. The group didn't have to use what we would call physical means to cause the organism to die, for the person would have died of his own accord (or occasionally have committed suicide). In the scheme of Western science, in contrast, individual life is tied to the spatio-temporal body.

Wamba-dia-Wamba related this example of the difference in the nature of individuals as well. In a palaver, or a discussion for settling some disagreement or difficult case, everyone would have talked until they said as much as they had to say. Age was respected in the speaking order. But age of a person present was calculated in terms of the line of ancestors he incarnated. And so the oldest might be what we would call a child—in terms of the emergence and maturation process of the *upper world*. But age for this purpose was calculated in terms of the whole upper and lower world cycles. Again in contrast, as posits of science, human individuals are born, grow old, and die in a way that is continuous in space and time.[6]

But my point in talking about the Kongo cosmovision is to show people and their world as generated in collective action. I assume community and nature to be a living process in which living beings generate the world and knowledge of the world—creating the environment and themselves. This interprets Quine's talk of posits and redistribution of truth values in terms of collective activity in making a world, not as a linguistic game. It gives us a different approach to scientific knowledge and the work of the scientists who posit the beings of the naturalized epistemology—and some of the dogmas they cling to in their practices.

One of the dogmas I mentioned in this chapter's first part was the dualism of knower and known. Another is the dogma associated with Merton's "universalism" norm—a norm of epistemic equality that claims any individual, no matter what culture, race, or class, can pursue science and come to know the truths that science uncovers. These are dogmas that legitimate the cognitive authority of science in the Western nations and much of the world. Taken together, they interpret the "posits" of science as the reality everyone should know and live by. They are dogmas defining the relations between knower and known. If the science of a naturalized epistemology is to be legitimated under these ideas of knowledge and reality, how can it satisfy Quine's pragmatism?

This dogmatic idea of objectivity in knowledge is a product of the long history of efforts to distinguish Western science from alchemy and astrology, and the modern idea of nature from the old one. Alchemists used a presentational symbolism, and the alchemical process was not one of a detached individual studying nature as an object. In the alchemical process, the alchemists and the world changed together. Knowledge was collectively made, materially and morally, as the relationship of knower and known was itself generated in the collective activity. Both knower and known were changed together.[7] The world was changed.

This is the idea of participatory knowledge. It seems to suit Quine's pragmatism about posits. To accommodate participatory knowledge, we would have to say that Quine's network and experience do not constitute some environment outside the knower. Knower and known are in the complex together—and Quine might agree to that. As R. C. Lewontin writes, organisms do not experience environments, they create them (Lewontin 1991, 109–10). And organisms are created in that reciprocal process. That follows from Quine's own effort to join epistemology and ontology.

The nature that natural scientists know is created in the process of knowing, and so are the scientists themselves. This is an old understanding that was put aside during the original scientific revolution. It is also a new understanding in social studies of science. Karen Knorr-Cetina (1999) writes that laboratories provide an "enhanced" environment that "improves upon" natural orders in relation to social orders. Laboratories presuppose that objects don't have to be taken "as they are." She goes on,

> There are at least three features of natural objects a laboratory science does not have to accommodate: first it does not need to put up with an object *as it is*, it can substitute transformed and partial versions. Second, it does not need to accommodate the natural object *where it is*, anchored in a natural environment; laboratory sciences bring objects 'home' and manipulate them on their own terms, in the laboratory. Third, a laboratory science need not accommodate an event *when it happens*; it can dispense with natural cycles. (Knorr-Cetina 1999, 27)

Knorr-Cetina goes on to write that scientists themselves are constructed as epistemic objects. She is giving an account of posits by reporting on how scientists construct natural objects, nature, and themselves in their pursuit of scientific knowledge. In fact, she offers an explanation of how the "physical objects" that Quine talks about as posits are explained through the processes of scientific positing. In the laboratory, the beings of nature are replaced by microorganisms, cell lines, strains of animals specially designed (142–45). Fruit flies become lab animals, through standardization, as do mice. The transformation takes place in the social sciences as well. Allan Pred commented on the "thingified, fragmented, and atomized" way of dealing with humans—humans regarded as producers, or as residents, or as perceivers of environment, or as consumers (Pred 1988, 7). If we rely on science, the beings of both nature and society become posits that are constructed in the practices of the sciences. Knorr-Cetina calls these sciences "epistemic cultures." Scientists participate in making themselves and their worlds, not just in observing them.

I've said several times that Quinean scientists exercise cognitive authority in providing knowledge of nature (conceived as Western science conceives it). This should be taken account of in interpreting posits and the participatory sort of knowledge that Western science yields. The Kongo picture has its four specialists—prophets, politicians, sorcerers, and healers. The world picture is quite different from the Western one, and so cognitive authority is granted differently. But it is cognitive authority all the same.

Expert knowledge is not all that is needed. In the Kongo picture, all people had knowledge through the rising and setting of their lives. It seems clear to me that not only did the herbalists and sorcerers and leaders have to know how to exercise their crafts, but the people as a whole had to know how to be healed and be led. The specialists and the people had to know how to create their environment collectively. This thought leads to a rather different perspective on knowledge and the language associated with knowledge. At the same time, it seems compatible with Quine's belief that the web that dips into experience is a continuous fabric, with mathematics and science at the center and everyday knowledge about physical objects at the periphery.

Could scientists acknowledge Quine's pragmatism in their practice? I'll close with a suggestion on reinterpreting the language of science in a way that could take account of science as being embodied in a living world that it helps create.

Sensitizing Quine's Net

Quine's effort at naturalized epistemology was a two-pronged effort to embody knowers as actors in making knowledge. According to the net metaphor, they were actively involved in weighing experience against theory and redistributing truth values. In naturalized epistemology they were actual scientists doing research that produced the account of the relations between knower and known—and so knowers were real, embodied knowers as well. How might the scientists of naturalized epistemology accommodate philosophical insights? I can't answer that because the answer must be discovered in practice, and the discovery (or invention!) requires an extensive social and political process of change. But I do have a suggestion that brings in some aspects of both the representational and the presentational use of symbols in science. It does so by taking the scientist as an embodied being who is a full participant in weighing experience, making posits, and redistributing truth values. It is the notion of sensitizing concepts, taken from interactionist sociology, which I'll extend to accommodate philosophical needs (see Addelson 1994).

Herbert Blumer developed the notion of sensitizing concepts to explain scientific language use in qualitative sociology, where researchers do small case studies, usually through participant observation and interview. The problem is to develop general theoretical constructs capturing interesting regularities among the case studies—examples of such constructs include *social problems*, *deviance*, *careers*, etc. Scientists here are *participant-observers*.[8] The empirical world under study is a process in which people interpret what they and others are doing—and they interpret what the scientists are doing as well, and change accordingly. This seems to capture something of Quine's net metaphor—it is a world continually remade and redescribed in interaction. Because of this, what Blumer called "definitive concepts" aren't suitable. "Definitive concepts" are those that have clear and fixed definitions and determinate references, to use Quine's language.

My philosophical interpretation is that the point of sensitizing concepts is to sensitize researchers (and eventually a more general group of knowers) to life processes in an ever changing world. Blumer writes that researchers "seem forced to reach what is common by accepting and using what is distinctive to the given empirical instance" (Blumer 1969, 148). They do so by a process of analogy, amplifying and extending meaning. One case is compared to others, and the understanding of concept and theory is enlarged. In this respect, the sociological language resembles the presentational. There is no rule that can tell the researcher how to go on, or how to classify the next case—an aspect that seems to capture

Quine's insight as well as Wittgenstein's. The embodied researcher, the trained researcher, is essential.

Understood in this way, scientific knowledge is not contained in theories, language, or textbooks and journal articles. I would say that knowledge is *embodied in sensitized people*. Knowledge (even knowledge in the sciences) is essentially something that people have and act upon. This seems plausible for the Kongo scheme, and it reduces the difference between their specialists' presentational use of symbol and the apparently representational use by our specialists.[9]

What is to be gained by taking the notion of sensitizing concepts seriously? I believe doing so would extend Quine's own beginnings in the net metaphor. He rejected the old, representational use of scientific (or ordinary) language because it seemed to require determinate reference. But he left us without a plausible understanding of scientific language and concepts. Weighing incoming experience against theory may be best understood as a move in the dynamic process of sensitizing researchers to both theory and experience—and so changing both.

Scientists and other "trained experts" also sensitize others to their theories and concepts that explain the world and guide action. They do this through the many ways of exercising their cognitive authority, through the educational systems, through the media, and so on. They exercise cognitive authority in contributing to decision-making, but this vast, institutionalized means of sensitizing ordinary folk is more powerful.

Because of all this, it is important that we must ask *who it is* that is sensitized, how they are sensitized, and within what range of experience. *Quine does not raise those questions, despite the fact that he takes knowers as agents in making knowledge*. If knowers are embodied, we must ask about their embodiment. Doing so immediately raises issues of cognitive authority and of gender, race, culture, class, and so on. It doesn't answer those questions, but it does open the door by providing a philosophical and theoretical justification for raising the questions out of Quine's own work. In the decades since Quine conceived the net metaphor, these questions have been raised and answers have been proposed many times—within feminist philosophy and elsewhere. If scientists understood themselves as developing and using sensitizing concepts, then the dynamic process of change could begin. And we might be able to reconcile Quine's pragmatism with his naturalized epistemology.

Notes

1. Except in quantum mechanics and the softer reaches of psychology, observation does not change the reality or its observer.

2. My discussion in this section relies heavily on conversations and correspondence with Ernest Wamba-dia-Wamba through the early 1990s. All quoted material comes from these sources. He has an article on the topic in Selin (1997), which post-dates my conversations with him.

3. It was also the primary use among alchemists and astrologers, and the impulse toward literal language and discursive knowledge that began as a seed among late 17th century fathers of science was in part prompted by their need to distinguish themselves from alchemists—and humanists. Hunt (1989) has a very interesting discussion of dreams.

4. I have my own example as well. Sullivan once wrote that in the late quartets, Beethoven solved the problem of evil (Sullivan 1942). I agree that he did.

5. There is, of course, a problem here because the old Kongo language was not a written language. Using Ernest Wamba-dia-Wamba's representation in English raises problems of its own for Quine. Since I believe Quine's way with translation is wrongheaded, I won't discuss these problems, except to offer a resolution in the idea of translation for a dissenting epistemology.

6. There are other example of the difference that would require longer explanations. For example, if an individual person of a classic Kongo community fell ill (in Western terms), it might have been necessary for the healer to heal the family, or the lineage, or even the community. Or it might have been necessary to call in a sorcerer as well, to bring in knowledge from the underworld. Family therapy heals families, it is true, but the families healed are composed of Western individuals in specific relations to one another.

7. See discussions in Berman (1981) concerning participatory knowledge among alchemists.

8. Given my remarks on participatory knowledge above, social scientists also change themselves and the worlds they study and theorize about. Many of them would agree that this is the case, but the ideology of science that supports their cognitive authority holds otherwise.

9. I believe this way of looking at things is the best interpretation of Thomas Kuhn's discussion of paradigms in the work of natural scientists. In *The Structure of Scientific Revolutions* (1970), at least, his perspective offers a strong argument for saying it is collectives, not individuals, who know. Researchers know how to approach a research situation because they have been trained and sensitized under a paradigm. "Paradigms" are poorly represented as sets of propositions or sentences, and it is only archaic methods that might lead scholars to represent them that way. Paradigms are better represented as practices—or as collective ways of knowing/doing. The fact that scholarly (including scientific) research is written up for journals, talked through at conferences, and embalmed in textbooks does not mean that scientific knowledge is essentially discursive knowledge, either in the social or the natural sciences. As with Wittgenstein's "language games," the sensitized scientist working under a paradigm *knows how* to go on.

References

Addelson, Kathryn. 1991. *Impure Thoughts: Essays in Philosophy, Feminism, and Ethics*. Philadelphia: Temple University Press.

———. 1992. "Knower-Doers and their Moral Problems." In *Feminist Epistemologies*, ed. L. Alcoff and E. Potter. New York: Routledge.

———. 1994. *Moral Passages: Toward a Collectivist Moral Theory*. New York: Routledge.

Alcoff, Linda Martín, and Elizabeth Potter, eds. 1992. *Feminist Epistemologies*. New York: Routledge.

Becker, Howard S. 1970. *Sociological Work: Method and Substance*. Chicago: Aldine.

———. 1973. *Outsiders*. New York: The Free Press.

Berman, Morris. 1981. *The Reinchantment of the World*. Ithaca: Cornell University Press.

Blumer, Herbert. 1969. *Symbolic Interactionism: Perspective and Method*. Englewood Cliffs, N.J.: Prentice Hall.

———. 1971. "Social Problems as Collective Behavior." *Social Problems* 18 (Winter): 298–306.

Bockie, Simon. 1993. *Death and the Invisible Powers: The World of Kongo Belief*. Bloomington: Indiana University Press.

Conrad, Peter, and Joseph Schneider. 1980. *Deviance and Medicalization: From Badness to Sickness*. St. Louis: C. V. Mosby Co.

Davidson, Donald. 1974. "On the Very Idea of a Conceptual Scheme." *Proceedings and Addresses of the American Philosophical Association* 47.

Dijksterhuis, E. J. 1961. *The Mechanization of the World Picture*. Oxford: Clarendon Press.

Fonow, Mary Margaret, and Judith Cook. 1991. *Beyond Methodology: Feminist Scholarship as Lived Research*. Bloomington: Indiana University Press.

Glaser, Barney, and Anselm Strauss. 1967. *The Discovery of Grounded Theory: Strategies for Qualitative Research*. Chicago: Aldine Publishing Co.

Goffman, Erving. 1961. *Asylums: Essays on the Social Situation of Mental Patients and Other Inmates*. Garden City, N.Y.: Doubleday.

Greenwood, John. 1991. *The Future of Folk Psychology: Intentionality and Cognitive Science*. Cambridge: Cambridge University Press.

Gusfield, Joseph. 1981. *The Culture of Public Problems: Drinking, Driving, and the Symbolic Order*. Chicago: University of Chicago Press.

Hunt, Harry T. 1989. *The Multiplicity of Dreams: Memory, Imagination, and Consciousness*. New Haven: Yale University Press.

Kim, Jaegwon. 1994. "What Is 'Naturalized Epistemology'?" In *Naturalizing Epistemology*, 2d rev. ed., ed. H. Kornblith. Cambridge: MIT Press.

Knorr-Cetina, Karin. 1999. *Epistemic Cultures: How the Sciences Make Knowledge*. Cambridge, Mass.: Harvard University Press.

Kornblith, Hilary, ed. 1985. *Naturalizing Epistemology*. 1st ed. Cambridge: MIT Press.

———. 1994. *Naturalizing Epistemology*. 2d rev. ed. Cambridge: MIT Press.

Kuhn, Thomas. 1970. *The Structure of Scientific Revolutions*. Chicago: University of Chicago Press.

Langer, Susan K. 1942. *Philosophy in a New Key: A Study in the Symbolism of Reason, Rite, and Art*. Cambridge, Mass.: Harvard University Press.

Levins, R., and R. C. Lewontin. 1985. *The Dialectical Biologist*. Cambridge, Mass.: Harvard University Press.

Lewontin, R. C. 1992. *Biology as Ideology*. New York: Harper Perennial.

Merchant, Carolyn. 1989. *The Death of Nature: Women, Ecology, and the Scientific Revolution*. San Francisco: Harper.

Nelson, Lynn Hankinson. 1990. *Who Knows: From Quine to a Feminist Empiricism*. Philadelphia: Temple University Press.

———. 1992. "Epistemological Communities." In *Feminist Epistemologies*, ed. L. Alcoff and E. Potter. New York: Routledge.

Pred, Allan. 1986. *Place, Practice, and Structure*. Cambridge: Polity Press.

Quine, W. V. 1960. *Word and Object*. Cambridge: MIT Press.

———. 1963. *From a Logical Point of View*, 2d rev. ed. New York: Harper and Row.

———. 1969. *Ontological Relativity and Other Essays*. New York: Columbia. University Press.

———. 1981. *Theories and Things*. Cambridge, Mass.: Harvard University Press.

Selin, Helaine. 1997. *The Encyclopedia of the History of Science, Technology, and Medicine in Non-Western Cultures*. Boston: Kluwer Academic Publishers.

Stich, Stephen. 1990. *The Fragmentation of Reason: Preface to a Pragmatic Theory of Cognitive Evaluation*. Cambridge: MIT Press.

Strauss, Anselm. 1987. *Qualitative Analysis for Social Scientists*. Cambridge: Cambridge University Press.

Strauss, Anselm, and Berenice Fischer. 1978. "Interactionism." In *A History of Sociological Analysis*, ed. T. Bottomore and R. Nesbit. New York: Basic Books.

Sullivan, J. W. N. 1958. *Beethoven: His Spiritual Development*. New York: Alfred Knopf.

Part III

Explications, Expansions, and Revisions of Quinean Positions

7

Feminism and Naturalism: If Asked for Theories, Just Say 'No'

Paul A. Roth

Men make their own history, but they do not make it just as they please; they do not make it under circumstances chosen by themselves, but under circumstances directly encountered, given, and transmitted from the past. The tradition of all the dead generations weighs like a nightmare on the brain of the living. And just when they seem engaged in revolutionizing themselves and things, in creating something that has never yet existed, precisely in such periods of revolutionary crisis they anxiously conjure up the spirits of the past to their service . . . in order to present the new scene of world history in this time-honored disguise and this borrowed language.

—Karl Marx, "The Eighteenth Brumaire of Louis Bonaparte"

Ah, the 1960s. Revolution everywhere. Indeed, the publication within that decade of *The Structure of Scientific Revolutions* and "Epistemology Naturalized" toppled a philosophical Bastille, overthrowing the *ancien régime* within philosophy generally and within the philosophy of science in particular. For the Quinean and Kuhnian turn in science studies signals

This paper incorporates much of a previously published paper, "The Epistemology of 'Epistemology Naturalized,'" *Dialectica* 53: 87–109. My thanks to Bob Barrett, Larry Davis, Richard Feldman, Jim Maffie, Peter Markie, Lynn Hankinson Nelson, Alex Rosenberg, Tom Ryckman, and Eleonore Stump for helpful criticisms.

the recognition that nothing but our artifices—not the world, not logic—undergird the cognitive authority of science.

But revolution is never easy. A new order must be legitimated—no simple matter. Shortcuts beckon. The rhetoric of the old regime has the virtue of familiarity. But, as Marx warns, the easy path just leads us back to repudiated practices and institutions. Indeed, the Quinean/Kuhnian turn in philosophy of science, once so promising, stands stalled, locked in a "legitimation crisis," an internal struggle regarding how to justify its own explanatory practices. Legitimation of claims to cognitive authority, like claims in the political sphere, comes most easily when its sources are seen as suprahuman—what the facts dictate or logic compels.

The revolution falters, in other words, because despite their having made a compelling case for taking the naturalizing/historicizing turn, many feminist and naturalist philosophers of science still "anxiously conjure up the spirits of the past to their service." They summon those very spirits the revolution seemingly laid to rest—progress, rationality, objectivity, and truth. Thus, one finds feminists recoiling from charges of relativism, naturalists insisting that they too have real epistemic norms, and everyone paying homage to the constraints that, of course, 'reality' exerts.[1] The revolution cannot have it both ways. The old forms of legitimation cannot coexist consistent with the Kuhnian and Quinean reasons for their delegitimation. A feminist philosophy of science will be best served—its agenda of reform forwarded—by freeing itself from any need of or nostalgia for special philosophical justification.

No small part of the problem here rests, I suggest, with the lack of consensus regarding either the meaning of 'naturalism' or the reading of Quine's now canonical essay. For while "Epistemology Naturalized" unquestionably excited a widespread revival of interest in naturalism, the status accorded the essay is ironic. One finds both friends and foes of philosophical naturalism denying that Quine does establish that the methods of naturalism can accommodate the problems of epistemology.

Diagnoses of the problems vary. Critics insist that a Quinean naturalism either cannot provide norms and so cannot be epistemology (Kim 1988), cannot legitimate its own basic presuppositions and procedures and so is essentially incomplete as an epistemology (Putnam 1982; van Fraassen 1995), or is just armchair speculation and so not interestingly different from the epistemological projects Quine rejects (Foley 1994). Self-described friends of naturalism (Goldman 1986; Haack 1993b) are equally uneasy, for they too doubt that Quine can successfully incorporate the substance of epistemology within the limits of his naturalism.

Is naturalized epistemology epistemology enough? Skepticism here is, I maintain, symptomatic of a pervasive misreading of the main line of argument of "Epistemology Naturalized." Consequently, its moral regarding naturalism remains misunderstood. This misunderstanding, in turn, encourages confusion or vagueness regarding what naturalism is and its sufficiency for the tasks of epistemology.[2]

Section I develops a characterization of philosophical theories generally and naturalist theories in particular. In the sense of "philosophical theory" discussed, naturalism does not constitute, I argue, a philosophical theory. Section II details an interpretation that challenges readings of Quine that construe his naturalism as a type of philosophical theory. My reading renders nugatory problems commonly attributed to Quine's naturalism. Seen aright, Quine's naturalism indeed radically reconceives the epistemological enterprise, but the reconception differs from that which has previously been emphasized. Section III examines how some recent efforts in feminist and naturalist philosophy of science lose their way by failing to be naturalist enough.

I

Bertrand Russell's theory of descriptions is, as Frank Ramsey famously observed, a paradigm of philosophy. The history of analytic philosophy subsequent to the publication of "On Denoting" proves Ramsey right. To anachronistically read Ramsey's remark as a Kuhnian might, Russell's analysis of "The present King of France is bald" or "George IV wished to know whether Scott was the author of Waverley" is paradigmatic in two distinct senses. One is as a problem-solving model. It greatly simplified the assumptions needed to analyze some standard "hard cases."

Yet Russell's analysis is also paradigmatic of a type of philosophical theorizing. For Russell has a philosophical theory of meaning of which the theory of descriptions is but a part. Meaning here becomes a function of a language possessing a particular logical structure, a structure revealed by proper analysis. This theory of meaning is not itself part of any natural science, but presupposes problematic philosophical views regarding "knowledge by acquaintance" and "knowledge by description." The Russellian paradigm reminds us of how a wrong-headed philosophical theory may lurk just below the surface of elegant and seemingly metaphysically pristine formal analyses.

Another important instance of how a logical analysis may overlie a contentious philosophical theory is the verifiability theory of meaning. It merits the title of a "philosophical theory" just because it too purported to explain, without the aid of science, why science works well when it works well.

My aim here is not to offer any general criteria for designating theories as philosophical, but only to note some features that can make them such, features I will later contend characterize (some) work in feminist philosophy of science. Primary among these features is that neither the theory of descriptions nor the verifiability criterion theory of meaning could be falsified by experience. Failure to solve conceptual puzzles represents a difficulty, not disconfirmation. In addition, as is notoriously the case in the various formulations of the principle of verifiability, the demarcation criteria kept coming out wrong. Various schemas invariably excluded from the realm of meaningful statements in science some sentences even positivists wanted to keep. *But the sundry shortcomings only whetted their philosophical appetite, inasmuch as the theories were held for reasons experiments could not touch, e.g., assumptions about the possible sources of human knowledge, the deep structure of natural language, and the requirements of cognitive significance.*

It is important to remember what separates the approach of a Russell and especially a Carnap from those of their empiricist and rationalist predecessors. It is their positive proposal to actually reconstruct the link between existing scientific theories and their empirical base. Somewhat ironically, what we owe to the decades of intensive work especially by Carnap is a deep appreciation of how resistant scientific theorizing is to this specification of its inferential relation to evidence.

This explicitly constructive aspect of the logical positivist project comes finally to define what empiricism is in the twentieth century.[3] "Rational reconstruction," Carnap writes, attempts "for the first time, the actual formulation of a conceptual system of the indicated sort" (Carnap 1967, vi),[4] i.e., our system of knowledge. Reconstruction would be proof positive of long-standing empiricist claims regarding what the "deconstruction" of empirical knowledge must yield. Rational reconstruction would have established the objectivity and rationality of scientific knowledge to anyone's satisfaction.

This defining characteristic of logical positivist epistemological theories is doubly philosophical. On the one hand, it is not tested via experiment; reconstruction is just an exercise in logical imagination. On the other hand, reconstruction provides the justificatory basis, in the best understood sense of that term—a formal logical derivation—of theoretical claims. Logical reconstruction is then a paradigm philosophical claim, a "first philosophy" that is prior to scientific knowledge.

Naturalism is *not* a philosophical theory of knowledge, at least in the senses outlined above. Some, to be sure, have tried to make it so. Naturalism in epistemology can be characterized negatively by its eschewal of any notions of analytic or a priori truths. Positively, naturalism asserts a normative and methodological continuity between epistemological and scientific inquiry.[5] The techniques endemic to the former are only a subset of the historically received and contingently held norms and methods of the latter.

So characterized, naturalism is frequently the object of two complaints. The first finds the positive characterization too vague to be of any use. Bas Van Fraassen, for example, remarks that "[t]o identify what naturalism is . . . I have found nigh-impossible" (van Fraassen 1996, 172). The second suggests that naturalism's link to scientific method precludes naturalism from fulfilling epistemology's normative role. In this version of the Humean is/ought paradigm, science describes, norms prescribe. Hence the latter cannot be derived from the former. Since naturalism has only descriptive scientific methods at its disposal, this forecloses the possibility of its justifying epistemic norms.

How vague is the notion of naturalism? No more vague, I suggest, than our ability to catalog the methods of science. Naturalism, moreover, does not yoke what counts as science to some philosophical characterization. It is ironic, then, to find philosophers such as van Fraassen making continued references to "science," as if they knew exactly what that means, and yet complaining all the while about the vagueness of naturalism.

What counts as a scientific method for naturalists is not itself limited to or defined by one particular science, or driven by a prior philosophical characterization of such. For Quine, as for American naturalists historically, the methods of science include the full panoply of procedures employed in fact-driven research programs in any area of inquiry.

The second complaint above rests on what I term the "naturalist's dilemma." For a naturalist, if philosophy does not utilize the methods of science, then it has no place on the roster of legitimate forms of inquiry. So philosophy could not contribute to a (naturalized) account of knowledge and justification. If it does employ such methods, then one or both of the following problems would seem to obtain. Either epistemological inquiry will be question-begging—it will evaluate the methods and results of inquiry by using some of those very methods or results—or impossible, since one cannot derive epistemologically prescriptive conclusions from empirical (descriptive) inquiry.[6]

Naturalists such as Quine subscribe to what I term "methodological monism."[7] What marks questions as epistemological for Quine is that they are about the processes sustaining and generating scientific beliefs. But he views such questions neither as receiving some distinctively philosophical answer nor as pursued by some special philosophical method.[8]

Three recent efforts to map systematically the peaks and divides within epistemological naturalism—James Maffie (1990), Phillip Kitcher (1992), and Hilary Kornblith (1994)—all situate Quine as a key point of contrast within the spectrum of naturalisms. Maffie offers the historically most comprehensive and philosophically sophisticated classification scheme of the three. But, even within his nuanced philosophical topology, the most basic divide—and the one of interest here—is between what he terms, on the one hand, "limited" and, on the other hand, "unlimited" naturalists. (Maffie 1990, 287ff.) Kitcher signals the split that concerns me by speaking of a distinction between "traditional" and "radical" naturalists (Kitcher 1992, 74ff., but especially 75). Kornblith develops a distinction between what he terms the "weak" versus the "strong" replacement theses (the replacement in question being the replacement of traditional epistemology by some form of psychology). In each case, the first-named category marks a space for those who hold that one can be both a naturalist and retain some separate role for epistemology—methodological dualism. The second category for each, however, marks those who do not conceive of any divide between philosophical and scientific method—methodological monism. All locate Quine in the latter category.[9]

Maffie's way of dividing the territory turns on whether or not one endorses full methodological continuity between epistemology and natural science. "Unlimited naturalism" tries to "fit epistemology into science" and so naturalizes epistemology "all the way up," inclusive of meta-epistemological issues (Maffie 1990, 287). In contrast, "limited naturalism" fits "science into epistemology" (288). Citing Alvin Goldman's work (through *Epistemology and Cognition*) as paradigmatic, Maffie contends that a limited naturalism holds that scientific methods do not play a role in practices such as explicating the meaning of epistemic terms or identifying the correct epistemological norms.[10]

Kornblith speaks, in this regard, of the "replacement thesis" (Kornblith

1994, 4)—the preemption or displacement of epistemological questions by psychological ones. Replacement may be strong or weak. Strong replacement opts for a description of the causal history of belief formation. Kornblith reads Quine as arguing for strong replacement: "psychological questions hold all the content there is in epistemological questions. In this view psychology replaces epistemology in much the same way that chemistry has replaced alchemy" (7). With weak replacement, however, the fields are thought to complement rather than preempt one another's areas of inquiry. In this regard, Kornblith holds that psychology and epistemology each ask different questions and "these questions are approached with different methodologies" (Kornblith 1994, 8). Weak replacement, unlike strong, preserves the autonomy of epistemology.

Kornblith does not indicate here in what "special method" the autonomy of epistemology consists that distinguishes it from the special sciences.[11] He rejects full-blown psychologism because it does not offer the desired transition from descriptions of belief-forming processes to epistemological advice giving. He plumps instead for a more moderate view, which he terms "ballpark psychologism" (10–11). What puts psychology and epistemology in the same ballpark is the antiskeptical assumption that we now do know a great many things (10–11). This antiskepticism implies that at least some of the processes actually used to form beliefs are ones we ought to be using. Reliabilist friends of weak replacement would envision epistemologists identifying what the truth-making features of processes are, while psychologists could investigate actual processes to learn whether or not they possess the desired qualities (7).

For Kitcher, the defining features of naturalism are, first, the resuscitation of psychology (and possibly biology) as relevant to epistemological analysis and, second, the denial of the legitimacy of claims to a priori knowledge. The primary point of philosophic contrast here, i.e., the positions taken to be paradigmatically non-naturalist, are the avowedly antipsychologist view of analysis championed by Gottlob Frege and the notably apsychologistic views of the early Wittgenstein (Kitcher 1992, 59).

While Maffie provides a careful schema that sorts and categorizes the wide variation of positions labeled as forms of naturalism, Kitcher sweepingly surveys the rise of a contemporary (post-Quinean, post-Kuhnian) variant. Like Maffie, Kitcher's positive characterization of naturalism emphasizes a methodological continuity between epistemology and natural science. But for Kitcher, what separates "conservative" or "traditional" naturalists from the more "radical" sort is that the former, but not the latter, believe that there are some perduring goals and strategies of scientific inquiry, however corrigible particular formulations turn out to be. Naturalism, conservatively construed, attempts "to fulfill traditional normative functions," while radical naturalism sees "in the collapse of apriorism the demise of any possibility for normative appraisals (or, at least, the need for relativizing any such appraisals to specific, local context)" (Kitcher 1992, 58).[12] For Kitcher, what separates traditional from radical naturalism is not just, as for Maffie, an issue regarding the continuity of methods, but also a concern regarding the nonrelativized character of the principles that naturalized inquiry seeks to uncovers.[13]

With regard to the traditional normative project of epistemology, Kitcher maintains that naturalists are primarily bent on improving epistemic performance. He terms this the "meliorative project." Its primary purpose "is to identify processes that are externally ideal" (Kitcher 1992, 66). Here, Kitcher's exemplar of a meliorative project within the bounds of naturalism is (again) Goldman's reliabilism (See Kitcher 1992, esp. sections 2 and 3). The twist here is that while Kitcher considers reliabilism "appropriate for the context of methodological improvement," he suggests that it is less clear how it applies to some other traditional normative concerns, e.g., "the context of epistemic appraisal" (Kitcher 1992, 68).

The relevance of reliabilism under Kitcher's interpretation to the meliorative project is straightforward. Stable standards allow for clear-cut advice on how to enhance epistemic performance. Appraisal, however, is more psychologically complex and multifaceted. The distinction reflects the differences between getting the right answer and getting the right answer for only the right reasons. Whether one has come to an answer in the "right" way is an issue, Kitcher suggests, best left to psychologists. Epistemologists can profitably separate themselves from such questions. As Kitcher notes, "the philosophical dichotomies rational/irrational and justified/unjustified may stand in need of replacement rather than analysis. . . . [D]ebate about whether the failure to undergo the epistemically optimal process is excusable or not can profitably be sidestepped in favor of a psychologically richer explanation of what occurred" (68). A consequence is that a naturalistic version of the meliorative project might fail to yield an analysis of, for example, justification.

Kitcher, then, while praising Goldman for promoting the epistemological relevance of psychology and other sciences, also notes two persistent anti-naturalist facets to Goldman's thought—an adherence to methodological dualism (natural science versus conceptual analysis) and a related concern with accomplishing more than just the meliorative project. Like Maffie, Kitcher questions Goldman's reluctance to fully naturalize his approach (69 n. 46).

However, it is unclear from Kitcher's remarks whether or not he opposes methodological dualism in any form. For some passages suggest that Kitcher himself conceives of philosophy as offering legitimate, non-naturalist methods. "Traditional naturalists ought to concede that there is a legitimate activity of using the arsenal of philosophical techniques (appealing to formal logic or probability theory, say) to articulate ideas about knowledge. The development of an account of epistemic value might well draw on such resources" (78). Unlike Goldman, however, Kitcher acknowledges that we stipulate what our epistemic values are. Thus, the dualism at issue in Kitcher's case concerns issues such as whether to count logic as a science, or as something else. The question here is what Kitcher, *qua* traditional naturalist, wants to say about how we come to knowledge outside the scope of science or, alternatively, how we define 'science.'

Another important problem with Kitcher's proposed way of differentiating radical and traditional naturalism concerns his attributing the meliorative project to the latter and denying it to the former. Kitcher, as do the others, views Quinean naturalization as effectively abandoning epistemology. "Radical naturalism thus abandons the meliorative venture . . . , letting epistemology fall into place as chapters of psychology, sociology, history of science" (96). Yet the "proof" that a view or method is actually reliable (and so genuinely meliorative) depends, in large part, on its historical record. Traditional naturalists, Kitcher believes, can counter the threat of "radically" relativizing epistemic standards by appealing to an emergent consensus in historically difficult cases (97–98). In other words, if a naturalist wants an epistemology that does more than relativize epistemic norms to received science, the historical record must be read so as to show that consensus emerges in the sciences due to certain stable principles guiding scientific investigation.

According to this account, radical naturalists are pessimists regarding stability; defenders of an optimistic version of traditional naturalism such as Goldman, Laudan, or Kitcher expect the discovery of stable principles that will improve epistemic performance. As Kitcher remarks, "[n]aturalism offers the optimistic picture of a particular type of organism, beginning with rudimentary representations of nature . . . and gradually replacing these with cognitively superior representations and strategies" (90).

This optimism is important, for it appears to be all that separates at any given time a Kitcher-type epistemological naturalism from the more radical varieties. Radical naturalism imagines that the best we can ever do is relativize epistemic norms to received science. However, Kitcher maintains that what would make naturalism genuinely meliorative (and so not radical) is if an account of science can be provided that shows that science allows us to possess "unambiguous possibilities of continual correction." These "unambiguous possibilities" would make the history of science something more than "a random walk" across time (93; see also 100). Indeed, only this optimism links naturalism to traditional epistemology: "whether naturalism allows any way to save the traditional meliorative project of epistemology" requires "the possibility of our sustaining the reliability of the historical process through which knowledge has emerged, given a naturalistic perspective" (113).

But is the difference between "radical" and "traditional" naturalism, as Kitcher labors to draw it, a difference that makes a difference? For what would distinguish the counsel given by a traditional as opposed to a radical naturalist? As Kitcher concedes, "[w]e hope, but cannot demonstrate, that the system of predicates we actually use will lead to success in the actual world" (88). The traditionalist possesses no epistemic wisdom that the radical lacks. The distinguishing feature would be the hope the traditionalist has that history will forever sanction the advice, for only that sanction makes it genuinely meliorative.

What traditional as opposed to radical naturalism achieves is not found anywhere in the present, but only in the future. "The ultimate goal of (traditional naturalistic) epistemology is to present a compendium of cognitively optimal processes for all those contexts in which human subjects find themselves" (76).[14] That is, in this view of what the meliorative project comes to, it remains incomplete until such time that we know that the processes in hand are optimal for all possible experiences of which we are capable.

So-called naturalist positions such as Kitcher's that promise more by way of normative edification than does Quine invariably turn out to fail to justify such normative claims naturalistically (or at all). As Miriam Solomon quite properly notes with regard to Kitcher's pseudo-naturalism—a position she dubs "Legend Naturalism"—his "naturalism does no work—no data or theories from psychology or sociology shape the epistemic account—the naturalism is just window-dressing for a previously and independently developed account of scientific rationality" (Solomon 1995, 207).[15]

A further problem is that what Kitcher advocates is, for all intents and purposes, a type of Kantianism naturalized. He hopes that the historical long run reveals what transcendental philosophy did not, viz., the perduring structure and operation of human cognitive capacities and the limits of inferences to be drawn about the world from experience. "The goal of pure inquiry is to produce a structured account of nature insofar as that is possible for limited beings like ourselves" (Kitcher 1992, 107).[16] Thus, Kitcher transforms traditional naturalism into a surrogate for the very type of a priori project the rejection of which he invoked when initially defining 'naturalism.'[17] Kitcher's nod toward taking into account social factors, for example, obscures the fact that all that separates "radical" from "traditional" naturalists is the latter's belief that it is our cognitive manifest destiny to get things right. But why naturalism, in order to be meliorative, must insist that history provides what transcendental philosophy did not, Kitcher nowhere explains.[18]

All three of the overviews just considered distinguish, in any case, radical naturalists such as Quine from moderates such as Goldman by the contention that a Quinean "radical naturalism" is somehow incompatible with normative concerns. In order to provide normative judgments, all agree that epistemology must at least have the resources to evaluate "the fitness of cognitive behavior" (Maffie 1990, 286) relative to truth. Maffie articulates a now common view when he maintains that Quine cannot accommodate normativity because by "integrating epistemology into science" a Quinean view "seems to leave us with no resources for making cognitively significant normative judgments" (285). Psychology provides only a list of processes we do, in fact, possess. But no description of processes or other natural properties tell us what norms to value. The received wisdom, in short, has Quine advocating the supersession of epistemology by a descriptive subject, psychology. There no longer is normative epistemology as we once thought we knew it.[19]

In sum, then, Quinean naturalism is not a philosophical theory in the previously specified pejorative sense of that term. It is empirical through and through, from its conception of logic to its conception of methods to what even to count as science. Quinean naturalism is untainted by prior philosophical commitments to reduction or to a hierarchy of sciences. No area of belief stands aloof from alteration or emendation in light of experience. Even the preference for naturalism itself is evidence-driven. Should some approaches other than those the sciences offer prove more efficacious in furthering our goals, the commitment to naturalism itself would then be jettisoned. There is no more vagueness to the notion of what naturalism is than there is to what the methods of the sciences themselves are. There is no more an obstacle to examining, emending, or excluding norms within a naturalistic approach than there is in any self-critical scientific approach. Which is to say, there is none at all.[20]

II

The preceding suggests that disputes about naturalized epistemology focus less on what it is for an epistemology to be naturalized than on what qualifies a naturalistic approach as epistemology. The substance of Quine's naturalism derives from his account of the "methods of science." Understood in this way, any case for Quine's naturalism must answer three critical challenges. It must first identify what science is and its methods are, and second provide good reasons for preferring these to other modes of inquiry. Finally, the argument must establish that these methods actually suffice for the prescriptive purposes of epistemology.

Criticism to date of Quine's naturalism focuses primarily on the last mentioned issue, with occasional allusion to the second. This fosters the illusion that the details of how Quine conceives of science are unproblematic or consistent with the answers imputed to Quine regarding the latter two challenges. In addition, a pervasive misreading of Quine's response to the second challenge results in the charge that Quine rejects the "doxastic assumption," i.e., that he wrongly tries to replace epistemology's normative/evaluative concerns with a causal/genetic enterprise. I propose a way to construe his responses to all three challenges so as to provide a cogent and coherent account of the hows and whys of naturalizing epistemology.

In my reading of "Epistemology Naturalized," that essay offers neither an argument for the naturalization of epistemology based upon some particular argument against foundationalism nor does it plump for some particular conception of science. Rather, Quine takes for granted that the history of post-Humean empiricism leads to holism. Consequently, questions about the justification of claims to *empirical* knowledge must be adjudicated intra-theoretically. *In other words, "Epistemology Naturalized" explicates the consequences of naturalizing epistemology for those prepared, for Quine's reasons or others, to take Quine's "holistic turn."*

The assumed question to which "Epistemology Naturalized" is to be the answer is: What becomes of empiricist epistemology if it is assumed that, working from within our current system of beliefs, we take 'science' as our best source of justification for beliefs about the world? What becomes of epistemology within those constraining assumptions? Quine's answer, I contend, is that the fate of empirical knowledge is no worse off in this (epistemological) regard than that of mathematical knowledge given the incompleteness theorems. The primary argument of the essay, in my reading, is to establish and defend this parallel. The consequence is the same for each as well: the epistemological limitations influence which problems to pursue and how best to pursue them.

Quine explicitly parallels foundational questions in epistemology with foundational studies in mathematics. "But still the success achieved in the foundations of mathematics remains exemplary by comparative standards, and we can illuminate the rest of epistemology somewhat by drawing parallels to this department" (Quine 1969, 69). The parallels, then, between the two forms of inquiry are to "illuminate" what Quine wants to say about epistemology. Yet it is precisely the nature of these parallels, and the critical role it plays in the argument given in "Epistemology Naturalized," that has been wholly ignored in efforts to ascertain and evaluate Quine's position. This distorts the focus of his argument in general, and of his position regarding naturalism in particular.[21]

Both foundational projects have two aspects: the conceptual and the doctrinal. Conceptual matters are semantic, concerning definition or explication (69). Doctrinal issues concern issues of justification and formal priority (69–70). Ideally, the definitions would generate all the concepts from clear and distinct ideas, and the proofs would generate all the theorems from these self-evident truths (70).

This suggests that the intended parallel to the foundational project in science is the logicist program for having a consistent, fully axiomatized, and complete set of rules adequate to all of mathematics. The parallel implies a concern with developing a consistent and complete system for evaluating all empirical knowledge claims (71).[22] Take sense impressions, and then either explicate or derive all statements about the external world. This formula, if successful, would have provided an analysis, in the best understood sense of the term, of the entire range of truths about the world.

Notice that rational reconstruction is just a method. *Qua* method, rational reconstruction has two aspects: one procedural, one normative. Procedurally, the question is what methods and evidence suffice to reconstruct all that the sciences teach us is true. Normatively, the question is what makes any such reconstruction rational, in a philosophically relevant sense. Philosophical foundationalists look for answers to both questions that hold the sciences to stricter standards than the sciences as we now find them hold themselves.

Yet the project of providing foundations for science discovers that it too is subject to forms of incompleteness, paralleling the fate of the logicist project in mathematics. Indeed, distinctive forms of incompleteness attend the doctrinal and the conceptual aspects of this model as an epistemological program in the foundations of science. On the doctrinal side, the project stumbles on Hume's problem—the simplest generalizations from experience outrun our evidence for them. Hence derivation of laws of science proves impossible (74).

The problem on the conceptual side is not quite as neat or accepted as that on the doctrinal. The principle difficulty on the conceptual side—the incompleteness of any explicatory project—turns on the fact that the relation of theoretical sentences and supporting evidence is never as it needs to be in order to make the desired translation possible (78–79). In short, holistic considerations regarding the language-evidence relation foreclose the possibility of an explication of the term-by-term sort that the foundational project requires.[23] Thus, there are two irremediable forms of incompleteness. Neither laws nor concepts can be justified as hoped. This forecloses the possibility of providing within empiricism a philosophical foundation for science.

But why is this a reason to prefer the methods of science? Quine's response is to suggest that the next best set of methodological norms are those that science itself offers. "To relax the demand for definition, and settle for a kind of reduction that does not eliminate, is to renounce the last remaining advantage that we supposed rational reconstruction to have over straight psychology; namely the advantage of translational reduction" (70). Yet Quine's response may appear both to assert dogmatically a preference for science and to shift illicitly the nature of the epistemological project to causal/genetic concerns.

The "suppressed" premise in the argument from the failure of foundationalism to the conclusion that we can do no better by way of justification than science self-applied is what I shall refer to as Quine's epistemic "scalar hypothesis." The "scale" here is one of degrees of strength of justification, with formal derivation constituting the strongest end of the scale. The hypothesis is that no standards lie between formal deduction and the more assorted methods of various sciences, i.e., that we can do no better than scientists do with regard to validating our beliefs.[24] Although a hypothesis about norms, it itself is based on observation and open to refutation by new facts, and so naturalistic.

Quine starts, in other words, with what are generally taken to be instances of knowledge—mathematics and natural science. He then asks, following the logicist lead, for a consistent and complete system for explicating and deriving these putative truths. Incompleteness does not motivate Quine to abandon the view that these are "best case" instances of what to take as knowledge. Rather, incompleteness forces Quine to settle for the next step down on the epistemic scale of justification.[25] This shift signals a lack of extrascientific means both for the reconstruction of scientific truths and for certifying what reconstructions count as rational.

Emphasis on the parallel between foundational studies in mathematics and those in science makes explicit how incompleteness in both cases shifts the norms for justification to the next best set of practices available. In logic this involves, for example, assessing the properties of different possible axiomatizations. In the case of empirical knowledge, the norms shift from those represented by explication and derivation to those embedded in the practice of science. *Foregoing foundationalism changes the understanding of the "best available epistemological standard."*

Making explicit the role of the "scalar hypothesis" in the argument for naturalizing epistemology permits identification of the source of epistemic norms, of the reason for their adoption, and of the conditions under which they might be subject to change. For insofar as the notion of what comprises science is not static but dynamic, so too will be the standards deemed appropriate or scientific. Quine is, as Kitcher charged, a "radical" naturalist. The third challenge too is met since, *ex hypothesi*, the methods of science circumscribe the bounds of knowledge.

But the criticism can be made that to claim that epistemology is concerned with the foundations of science appears to arbitrarily circumscribe the concerns of epistemology. Why just the foundations of science as opposed to, say, the bases for all human beliefs? What licenses Quine's assertion that science encompasses what we can be properly said to know?[26] Yet these criticisms presuppose that whatever "science" is for Quine would preclude the study of some area or other of human belief. But Quine does not start with some prior conception of what science is, and then insist that all legitimate empirical inquiry fit this procrustean bed. Rather, Quine's conception of science is quite liberal.

The opening sentence of "Epistemology Naturalized" is: "Epistemology is concerned with the foundations of science" (Quine 1969, 69). Reading this sentence as *narrowing* the scope of epistemology misreads it. Quine countenances as a science any form of inquiry that respects the experimental method. He does not mandate invidious distinctions between types of sciences—"hard" or "soft," natural or social.[27]

The charge that Quine illicitly infers epistemic virtues from the pragmatic and instrumental ones science offers simply misses the implications of conjoining the failure of foundationalism with the consequences of holism. For a holist *cum* naturalist, there is no alternative to beginning with all methods of empirical inquiry—from physics to history—as we find them. "Unlike Descartes, we own and use our beliefs of the moment, even in the midst of philosophizing, until by what is called scientific method we change them here and there for the better" (Quine 1960, 24–25).[28] "Best" and "better" are clearly provisional characterizations for Quine; there is no point of cosmic exile. Epistemology starts with what we now have, and goes from there. Quine does not need to defend adverting to scientific standards in this case. Rather, for this time and culture, the burden of proof is on those who would claim extra-scientific bases for knowledge.

Quine's version of naturalized epistemology naturalizes epistemology in two related but distinct ways. One level is explicitly normative, in which the naturalized epistemologist uses and refines whatever the standards of proofs, techniques of inquiry, or other methods are among those that are already in use in the sciences. This follows directly from endorsing these standards as the ones best available to us for justifying our beliefs about the world. The second level is explanatory, and involves the construction of scientific—causal—explanations.

In a completed scientific world picture, the first (normative) level would be the proverbial ladder that is kicked away after it is ascended. Short of that point, however, naturalized epistemologists proceed in both of the aforementioned ways that scientists do. The naturalistic/pragmatic turn embraces not only the descriptive results of scientific inquiry, but also the prescribed practices for conducting such inquiry. For doing science involves both.[29] In this regard, Quine's writings advocate a paradigm shift in epistemology—a change in the methods, problems, and standards previously invoked in the subject.[30]

Thus, when Jaegwon Kim complains that "Quine is asking us to set aside what is 'rational' in rational reconstruction," he misses the point (Kim 1988, 389). For what Quine has understood is the need to alter what counts as an epistemologically satisfactory *reconstruction* of science (Quine 1969, 76). For a foundationalist, a rational *reconstruction* was to reconstruct science by derivation from sensory evidence. Such reconstruction is now understood to be impossible due to both forms of "epistemological incompleteness." This shifts not only what counts as a possible reconstruction from a derivation or explication to a causal analysis, but also changes what makes the reconstruction *rational*. It is rational if done in a scientific way.

Kim reacts incredulously to the suggestion that any causal account could be of epistemological interest. He asks "in what sense is the study of causal relationships between physical stimulation of sensory receptors and the resulting cognitive output a way of 'seeing how evidence relates to theory' in an epistemologically relevant sense?" (Kim 1988, 390). But a question of how evidence relates to theory is either a question of what *methods* a science employs, or it is a request for a causal story, to the extent there is one. In either case, the answer must employ those inferential procedures belonging to the repertoire of methods in the sciences.

On the one hand, a question about scientific justification might be taken as a request for a scrutiny of the type of confirmation theory and other inferential practices employed by some portion of the scientific community. Are their conclusions licensed by acceptable inferential procedures? The question here is normative, i.e., whether or not they are acting in accord with the best recognized standards given what else is known.

On the other hand, one might interpret the question causally, as one of how we human beings might ever have come up with scientific theories such as those we possess, given our information about the world—our stimulus input. This way of interpreting the question accords with the second level previously noted, i.e., a demand for a causal/developmental story of belief acquisition. Each of these two readings raises questions about the theory-evidence relation. Epistemologists might conceivably take an interest in either question. But one asks what makes such reconstructions rational, and the other asks by what methods we reconstruct truths. Each is a question asked about science from within science.

Here, then, is the full philosophical import of Quine's initial parallel between the foundational aspirations in mathematics and those in epistemology. The causal story is what rational reconstruction becomes once demands for stricter reconstructions are seen as futile. Any other interpretation either confuses both the first question and the second, or is a demand, *per impossible*, for a better reconstruction than science itself provides.

This confusion of justificatory practices and rational reconstruction is also manifest in the charge that Quine violates the "doxastic assumption," i.e., the view that only beliefs can justify other beliefs (See especially Koppelberg 1990; also Gibson 1995). On the one hand, philosophers understand justification in terms of inferential relations. But, on the other hand, scientists characteristically explore causal relations. Naturalism, once again, appears to confusedly substitute a causal story for a rational/inferential one.

Koppelberg notes the resistance to accepting this switch and gives voice as well to his own suspicions, however inchoate his reasons, of this resistance (Koppelberg 208–9).[31] But, we can now say, what Quine provides is precisely this: a *theory* that tells us what justification consists in. The theory unfolds by appreciating the paralleling of mathematics and science as paradigm cases of knowledge, by identifying the foundational projects associated with each, and by apprehending what the failure of each such project implies, particularly with regard to the changes effected on the notion of rational reconstruction. In Quine's naturalism, the causal and the normative are just opposite sides of the same scientific coin.[32]

Richard Foley rightly rejects criticisms such as Kim's that impute to Quine's procedure an abandonment of a concern with the normative project of epistemology (Foley 1994, 246–48). Foley has a different question: just how does Quine's approach differ from the non-naturalist epistemological tradition? (245). He suspects that the differences are more illusory than real (256).

He discerns two possibilities for distinguishing Quine's way of doing epistemology from that of, for example, Descartes or Roderick Chisholm. The first, albeit "uninteresting," differentiating factor is that "the canons of rational belief just are the canons of science, broadly conceived" (258). This move is uninteresting, Foley suggests, inasmuch as it simply marks out the substance of Quine's epistemic advice; by itself, this does not differentiate Quine's way of determining what advice to give from that of his non-naturalistic predecessors (255).

Foley's second way of distinguishing Quine from non-naturalists emphasizes Quine's rejection of the analytic/synthetic distinction, a move that leads to the conclusion that "the fundamental epistemic norms in his system cannot be known a priori, nor are they necessary. Rather, they are continuous with science" (258). If these norms were themselves shown to be *part* of science, Foley acknowledges, then a genuinely important and interesting difference between Quine and the tradition would have been identified. For then the normative issues become one with other scientific questions.[33]

The problem here, Foley maintains, is that Quine's commitment to the revisability of norms is hardly more than a *façon de parler*, inasmuch as Foley believes that Quine's commitment to empiricism is such as to make it effectively unrevisable. Foley's evidence that Quine is a closet traditionalist is that Quine offers no scientific defense of the very norm—empiricism—that Foley takes to be central to Quine's conception of the scientific project.[34] "The specific norms Quine favors are ones that he recommends from his philosophical armchair, with little or no concern for an empirical defense of them" (258–59).[35] Quine's procedures are, Foley concludes, only "tub-thumping" (as Kitcher puts it) for his favorite epistemic values.

Yet Foley concedes Quine's philosophical point, viz., that it is our most successful scientific practices that delimit the acceptable epistemic norms for a naturalized epistemologist.[36] As Foley acknowledges, there exist tests for ascertaining the correctness of the tenets Quine favors. More generally, as Foley notes, the "interesting conception [of Quine's] epistemology is one that makes his epistemology part of science, but this requires that even his most fundamental norms . . . be products of science" (255). Can this be done in a manner consistent with the approach Quine advocates? Foley allows that it can.[37] In the end, then, Foley acknowledges that Quine can be read as "doing epistemology" in an interestingly and importantly different fashion, one in which the norms of science are taken as findings of science. *But all that one needs to defend the consistency and normativity of naturalized epistemology is this sense.* For Quine, axiological claims about ends are to be made a posteriori through experimental practice, rather than a priori through conceptual analysis or appeal to intuition, and this is what distinguishes Quine from traditional epistemology.[38] His is the practice of epistemology *within* and *as* science.

Peter Hylton argues for an interpretation related to the one I offer above (Hylton 1994), but draws some different conclusions from those I defend. In line with the view developed here, Hylton maintains that for Quine, "[n]aturalism can be equated with the failure of foundationalism" (Hylton 1994, 268). As a consequence, there is for a Quinean naturalist no distinction to be drawn between philosophy and science. "What is crucial to Quine's naturalism is the negative point, that there is no theoretical perspective other than the general perspective of natural science—and, in particular, no distinctively philosophical perspective" (267). Hylton emphasizes, rightly in my view, that Quine's conception of science is primarily methodological (278).[39]

Where I take exception to Hylton's otherwise thoughtful and penetrating analysis is the account he offers of what follows from the failure of the foundational program in epistemology. Hylton finds in "Epistemology Naturalized" no reason to accept science self-applied as the obvious surrogate project with which to replace foundationalism (269). Hylton's complaint underscores the significance of the epistemic scalar hypothesis for Quine's argument, as well as the fact that it is commonly overlooked. For this shifts the burden of proof to those who would resist or deny the naturalistic turn.

Against the shared concerns of both Hylton and Foley that any attempt to justify basic norms must be, to a greater or lesser extent, circular (Foley 1994, 256; Hylton 1994, 269–70), my reconstrual eliminates the need to simply assume the truth of naturalism. In my account, naturalism follows from two assumptions: first, the fact that there are apparently sound arguments to the conclusion that foundationalism is impossible, and second, the normative scalar hypothesis, i.e., the claim that we possess at present no better standards of validation for empirical knowledge claims lying between what foundationalism promised and what science itself offers.[40] Given the normative scalar hypothesis, Quine's naturalism subsumes the is/ought gap.

Quine starts, not with appeal to any a priori truths or incorrigible beliefs, but with just the best explored systems of inference and evidence he has available. The focal point, the crux of the whole matter, is *not* a contrast between the normative and the descriptive. The epistemologically significant contrast with which Quine is working, rather, is *extrascientific* versus *intrascientific*. This, of course, is the point of his inveighing against "first philosophy"—the presumption that we have access to methods and evidence better than those that science itself underwrites. The issue throughout "Epistemology Naturalized" is not whether to be normative, but how.

Quine views science as self-correcting, and so as incorporating a concern for norms within its ongoing practice. Even the bias in favor of empiricism as a theory of evidence is one that Quine believes science to underwrite.[41] Can a naturalized epistemology be normative? Quine, for one, would not expect it to be otherwise. But this means only that the rules for engineering the success of science are not themselves discovered by some special nonscientific form of inquiry. *Contra* Kitcher, "radical naturalism" does engage in a meliorative project.

The issue for Quine with regard to naturalizing epistemology is which set of norms to settle for. Having tried to improve or clarify the intuitively most plausible set of truths and practices by a standard stricter than current science supplies, Quine concludes that there are no normative precepts available superior to those that scientists employ. The description of what it is to do science includes, *inter alia*, the norms relevant to that practice.[42] *The justification of this set of norms, in turn, is given by the success of the practice (relative to other options) in attaining a desired end.*[43]

Following science, much may be let go, for example, belief in physical bodies as basic.[44] Quine suggests that even if, for some reason or other, we gave up empiricism as our theory of what counts as scientifically acceptable evidence (and so granted legitimacy to clairvoyance, for example), the test of a science of clairvoyance would still be successful prediction. Could even this benchmark of science be altered? "In that extremity [of countenancing clairvoyance] it might indeed be well to modify the game itself, and take on as further checkpoints the predicting of telepathic and divine input as well as of sensory input. It is idle to bulwark definitions against implausible contingencies" (Quine 1990, 20). The parameters of the scientific language game, defeasible though they may be, are for Quine animated by purposes tied to technology and understanding, and defined by prediction. If inquiry yields no predictive test, then it is not a Quinean science.

But, now, if worthwhile purposes may be so diverse as to include interest in understanding, then what counts as a scientific explanation, and so a scientific method, is any inquiry and practice that satisfies understanding and has empirical checks. For naturalism is *not* a theory of how to decide among competing or incompatible accounts of science. An irony here is that the "naturalists return" is coincident with the departure of faith that the term 'science' marks out fields of inquiry by methodological kind (See Roth 1996b). The ghost of the demarcation problem haunts naturalized epistemology insofar as opting for a naturalized epistemology does not settle which type naturalistic theory to prefer.

III

Feminism as I see it is concerned with the oppression of women. Feminist philosophers of science examine both how and why the sciences have been utilized, wittingly or not, as institutions and instruments of this oppression. But the theoretical alternatives for legitimating a feminist challenge to scientific practice offers them, or so it might appear, only a Hobson's choice. On the one hand, the sciences have no lack of defenders even among feminists regarding the objectivity, rationality, and truth production of their theories and methods. Defenders of the scientific faith account for any aberrant instances—be they Nazi medicine or primatology research—as just cases of bad science. But then they are stuck with the old vocabulary of legitimation, one that has not served them at all well. Thus, tradition "weighs like a nightmare on the brain of the living."

On the other hand, as has been by now compellingly documented (and not just in the case of women), scientific theories have been used to legitimate various oppressive social policies, to embody prior commitments to social values, and to influence in their most basic formulations by prejudicial forms of thought at play in the culture. So some critics, both feminists and others, respond to claims of scientific objectivity with "*Écrasez l'infâme.*" But this appears to be a case of tossing out both the baby and the bath water.

Charting a *via media* between these unattractive alternatives motivates a melding of feminism and naturalism into a social empiricism. Such views are naturalistic and empirical by virtue of their conception of what the possible evidence is and what is the source of methods for assessing evidence. They are social insofar as they maintain, paraphrasing Quine, that science is a social art and that in acquiring it, one depends entirely on intersubjectively available cues as to what to say and when. Terming science a "social art" implies, *inter alia,* that scientific inquiry and scientific communities do not operate in splendid (epistemological) isolation from the world around them. Finally, a specifically *feminist* social empiricism concerns how gender-nuanced patterns of reasoning and theorizing result in scientific inquiry abetting forms of oppression.

But even here anxiety about the legitimacy of the naturalist project is evident. For feminists subvert their achievement—the unmasking of science so as to expose social agendas at work beneath the veneer of dispassionate inquiry—by propounding philosophical theories that only function to help perpetuate old illusions. Indeed, they do this using philosophies of a thoroughly discredited sort—a "conjuring up of the dead" to the new scene in "time honored disguise and . . . borrowed language."

Recall the hallmark of logical empiricism, viz., its claim to offer a reconstruction of knowledge claims in empiricists terms. Feminist critics then emphasized how this specific pretension about the relation of evidence to theory only served to hide a social agenda behind the mask of methodology. But with the Kuhnian turn, the notion of social construction replaces that of rational reconstruction. Encouraging this replacement was pioneering work in the sociology of science by Barry Barnes and David Bloor—the self-named Strong Programme in the sociology of scientific knowledge. I think their work and what follows can stay, but it needs a turn to Quinean themes afterwards.

Barnes staked out early on a conception of what he termed "natural rationality" as central to the underlying intellectual presuppositions of this sociological approach. As he conceived it, a study of "natural rationality" examines "how people actually reason rather than how ideally they should reason" (Barnes 1976, 115), a deliberate contrast to idealized accounts of reasoning he finds in the philosophy of science.

Two features of natural rationality are particularly salient for subsequent critiques of conventional philosophy of science. First, Barnes maintains, for "inductive inference to be possible, observations have to be taken as instances of something or other. . . . Hence a *fundamental* distinction between 'theoretical' and 'observational' discourse cannot be sustained in any culture" (122). Second, "[n]atural rationality operates in the context of a pre-existing set of concepts and beliefs. . . . No unique set of beliefs is thrown up spontaneously by the interaction of an unsocialized naturally rational actor with the world" (122).[45] Barnes' insight is that "no distinctiveness can be attributed to our existing natural science. All institutionalized systems of belief and action appear to embody natural rationality alike—science no more or less than any other institution" (122). He derides, in this context, "virgin birth" views of scientific rationality.

But their well-motivated studies of natural rationality at work in laboratory settings notwithstanding, the claim by social scientists to have privileged access to the factors explanatory of what natural scientists do is ironic. For the social sciences are where positivism had its strongest and most enduring impact on disciplinary practices and self-image. Texts in these areas still serve up potted versions of Carl Hempel's *Philosophy of*

Natural Science as received philosophical truth. Moreover, hand-wringing about their status as "real sciences" remains endemic in the social sciences. A positivist conception of science, in turn, is still taken as their legitimation. Follow the methodological recipe, and "real" science results.

Indeed, a basically positivist view of what it takes to be a science is as much a part of the Strong Programme as it is of other social sciences. The red flag is their claim to provide causal explanations of the cases they study, from turn-of-the-century phrenologists to Weimar physicists, and from contemporary high-energy physicists to cancer researchers. Claims for the causal adequacy of their explanations also signal where these sociologists go off the naturalistic track. But it is sheer pretense on the part of these sociologists to maintain that any of their case studies yield causal explanations. There are no causal explanations, because they can cite neither laws nor regularities; there are not even passable facsimiles of ones. Nor do the sociologists have some special account of "causal explanation" to which to appeal. They write as if they could provide *Der Logische Aufbau der Welt* done up in sociological dress. The sociological claim to have uncovered the secret engine of scientific cognition reveals only that social constructionists are themselves true believers in scientific rationality. But there are no such reconstructions. An inability to detail how the social is in fact "constructed" comes as no philosophical surprise.[46]

My endorsement of Barnes' notion of natural rationality still stands. The pervasive presence and influence of social factors on what is termed 'scientific reasoning' goes without saying. But if the question is one of determining the relation of values to practices, taking sociological construction as the replacement program for rational reconstruction is simply a nonstarter. If experience teaches anything, it is the virtual impenetrability of whatever processes there are that lead people to associate beliefs in the way they do. There is no saying exactly how, given knowledge of someone's interests, education, gender, and so on, these factors then determine what other sets of beliefs, especially scientific beliefs, a person is going to hold.

A recent essay by political scientist Joyce Mushaben, "Collective Memory Divided and Reunited," provides an illustration of how varied is the way that individuals understand (Mushaben 1999). Mushaben, an expert in post–World-War-II German politics, focuses on the impact that reunification has had on the self-understanding of German feminists as they examine women's roles in Germany's troubled history since the 1930s.

The particular problem that Mushaben ponders involves the fact that reunification brought together two groups of feminists—East Germans and West Germans—each raised in a different understanding of both Germany's and women's responsibility for German actions during World War II. Unification accelerated the challenges of later feminists to the avoidance strategies of their sisters-in-arms. For when the Wall came down, those living east of the old divide found themselves faced with what appeared to be unmodified and unrepentant German nationalism, while those in West Germany could see only vestiges of a militaristic and authoritarian state that they had repudiated. In broad strokes, what Mushaben examines is how feminists in both the GDR and the FRG early on took refuge in the view of women as among the victims and the oppressed during the Nazi regime. Yet, she notes, the feminist slogan "the personal is the political" worked against this view as an ultimate refuge from participation in and responsibility for the events of that era. Feminist scholars and writers from both East and West Germany increasingly produced works challenging the sanguine assumptions of the "women as victims" view.

Mushaben highlights a controversy that has developed over the appropriation of feminist doctrines by women committed to Germany's New Right, i.e., neo-Nazis and ultra-nationalists. She observes that "many women of the New Right see their own behavior as the logical extension of feminism's self-empowering legacy" (Mushaben 1999, 31). This puts contemporary feminists in a special "double bind": first, in deepening their already problematic and largely unexplored relationship to their mothers and the behavior of German women of that generation, and second, in assessing their own doctrines and how they are open to neo-Nazi appropriation (31–32).

Once again, the historiographical moral cautions against an assumption of "obvious" connections within the web of beliefs. Mushaben nicely summarizes the difficult lesson her study suggests: "This treatment of mothers, daughters and the fascist experience confirms the existence of 'competing generations of collective memories'—fractured further still by the prism of gender—'which are not linear and progressive but circular, repetitious and profoundly unpredictable'" (33). Her analysis nicely illustrates ways in which feminist doctrine underdetermines beliefs about history, agency, and appropriate forms of government.

Theorizing as if social construction could do the job that rational reconstruction could gets us nowhere, I am suggesting, because there is no discernable structure at work. Only adherence to some prior philosophical theory could foster the belief that a structure must be present. Such prior philosophical commitments frustrate the efforts of some feminist and naturalist philosophers of science to pursue a naturalized and socialized study of scientific reasoning.[47]

Helen Longino's effort to sketch a type of social epistemology, I contend, runs aground on the shoals of philosophical theory as well. In Longino's case, she evinces a felt need to steer between the fear of relativism and the charge of what one might call standpoint elitism. "The problem with recognizing the social locatedness . . . of individual epistemic subjects is that it seems to force us into choosing between relativism and demonstrating the epistemic superiority of one among the various social locations. I wish to reject this choice" (Longino, in Schmitt 1994, 139). Her alternative is to conceive of scientific inquiry on the model of a Habermasian idealized speech community (56).

Longino goes so far as to formulate her account in the great Justified True Belief tradition. Her analogue to the justification condition, where S is the member of an epistemic community, W a real-world system, M a model of that system, and C a variable ranging over communities, is as follows (153):[48]

> $S_1 \ldots S_n$'s representing W as M is the result of warranting practices adopted by C in circumstances characterized by
>
> a. public forums for critical interaction,
> b. uptake of criticism,
> c. public standards, and
> d. equality of intellectual authority among diverse perspectives.

This avoids, Longino maintains, the relativism endorsed by sociologists of science.

In particular, she opposes Karin Knorr-Cetina's sociological version of the epistemological question "How is that which we come to call knowledge constituted and accepted?" (137) and seeks instead "an account of knowledge that incorporates the social dimensions of science into the epistemology of inquiry," i.e., one that demonstrates "that good science does not express the biases decried by feminist critics" (138). Longino opts for a less social epistemology than Knorr-Cetina certainly because she believes than an account of how science works must put a positive philosophical face on that epistemic community's justificatory practices.

Her schematic accounting of warranting procedures, Longino believes, gives us all we can have. At the end of the day, scientists can only argue in terms of practices they know and use. "The point is that there is nothing further—that appeal to standards or methodological norms beyond those ratified by the discursive interactions of an inquiring community is an appeal to transcendent principles that inevitably turn out to be local". Once a community has responded to "free and open" criticism, "then it is not clear that there are any further grounds (beyond simple disagreement) for criticism" (155). Longino's account assumes that ongoing dialogue is the best (because the only) corrective possible for distortions in the process of inquiry.[49]

Longino wants a difference (in warranting practices) that actually differentiates her proposal from Knorr-Cetina's forthright relativism, which settles for "answers invoking the social processes and interactions in the laboratory and between the laboratory and its worldly environment". But has Longino shown, as she intends, "[w]hat distinguishes knowledge from other doxastic states" (137)?

Note first that her model of warranting practices is, at best, a model of normal science, in the straightforward Kuhnian sense. Almost any case of the scientific outsider—from Copernicus to Barbara McClintock—cannot be a knower by her account. This is by definition—by failing to use warranting practices adopted by their community. This is an unavoidable result of any positive explication of scientific knowledge that puts the weight on public, and not impersonal, standards. The other clauses are idle, pending further explication of 'public' and 'equal intellectual authority.'

Individualistic models of scientific reasoning, the very ones that are rejected by Longino and others because they present an inappropriately abstract and abstracted view of how deliberation can or even should proceed, were in fact tailored for "rebels." It is precisely the cases in which outsiders are later "vindicated" that those who oppose social epistemology such as Larry Laudan want to rescue using nonsocial accounts of what good scientific reasoning is. Longino's exclusion as knowers those whose cases motivate, in the first place, a revised account of scientific knowledge suggests that the account has gone terribly wrong.

It goes wrong not because individualism in epistemology needs to be brought back in, but because Longino lacks the courage of her own philosophical convictions. If the best sense to be made of good reasoning is what the community of practitioners, in their collective wisdom, take it to be, then no matter how openly or freely they arrive at that view, there are no transcendent principles, only local ones. But although she says that there are no transcendent principles to which to appeal to bail us out, she just cannot stop herself from still looking. So her account instead simply designates that a particular institutional arrangement instantiates the desired doxastic state. But this is only a relabeling of Knorr-Cetina's relativism, not a proof that she has transcended it.

Naturalism in the Quinean and Kuhnian senses is the realization of what philosophy of science comes to once we acknowledge that there is no special formula, were we but to know it, that would redeem us from our epistemic sins. From this perspective, "feminism" is best taken as marking a particular hermeneutics of suspicion that investigators may bring to bear on scientific practices as they find them. But a "feminist perspective" is not a corrective of distortions in research. There is no methodological template that will do this for us. Rather, the goal must be to find ways to prevent or deflect whatever we term 'science' from becoming complicit in oppression.

Nothing of interest follows, I believe, from calling knowledge 'social.' For it is either tautological—redundantly emphasizing what one means, in part, by knowledge—or unhelpful—serving only to summon the ghosts of dead philosophies. Naturalism, however, adds to knowledge that the sciences provide our best institutional approaches for enhancing the project of epistemology. Taking naturalism seriously requires, however, renouncing the old modes of legitimation and settling for the limits of the new. Doing this leaves us still very much at the beginning of the project of understanding science.

Revolution remains unfinished unless and until we learn to forego the old vocabulary of legitimation and instead become fluent in the new. As Marx observes in concluding the passage I quoted at the outset: "In like manner a beginner who has learned a new language always translates it back into his mother tongue, but he has assimilated the spirit of the new language and can freely express himself in it only when he finds his way in it without recalling the old and forgets his native tongue in the use of the new."

Bertrand Russell observed early in this century that "every advance in knowledge robs philosophy of some problems which formerly it had, and . . . it will follow that a number of problems which had belonged to philosophy will have ceased to belong to philosophy and will belong to science" (Russell 1918, 34). So while some, such as Kim, read Quine's naturalized epistemology as surrendering to the skeptic, I read it as indicating the limits of reason in light of the science of the late twentieth century. We are now in a position to forego intuition-mongering and simply settle for science. The so-called epistemology of empirical knowledge has ceased to be a *philosophical* problem.

Notes

1. See, for example, the following expressions of such epistemological anxiety: Evelyn Fox Keller (in Kourany 1998, 397–98); Elisabeth Lloyd (in Nelson and Nelson 1996, 242); and Helen Longino (in Schmitt 1994, 138).

2. For lamentations regarding the presumed vagueness of naturalism, see Conee (1996) and Plantinga (1996). Bas van Fraassen complains: "To identify what naturalism is . . . I have found nigh-impossible" (van Fraassen 1996, 172). Yet van Fraassen writes throughout his essay about "science," as if he knew exactly what that is. As I argue below, the terms 'naturalism' and 'science' should be seen as equally clear or equally problematic since the latter is central to the definition of the former. See Roth (1996b).

3. "I had realized, on the one hand, the fundamental importance of mathematics for the formation of a system of knowledge and, on the other hand, its purely logical, formal character to which it owes its independence from the contingencies of the real world. These insights formed the basis of my book. . . . This orientation is sometimes called 'logical empiricism' (or 'logical positivism'), in order to indicate the two components" (Carnap 1967, vi).

4. Ibid.

5. See Maffie (1990) and Kitcher (1992). For an especially insightful overview of contemporary variants of philosophical naturalism, see Rosenberg (1996).

6. The "naturalist's dilemma" is just the epistemological analog of Hume's is/ought problem. The charge against naturalism in either case—the ethical or the epistemological—is that one cannot read off what it is best to do from descriptions of what is the case. See Alston (1989) for related discussion, especially sections III and IV.

7. I discovered that Quine uses the term 'methodological monism.' For Quine, methodological monism follows from his rejection of the analytic/synthetic distinction and his consequent acceptance of holism. The 'monism' signals that he recognizes no principled distinction in kind (e.g., empirical versus non-empirical; revisable versus non-revisable) among sentences in a language. The monism is methodological inasmuch as the means of evaluating statements is scientific (see Quine 1981, 70–71). Arthur Danto also identifies methodological monism as the defining feature of naturalism. See Danto (1967, 448–50).

Having elsewhere (Roth 1987) argued for "methodological pluralism," does the present account of naturalism represent a change of view on my part? My position is now somewhat more radical. In Roth (1987), the "pluralism" that I defend urges *broadening* the notion of what counts as science. I no longer believe that there is any point to arguing about what is or is not a science (see Roth 1996b). There are only different ways of doing empirical inquiry.

8. Self-described naturalists such as Alvin Goldman attempt to escape such criticisms by construing the analysis of knowledge as tolerating "methodological dualism." Goldman would like to have matters both ways, i.e., to separate himself from those who insist on pursuing a purely a priori analysis of epistemic notions but yet still maintain that there are techniques—specifically philosophical ones—distinct from what we now classify as science. Goldman, *pace* Quine, construes naturalized epistemology as a "liaison" of two distinct forms of inquiry. In this view, philosophy makes

an independent contribution to the analysis of knowledge. I discuss these issues in Roth (1996a) and Roth (1999).

9. Rosenberg agrees in general with this diagnosis, but goes on to suggest, correctly in my view, that Quine is the *bête noire* of other erstwhile naturalists because he (Quine) decouples naturalism from realism, progressivity, and other "philosophical" theses.

10. Maffie argues that limited naturalism preserves a type of fact-value bifurcation, and so "undermines the integrity of naturalism as a comprehensive methodological and epistemological program" (Maffie 1990, 289). For a related discussion of Goldman's work, see Markie (1996).

11. But see Kornblith (1993) for one account of how this might be accomplished.

12. Kitcher adds, in a footnote at this point, the following observation: "The *denial* [my emphasis] of normative appraisal flows from the relativization of such appraisals, if one also accepts the idea that there are always available changes of context that would reverse any piece of normative advice" (Kitcher 1992, 58 n. 16). Quine is later identified as someone holding exactly that radical naturalist position (Kitcher 1992, 69–70).

13. This project is clearly reminiscent of Larry Laudan's views. See, e.g., Laudan (1986) and Laudan (1987). Kitcher here distinguishes himself from Laudan by looking to psychological processes for stable principles, and not just the history of science. Historical stability for Kitcher, I take it, is itself to be explained by pointing to the stability of underlying cognitive structures. Kitcher, unlike Laudan, also believes that social processes can enter into epistemic analysis in positive ways. See discussions by Kitcher (1993), especially chapters 5 and 8.

14. Kitcher (1992, 77 n. 72) makes clear that this is Kitcher's position.

15. Solomon thinks this is the case for Quine as well, and here I disagree.

16. A Kantian reading of Kitcher's view is strongly suggested by the characterization of "minimal realism" and cognitive value that he develops in pages 104–8.

17. For a related criticism, see Solomon (1995), but especially her observation that for Kitcher "naturalism is just window-dressing for a previously and independently developed account of scientific rationality" (Solomon 1995, 207). Nor is Kitcher alone in doing this in the name of naturalism. See Richard Bernstein's complaints regarding McDowell's "naturalized platonism" (with Kantian overtones) (Bernstein 1995).

18. Rosenberg (1996) rightly emphasizes the importance of the "Darwinian paradigm" to both Kitcher's project and other recent species of naturalism. This paradigm fuels the hopes of Kitcher et al. that some traditional philosophical theses, e.g., that science progresses or that realism is correct, can piggy-back on a naturalist project. For a corrective to Philip Kitcher's enthusiasm for the Darwinian paradigm, see Patricia Kitcher (1992), especially chapter 7.

19. I owe the last two sentences to Jim Maffie.

20. Over fifty years ago, Abraham Edel mounted a defense of naturalism in ethics germane to this discussion of naturalism as a source of normative insight for the sciences. He there nicely articulates just why naturalism is reflexive regarding its normative commitments. In the quote that follows, imaginatively replace each use of "ethics" or cognate terms with the appropriate form of the term "science."

> The whole articulation of a morality within a society under given conditions, the problems of change and adjustment within it, require constant valuational activity. We find our commitments as what we are committed to in the specific lines of choice and directions of striving in which we are engaged. Even the major permanent ends we may thus elicit on analysis . . . do not become the objects of isolated independent selection. Their evaluation rests on the whole network of choices and the kind and quality of life to which they commit us.
>
> . . . Mr. Murphy seems to me to pose the question almost as if an ethical theory must somehow equip a hypothetical man who holds no values to choose between conflicting

> values. If he means to eliminate all reference to an existent value-pattern of the self as already settling the moral problem, then he poses an impossible task. The question "What values should I choose if I had no values?" is meaningful only if it asks what other who had values would recommend for a person in my position. All justification is in a matrix of existent values. Scientific method is applicable to values in so far as it provides a way of identifying one's existent values, testing them, and refining or revising them in choice. (Edel, "Is Naturalism Arbitrary?" *Journal of Philosophy* 43: 146–47)

We have ends important to us, and we have systems that, we hope, will abet us in achieving those ends. If the ends seem to require rules we find overly restrictive, we can alter or drop the goal; if a rule does not function well relative to the end in view, we can change the rule. This is as true for science as for ethics. Nelson Goodman offers a similarly naturalistic justification of deduction: "Principles of deductive inference are justified by their conformity with accepted deductive practices. Their validity depends upon accordance with the particular deductive inference we actually make and sanction. If a rule yields unacceptable inferences, we drop it as invalid. Justification of general rules thus derives from judgments rejecting or accepting particular deductive inferences. . . . A rule is amended if it yields an inference we are unwilling to accept; an inference is rejected if it violates a rule we are unwilling to amend. This process of justification is the delicate one of making mutual adjustments between rules and accepted inferences; and in the agreement achieved lies the only justification needed for either" (Goodman 1979, 63–64).

21. Roger Gibson, in otherwise very careful exegetical accounts of Quine's naturalism, completely misses the importance of the parallelism (Gibson 1987, 1995).

22. "Just as mathematics is to be reduced to logic, or logic and set theory, so natural knowledge is to be based somehow on sense experience. This means explaining the notion of body in sensory terms; here is the conceptual side. And it means justifying our knowledge of truths of nature in sensory terms; here is the doctrinal side of the bifurcation" (Quine 1969, 71).

23. This is explicit in any number of places in Quine. See, e.g., Quine (1981), 70–71.

24. This is, of course, the position of epistemology as Quine portrays it in Quine (1973), 1–4.

25. The scalar notion is suggested by Quine's remarks such as the following: "The fifth move, finally, brings naturalism: abandonment of the goal of a first philosophy. It sees natural science as inquiry into reality, fallible and corrigible but not answerable to any supra-scientific tribunal, and not in need of any justification beyond observation and the hypothetico-deductive method. Naturalism has two sources, both negative. One of them is despair of being able to define theoretical terms generally in terms of phenomena, even by contextual definition" (Quine 1981, 72).

26. The points raised here were emphasized to me by both Peter Markie and Jim Maffie, and I owe the formulation of the problems to their remarks.

27. The question is explicitly raised by Quine, and answered as sketched, in Quine (1995), 251–52. Quine expresses the basic epistemological question in the following way: "Given only the evidence of our senses, how do we arrive at our theory of the world?" (Quine 1973, 1). The "theory of the world" in question embraces both our acquisition of language (in infancy) and the development of mature science. Our mother tongue is our first theory of the world, and natural science is its refinement and extension. The epistemological relation of ordinary language to natural science is fundamental for Quine, and he never substantively alters from the account he gives of it in his 1954 essay, "The Scope and Language of Science" (Quine 1976).

28. The issue of what privileges scientific evidence is an important one, but is tied to considerations involving Quine's understanding of language acquisition. See n. 40.

29. Quine has recently put the matter this way: "Is this sort of thing still philosophy? Naturalism brings a salutary blurring of such boundaries. Naturalistic philosophy is continuous with natural science. It undertakes to clarify, organize, and simplify the broadest and most basic concepts, and to analyze scientific method and evidence within the framework of science itself. The boundary

between naturalistic philosophy and the rest of science is just a vague matter of degree" (Quine 1995, 256).

30. This point is also emphasized in Rosenberg (1996).

31. "Davidson, Rorty and Stroud agree that evidential and causal questions have to be kept strictly apart. I am not sure Quine would agree. . . . I think that a thorough-going naturalism should try to combine them systematically.

"A naturalist in epistemology has the task of showing how any interest in factual and empirical matters can help to explicate and to explain questions of justification. . . . [M]any traditional epistemologists do nothing more than rely upon their intuitions about epistemic justification. . . . What we really need is a theory that tells us what justification consists in" (Koppelberg 1990, 208).

32. Can reasons be causes for Quine? I find nothing in Quine's work to suggest that they cannot.

33. Quine, of course, does take it that, e.g., empiricism is a norm which results from the *findings* of science. "The crucial insight of empiricism is that any evidence for science has its end points in the senses. This insight remains valid, but it is an insight which comes after physics, physiology, and psychology, not before." (Quine 1976, 225)

34. The work of van Fraassen (1995) contains a similar charge, viz., that Quine's empiricism is an inadequate account of how science proceeds. However, van Fraassen's account is not Quine's. For one, van Fraassen's empiricist identifies experience as the "one and only source of information" (van Fraassen 1995, 69). But Quine's "unassailable tenets of empiricism" only claim that sensory stimulation is our sole source of *evidence*. And for Quine, evidence is not the same as what van Fraassen takes as information. For example, van Fraassen claims that a Quinean naturalist could not accommodate taking instinct to be the explanation of an infant's breast-feeding behavior (van Fraassen 1995, 76). But this clearly is not correct since Quine allows, e.g., innate quality spaces as an explanation of color perception (Quine 1969, 126; also elaborated in Quine 1973).

35. See also Foley (1994), 257. For a similar complaint, see Solomon (1995, 207 n. 2).

36. Even Quine's views on empiricism are subject to revision. See, e.g., Quine (1995), 257.

37. Foley (1994, 255). For reasons given below, it is not quite correct to say, as Foley here does, that empiricism defines what science is for Quine.

38. I owe this formulation to Jim Maffie.

39. The link Hylton stresses between, on the one hand, ordinary language as embodying our proto-scientific theory and, on the other hand, the role of language learning in guiding our understanding of theory acquisition and development is of the very first importance in understanding Quine's epistemology (Hylton 1994, 270–77). It is a point I have attempted to highlight in my own writings on Quine. See, in particular, Roth (1978) and Roth (1987), chapters 1 and 2.

40. For related remarks, see Quine (1981, 71–72).

41. Quine, in writings of recent vintage, nicely summarizes these aspects of his views.

> Insofar as theoretical epistemology gets naturalized into a chapter of theoretical science, so normative epistemology gets naturalized into a chapter of engineering: the technology of anticipating sensory stimulation.
>
> The most notable norm of naturalized epistemology actually coincides with that of traditional epistemology. It is simply the watch-word of empiricism: nihil in mente quod non prius in sensu. This is a prime specimen of naturalized epistemology, for it is a finding of natural science itself, however fallible, that our information about the world comes only through impacts on our sensory receptors. And still the point is normative, warning us against telepaths and soothsayers. Moreover, naturalized epistemology on its normative side is occupied with heuristics generally—with the whole strategy of rational conjecture in the framing of scientific hypotheses." (Quine 1990, 19–20)

See also Quine (1986, 664–65).

42. Susan Haack is clearly correct to complain about ambiguities in Quine's notions of science, and so his attendant account of naturalism. See, e.g., Haack (1993b), and especially chapter 6 of Haack (1993a). However, as I argued in chapter 2 of Roth (1987), Quine's reductionist and scientistic proclivities about which Haack complains can be separated from his naturalism.

43. There is an additional problem here. As Peter Hylton notes, when Quine asserts that all "genuinely factual questions" are scientific ones, the "phrase is of course the location of a problem: exactly what constitutes a genuinely factual question? Quine's answer here is far from straightforward" (Hylton 1994, 280 n. 18). The terms "genuinely factual" and "science" cannot be defined without reference to one another.

44. Examining what Quine says with regard to a science/non-science partitioning is helpful, if only as a starting point of investigation. To begin, he denies that specifying a demarcation criterion is any part of his project (see Quine 1995, 252). Nor he does require that a science be extensional (see Quine 1990, 72, noting the liberal implication of his "ecumenical" conception of truth in §42). Further, he maintains that prediction is not a norm of science, but that prediction is probative of claims (for individual sentences or groups of them) to scientific status.

> But when I cite predictions as the checkpoints of science, I do not see that as normative. I see it as defining a particular language game, in Wittgenstein's phrase: the game of science, in contrast to other good language games such as fiction and poetry. A sentence's claim to scientific status rests on what it contributes to a theory whose checkpoints are in prediction.
> ... [P]rediction is not the main purpose of the science game. It is what decides the game, like runs and outs in baseball. It is occasionally the purpose.... But nowadays the overwhelming purposes of the science game are technology and understanding. (Quine 1990, 20)

As Laudan persuasively argues, considerations drawn from the history of science might well yield normative considerations without abetting demarcation criteria (Laudan 1990).

45. Indeed, in work of later vintage, Barry Barnes cites Quine favorably as an advocate of the study of "natural rationality" in Barnes' sense of the term. In its heart, the sociological project aims, then, to be a naturalistic one (Barnes 1992, 334).

46. There is a disanalogy here I need to acknowledge. Carnap's concern in rational reconstruction was explicitly non-psychological, at least in the sense that he had no interest in the actual genesis of any (scientific) concept. He concern was, for any given theoretical notion, not in showing how it actually might have been acquired, but in revealing a line of reasoning that would show why the concept was rationally justified, i.e., inferable from the evidence in a logically appropriate manner. Social constructionists, however, characteristically write as if they are detailing the genesis of a view, i.e., tracing how it actually was inferred on the basis of prior beliefs. In this sense, the social constructionist view owes more to the phenomenological tradition than the analytic, e.g., to Peter Berger and Thomas Luckmann or Alfred Schutz, than to the Vienna Circle. Nonetheless, my point of analogy rests on the idea of a traceable logical structure from base beliefs to theoretical ones, and on this point the analogy remain valid and is all, I believe, I need.

47. Such prior philosophical commitments frustrate the efforts of some feminist and naturalist philosophers of science to pursue a naturalized and socialized study of scientific reasoning. On the naturalizing side, Miriam Solomon, for example, defends a "social empiricism" (Solomon, in Schmitt 1994). What makes her empiricism social is her view that the attainment of scientific goals is best understood as following a path that leads not through individually selected cognitive processes but, rather, through ones which "aggregate individual and social processes (epistemic, cognitive, motivational, sociopolitical) which are, as a whole, adequately responsive to empirical successes" (Solomon, in Schmitt 1994, 219–20). She suggests that explanations of theory change that screen out everything but scientific success will invariably prove unsatisfactory.

For example, she takes the empirical success of the theory of plate tectonics as insufficient to explain a shift in the scientific community to that view. All fuller explanatorily correct stories involve, she believes, "mechanisms that are traditionally viewed as 'biasing': cognitive salience and availability; motivational biases such as self-interest . . . ; and social factors such as the influence of institutional training and institutional structure" (221). Solomon's social empiricism, then, seeks to demonstrate that the various factors she cites are not necessarily in opposition to one another; biasing factors are not a distortion of the process but part of its natural history. Whatever influences (real world) reasoning of scientists she incorporates as part of a social theory of scientific reasoning.

The key distinction with which Solomon works is the one between "biasing factors" and "empirical success," with the latter defined as "engagements with the world which include experimental, observational, predictive, and some technological successes" (226). But what marks "real" empirical success? For, I would have thought, it is the very lack of a philosophically reputable notion of empirical success that is the reason, in the first place, to look to other sorts of explanatory factors.

Indeed, while her account relies on "empirical success" and "biasing factors" as independent elements of explanation, her case studies suggest a murkier picture in which "success" may not be distinguishable from so-called biasing factors. For example, Solomon contests the view that the plate tectonics revolution is best explained by examining how individual geologists each assessed the data. What then is Solomon's story?

> Consensus took place when plate tectonics had universal (in the scientific community) empirical successes, so that even biased evaluations of the importance of some successes led to the same choice of plate tectonics. That consensus was helped along by salient advertising of new results . . . and bandwagon phenomena. I contend that the successes of plate tectonics were necessary for consensus on the theory, but not sufficient. It makes sense to say that the scientific community as a whole selected plate tectonics because of its universal successes, while no individual did so. Furthermore, the scientific community did so only via mechanism that are traditionally viewed as "biasing." (221)

The picture she wants to promote is that, as it were, no one person's vote is determinative. It is only when different groups, deciding more or less autonomously of one another, arrive at the same decision that the theory in question "wins." Universal success is success within each subgroup that has a vote on such matters. Individuals acts only derivatively affect change, through membership in relevant groups with a vote in the outcome. In this respect, theory change is a social achievement, not an individual one.

But even if the decision is social in the above sense, how does this make it a story at odds with the one she sets herself against? In the end, the evaluators are individuals, and she says explicitly that empirical success created the consensus. Within each subgroup, either the decision-making process is driven by the empirical successes or by them in some combination with biasing factors. If the former, the biasing factors drop out as a necessary element of the story. But if the latter, we are left again with the problem of how to distinguish what counts as an "empirical success" independent of alleged "biasing factors." So either empirical successes are sufficient to tell the story of change, or they remain obscurely bound up with "biasing factors."

Either so-called biasing factors are constitutive of what counts as empirical success or they are not. If not, as Solomon would prefer, I do not see how empirical success could fail to be sufficient on the story as she tells it. For she says, "Consensus took place when plate tectonics had universal . . . empirical successes, so that even biased evaluations of the importance of some success led to the same choice of plate tectonics" (220). Universal empirical success—successes acknowledged within each subgroup—trumps bias on her own account. Perhaps the other factors she mentions help explain the quickness with which this theory gained acceptance. But what she says appears disconcertingly similar to what she purports to oppose, viz., that "geologists were each persuaded of continental drift by objective assessment of the implications of new geophysical and paleomagnetic data" (220). What her account suggests is only that a theory needs empirical successes within each subgroup, not that non-epistemic factors are necessary to explain success.

Any effort to "split the difference" among the factors would require a reconstruction of how each factor must weigh in judgment. But the historical tapestries are not so woven that we perceive the threads , some white with theory, others black with fact, that we can then neatly unravel and determine how exactly each contributed to the larger picture under study. For, given the concerns that drive one in the first place to doubt efforts at line-drawing between theory and observation or the social and the scientific, Solomon's two factor theory—"biasing" and "empirical success"—is bound, absent a robust philosophical theory of "empirical success," to reduce to one for purposes of explanation. Such reconstructionist gambits are the poisoned pawns of philosophy.

48. Obviously worrisome is d—the "equality of intellectual authority among diverse perspectives." Longino's concern, in formulating d, is an attempt to ensure "free and open criticism referencing some goals" of the community in question (155). I am not aware of actual intellectual communities that satisfy this, and with good reason. Some perspectives do not merit intellectual authority.

49. This account, as I read it, is an elaboration of the "social account of objectivity" broached in chapter 10 of *Science as Social Knowledge*.

References

Alston, W. 1996. "A 'Doxastic Practice' Approach to Epistemology." In P. Moser, ed. *Empirical Knowledge*, 2d ed., ed. P. Moser. Lanham, Md.: Rowman & Littlefield.

Anderson, Elizabeth. 1999. "Feminist Epistemology: An Interpretation and a Defense." In *Readings in Epistemology*, ed. J. Crumley II. Mountainview, Calif.: Mayfield Publishing.

Barnes, Barry. 1976. "Natural Rationality: A Neglected Concept in the Social Sciences." *Philosophy of the Social Sciences* 6: 115–26.

———. 1991. "How Not to Do the Sociology of Language." In *Annals of Scholarship* 8: 321–35.

Bernstein, R. 1995. "Whatever Happened to Naturalism?," *The Proceedings and Addresses of the American Philosophical Association* 69: 57–76.

Carnap, Rudolf. 1967. *The Logical Structure of the World: Pseudoproblems in Philosophy*. Berkeley: University of California Press.

Conee, E. 1996. "Plantinga's Naturalism." In *Warrant in Contemporary Epistemology*, ed. J. Kvanvig Lanham, Md.: Rowman & Littlefeld.

Danto, A. 1967. "Naturalism." In *Encyclopedia of Philosophy*, Vol. 5, ed. P. Edwards. New York: Macmillan.

Edel, Abraham. 1946. "Is Naturalism Arbitrary?" *The Journal of Philosophy* 43: 141–52.

Foley, R. 1994. "Quine and Naturalized Epistemology" In *Midwest Studies in Philosophy*, Vol. 19, ed. P. French et al.

French, P., et al, eds. 1994. *Midwest Studies in Philosophy*, Vol. 19. Minneapolis: University of Minnesota Press.

Gibson, R. 1987. "Quine on Naturalism and Epistemology." *Erkenntnis* 27: 57–78.

———. 1995. "Quine on the Naturalizing of Epistemology."In *On Quine: New Essays*, ed. P. Leonardi and M. Santambrogio.

Goldman, A. 1986. *Epistemology and Cognition*. Cambridge, Mass.: Harvard University Press.

———.1992. *Liaisons: Philosophy Meets the Cognitive and Social Sciences*. Cambridge: MIT Press.

———. 1994. "Naturalistic Epistemology and Reliabilism." In *Midwest Studies in Philosophy*, Vol. 19, ed. P. French et al.

Goodman, Nelson. 1979. *Fact, Fiction, and Forecast*. 3d ed. Indianapolis: Hackett.

Haack, S. 1993a. *Evidence and Inquiry*. Cambridge, Mass.: Basil Blackwell.

———. 1993b. "Two Faces of Quine's Naturalism." *Synthese* 94: 335–56.

Hylton, P. 1994. "Quine's Naturalism." In *Midwest Studies in Philosophy*, Vol. 19, ed. P. French et al.

Keller, Evelyn Fox. 1988. "Critical Silences in Scientific Discourse." In *Scientific Knowledge*, 2d ed., ed. J. Kourany. Belmont, Calif.: Wadsworth.

Kim, J. 1988. "What is 'Naturalized Epistemology'?" In *Philosophical Perspectives*, Vol. 2, ed. J. Tomberlin. Atascadero, Calif.: Ridgeview.

Kitcher, Patricia. 1992. *Freud's Dream*. Cambridge: MIT Press.

Kitcher, Phillip.1992. "The Naturalists Return." *The Philosophical Review* 101: 53–114.

———. 1993. *The Advancement of Science*. New York: Oxford University Press.

Koonz, Claudia. 1991. "Genocide and Eugenics: The Language of Power." In *Lessons and Legacies*, ed. P. Hayes.

Kornblith, H. 1993. "Epistemic Normativity." *Synthese* 94: 357–76.

———. 1995. "Naturalistic Epistemology and Its Critics." *Philosophical Topics* 23: 237–55.

———, ed. 1994. "Introduction: What is Naturalistic Epistemology?" In *Naturalizing Epistemology*, 2d rev. ed. Cambridge: MIT Press.

Koppelberg, D. 1990. "Why and How to Naturalize Epistemology." in *Perspectives on Quine*, ed. R. Barrett and R. Gibson. Cambridge, Mass.: Blackwell, 1990).

Kvanvig, J., ed. 1996. *Warrant in Contemporary Epistemology*. Lanham, Md.: Rowman & Littlefeld.

Laudan, L. 1986. "Testing Theories of Scientific Change." *Synthese* 69: 141–224.

———. 1987. "Progress or Rationality: The Prospects for Normative Naturalism." *American Philosophical Quarterly* 24: 19–31.

Leonardi, P., and M. Santambrogio, eds. 1995. *On Quine: New Essays*. New York: Cambridge University Press.

Lloyd, Elizabeth A. 1996. "Science and Anti-Science: Objectivity and its Real Enemies." In *Feminism, Science, and the Philosophy of Science*, ed. L. H. Nelson and J. Nelson. Boston: Kluwer Academic Publishers.

Longino, Helen E. 1990. *Science as Social Knowledge*. Princeton: Princeton University Press.

———. 1994. "The Fate of Knowledge in Social Theories of Science." In *Socializing Epistemology*, ed. F. Schmitt.

Maffie, J. 1990. "Recent Work on Naturalized Epistemology." *American Philosophical Quarterly* 27: 281–93.

———. 1995a. "Naturalism, Scientism, and the Independence of Epistemology." *Erkenntnis* 41: 1–27

Markie, P. 1996. "Goldman's New Reliabilism." *Philosophy and Phenomenological Research* 56: 799–817.

Mushaben, Joyce Marie. 1999. "Collective Memory Divided and Reunited." *History and Memory* 11: 7–40.

Plantinga, A. 1996. "Ad Conee." in *Warrant in Contemporary Epistemology*, ed. J. Kvanvig.

Putnam, H. 1982. "Why Reason Can't Be Naturalized." *Synthese* 52: 3–23.

Quine, W. V. 1960. *Word and Object*. Cambridge: MIT Press.

———. 1961. "Two Dogmas of Empiricism." In *From a Logical Point of View*, 2d rev. ed. Cambridge, Mass.: Harvard University Press.

———. 1969. "Epistemology Naturalized." *In Ontological Relativity*. New York: Columbia University Press.

———. 1973. *The Roots of Reference*. LaSalle, Ill.: Open Court Publishers.

———. 1976. *The Ways of Paradox*. 2d. rev. ed. Cambridge, Mass.: Harvard University Press.

———. 1981. *Theories and Things*. Cambridge, Mass.: Harvard University Press.

———. 1986. "Reply to Morton White." In *The Philosophy of W. V. Quine*, ed. L. Hahn and P. Schilpp. LaSalle, Ill.: Open Court Publishers.

———. 1990. *Pursuit of Truth*. Cambridge, Mass.: Harvard University Press.

———. 1995. "Naturalism; Or, Living Within One's Means." *Dialectica* 49: 251–61.

Rorty, Richard. 1980. "A Reply to Dreyfus and Taylor," *Review of Metaphysics* 34: 39–55.

Rosenberg, A. 1996. "A Field Guide to Recent Species of Naturalism." *British Journal for the Philosophy of Science* 47: 1–29.

Roth, P. A. 1978. "Paradox and Indeterminacy." *Journal of Philosophy* 75: 347–67.

———. 1987. *Meaning and Method in the Social Sciences*. Ithaca: Cornell University Press.

———. 1996a. "Dubious Liaisons." *Philosophical Psychology* 9: 261–79.

———. 1996b. "Will the Real Scientists Please Stand Up?" *Studies in History and Philosophy of Science* 27: 43–68.

———. 1999. "Naturalizing Goldman." *Southern Journal of Philosophy* 37: 89–109.

Russell, B. 1918. "What There Is." In *Classics of Analytic Philosophy*, ed. R. Ammerman. Reprint, 1990. Indianapolis: Hackett.

Schmitt, Frederick F., ed. 1994. *Socializing Epistemology*. Lanham, Md.: Rowman & Littlefield.

Solomon, M. 1994. "A More Social Epistemology." In *Socializing Epistemology*, ed. F. Schmitt.

———. 1995. "Legend Naturalism and Scientific Progress: An Essay on Philip Kitcher's *The Advancement of Science*." *Studies in History and Philosophy of Science* 26: 205–18.

van Fraassen, Bas. 1995. "Against Naturalized Epistemology." In *On Quine: New Essays*, ed. P. Leonardi and M. Santambrogio.

———. 1996. "Science, Materialism, and False Consciousness." In *Warrant in Contemporary Epistemology*, ed. J. Kvanvig.

8

The Last Dogma of Empiricism?[1]

Jack Nelson

This is, in the jargon of twenty-five years ago, a paper about the fact/value distinction, or, better, the science/values distinction. The question mark in the title concerns whether the science/value distinction is a dogma or a defensible distinction to be drawn within holism. I begin from the position of a Quinean holist and argue that value claims should be seen as part of our holistic world theory that is, as a whole, supported by experience. However, I do conclude that there may still be a distinction, though perhaps one of degree, to be drawn between values and value-laden claims and other parts of our world theory. The moral of this paper will be that whether there is a science/values distinction of some sort is far less important than is the recognition of two "facts" about "values," that values frequently do influence the course of science and that we cannot, for this very reason, afford to treat values as matters of personal preference or as subjective or as in any other way wholly or even largely exempt from the standards of evidence and evaluation that apply to science itself.

Starting Points

It will be useful to enumerate at the start what I take to be some fairly noncontroversial boundary conditions for any view about the relation between facts and values and about the nature of science. I assume that in any acceptable view of science and values there must be room for social, political, and moral theory as well as for physics, chemistry, and biology, that there must be room within all of these areas of inquiry for arguments and for evidence. Within the sciences, however broadly construed, there must be a place for testability and empirical confirmation. I am a holist, and as such believe that none of our currently accepted theories, either in part or in whole, are immune from possible revision and even abandonment. I think it is a consequence of holism, though not one Quine fully recognizes, that it is we, and not I, who know, in more than the editorial sense (see Nelson, 1990). As a holist, I believe that no theory or thesis that we are now in a position to put forward that challenges the basic success, accuracy, or objectivity of science, or large parts thereof, will be viable. We are too close to current science, our standards of evidence and reasonableness are too much part and parcel of our science, to be in a position to reject that science in total. And this is as it should be. But it does not follow that all intelligent creatures, everywhere, and for all time, will be subscribers to science as we now know it. There is no paradox here.[2]

Like most philosophers of science, I hold both that science does not rest on a priori truths that it is the business of philosophy to lay bare and, where necessary, explain, and that the philosophy of science should be equated neither with the history of science nor with the sociological description of the activity of scientists. Rather, philosophy of science is, despite the ill repute into which the phrase has fallen, the identification and *rational reconstruction* of good science. As such it presumes that it is possible to distinguish good from bad science, and to say what it is about each that makes it so. But there is no presumption here that there are any standards other than those of science itself, broadly construed, for so doing.

One of the great failings of the naive empiricism of logical positivism is that the story it told about scientific investigation failed, almost completely, to match the actual practices of scientists. Logical empiricism (or immediate postlogical positivist philosophy of science)[3] adopted, as a proposed remedy for this failing, the context of discovery / context of justification distinction, and, at least apparently, abandoned all pretext of giving an account of the practice of scientists in favor of a way of distinguishing good theories, however arrived at, from bad theories. This is not, as most philosophers of science now recognize, a viable position, for to suggest that there is no discoverable connection between how science is done and whether viable theories are produced is to assign a substantial part of the process of science to the realm of the irrational, or at least the nonrational.

Any viable philosophy of science must recognize the indisputable success of science. But what does this mean? At least this: we are able to build automobiles and nuclear reactors, and to explain why both run and, normally, neither explodes. We understand something about how diseases spread and can, sometimes, intervene to cure or control them. We can relate the gross structural properties of middle-sized objects to properties attributed to molecular, atomic, and subatomic particles. For a wide range of events and actions, we can predict at least some ensuing events and actions. We have organized our knowledge into broad fields, and know something of the connections between and across those fields. And so on.

The success of science is due, in large part, to the stress it places on empirical confirmation. The traditional view has been that the questions science deals with can, in principle, be settled by the normal techniques of science, including empirical confirmation, whereas questions of value cannot. Hence, if the norms of objectivity, accuracy, and the goal of truthfully representing nature are to be accomplished, values must be excluded from science. Since anything goes in the realm of values, the success of science can only be accomplished by building and maintaining an absolute wall between science and values.

For these reasons, scientists are trained to "leave their values at the laboratory door." And, by and large, good scientists do leave at least their most obviously value-laden views at the laboratory door. That is, for the most part the various sciences have been fairly successful in developing and enforcing canons of intellectual responsibility that have either prevented, or exposed and condemned, the blatant intrusion of values into research. However, over the past twenty years research into the theory and practice of science, including research by feminist science critics and by practicing scientists—some of which is presented in papers in this volume—has shown that values do influence science more frequently and in more subtle ways than positivist and postpositivist philosophy of science would have us believe. Personal and societal norms and values do influence, for better and for worse, the selection of research agendas, the way research is carried out, what is counted as "data" and as "results," and when a hypothesis or theory is counted as confirmed or disconfirmed. The norms and values that affect science include not only what are taken to be constitutive values of science (e.g., simplicity, explanatory power, fecundity . . .) but also traditional moral values of various sorts, broad and usually unexamined views and presuppositions about what research agendas are important and worth pursuing, about what is and is not relevant to those agendas, about the standards for what constitutes good scientific practice and good scientific theories, about what the relation of science to society and social values is, and about what is and is not obvious. Often cited examples of social values influencing science include the long unchallenged dominance of "man-the-hunter" theories in anthropology, the unwarranted and widespread acceptance of Wilson's sociobiology, the emphasis in medical research on diseases and ailments primarily affecting males, and the continuing currency of the view that women and minorities "can't do science and math."

Reactions to the litany of cases in which values seem to have influenced science range from attempts to deny or dramatically minimize the effects of such influence, to pronouncements that these are examples of bad science and that the scientific community must hereafter be more vigilant about keeping values out of science (Haack 1993), to suggestions that the problem is not that values influence science, but rather that *the wrong values* have influenced science (along with suggestions as to what the right values might be) (Longino 1990), to proposals to reconstruct science with values but without empiricism (Harding 1986). A few have argued that the notion of evidence can reasonably be construed so as to include value-laden assumptions broadly held within the relevant research community without transforming science into a radically different enterprise (Nelson 1990).

I end this section with what may seem a digression. Many years ago I was discussing meta-ethics with a colleague. I was maintaining that, despite all of the problems with utilitarianism, it is still the only theory that makes sense, in the end, in a world in which determinism or something very like it holds. After a lot of verbiage, my colleague, who was defending a deontological view, said, in exasperation, "Well, *everyone* is a utilitarian in your sense," by which he meant that everyone, or everyone who has thought seriously about the matter, agrees that in the end what is of concern is maximizing the welfare and happiness of individuals. He thought the only interesting disputes are about what sort of a society is likely to best address those concerns, his own view being that the notion of justice or fairness must play a pivotal role in any such society.

In recent years it has become fashionable to announce that empiricism is dead and that we must move beyond that naive approach to science. The context within which such claims have been made is not that of a discussion of philosophical empiricism versus philosophical rationalism, both of which grant experience an important role in theory formation and confirmation, but differ on whether, in epistemic activities, the mind is "active" or "passive." That is, the empiricism under attack is that which is assumed by both philosophical empiricism and philosophical rationalism, and is the touchstone of modern science. It is the view that our knowledge of the natural world is built on sensory experience and is intended to predict, explain, and integrate that experience, present, future, and past. I feel about pronouncements of the death of this minimal kind of empiricism, call it science empiricism, much as I do about the professed demise of utilitarianism—that people who reject either utilitarianism or science empiricism are being disingenuous. What they are really saying is that certain unduly restrictive or naive formulations of utilitarianism or of science empiricism must be rejected. This is of course true. But in the end we are all utilitarians, and, I think, science empiricists. Those who deny a connection between knowledge and experience, and are not disingenuous in doing so, are unlikely to successfully cross a street on which there is even a moderate amount of vehicular traffic.

The point of this disgression is that some recent attacks on science, and more specifically on empiricism, including those motivated by the revelation that values have influenced various sciences, are either disingenuous or very badly stated, mistaking science empiricism for logical positivism or for a naive inductivist view of the growth of scientific knowledge by accretion, or for the postpositivist distinction between the context of discovery and the context of justification and the deductive nomological model of explanation developed in tandem with that distinction (see, for example, Harding 1986, 1993). But science empiricism is not any of the above positions. The core of science empiricism is simply that experience matters, is the touchstone of knowledge claims and theory formation.

The Quinean Context

Quine's legacy will surely include the lesson that what we have come to think of as natural, intuitive, and structure-yielding distinctions and boundaries are frequently anything but natural, seem intuitive only because we have learned to see philosophy, science, and the world through their blinders, and that the structures they impose are not always the most useful ones. There is no analytic/synthetic distinction because there are no analytic truths. There is at least no sharp theory/observation distinction because all, or almost all, sentences are theory-laden.[4] No sentences of our accepted theories, including definitions and observation sentences, are immune from possible revision or abandonment in the light of new experience or of reconsidered past experience. Truth can be defined, *à la* Tarski, for a language and hence for a theory, but the old notion of a naive correspondence theory of truth, with its simplistic dichotomy between words and world, goes by the way, as, in the end, do reference and meaning, at least in the sense of intension. Confirmation and testability are viable and useful notions, but it is theories as wholes that face the tribunal of experience, not individual sentences, be they putative laws, observation sentences (except as construed holophrastically), or proposed definitions.

Science itself is "a conceptual bridge of our own making, linking sensory stimulation to sensory stimulation" (Quine 1981d, 2). We, as a species and as individuals, are as much posits of our theories as are quarks, atoms, tables, and chairs. Hence, we are as much creatures of our theories as they are of us. And once we have posited *us*, *Homo sapiens*, the data that science must accommodated come to include our reactions to the firings of our sensory receptors.

Some have concluded that for all of these reasons we are trapped by our own conceptual scheme, powerless prisoners of our past, and have turned to Kuhn's account of scientific revolutions for an explanation of theory change. But the proper metaphor is not that of being trapped or constrained by our own theories. The proper metaphor is rather that of being enabled and empowered by our best going theories, for these theories not only structure our view of the world and our place in it but also themselves provide us with the tools whereby we can reshape those very theories, though not, of course, "all at once." The history of science is the history of our doing so, with varying degrees of competency and success.

Given that Quine has challenged so many traditional distinctions and dogmas, one might expect him to reject the science/value distinction as well.[5] But Quine has a foot firmly in the tradition of Carnap and the empiricism of the first half of this century. He would certainly defend many views and policies that are taken to follow from the science/value distinction, for example that religious, political, social, and moral values have no place in the laboratory, that social and political policies are not logical consequences of scientific discoveries, and that "good" science (i.e., technically well done research and the theories resulting from it) can lead to, or at least make possible, horrendous social and political acts. And in a relatively late piece, "On the Nature of Moral Values," in *Theories and Things*, he does explicitly defend a distinction between values and science.

There are a number of real, or presumed, difficulties about value sentences that are not, I suggest, the basis for Quine's insistence upon a science/values distinction. The truth conditions for value claims are often seen as problematic, but this is not why Quine excludes such claims from science. In "On Austin's Method" Quine notes that "The paradigm [Tarski's theory of truth] works for evaluations . . . as well as for statements of fact . . . 'Slander is evil' is true if and only if slander is evil. . . . " (Quine 1981b, 90). There is a difficulty in accommodating value claims to the extensional logic of first-order quantification theory, but this is not, I think, Quine's reason for excluding values from science, for the same concern holds for a vast range of sentences that we are not now in a position to treat within first-order quantification theory but are also not prepared to abandon, including, for a start, the whole range of sentences ascribing intensional states to agents, many principles and claims of the social sciences, and much of psychology. Nor does Quine exclude values from science because he is a reductionist and value sentences are not reducible to sentences of physics. Whether Quine is a reductionist, and if so of what sort, need not be settled here, for there are, again, a whole host of sentences that are not obviously reducible to sentences of physics that Quine does include within science, including most of the substance of the life sciences and the social sciences.[6]

Finally, Quine does not exclude value sentences from science because there is *no* evidence for value claims. In "On the Nature of Moral Values" Quine allows that holism does place constraints on the values we posit as well as on the scientific theories we construct. He also recognizes the constraint imposed by the survival value to societies of moral, social, and political systems that serve to promote at least minimal cooperation and to prevent behavior that works against the smooth functioning of society. "[W]e can expect a common core, since the most basic problems of society are bound to run to type. Morality touches the common lot of mankind" (Quine 1981c, 62). Of course, sentences that *ascribe* likes and dislikes, values, or value systems to individuals or societies *are* part of science, for they do support predictions. People who like raw oysters behave differently from those who do not, at least in the presence of raw oysters and with all other things being equal. So too, there are situations in which racists and non-racists behave, predictably, differently.

The primary reason Quine excludes values from science is, I think, that in his view "empirical controls" work only on science: "Science, thanks to its links with observation, retains some title to a correspondence theory of truth; but a coherence theory is evidently the lot of ethics" (Quine 1981c, 63). The empirical controls on science function via observation conditionals. "A reasonably inclusive body of scientific theory, taken as a whole, will . . . imply a lot of observational conditionals, as I call them, each of which says that if certain observable conditions are met then a certain observable event will occur" (Quine 1981a, 70). But no set of nondescriptive value sentences will, Quine apparently believes, imply any observational conditionals not derivable without the value sentences.[7] There is also, for Quine, the stumbling block of modal logic. Quine believes that all of modal logic rests on a confusion, and the "logic" of values (deontic logic) seems to be a variety of modal logic.

Arguments Against a Science/Values Distinction

A compelling reason for seeking to accommodate value claims within science is the hope of bringing something of the "objectivity" and openness that are characteristic of science to bear on value claims. The hope here is that rejecting the science/value distinction would result not, as many scientists and traditional epistemologists and philosophers of science assume, in relativism, in everything becoming a matter of personal or group preference, but rather in all claims, including value claims, becoming subject, more or less, to the same canons of evidence and evaluation. Values, that is, might become more like facts than facts become like values. And were this to happen, the fact that values do, to whatever extent, influence science would be less of a concern than it is now.

I find two interlinked themes within Quine's work that argue against a complete science/value distinction. The first is Quinean holism, the second Quine's notion of posits and reality. I begin with holism.

Quinean empiricism, as I interpret it, is the view that experience is the firings of sensory receptors, and that science is a set of theories whose aim is to explain, predict, and systematize experience. Quinean holism is the story of how this is accomplished. (I take Quinean empiricism to be a theory of evidence, not a theory of meaning, although Quine's talk of words and sentences as having meaning only within the context of larger theories sometimes makes it seem as though he were offering a theory of meaning.)[8] Quine's earliest, and perhaps clearest, statement of holism is in "Two Dogmas of Empiricism":

> The totality of our so-called knowledge or beliefs, from the most casual matters of geography and history to the profoundest laws of atomic physics or even of pure mathematics and logic, is a man-made [*sic*] fabric which impinges on experience only along the edges. Or, to change the figure, total science is like a field of force whose boundary conditions are experience. A conflict with experience at the periphery occasions readjustments in the interior of the field. Truth values have to be redistributed over some of our statements. Reevaluation of some statements entails reevaluation of others, because of their logical interconnections—the logical laws being in turn simply certain further statements of the system, certain further elements of the field . . . the total field is so underdetermined by its boundary conditions, experience, that there is much latitude of choice as to what statements to reevaluate in the light of any single contrary experience. No particular experiences are linked with any particular statements in the interior of the field, except indirectly through considerations of equilibrium affecting the field as a whole. (Quine 1963, 42–43)

What counts for or against a claim or theory is how it is integrated in a larger theory or set of theories, and how well these interconnected claims and theories collectively predict, explain, and integrate the firings of our sensory receptors. All of this seems to invite, or at least allow, the inclusion of value claims, or value laden claims, within science—or at least within the holistic web consisting of "[t]he totality of our so-called knowledge or beliefs."

Consider now Quine's view of posits, reality, and conservatism. Quine is neither a realist nor an instrumentalist. Theories are sets of sentences. Our ontic commitment is to those things that we must posit to make the sentences of our theories come out true. To ask what there is is to ask what posits we must make for our theories to come out true. Among the posits of the going theories of the natural and social sciences are atomic and subatomic particles and middle-sized bits of animate and inanimate stuff, including us, *Homo sapiens*. While we do, at times and for certain purposes, make use of theories whose posits include only esoteric objects, e.g., chunks of space-time, we are not prepared, at least yet, to dispense with theories that do include more standard objects, including *us*. Indeed, the theories within which we do most of our applied and theoretical work do posit the mundane objects of ordinary life.

To the extent that we are concerned to understand us, *Homo sapiens*, our theories also posit social structures and individual and social goods and rights. For good and not so good reasons we have posited racial and sexual categories, and have constructed notions of sexuality, most of which are value infused. We collectively construct a world in which pain, suffering, happiness, joy, and prejudice are as real as trees, cars, political entities, and quarks. The social and the physical worlds are both posits, and the very distinction between these is itself a boundary of our own making and open to revision. If this is indeed the boat of Neurath, within which we collectively find ourselves, then values and value theory are important parts of the holistic web that, as a whole, confronts experience. And the evidence of holism is available as much for value claims as it is for claims of logic and number theory. In these as in all cases we appeal to how the claims or theories in question help to integrate our experience, including our social experience, how they connect with other going theories, and how they together help us predict future experience, including our own and others' reactions to the violence, kindness, rudeness, and considerateness we encounter.

A More Modest Holism

But there is good reason to think the foregoing view is not Quine's view, or at least not Quine's most recent view. The last sentence of Quine's statement of holism in "Two Dogmas" (quoted above) is "The unit of empirical significance is the whole of science." I have always been inclined to read Quine, in passages such as this, as including within science all beliefs worth holding. So, since beliefs concerning values are worth holding, they must be included within that holistic system. But I now think this is a misreading of Quine. Even in "Two Dogmas" Quine probably includes within science only the natural and social sciences (he explicitly includes geography and history), not all of our seriously held beliefs. In "The Nature of Moral Values" Quine does, as noted above, explicitly advocate a science/values distinction. And Quine's views have evolved. In his conversation with Giovanna Borradori in *The American Philosopher* Quine says:

> I have actually tempered the extreme holism of my first writing. . . . The way I look at things today is that there isn't only one science, but a big enough bundle of laws not to be comprehended as a single hypothesis. The big enough bundle implies logically some observational conditions,[9] namely some categories defining observable situations. . . . [H]olism is needed to the extent that you have a big enough combination to apply some of these testable categories. (Borradori 1994, 36)

The theme of a more modest holism is also to be found in "Five Milestones of Empiricism," where Quine writes:

> When we look thus to a whole theory or system of sentences as the vehicle of empirical meaning, how inclusive should we take this system to be? Should it be the whole of science? or the whole of *a* science, a branch of science? This should be seen as a matter of degree, and of diminishing returns. All sciences interlock to some extent. . . . It is an uninteresting legalism, however, to think of our scientific system of the world as involved *en bloc* in every prediction. More modest chunks suffice, and so may be ascribed their independent empirical meaning, nearly enough. . . .

> Thus the holism that the third move brings should be seen only as a moderate or relative holism. (Quine 1981a, 71)

Finally, there is a clear difference between Quine's use of Neurath's metaphor of sailors rebuilding a ship while on the open sea in *Word and Object* and in "Five Milestones of Empiricism." In the former, the metaphor is parsed as follows: "Neurath has likened science to a boat which, if we are to rebuild it, we must rebuild plank by plank while staying afloat in it" (Quine 1960, 3). In "Five Milestones of Empiricism" the crew of Neurath's boat is not the inclusive "we" but rather "the naturalistic philosopher":

> The naturalistic philosopher begins his [*sic*] reasoning within the inherited world theory as a going concern. He tentatively believes all of it, but believes also that some unidentified portions are wrong. He tries to improve, clarify, and understand the system from within. He is the busy sailor adrift on Neurath's boat. (Quine 1981a, 72)

Here the holistic story is the story of the *naturalistic* philosopher, the scientist. The story is that she or he begins with the sum of the sciences of her or his time (presumably including the social sciences, for though Quine uses the expression "naturalistic philosopher" he also talks of the "inherited world theory as a going concern") and goes on to refine and expand that body of knowledge, or a chunk thereof.

Should we restrict the web or network of sentences and theories that constitutes Quinean holism to sentences and theories of the sciences, and retreat from the view that it is the totality of those sentences and theories that confronts experience? Doing so would certainly make it easier to maintain the science/values distinction. Here it will help to remind ourselves of how an individual acquires "a world theory as a going concern."

As individuals we begin neither with a manageable chunk of science, nor with all of science, narrowly construed. The body of beliefs we inherit from our parents and our culture does not come to us separated into science/non-science components. We do not make the move from infancy to childhood to adolescence to adulthood by acquiring only, or in clearly delineated categories, a rudimentary knowledge of physics, chemistry, mathematics, logic, and other disciplines Quine includes within science.

What we acquire is a much more comprehensive and frequently inconsistent theory of physical objects, including human beings, of their patterns of behavior, and of our and others' reactions to that behavior, along, in some cases, with some ill-defined views about gods, extrasensory perception, magic, and whatever. Mixed in with all of this, not always in clearly distinguishable ways, are our values, what we like and dislike, what is worthwhile and what isn't, what is right and wrong. As we mature we refine our theory, throwing out gratuitous and distracting talk of extrasensory perception, magic, and, with any luck, of gods and the efficacy of prayer. Our theory comes to include more and clearer sentences about physical objects and physics, logic and mathematics, and about psychology, history, geography, morality, social theory, our likes and dislikes, and perhaps the meaning of life, or at least about what is worth doing. The educational system, with its traditional disciplinary distinctions, works its way and we come to see the world and our own beliefs largely in disciplinary terms, with values largely relegated to a separate domain. Some beliefs do persist that, when pressed, we would be hard put to label as purely factual or purely valuational, e.g., beliefs about what is "natural," medical beliefs about what constitutes health, disease, successful treatment, and beliefs about social and political structures and practices.

The evolution in our beliefs is in part the evolution from "I" to "we." The beliefs we retain are the beliefs we find others in our communities holding or amenable to holding. We learn that most of our beliefs are shared with some, but not all, and not always the same, members of society at large. (Those that are shared with no others tend to wither away.) That is, we become members of distinct but overlapping communities, each with an associated set of beliefs. Some communities are based on loyalty to these particular kith and kin, deriving from a shared and idiosyncratic family upbringing, others on broader beliefs about the proper organization of society and socially acceptable behavior (deriving from cross-family training and experience), others on shared religious beliefs derived from a community broader than the family but narrower than one's political and economic community, others on one's exposure to or inclusion in the natural science community, with its commitment to standards of evidence and testability. Experience shows, by and large, that we cannot expect all others to share our views about our own kith and kin, our religion or lack thereof, our views of government and social organization. We are, in fact, taught to tolerate if not encourage differences in beliefs about religion, politics, social structures, and appropriate behavior (within limits). But we do think everyone will share, or can be brought to share, the claims that are constitutive of the sciences. We are taught that differences in belief within the natural sciences must be resolvable. Given this view, holism, the view that every claim is connected, however remotely and tenuously, with every other claim, can work only within the natural sciences, for elsewhere we are prepared to tolerate conflicting claims. And the only posits that deserve to be thought of as constitutive of reality will be those required to make the sentences constitutive of the holistic web of the natural sciences true. An implication of this view is, of course, that rationally based agreement is obtainable on all and only the claims of the traditional sciences.

Two untoward results are likely to follow: first, we are likely to mistake broad agreement concerning a belief with that belief's being part of science (for we expect broad agreement only within science), and, second, we may be too ready to tolerate divergence of belief in areas outside the traditional sciences.

A Broader Holism

A preferable view is surely that the crew of Neurath's boat is indeed "we" and not "I," and that the boat itself consists of all our seriously held beliefs, our whole world view including beliefs about values in so far as we expect to be able to achieve community-wide consensus about those beliefs. This is our "world theory as a going concern." To Quine's remark, quoted earlier, that "Science, thanks to its links with observation, retains some title to a correspondence theory of truth; but a coherence theory is evidently the lot of ethics" we can reply that, on Quinean grounds, neither a correspondence nor a coherence theory of truth is viable. The only viable theory of truth is Tarski's semantic theory, and that theory accords well enough, as Quine recognizes, with value claims.

The broader holism I am urging will grant that some beliefs included in our world theory will express values or be value laden. For example, until recently the inherited world theory of most scientists included the view that women are less intelligent and less capable than men, that the activities of men (and not those of women) are at the heart of the explanation of the development of civilizations and culture, and that there are racial differences in intellectual abilities. In the view I am urging, once these and other views are seen to be value laden they will not be for that reason expelled from our going world theory (and thus exempted from the demand for evidence and justification), but scrutinized and adjusted as the (holistic) evidence warrants.

There are, I think, two ways in which we might see the science/value distinction given the broader holism I am urging. Both involve including value and value-laden beliefs within our holistic world view. The first would be analogous to the way Quine thinks the work of the analytic part of the analytic/synthetic distinction is diffused throughout science. Recall that the analytic/synthetic distinction presupposed two grounds for truth, linguistic convention and correspondence to the world. In abandoning the distinction we do not abandon the view that world and language both contribute to the truth of our claims:

> Taken collectively, science has its double dependence upon language and experience; but this duality is not significantly traceable into the statements of science taken one by one. (Quine 1963, 42)

And in "Five Milestones of Empiricism" Quine says:

> Holism blurs the supposed contrast between the synthetic sentence, with its empirical content, and the analytic sentence, with its null content. The organizing role that was supposedly the role of analytic sentences is now seen as shared by sentences generally, and the empirical content that was supposedly peculiar to synthetic sentences is now seen as diffuse through the system. (Quine 1981a, 71–72)

Analogously, perhaps, we might see views about *what is* and *what is of value* as jointly contributing to our understanding of the world, but with these contributions also not being "traceable into the statements" of our world view taken one by one. On this suggestion we would see our valuational concerns as "shared by sentences generally," and both factual concerns and value concerns as "diffused through the system."

The work of "analytic" sentences is spread across the linguistic net in the sense that the "meaning" of a term is given, not by a set of analytic truths containing that term, but by all the sentences containing that term, embedded as they are in a wider theory from which observation conditionals can be derived.[10] Similarly, the "meaning" of a value term is given by the totality of sentences in our theory in which that term occurs. The question is what the connection or overlap is between our commitment to sentences containing value terms and the rest of our world theory. Are all the observation conditionals derivable from our world theory also derivable when all sentences containing value terms are excluded? I do not know what the answer to this question is, in part because I am not sure we are clear about the distinction between "value term" and "non-value term." However, if pressed to supply evidence for the minimal utilitarianism to which I subscribe, I would be tempted to say that the evidence is diffused throughout the world view to which I subscribe, flows from the way that view pictures individuals and their place in the world and their relations to other individuals. If this is so, it suggests that the value content of utilitarianism is spread through at least large parts of our world theory.

The second way in which we might bring values within our holistic world theory is by simply extending that theory so as to include as disciplines within it moral theory and social and political theory. We would then come to see our world theory as a continuum, with values and value issues being largely if not entirely excluded from the physical sciences, having some substantive connection with the biological and biobehavioral sciences, more with the traditional social sciences, and of paramount importance in social and political theory and moral theory. This would retain something of the science/value distinction, but as a distinction drawn as a matter of degree, and within the holistic world theory. The overall goal would remain that of delineating, explaining, and predicting experience, the firings of our sensory receptors, and our reactions thereto. The degree to which theories and parts of theories are removed from the experiential edge of this web will, of course, vary, and it is not clear that all parts of the physical sciences, e.g., high energy physics, will be closer to the experiential edge than all parts having a clear value component, e.g., social theory.

Does the foregoing view place science and values on the same footing, obviating any need to disentangle the two wherever they are intertwined? Does it address Quine's concern for empirical adequacy, for the requirement that to be part of a serious theory of nature beliefs must be constituents of some block of theory that does imply observation conditionals? Is it enough that the world theory as a whole does imply observation conditionals? We might note here that pure logic and number theory do not themselves imply observation conditionals. They are, however, infused in chunks of our world theory, e.g., physics, that do imply observation conditionals. Are value claims similarly infused in parts of social and political theory? Might it be the case that values and value theory serve to enhance the explanatory power of our broader biological, biobehavioral, and social theories, not by implying observation conditionals, but by shaping the way in which we look at the world, by highlighting certain aspects of experience? Might not value claims and value theory, including a commitment to a minimal utilitarianism, help us make sense of and integrate the firings of our sensory receptors, past, present, and future, and *our reactions thereto?*[11] For example, might value-laden claims help us make sense of our and others' reactions to natural and human-caused disasters? Does positing that human suffering is evil perhaps make our reactions to suffering more comprehensible than it would otherwise be?

I am not sure what the answers to the foregoing questions are. Nor do I think answering those questions is as important as is recognizing that values and value theory are not everywhere a matter of personal taste or preference, that a minimal commitment to utilitarianism and a recognition of the interconnections among the biological, the biobehavioral, and the social sciences, and value theory yields a more viable and valuable world theory than does any sharp science/values distinction that excludes values and value theory from the realm of evidence and evaluation.

For example, the work of feminist science critics of the last twenty years suggests that the history of science is replete with examples of value-laden beliefs, social, political, and moral, influencing what research project is undertaken and what hypotheses entertained. If this is so, an alternative to striving even harder to exclude those beliefs would be to work harder to make sure such beliefs are reasonable beliefs, are congruent with our collective wider network of beliefs. This will require dropping the assumption that in all value-laden areas agreement is not to be expected, that wildly differing views are to be tolerated, if not encouraged, but excluded from science. Given a commitment to a minimal utilitarianism, it does not seem crazy to think we might obtain agreement about such issues as social and political policies, as well as about standard moral issues.

The attempt to isolate science from values can be traced back a long way, and has in some clear ways contributed to the advancement of science. One can, for example, read Descartes's *Meditations* as a subversive tract designed to show that god is unnecessary (the epistemic arguments of the *Meditations* work as well without any theistic assumptions) in ways that clerics would not understand, and, more to the point here, to get the

Church off the back of science. That is, one can read Descartes as providing a pretext for the Church's giving free reign to science, since the latter deals only with the material world, a world, as Descartes showed, of little or no importance compared to the world of the mental.[12] One can also see Descartes' gambit as having worked. Science prospered. But this gambit, which might be termed "Descartes's Compromise," had a price: it left religion and ethics within the domain of the Church and, wittingly or not, laid the groundwork for a strong science/value distinction and the ensuing view that there is no settling issues involving values (except perhaps by appeal to religion).

Had this dichotomy not been established, whether by Descartes or the larger intellectual tradition, science and the industrial revolution might not have progressed as quickly. On the other hand, had it not been put in place we might now have a more sophisticated view of value issues and of the interplay of values and what became traditional science. While allowing that "anything goes" in the areas of values and religion mitigates against holy and ideological wars (if anything goes, then whatever my views are, they are not worth fighting and dying over), it also mitigates against the development of a broader perspective in which it becomes apparent how "facts" and "values" intertwine.

Holism with Distinctions

Without assuming that the issue of the coherence and usefulness of the science/value distinction has been settled, I do want to explore the consequences of a science that, minimally, makes less of that distinction. In no sense would it follow from such a down-playing of the science/value distinction that "anything goes" in theory construction and testing, be it in evolutionary biology, social theory, or theories of the hormonal determination of sex-linked differences in cognitive ability. There are constraints on all, constraints traceable to our best going theories of the world and its contents, and to experience, upon which those theories collectively impinge. If well done, none of our theories will be arbitrary or capricious. Accordingly, it would be a mistake to conclude that if we allow both science and values into our going world theory we will, as a result, everywhere mix values and science and that as a result everyone will be free to bring her or his own preferred values into science.

At any given point in the history of research our world theory will be a collection of more modest theories, some well advanced, others in their infancy, still others ripe for abandonment, and together almost certainly inconsistent. There are, therefore, practical limits to applying the results of one field to another, even where they are related. For example, E. O. Wilson's own research, limited as it has been in the main to ants and termites, seems obviously not at a stage where it can serve as a model for sociobiology applied to humans, even if sociobiology ultimately proves to be a viable field. The second reality is that researchers are often not broadly educated, their expertise being limited to the narrowly defined segment of the research program for which they are responsible. Finally, researchers holding almost every imaginable combination of political, religious, ethical, and social views do participate in science.

Traditional science accommodates these realities by denying holism—not all of our seriously held beliefs are relevant to all other beliefs, and by denying that values are relevant to any part of science. One advantage of so doing is that it makes the qualifications for doing science very modest indeed. When taught the scientific method and accepted research procedures (which has generally come to mean the method and procedures of one rather narrowly defined field), those of all political, religious, ethical, and aesthetic persuasions, no matter how ignorant of virtually everything except what is narrowly involved in the research project in question, can and do pursue science. The fact that researchers believe the silliest things, and engage in the silliest, or most heinous, practices outside their laboratories, or are woefully ignorant outside their own field, is taken to be no indicator whatsoever of the quality of their scientific research. All traditional science asks is that when doing science researchers neither appeal to nor let their research be influenced by their nonscience views and opinions.

To what extent can, and should, a holism that allows values within our world theory seek to accommodate the above realities of scientific practice? As a first step, we must follow Quine in conceding that a more manageable holism, a holism that most often works in terms of chunks of particular theories of particular disciplines, will generally suffice for the *bench scientist*. The theorist will have to deal with larger chunks or whole disciplines, and sometimes, when disciplines are in conflict, with our entire world theory. But the latter will be a very rare exception, not the rule. We can have, that is to say, holism *with distinctions*. We can allow for differential progress across the holistic world theory and can demand far less of bench researchers than a mastery of all of science. In the present taxonomy of disciplines, physics is not political theory, biology is not psychology, and population genetics is not social theory, though in each case the first may have important implications for the second, and in the last case at least, the second for the first.

At the same time we can hope that a broader holism of the sort I am advocating will bring with it a greater willingness to reexamine and redraw disciplinary boundaries as needed and to recognize connections between disciplines, perhaps thereby lessening the disparity in rates of progress among related disciplines, including areas of value theory. Disciplinary boundaries are, after all, of our own making. They evolve as our ongoing theories evolve. They are artificial but not imaginary.[13]

The acceptance of holism may also encourage individuals and society to take research in moral theory and in social and political theory more seriously. This, in turn, might mitigate against both individuals and groups holding and espousing ill-thought-out views about all manner of topics, including race, gender, and class. We can grant individuals the right to hold whatever views they want, while insisting that they are responsible for the views they hold. While we cannot expect individuals to examine, *à la* Descartes, every view they hold, we can expect them to examine views that are called into question by new or reconsidered experience or by other views they or others hold. And holism will reveal that there are more connections between seemingly disparate views than previously thought, e.g., connections between views about race, class, and gender and specific research projects concerning cognitive abilities and sexual preferences.

Suppose we do, as individuals and as communities, take values more seriously and countenance the kinds of evidence holism affords for and against value and value-laden claims. When this is so, should researchers be debarred from doing research when their views on value-infused issues are not those of the larger research community or society at large? No, of course not. But the larger research community, and society at large, will appropriately view the results of the research in question as in part a function of views and assumptions that they do not share with the researcher. Should funding agencies refuse to fund researchers whose value-infused views about the proposed research are other than those of the larger research community? Perhaps it depends on how divergent the views are, whether the researcher can give good (even if not compelling) arguments for those views, and the availability of funding and nature of the research project. The openness of science allows for a renewed defense of the Ptolemaic system. But most of us have a very hard time imagining the NSF funding a research proposal to do so.

To take an extreme case, can a researcher who believes that both euthanasia and infanticide should have a place within socially sanctioned practices usefully and appropriately engage in social policy development? There is certainly no reason to prevent such a person from proposing a social policy that sanctions both euthanasia and infanticide. The proposal will be evaluated on its merits by the larger community. Is there a reason to fund such research? Perhaps, though the reality of the current political climate is surely that it will not be funded. Can such a researcher reasonably work on the development of a social policy as part of a larger research group, a group that may have public funding? I think the answer is "yes." If the working assumptions of the research group include the view that infanticide and euthanasia are not to be tolerated, then our more radical researcher will either have to challenge those assumptions or agree to work within their confines. That is, if our researcher wants to work with the group, without challenging, or after unsuccessfully challenging, their assumptions, then she or he will have to leave all views about the merits of infanticide and euthanasia at the laboratory door. And this may be a perfectly reasonable accommodation, for there may be large areas of social policy where our researcher and the larger group are in agreement.

In general, then, while the inclusion of values and value theory within the web of seriously held beliefs challenges the view that values have nothing to do with research, it remains appropriate to require that researchers who are engaged in research whose assumptions are at odds with their own views must either challenge those assumptions or set their own conflicting views aside while engaged in that research.

We must also remember that the value-infused views and assumptions that influence research are not always consciously held or made. They are equally or more frequently non-consciously held biases, prejudices, or general but unwarranted or at least untested assumptions about, for example, race, class, and gender. They also include naive views about the nature of science, about the theory/observation distinction, about naive induction and theory formation, and about the relation of science to society. They include, finally, unspoken assumptions about the privileged status of the experience and views of white middle class males and of women and minorities who have been made into surrogates for white middle class males. There is no panacea for this problem. We can only work to make individuals more conscious of their own views, more aware that there may be connections between those views and what previously seemed to be wholly unrelated views. Making values and value theory a legitimate area of investigation, where rational discussion, argumentation, and connections with various of the traditional sciences are expected, is a good step in this direction.

The holism I am advocating also suggests we need to reconceptualize the way we train scientists. A reasonable (and not a rationalized) knowledge of the history of science should be required of all science majors. Ph.D. programs should place more emphasis on understanding the broad field and its presuppositions, including its relation to society and social issues, and less on purely technical skills. While mastering those technical skills allows Ph.D. students to replace traditional laboratory assistants in the research programs of their mentors (frequently without understanding the significance of those programs), it too often prepares those students only for specialized laboratory work, the demand for which has often disappeared by the time they graduate.[14] We need, in short, a better and more broadly educated, as well as a more diverse, research community.[15] We need to challenge the misconception that "anything goes" in the realm of religious, social, political, and personal views without inciting holy or ideological wars and while preserving an open society. We need to allow members of society to believe the silliest of things, but we need not deny that they are silly.

Will we ever, however we reform science and research, be in a position to be sure that some unseen prejudice or unwarranted assumption has not biased the results of a particular piece or whole area of research? The answer here is clearly "no." We can be more careful, we can make the science community more diverse, we can urge that problems and research agendas be viewed from various perspectives, but we cannot know that nothing has biased our research. We can only do our best and accept our results tentatively. But what else could we ask for?

Postscript

One commentator has suggested, in less bald terms than these, that my thesis is muddled. When unmuddled it comes either to the view that value-laden beliefs are, at times, actually nodes in the theories and reasoning that lead ultimately to observation conditionals—in which case it is false—or to the view that values do sometimes influence the formation of research agendas and of perspectives taken, the range of experiments deemed relevant, and the use to which research results are put, but *not* the actual findings of science, in which case it is obvious (and uninteresting). In many ways, I am content to accept the interpretation that makes my position obvious and uninteresting, for I think that, in the end, the business of philosophy is in large part to make the obvious obvious. But I also think that what comes to be seen as obvious is not always uninteresting and unimportant. If we can establish the principle that not anything goes in the realm of values and value theory, then the influence values have on science, on the selection and delineation of research agendas, on the range of experiments deemed relevant, and on the use that is made of the findings, will become less pernicious.

It also seems to be the case that when one explores actual research programs that have been influenced by values, it becomes very hard to decide whether the best description of that influence is that of value-laden views that are clearly separate or separable from science influencing and shaping research agenda, or that of value-laden views becoming nodes in the theory and reasoning within which the research takes place. Consider, for example, research in neuroendocrinology in fetal development. The work of biologist Anne Fausto-Sterling and others makes it clear that this research presumes that it is only male development that is to be explained, and that it is only male hormones that are seen as having "organizing effects" on development (Fausto-Sterling 1991). Fausto-Sterling notes that textbook accounts of "fetal sexual development" are accounts of male sexual development. One such text includes the assertion that it is "the natural tendency of the body to develop along female lines in the absence of other modifying influences" (Carlson 1981 as quoted in Fausto-Sterling 1991). As Fausto-Sterling notes, the question "How does [the female direction of development] *happen*, what are its mechanisms?" is, by and large, not asked. So too, it is only the effects of androgens, not those of estrogens, that have been widely studied, including their effects on the morphology of rat brains and subsequent changes in maze-negotiating skills (with some taking the results to be relevant to an explanation of why males are purportedly better than females at science and mathematics). This assumption of what needs to be explained and what the explanatory mechanisms might be is clearly value-laden and seems to be central to the research conducted. But it is not clear that the research in question is bad research; in fact Fausto-Sterling takes it to be commensurate with and supported by accepted theories (see also Nelson and Nelson 1995).

Feminists have seen a broader assumption at work, the assumption that it is males and male activity that are the appropriate focus of explanations in the social and biobehavioral sciences, as shaping and limiting, if not distorting, work not only in neuroendocrinology but also in evolutionary theory, primatology, and anthropology. Whether the narrow assumption about what is to be explained in fetal development, and the broader assumption about the centrality of male and maleness are seen as value-laden cultural beliefs that have influenced science or nodes within the theories of science matters less, as I suggested in my opening remarks, than does challenging those assumptions and modifying them as the evidence warrants, and this requires serious discussion and evaluation, not relegation to somewhere outside our world theory where evidence is of no consequence.

Postscript to "The Last Dogma of Empiricism"

When asked to co-author *On Quine* I reread many of Quine's works, and gained a better understanding of how they are interrelated and indeed part of a protracted argument. In the course of doing so I realized in rereading "The Last Dogma of Empiricism" that in that paper I concentrated on Quine's holism to the detriment of my understanding of his empiricism. Consequently, I did not address, head on, what is surely the strongest argument against the view I was there defending—namely that ethical claims are part of the web formed by our best going theories of the world, and are therefore empirical claims. The argument I failed to consider can be put this way. In the history of science, as disciplines emerged or were brought within science, the range of what counts as Quinean observation sentences and their kin (observation categoricals) has steadily expanded. For example, as alchemy grew into chemistry the range and number of observation sentences that constitute the base level claims of science increased. Why, then, if ethical claims are part of the corpus of science, can we not identify a range of observational sentences that are particularly germane to the determination of the truth or falsity of ethical claims? Alternatively put, if ethical truths are empirical truths, why cannot we identify instances of the firings of exteroceptors that are particularly relevant to determining the truth or falsity of ethical claims? There appear to be only two possible responses to this argument.

The first is that there are such observation sentences, such instances of the firings of exteroceptors. These will include, it can be argued, those that are associated with the witnessing of particularly horrific instances of human cruelty, or of disinterested acts of generosity, or of the defense of principle at considerable personal cost, and so on. But this response now seems unpromising to me. These experiences give us information about the psychological makeup of at least some of us, of how we react to various sorts of events, but it is not clear they constitute the observable basis of morality.

The second response to the above argument holds that ethical claims are like the claims of mathematics and logic in that they are spread throughout the web that consists of our best going theories and are somehow integral to those theories. If so, then despite the fact that there is no special experiential basis either for ethics or for mathematics and logic, these are nonetheless empirical disciplines. They are so because they are integral to all of science broadly construed, and because there is in the end no evidence other than empirical evidence. Quine neatly dispensed with the view that there is a different basis for mathematics and logic, namely that the claims thereof are true by convention, by noting that attempts to specify these conventions inevitably make use of the key logical notions we are trying to define, e.g., 'and,' 'or,' and 'not.'

But is it the case that ethical claims and ethical terms are spread through all of science in anything like the way the claims and vocabulary of mathematics and logic are spread through all of science? I now think that my argument in "The Last Dogma of Empiricism" was, in effect, that they are. But I also now think that my argument was inconclusive. More work needs to be done. In particular, I think it might be useful to explore whether the norms characterizing science, such as intersubjectivity and being unbiased, and those characterizing the doing of science, such as not giving special weight to the experiences of any subset of individuals and such as valuing consistency, generality, and even-handedness, might be such as to foster and support the development of enlightened ethical views.

Acknowledgments

I thank Steve Cohen, Michael Shepanski, and Richmond Campbell for helpful comments on several earlier versions of this paper. I thank the members of the Institutionen för filosofi och vetenskapsteori at the

University of Umeä, and in particular Sten Lindström, for enduring the reading of a much longer and denser version of this paper, and for convincing me that major changes were required. Finally, I thank Lynn Hankinson Nelson for valuable comments on many versions, and the moose and loons of Maine, who provided welcome interruptions to two summers of work on this paper.

Notes

1. There are two plausible claimants to this title, epistemic individualism, which has already been undermined by Lynn Hankinson Nelson and others, and the science/value distinction. This is a paper about the latter.

2. The view just expressed is, however, controversial. It is not held, for example, by Sheldon Glashow, who made the following remarks at a Nobel conference in 1989:

> We [scientists] believe that the world is knowable, that there are simple rules governing the behavior of matter and the evolution of the universe. We affirm that there are eternal, objective, extrahistorical, socially neutral, external and universal truths, and that the assemblage of these truths is what we call physical science. Natural laws can be discovered that are universal, invariable, inviolate, genderless and verifiable.
>
> They may be found by men or by women or by mixed collaborations of any obscene proportions. Any intelligent alien anywhere would have come upon the same logical system as we have to explain the structure of protons and the nature of supernovae.
>
> This statement I cannot prove. This statement I cannot justify. This is my faith. (Glashow 1989)

3. I include as postpositivist philosophers of science Carnap, Hempel, Nagel, Popper and others who recognized the failure of logical positivism but still sought to retain the analytic/synthetic distinction and the theory/observation distinction.

4. Quine does exempt occasion sentences viewed holophrastically from the charge of being theory-laden (see Quine 1990).

5. In one sense, of course, whether there is a science/value distinction is an issue that cannot arise at all for Quine, for his most serious ontology presumably includes neither facts nor values. But there are sentences that include value terms, and whether the evidence that bears on these sentences is substantially different from the evidence that bears on sentences not containing value terms is an issue that can and does arise for Quine.

6. In fact, I do not think Quine is a reductionist. That is, I do not think he holds the view that the relation between our most serious theory, whatever that turns out to be, and the multiple theories we use in various contexts, is one of reduction. To the extent and for the period that it suits our purposes, we may talk within a theory that countenances Tom Sawyer, Lady Macbeth, and Calvin and Hobbes, not as fictional entities with some kind of funny ontological status, but as straightforward members of our current theory's domain. When we move or retreat to a theory whose domain includes only entities to whose existence we are more seriously committed, the move is not one of reduction, but rather one of shifting from one theory to another. So too, it may be that at some point Quine shifts from a theory that includes people, table, chairs, and other middle-sized bits of dry goods to one that includes only chunks of space time. At that point, at the point where we give up talk of people, it may be that we also give up talk of values.

7. Michael Shepanski has pointed out that non-value claims are readily derivable from value claims. His example is this: "All blue-eyed people are evil" and "Jones is not evil" (both value claims) logically imply "Jones is not blue-eyed," a non-value claim. Shepanski also suggests, and I think rightly, that the view Quine holds or would agree to is that "evaluative claims generally never 'add' to the total observable consequences of our theory," that is, whatever observable claim, or even observation conditional, we derive from value claims we will always be in a position to derive without those value claims.

8. To the extent that Quine has a theory of meaning it might be termed the disappearance theory, for in the end meaning does disappear, except in the sense that the meaning of holophrastically construed observation conditionals can be specified, in terms of their verification conditions, and in the sense that we can still say, e.g., that "Maine" denotes Maine.

9. One suspects that the phrase should be "observation conditionals"—Quine's knowledge of Italian is almost certainly impeccable, but perhaps Borradori's knowledge of English is not.

10. I am here indebted to Michael Shepanski.

11. Quine will note that our reactions to our experiences, pain, pleasure, horror, approval . . . will vary more than will our acceptance or rejection of observation sentences. That this is so will matter less if we adopt a community-based rather than an individual-based epistemology (see Nelson 1990).

12. I am aware that Cartesian scholars will see this reading of the *Meditations* as, at best, attributing to Descartes something that he might have been, but almost certainly wasn't, about.

13. "Boundaries between disciplines are useful for deans and librarians, but let us not overestimate them—the boundaries. When we abstract from them, we see all of science—physics, biology, economics, mathematics, logic, and the rest—as a single sprawling system loosely connected in some portions but disconnected nowhere" (Quine 1966, 56).

14. Jules Lapidus, President of the Council of Graduate Schools, likes to remind us that there was a time when we hired faculty to teach our undergraduates and train our graduate students. Now we recruit graduate students to teach our undergraduates and assist faculty with their research.

15. *On Being a Scientist*, a publication intended for, among others, new graduate students in the sciences, reflects a similar concern about the training of scientists. (Committee on Science, Engineering, and Public Policy, NAS, NAE, IOM, 1995).

References

Borradori, G. 1994. *The American Philosopher: Conversations with Quine, Davidson, Putnam, Nozick, Danto, Rorty, Cavell, MacIntyre, and Kuhn*. Chicago and London: University of Chicago Press.

Carlson, Bruce M. 1981. *Patten's Foundations of Embryology*. New York: McGraw-Hill.

Committee on Science, Engineering, and Public Policy. 1995. *On Being a Scientist*. Washington, D.C.: National Academy Press.

Fausto-Sterling, A. 1991. "Society Writes Biology/Biology Constructs Gender." *Daedalus*, 61–76.

Glashow, S. 1989. Remarks at a Nobel conference, as reported in *The New York Times*, 10/22/89.

Haack, S. 1993. "Epistemological Reflections of an Old Feminist." *Reason Papers* 18, 31–43.

Harding, Sandra. 1986. *The Science Question in Feminism*. Ithaca: Cornell University Press.

———. 1993. "Rethinking Standpoint Epistemology: What is Strong Objectively," in L. Alcoff and E. Potter, eds. *Feminist Epistemologies*. New York: Routledge.

Longino, Helen E. 1990. *Science as Social Knowledge*. Princeton: Princeton University Press.

Nelson, Lynn Hankinson. 1990. *Who Knows: From Quine to a Feminist Empiricism*. Philadelphia: Temple University Press.

Nelson, L. H., and J. Nelson. 1995. "Feminist Values and Cognitive Virtues," in *PSA* 2. East Lansing, Mich.: PSA.
Quine, W. V. 1960. *Word and Object*. Cambridge, Mass.: Harvard University Press.
———. 1963. "Two Dogmas of Empiricism," in *From a Logical Point of View* (rev. ed.). New York: Harper & Row [1953].
———. 1966. "Necessary Truth," in *The Ways of Paradox*. Random House, New York.
———. 1981a. "Five Milestones of Empiricism," in *Theories and Things*. Cambridge, Mass.: Harvard University Press.
———. 1981b. "On Austin's Method," in *Theories and Things*. Cambridge, Mass.: Harvard University Press.
———. 1981c. "On the Nature of Moral Values," in *Theories and Things*. Cambridge, Mass.: Harvard University Press.
———. 1981d. "Things and Their Place in Theories," in *Theories and Things*. Cambridge, Mass.: Harvard University Press.
———. 1990. *Pursuit of Truth*. Cambridge, Mass.: Harvard University Press.

9

Feminist Epistemology Naturalized

Richmond Campbell

My plan is this: first to defend the possibility of feminist empiricism, then to analyze the logical structure of epistemology when it is, in Quine's sense, "naturalized," and finally to interpret feminist empiricism as a form of naturalized feminist epistemology. In developing this epistemology, I will draw on Quine's holistic conception of evidence and meaning to show the untenability of his fact-value dichotomy and to defend a feminist normative realism.

I am grateful for the comments I received from the editors some nine years ago when this volume was first conceived. The draft they commented on grew into a book (Campbell 1998) from which many parts of this chapter are drawn.

1. Internal Feminist Empiricism

Feminist epistemology comes in a variety of forms. Those that combine empiricist methodology with feminist political goals are forms of feminist empiricism.[1] It has been a matter of some controversy whether such a combination is viable, for it is often charged that using empiricist methodology is incompatible with being motivated by political goals of any kind.[2] The assumption has been that when empiricist methodology is properly applied, it is value-free—at least that is the ideal—so that the idea of feminist empiricism as a norm for scientific practice is seen as a contradiction in terms.

It might be thought that feminist empiricism can be defended by construing empiricist methodology narrowly to cover only the testing of hypotheses by experiment. The argument would be that a scientist might be influenced by her political commitments in forming her research agenda and conceiving of hypotheses to test, but be utterly dispassionate and impartial in designing, running, and evaluating empirical tests. To adopt a terminology that I have used elsewhere, she could practice an *external* form of feminist empiricism,[3] keeping her feminist politics separate from and hence external to her narrowly construed empiricist methodology.

This defense of feminist empiricism is unsatisfactory for two closely connected reasons.[4] First, it rests on the positivist principle that the context of discovery, which concerns matters like the "discovery" of a theory or data, can be separated from the context of justification, in which a theory or hypothesis is tested against the evidence to see whether or not it is empirically supported. It is not hard to show that the context of discovery plays an essential role in the process of deciding whether any hypothesis or theory is supported by the data. Consider that whether a hypothesis h is confirmed by evidence e depends on whether there is any alternative hypothesis h^* that explains the evidence equally well. The discovery of h^* would directly undercut the presumption that e supports h better than some alternative hypothesis; hence any sufficient ground for believing that h is confirmed by e depends on matters of discovery, contrary to the positivist principle that the two contexts are fundamentally separate.

An example should bring the point home. Coronary heart disease is the single most frequent cause of death in women and men alike. A common initial manifestation of the disease is myocardical infarction (death of some of the muscular tissue of the heart due to blockage of blood supply). Consider then the hypothesis that the disease initially manifests itself in this manner. A number of studies of coronary heart disease were done to test various other hypotheses, such as that low-dose aspirin reduces the risk of myocardial infarction. One controlled study involved 12,866 high risk subjects between the ages of 35 and 57; another involved 22,071 physicians. In each case the first hypothesis was consistent with the evidence. This hypothesis predicts that myocardial infarction is the most common initial manifestation of the disease in the massive samples, and the prediction is correct. But, as it happened, the tests were carried out exclusively on men. An alternative hypothesis is that although men initially manifest the disease in this way, women do not. This hypothesis is also consistent with the evidence and, moreover, it predicts the data better than the first hypothesis when women are included in the trials. Indeed, myocardial infarction is rare in women under the age of 65, and the disease is usually manifested initially in women by angina pectoris (chest pain due to reduced coronary blood supply) (Committee on the Ethical and Legal Issues Relating to the Inclusion of Women in Clinical Studies 1994, 64–66). In this example the context of discovery, which includes political motives to advance women's health, leads to an objectively more adequate hypothesis. Further examples demonstrating interaction between the two contexts are not hard to find (e.g., Fausto-Sterling 1985; Longino 1990; Tuana 1993; Spanier 1995; Campbell 2001).

Positivists have always acknowledged that matters of discovery can be influenced by a great variety of factors: social, economic, religious, political, and so on. Feminist motivation in particular can play a significant role in determining which alternative explanations of the evidence are available for comparison. But, contrary to positivism, such motivation can enter into the context of justification and be instrumental in showing whether given data *e* confirms a given theory *h*. The example just presented makes clear how. Political motivation led to the discovery of an *h** that predicts *e* as well as *h*, undermining the putative justification for *h*. This example reveals also a second reason why a defense of feminist empiricism should not appeal to the externalist interpretation. A goal common to many feminist scientists is the removal of sexism and androcentrism from scientific practice. That goal will be misconceived if it is supposed that these ills cannot affect the context of justification when empiricist methodology is properly applied. If feminist political motivation can enter directly into this context for the reason just given, so can motivation that is sexist or androcentric. In short, the false assumption that the context of justification is value free can only hinder the effort to combine feminist political aims with empiricist methodology.

Internal feminist empiricism rejects that assumption and therefore does not suffer this impediment to opposing sexism and androcentrism in science. It is ironic that feminist standpoint theorists and postmodern feminists who have dismissed feminist empiricism on the grounds that feminism and empiricism are in irreconcilable tension have based their opposition on the very positivism that they have thought made any form of empiricism untenable. Once it is understood, however, that standard norms of empirical testing like predictive success and explanatory power[5] cannot be separated in their application from influences that arise within the context of discovery, the self-consistency of an internal feminist empiricism is no longer problematic.

An unexpected by-product is a more defensible conception of objectivity than is found in positivist forms of empiricism. The positivists (or logical empiricists, as they are also called) have supposed that objectivity consists in not allowing norms other than the strictly empiricist ones to guide the logical process of confirming or disconfirming hypotheses and theories on the basis of evidence. This same understanding of objectivity has been taken over in popular culture, which understands good science to be value free, or at least free of all values except those norms that define the essence of empirical controls. Given the argument presented thus far, this conception of objectivity is inconsistent with the nature of the empiricist norms in question.

Fortunately, there is another conception of objectivity in empirical testing, which has at least equal claim to being fully empiricist. I have in mind the view that objectivity in testing is to be found in faithfully applying empiricist norms.[6] This conception allows for political motivation to play a significant part in a testing process that is objective in the relevant sense. In this conception of objectivity, internal feminist empiricism would be no less objective in its results than other varieties of empiricism, even though it combines feminist with empiricist norms.

2. What Is Epistemology Naturalized?

Can such empiricism be naturalized in Quine's sense? I will argue that it can be, but there is an irony in my invoking Quine's standard for good epistemology. My argument that political motivation naturally and legitimately enters into the application of empiricist norms derives from the Duhem-Quine thesis that empirical tests are holistic in nature, depending on a network of theoretical background assumptions. To introduce the concept of internal feminist empiricism, I have simply pointed out that these background assumptions form part of the context of discovery and hence cannot be insulated from the effects of contextual values. The irony is that Quine himself has maintained that science is free of such effects. In his words: "Scientific theory stands proudly and notoriously aloof from value judgments" (Quine 1974, 49).[7] Relying implicitly on the Duhem-Quine thesis, I am led, therefore, to a conception of epistemology that Quine thinks is at odds with the nature of science.

To compound this irony, a common criticism of naturalized epistemology is that in turning epistemology into science Quine is destroying the normative content of epistemology. Quine conceives naturalized epistemology as an attempt to understand the link between observation and theoretical science by appeal to (in his words) "the very science whose link with observation we are seeking to understand" (Quine 1969, 76). A common objection, which has been advanced independently by Hilary Kornblith (1994, 1–7) and Jaegwon Kim (1994), is that epistemology cannot be reduced to science in this way, because epistemology as such (never mind feminist epistemology) is normative through and through. Astonishingly, Quine shares with his critics the assumption that science, and hence naturalized epistemology, is *not* inherently normative.[8] But if I am right that science is inherently normative, then not only does the objection rest on a false premise, but Quine has in an important way misconceived his own project.

We should, then, look more carefully at what that project is. Quine tells us that naturalized epistemology seeks to understand through science the link between observation and science, but taken in isolation this description is seriously misleading. It makes it sound as if the goal of this epistemology is merely to identify the psychological and perhaps social mechanisms for generating scientific theory on the basis of sensory stimulation. It thus invites the objection that naturalized epistemology only answers the factual question of how we come to have the scientific beliefs we do, without answering the normative question of why we *ought* to have the scientific beliefs we do. Without an answer to the latter question, the issue of justification, which has been central to traditional epistemology, goes unresolved.

In some interpretations, Quine deliberately sets aside the traditional issue of justification as unresolvable and outmoded. This interpretation, however, is not supportable. Quine rejects traditional conceptions of justification, both foundational and coherentist,[9] because they seek to provide an understanding of the nature of knowledge that is prior to and hence not dependent upon science. That understanding, based ultimately on the possibility of a priori knowledge, is not viable in Quine's view.[10] But Quine does not reject the issue of justification itself.[11] Rather, he sees naturalized epistemology as providing an explanation of how beliefs can be justified by relying on some of the very beliefs whose justification may be called into question. He thus sees naturalized epistemology as addressing the traditional problem of skepticism, but in a new a way.

Is Quine's new way question-begging? To see more clearly the logical structure of naturalized epistemology, we need to look at how justification is supposed to work when it is internal to science. A paradigm of explaining science by science is provided in Quine's sketch of how science might explain inductive reasoning. Inductive reasoning is itself a method of justifying beliefs. The traditional problem introduced by Hume is to justify this method of justification. How do we know that reasoning inductively, itself a method of justifying beliefs, is reliable? Following Hume, Quine takes inductive reasoning, at least in its primitive stages, to consist in a habit of mind through which we come to expect that similar causes will have similar effects (Quine 1969, 125). We project our sense of similarity into the future, expecting that our subjective spacing of qualities matches the way things are. The problem of induction is thus "why does our innate subjective spacing of qualities accord so well with the functionally relevant groupings in nature as to make our inductions tend to come out right?" (126). As an example of naturalized epistemology, Quine suggests on the same page the following answer: "If people's innate spacing of qualities is a gene-linked trait, then the spacing that has made for the most successful inductions will have tended to predominate through natural selection. Creatures inveterately wrong in their inductions have a pathetic but praiseworthy tendency to die before reproducing their kind." Famously, Quine appeals to science, and in particular to Darwin's theory of evolution by natural selection, to explain the inductive basis of science.

What does this example tell us about the structure of naturalized epistemology? In particular, does it reveal how an explanation of the origins of induction can provide a justification of induction and thereby address the traditional problem? I think it does. The easiest way to see how is to consider how naturalized epistemology could resolve the following Humean dilemma. Suppose the story about how we come to reason inductively is true. Is this a story about how we *ought* to reason "to make our inductions tend to come out right"? If we assume it is, we commit the naturalistic fallacy of inferring what we ought to do from what we do. Worse than that, we reason in a circle, assuming that we reason the way we ought to, which is exactly what we were supposed to establish. If, on the other hand, we don't make this assumption, our story fails to provide a justification for what we do, and of course fails to address the traditional problem.

Let us take up the horns of this dilemma, in order, one at a time. It is true that Quine's story derives from the use of induction, but that is not the same as it being based on the assumption that induction is justified. In particular, the story employs Darwin's theory of natural selection and the auxiliary assumption that people's innate spacing of qualities is a gene-linked trait. Though these are derived from induction, one or both assumptions can be mistaken, and science could arrive at that conclusion based on induction. If it did, then this particular effort at explaining science would fail. It does not, therefore, assume its own success. But the point is general. Nothing in the method of vindicating induction in the style of naturalized epistemology guarantees that the method will succeed. For science, in applying induction, may not settle on *any* theory that would vindicate induction. Science may never be able to vindicate itself; naturalized epistemology allows that possibility. "Science is," as Quine writes, "vulnerable to illusion on its own showing" (Quine 1981, 22). Naturalized epistemology does not imply, therefore, that our methods of inductive reasoning must be the ones we ought to have if we want our inductions to come out right.

Now the other horn. How does Quine bridge the gap between the putative facts of evolution and the "ought" of justification? The answer resides in a feature of his story that is frequently overlooked. Quine supposes that there is a point to induction. In his story the understood point of induction is that our innate subjective spacing of qualities accords so well with functionally relevant groupings in nature as to make our inductions come out right. The purpose of our inductions is, in short, that they are reliable. Since this point is apparently easily missed, let me quote Quine again. "For me then the problem of induction is a problem about the world: a problem of how we, as we now are (by our present scientific lights), in a world we never made, should stand better than random or coin-tossing chances of coming out right when we predict by inductions which are based on our innate, scientifically unjustified similarity standard. Darwin's natural selection is a plausible partial explanation" (Quine 1969, 127).[12] It is clear that for Quine, standards used in our inductions are good or bad depending on their usefulness in achieving the aim of "coming out right." In this respect naturalized epistemology involves normative assessment in a straightforwardly instrumental sense. Inductive methods are explained and, indeed, *justified* to the extent that they are shown to be a good means to achieving our aim, given how "we now are . . . in a world we never made." How we are is of course to be explained by our best science, itself based on induction, but this, as we have already seen, does not guarantee that our inductions will be justified as being a good means to achieving our aim of having our inductions come out right.

What has emerged is a fairly complex dialectical structure. Let me try now to give a schematic representation of its main elements. For the sake of simplicity and generality I will speak of inductive norms rather than methods, allowing that some may be innate, as Quine suggests, while others may evolve socially and be socially maintained.[13] The traditional problem has been to justify the methodological norms of inductive reasoning (be they innate or learned). Quine's story reveals the relevance of another kind of norm, one that gives the aim of applying the methodological norms. Call the norms of *method* M norms and norms that specify their purpose or *end* E norms. In these terms, the traditional problem has been to show that the M norms are a reliable means to fulfilling the E norm of making inductions that come out right. Schematically, naturalized epistemology proposes to solve this problem by seeing whether or not the body of theory that evolves from applying the M norms can explain how the application of those norms achieves the satisfaction of the E norm in question. Whether this reflexive exercise succeeds is obviously an empirical matter. If it does, there is a clear sense in which the M norms are justified relative to the given E norm. We have thus a procedure that is at once empirical, nontrivial, and plainly normative.

3. How to Naturalize Feminist Empiricism

To see how naturalized epistemology might apply to feminist empiricism, we need to reflect first on the general form of naturalized epistemology. I take it that the M norms are not restricted in any specific way. These are norms that guide scientists (largely implicitly) in testing theories against experience. I suspect that no unique set of such norms exists for science or indeed for any discipline within science. Once more, such norms change over time for any given community. Perhaps the most we can say is that some subset of these norms must bear on the relevance of observation to theory if the norms are to be empiricist in any recognizable sense. The E norms are also similarly unrestricted. They concern the implicit purposes of scientists in using the M norms. It is plausible to suppose that chief among these will be the aim of using M norms that are apt to lead to reliable models. But if we are true to the naturalizing spirit of naturalized epistemology, we should not restrict the content of E norms a priori. How, indeed, could Quine allow any such restriction without compromising his naturalism in explaining science?

Adopting this tolerant attitude toward the content of norms, it is not hard to see how an internal feminist empiricism might be naturalized along the lines just sketched. Feminist political norms are E norms, but operate at both levels. Methodologically, they affect the evaluation of test results, by combining with empiricist M norms to support or undermine the confirmation or disconfirmation of theories. In this respect, they function as norms that are internal to the methods of testing. But they also function externally in the construction and refinement of theories, in the planning of research agendas, and in numerous other ways that affect what models are ultimately generated by scientific research. Scientists want norms that aid in identifying reliable models; they also want reliable models that serve their broader interests. We should, therefore, consider the *full* set of M and E norms and ask whether the body of theory generated by all the norms taken together could, when turned reflexively to explain itself, explain how the M norms succeed in satisfying the E norms. As before, the question is empirical, nontrivial, and normative.

This is the barest sketch of how to naturalize feminist empiricism. As a first step toward clarification, I will close this section by addressing two objections to the inclusion of feminist norms that are apt to be raised at the outset.

The most obvious is that feminist political norms, like so many other norms, are norms of action rather than of belief formation. The feminist norm that prohibits the systematic subordination of women to men is not about what to believe. Instead it pertains to political action and the reform of social arrangements. Such norms, it seems, do not provide a method for generating a body of theory about what the world is like. Naturalized epistemology, on the other hand, is structured so as to apply to the justification of norms that are directed toward belief formation, and not to the justification of norms that pertain to political action and the reform of social arrangements. Bluntly put, naturalized epistemology is an epistemic theory, not a theory of moral or political action.

The fundamental error of this objection is that it fails to appreciate the radical character of the initial argument for feminist empiricism. In its internal form, feminist empiricism denies that standard empiricist norms succeed in determining confirmation and disconfirmation in isolation from other norms operating in the context, such as norms of moral and political action. Feminist empiricism implies that empiricist norms do not operate alone but in tandem with other norms. Therefore, if the original argument for feminist empiricism is sound, the objection rests on a false premise.

The second objection is that naturalized epistemology provides no account of how the E norms themselves might be justified, including the political norms that define some of the aims of feminists. Without such an account, naturalized epistemology does not fully succeed in its normative project of justifying the norms that it counts as epistemic norms.

Note first that if naturalized epistemology failed in this way it would not be worse off than traditional theories of justification regarding induction. These theories simply assume as relevant the end of having inductions come out right. The end serves to define the nature of the problem, and thus the question of *its* justification doesn't arise. What is almost always at issue is not the end, but rather the justification of the methods of reasoning that are supposed to be an adequate means for achieving the end.

But, in fact, naturalized epistemology has within it the resources to call into question the E norms themselves. Suppose that the M norms fail to yield a body of theory that is capable of explaining how certain M norms are a good means to E norms. Then the justification project fails for those particular M norms. But there may be reason to suspect that it will fail for other sets of M norms as well, given the same E norms. What may need to change are the E norms, on the ground that there is not much hope of satisfying them. For a nonfeminist example, the goal of having inductions come out right might be interpreted in realist terms initially and then modified in light of arguments that the norm cannot be satisfied when it is construed this way. Likewise, feminist norms can be modified in light of an evolving body of theory about the causes of women's subordinate position. As conceptions of sexism change, so does the content of norms prohibiting it. It is even theoretically possible that the central feminist norms could be rejected. Feminist empiricism doesn't guarantee its own success. Contrary to the last objection, in feminist naturalized epistemology, both M and E norms are subject to revision in light of the theory that they generate.

4. Realism and Objectivity

The revisability of E norms is important. For a naturalized epistemology to be feminist, it must contain a norm or norms that oppose the subordination of women to men. (Whether or not that is sufficient for it to qualify as feminist, I will assume that it is necessary.)[14] Yet, for reasons just given, even norms that oppose the subordination of women to men are subject to possible revision or rejection. Were this not so, some part of feminist naturalized epistemology would entail a standpoint or foundation that is logically prior to and separate from any evolving theory of the natural world. Hence for the same reason that the skepticism about induction is not rendered incoherent or dismissable a priori by naturalized epistemology, a skeptic of the legitimacy of gender equality cannot be dismissed out of hand on grounds that are external to empirically grounded theory.

But granted that there can be a pragmatic basis for norm revision, is there any firmer ground for maintaining a norm than the absence of pragmatic reasons for change? Can there be an *objective* basis for feminist norms? Indeed, can there be an objective basis for any norms that lie within naturalized epistemology? Such questions are not easy to answer. A large part of the difficulty is that it is not clear what we are asking when we inquire about the objectivity of norms in the context of naturalized epistemology. We need a suitable way to interpret the concept of objectivity within this context.

The question of objectivity arose earlier. In the first section I suggested that objectivity in testing consists in being guided by certain empiricist norms (such as predictive success and explanatory power). That suggestion, on reflection, appears to be incomplete for two reasons. First, we can ask: Why should *these* norms and not others determine objectivity? Second, how could such norms ever explain the objectivity of *end* norms?

For example, feminist norms that oppose the subordination of women to men are among the E norms of any naturalized epistemology that is feminist. How could an empiricist standard of objectivity for testing hypotheses about the world be relevant to determining the objectivity of such norms? The first question is easier than the second, so I will begin there, reserving discussion of the objectivity of E norms for sections 5–7.

What would make empiricist norms the right standard for objective testing rather than some other set of norms? My answer is that they are the right standard just in case they are better than their alternatives for arriving at reasonably accurate models of what the world is like. This answer links norms for objective testing with norms for selecting accurate models of the world, and thus implies a realist interpretation of objectivity in testing. Can it be reconciled with Quine's conception of naturalized epistemology? I think it can.

For Quine, what exists is what our most serious theory of the world posits as existing. He is emphatic on this point in "On What There Is" (Quine 1953, 1–19) and "Posits and Reality" (Quine 1976, 246–54). We have, he believes, no access to reality that is independent of science. There is no "first" philosophy, no way to establish ontology outside our developing, continually revised understanding of nature. But that very understanding, Quine has noted, posits a world that existed before we did and that is responsible for our evolution through natural selection. By our present lights, therefore, it is a world that is not bounded by our present understanding of it. This is Quine's implicit realism.[15] Since it is empirically based and open to revision or rejection in light of further experience, it is distinct from traditional forms of realism that are held to be demonstrable a priori. But it is realism, nonetheless; it implies access to a world that exists beyond us and is not reducible to what we may desire or believe. Hence the realist interpretation of objectivity is not incompatible with Quine's naturalism, so long as the realism implied by it is naturalized, that is, contained within science.

Let us, then, ask again: "Are the empiricist norms the right standard for objective testing?" It should be clear now, based on our discussion of induction, how naturalized epistemology would deal with this question. Naturalized epistemology must attempt to determine whether or not the body of theory generated by an application of these norms vindicates their application, *given* the end of arriving at reasonably accurate models of what the world is like. This, like the matter of vindicating our innate similarity spacing, is not a trivial question. Of course, what the world is like from our present standpoint is nothing more than what our present theories say it is; but from this it doesn't follow that the norms that generate these theories will be vindicated. Empiricist norms of the kind discussed above are norms of inductive reasoning, and we have already seen that such norms can fail to be vindicated by this process. Whether or not they are the right standard for objective testing is an empirical question that cannot be decided except within science itself.

5. Fact-Value Holism

We now have an interpretation of what it is for M norms to be objective within the context of naturalized epistemology. This brings us to the thorny issue of how to determine the objectivity of E norms. Suppose that empiricist M norms of the kind indicated are by present lights the right ones for objective testing, and that naturalized epistemology determines this through the process just described. This process of vindication is relative to the goal of arriving at reasonably accurate models. That goal embodies a particular E norm, and we should now ask whether this norm has any objective basis itself. Indeed, we can ask this question of any E norm contained within naturalized epistemology. The problem is: How is naturalized epistemology to answer this kind of question? The empiricist M norms would seem to be irrelevant to answering it, and presumably we cannot appeal to some further E norm without inviting the same question all over again. When it comes to finding an objective basis for E norms, we seem to be left tugging at our bootstraps.

The present difficulty is generated, I think, by a nest of connected confusions. To get at them, let us take seriously the commonly acknowledged difference between making a purely descriptive statement that is devoid of normative content and making a statement that has normative content. It is of course controversial how to draw this distinction, but I will assume that there is an important difference between, for example, saying that women earn on average less than men and saying that this is unjust. The latter claim is clearly normative in a way that the former is not. Allowing borderline cases, I will assume that, in general, statements can be divided between those with explicit normative content and those without it. Call this the "weak normative/descriptive thesis," or simply the "weak thesis."

Much more controversial is the thesis called "noncognitivism," which contends that normative statements have no truth value. Later I will offer reasons to reject noncognitivism, but for the moment I will assume this thesis too for the sake of argument. As will become clear, the arguments to follow do not depend on either the weak thesis or noncognitivism. If anything, these theses make it more difficult to explain how E norms can have an objective basis. It will not be question-begging, then, to let these theses stand for the moment.

Given noncognitivism, it is tempting to say the following. Purely descriptive statements can have an objective basis in how the world is because they can be known to be true, but normative statements, since they cannot be known to be true, cannot have an objective basis. Since normative statements expressing the content of norms cannot have an objective basis, neither can norms themselves. In short, given noncognitivism, both M and E norms would be devoid of any objective basis. Still, M norms have an advantage over E norms. For although M norms would not, in a strict sense, have an objective basis, they can generate a body of theory consisting of true descriptive statements that would have an objective basis. Thus, M norms can acquire an objective basis *indirectly* by generating a true theory. E norms, however, would not have an objective basis even indirectly, since they have no truth value themselves and do not provide a method to generate statements that do have truth value.

Something like this picture seems to underlie the resistance to regarding E norms as having an objective basis. But this picture cannot be right, even assuming that noncognitivism is true. This picture supposes that M norms are capable of guiding us to true theory independently of the influence of any E norms. This supposition is manifestly false. Our interests play a fundamental role in developing research agendas and fueling our imaginations in the construction of theories, and these interests are significantly shaped by norms regarding the goals we ought to be pursuing, that is, by E norms. Moreover, as argued earlier, E norms can enter into the application of M norms in the context of justifying theories on the basis of data. We have already seen this to be true when M norms are empiricist. It follows that M norms cannot acquire an objective basis indirectly unless E norms do so likewise. The two kinds of norm work together in generating and empirically confirming theories. One is as tied into reality as the other, and this is so whether or not noncognitivism is true.

The reasoning that leads to the illusion that E norms have no objective basis in empirical reality contains a fundamental error. This is the assumption that we can know the truth of descriptive claims about the world independently of relying on a combination of M and E norms to guide us in testing these claims against experience. In fact, true descriptive claims stand in a reciprocal relationship with justified normative claims. On the one hand, normative claims about specific things can be justified only against a background of descriptive claims that are held to be true. If something *x* is judged good or bad, right or wrong, and so on, we cannot support this claim, even by appeal to further normative claims, except on the basis of some descriptive account of *x*. Conversely, for the reasons already marshaled, support for a descriptive claim will ultimately depend explicitly or implicitly on norms.

I call this reciprocal relationship "fact-value holism."[16] Thus defined, fact-value holism presupposes the distinction between purely descriptive claims and normative ones (in compliance with the weak thesis). Note, however, that if the weak thesis is false, the spirit of fact-value holism would be preserved, since there would be no way to identify facts independently of values. This would be a trivial consequence of fact that there would be no "purely" descriptive claims. Let us, therefore, extend our use of "fact-value holism" to cover this case too. In the case where the weak thesis is true but noncognitivism is false, the spirit and the letter of fact-value holism would be intact. Indeed, even if both the weak thesis and noncognitivism are true, fact-value holism remains defensible. Fact-value holism is a remarkably robust thesis that is unaffected by conventional ways of drawing or rejecting a distinction between facts and values.

Interestingly, fact-value holism undermines two of the most influential arguments in favor of noncognitivism. One of these arguments derives from internalism.[17] This is the view that values have a direct or "internal" connection with our reasons or motives for action. If facts are by themselves inert in this regard, values cannot be facts. This is the same reasoning used by Hume to claim that morals are based on sentiment rather than reason. Hume reasoned that, because facts in themselves cannot move us or give us reason to act yet morals can, there are no moral facts to be discovered by reason (Hume 1978, 457). To see the relevance of fact-value holism, consider the premise that, by themselves, values move us and give us reason to act. To be at all plausible, this premise must mean that acceptance of a value or norm (that is, acceptance of something expressed by a normative claim) by itself moves us and gives us reason to act. But then, in order for the logic to work, the premise that facts are inert must be read to mean that the *acceptance* of a fact, and thus acceptance of a purely descriptive statement, cannot by itself move us or give us reason to act. But this premise flies in the face of fact-value holism, which implies that acceptance of a fact, at least when it is a reasoned acceptance, directly involves motives and reasons for action and therefore can by itself move us and give us reason to act. If fact-value holism is true, a premise of the argument from internalism has to be false.

The other influential argument is this: (1) values play no essential role in explaining facts that are accessible to direct observation and, thus, (2) there is no need to posit values or "normative facts" as part of the natural world. But (3) if normative claims are not about normative facts, they are best construed as having a purely noncognitive function, such as to express commitment to norms or to exhort people to action.[18] As with internalism, this argument has inspired a large and tangled literature. We need not engage this literature, however, to see that fact-value holism is in conflict with the first step—that values play no essential role in explaining observable facts. It may be that there is no need to posit normative facts as part of the natural world. (I will dispute this second step later.) But the reason behind the second step, that we can discover all the relevant facts about the world independently of appeal to norms, is not supportable. Even if the weak thesis is true and we can describe such facts in purely descriptive terms, these facts will not be accessible without appeal to norms.

Noncognitivism does not thereby stand refuted. But in undermining the arguments from internalism and explanation, fact-value holism blocks two prominent reasons for believing noncognitivism. Section 7 contains a more direct criticism.

6. Of Models and Norms in Okin's Theory of Justice

In this section I want to consider how fact-value holism bears on a specific example of feminist moral and political theory. To do this I need first to clarify the relation of models to norms. Fact-value holism has the consequence that the models and norms of science have distinct functions. Indeed, their distinctness reflects a kind of fact-value dichotomy, but one I believe we should respect. The primary function of models is to represent the structure of actual systems in nature. At least that is the view I have defended above in the form of naturalized realism. The function of norms, however, is not to represent the structure of things as they are, but to set a standard for how things ought to be.

This difference in function between models and norms is implied in the preceding account of how norms enter into the practice of science. For example, the empiricist M norms cited earlier set a standard for testing theoretical hypotheses. These norms do not necessarily represent the practice of science as it is; nor are they designed to do so. They are not models of science in that sense. Rather, they are designed to represent how testing ought to be carried out. E norms set a standard of another kind. They set the goals that ought to be achieved, such as goals to be achieved in scientific testing.

It is easy to suppose that the difference between models and norms plays into the hands of noncognitivists who hold that the descriptive and normative functions of language are independent. But this independence does not follow, for reasons that are (ironically) Quine's. Though models and norms serve distinct functions, there is no reason to suppose that the linguistic functions of description and of normative expression cannot be simultaneously exemplified.[19] Nor do the distinct functions of models and norms call into question the fact that these functions are interdependent. Successful representation still depends on the guidance of M and E norms, and this guidance plays a critical role in the production and assessment of models. Conversely, the application of such norms depends on representing in some suitable fashion the situation to which the norms are to apply. The norm of predictive success, for example, depends on the reliability of auxiliary models for the purpose of making a testable prediction.[20]

The distinct but complementary character of these functions permits a richer conception of justification than we have allowed up until now. Recall the general structure of naturalized epistemology. The central question in naturalized epistemology is whether the models of nature generated by the M and E norms can explain how the M norms satisfy the E norms and thus can vindicate themselves. Thus, the Darwinian model of evolution explains how innate standards of similarity spacing used in inductive reasoning are reliable, thereby partly vindicating our methods of arriving at that model. The direction of justification, if I can call it that, is from models to norms and back to models. That is, the norms are justified by the models they yield, and this in turn partly vindicates the models themselves. It is, in effect, how the natural world is—or at least how it appears through the lens of our best models—that ultimately explains the representational and normative aspects of the science. But might not the direction of justification go in the other direction as well? Might not our best norms explain why the natural world is (or appears) as it is, and this in turn explain why we have the norms we do? Of course, neither mode of justification need succeed in any given case. The question is whether the second direction makes sense.

Susan Moller Okin's revision of John Rawls' theory of social justice provides a striking illustration of how the direction of justification can be from norms to models and back to norms (Okin 1989). Okin argues that Rawls' use of an "original position" to justify certain principles of justice is gender biased. In the original position, free and rational representative members of society who are motivated to increase their individual shares of primary goods are to choose principles for determining the structure of the major social institutions, and are to do so behind a veil of ignorance that keeps them from knowing their individual identities. The veil of ignorance is supposed to eliminate bias regarding such matters as race, religion, class, and perhaps even sex. But, as Okin convincingly argues, the fact that Rawls has selected "heads of households" for the representative persons in the original position significantly skews the outcome of the choice problem. Not only are those who would count as being heads of households likely to be males, but there is a tacit assumption that what transpires within the family and how it is affected by what goes on in the public realm are matters beyond the reach of the principles of justice. The principles would be chosen to govern relations between heads of households, and hence relations that exist mostly in the public realm, rather than to govern as well relations that exist *within* families.

The inevitable effect of structuring the choice situation in this way is to make gender inequalities largely invisible to the principles of justice, since such inequalities are rooted in the domestic-public dichotomy itself. It makes invisible, for example, the injustices that arise from the fact the care and nurturance of preschool children is largely the responsibility of women. To correct this bias, Okin restructures the original position so that the choice of principles is to be made by all members of society and to apply to relations within the family and to the way that those relations are affected by institutions in the public realm. Moreover, the choice is to be made in light of information about the nature of the gender inequalities that now exist and their causes.

Note the direction of justification in Okin's discussion. Her point of departure is normative: that an adequate theory of social justice ought to have the power to discern injustice with respect to gender. In this respect the situation isn't parallel to the case of justifying norms for testing scientific models. One begins there by assuming certain models of the world (for example, natural selection). But here another important difference exists as well. The initial norms do not exist to generate models of what the world is like, which may then be used to justify these norms and finally themselves. Rather, the norms serve, when coupled with views about gender inequality and Rawls' norm of justice as fairness, to generate a new, much more complex, normative structure for justifying principles of social justice. Norms exist in this instance to generate more refined normative structures. Norms serve other norms rather than models.

Norms are not invoked to identify reliable models. Instead it is the other way around: reliable models (e.g., regarding the causes and consequences of gender inequalities) are needed by the parties to the original position in order to make a fair choice of principles for social justice. Reliable models are deemed worthy of notice only in respect to their usefulness in applying the norm in question. Their existence is justified because of their relevance to certain norms. The reversal goes even deeper. If the justification project succeeds, so that the norms of social justice with which we began or a refined version of them is vindicated through this process, these norms will have been justified ultimately by reference to themselves, much as models were in the previous case. Though models and norms remain interdependent for justification, norms occupy here the central point of reference.

Does this mean that E norms can explain what the world is like? To a significant extent they can, at two levels. They determine what models are relevant, and hence can determine how we see the world. That this is true in general is already a consequence of fact-value holism. But in feminist theory the determination is apt to be explicit. Compare Rawls unrevised. Contractors in the original position, though ignorant of their identities, have general knowledge of economics, psychology, and social theory. But which general knowledge? General facts about gender inequality will not come to light in a relevant way apart from a normative structure that renders their importance visible. In Rawls' original normative structure, such information is not important. Indeed, even in Rawls' latest work, the relevance of models of gender inequality is obscure (Okin 1994). It is only in Okin's radical restructuring of the normative standard for justifying principles of social justice that the relevance of such models to the original position becomes clear.

This is to say that norms can explain what the world is like to us, that is, how we see it. But norms can also explain the shape of the world more directly: they can guide actions that effect change in the world and in this way play a direct role in making the world conform more closely to their standards. Consider, for example, the norm of men sharing equally with women in child care—a norm Okin thinks would be chosen behind the veil of ignorance in her revision of Rawls' original position. If it were to be widely internalized, present society would be changed in a fundamental way. Suppose that happened. Then to the question "Why have things changed in this regard?," we could answer that the new arrangement for child care is more fair. Reversing the earlier direction of justification, we would be justifying how the world is by appeal to a normative standard, one justified in turn by appeal to another standard: choice in an original position of equality. This direction of justification is no less basic or explanatory than the other.

7. Meaning-Value Holism and Feminist Normative Realism

In developing these implications of fact-value holism, I have not assumed that there is any fact of the matter about whether something is fair or just. I have not assumed, for example, that the justness of gender-equal child care could be a fact about the world that obtains independently of whether anyone now thinks it is a fact. I have thus steered clear of normative realism, the doctrine that implies that there are such normative facts. This is consistent with Quine's well-known anti-realism regarding moral value (Quine 1981, 55–66). But it is not obvious how anti-realism about values is consistent with Quine's views about the nature of definition and meaning. Given his holism about meaning, I shall argue, Quine should accept rather than reject the possibility that a statement might function both as a representation of the world and as an expression of normative commitment. Using his views on analyticity, I shall defend a form of meaning-value holism and the possibility of feminist normative realism.

Traditionally, analytic truths have been regarded as truths that can be known a priori. This is because they are, as a matter of definition, truths that can be known in virtue of their meanings *alone*, and hence truths that can be known independently of sense experience. Quine has attacked this idea at two levels. At one level he calls into question whether or not there is a satisfactory explanation of the notion of meaning on which the concept of analytic truth depends. How can an analytic truth be known from meaning alone? Quine suggests that such knowledge is thought to be possible because, when synonyms are substituted for synonyms, analytic truths can be transformed into logical truths. But, Quine contends, the notion of synonymy presupposed here cannot be explained without appealing sooner or later to the concept of analyticity itself.[21]

This attack led Paul Grice and Peter Strawson to try to find an independent account of synonymy and to charge Quine with self-contradiction at points where he seems to grant that synonymy is possible (Grice and Strawson 1956). They suggested an informal test for synonymy and analyticity. The trouble with their reply is that Quine's attack is not merely on the lack of clarity in the notion of meaning invoked by defenders of analyticity. He is also arguing at a deeper level that meaning as it is informally understood cannot sustain the concept of a priori knowledge. It is this second level of argument that we need to pursue.[22]

Quine's argument is in essence simple. Meanings cannot be grasped apart from making assumptions about which truths prevail, and these include truths that virtually everyone concedes are known partly in virtue of sense experience. Meanings, in short, stand in a reciprocal relationship with empirical truths; we cannot know one without some knowledge of the other. Hence there cannot be knowledge based on meanings alone, at least not in the strong sense that requires meanings to be identified independently of knowledge based on sense experience. Since the concepts of analyticity and a prioricity both presuppose that meanings can be identified independently of knowledge based on sense experience, the argument against analyticity is at the same time an argument against a priori knowledge.

Quine's reasons why the reciprocal relationship holds between meaning and empirical truths are, however, not simple, and involve issues too complex to examine here in any detail. In outline, his argument has two steps. First, there are no language-independent meanings, i.e., no meanings that can be known apart from knowing a particular language.[23] Second, we learn meanings either firsthand in conjunction with learning truths about things with which we have more or less direct sensory experience, or else through translation into a language whose meanings are already known. In the latter case, discovering the best translation depends on what we believe is empirically true, including what we believe (other) native speakers believe is empirically true. Either way meanings cannot be understood a priori.

The upshot is that ordinary meaning, that is, language-dependent, empirically grounded meaning, is reciprocally tied to our empirical understanding of the world. Each plays a role in fixing the identity of the other. In Quine's words, "it is nonsense, and the root of much nonsense, to speak of a linguistic component and a factual component in the truth of any individual statement. Taken collectively, science has its double dependence upon language and experience; but this duality is not significantly traceable into statements of science taken one by one" (Quine 1953, 42). We could call this "fact-meaning holism," understanding the terms "fact" and "meaning" loosely and informally. Quine's argument against analyticity and the doctrine of a priori truth generally is that each requires a language-independent conception of meaning. We can talk about synonymy, but language-dependent synonymy will be always inexact and empirically grounded, and our talk will not imply that there is any fundamental difference between dictionaries and encyclopedias. Such meaning is of no use to those who believe that we can understand the content of truths without any recourse to empirical knowledge.

We can even construct a notion of analyticity based on language-dependent meaning. We might say that a sentence is analytic, relative to a certain empirically based specification of its meaning, if, given that meaning (together with the relevant synonyms), the sentence can be seen to be true. But this notion of analyticity would obviously have no interest to believers in a priori truth. It may be that students internalize just such a relativized notion of analyticity when they learn to distinguish analytic from synthetic truths. How else do they learn to apply the distinction more or less consistently to an open class of cases?[24] The difficulty is that any construction of this kind, being compatible with fact-meaning holism, can add nothing to the credibility of analyticity as traditionally understood.

When fact-value holism is combined with fact-meaning holism, they have the important consequence that meaning and value are reciprocally related to each other. Meanings are based on empirically grounded facts that are in turn shaped by various normative commitments; the latter are based in part on empirical truths that are in their turn understood in relation to the meaning of sentences through which the truths are expressed. This "meaning-value holism," though implicit in Quine's understanding of meaning and evidence, suggests a broader web of belief than he officially allows.

Might this web not have within it definitions linking normative and non-normative expressions? And if so, would this not allow for expressions that function both to represent the world and to express normative commitment? Return for a moment to Okin's Rawlsian theory of justice. According to this theory, for a major social institution like the family to be just *is* for it to conform to principles that would be chosen in the original position (structured in the new way that Okin suggests). Question: What is the force of "is" in this claim? Could it be construed as conveying identity? Suppose for the sake of argument that whether or not a social institution conforms to principles that would be chosen in Okin's original position is a matter that is, at least in principle, empirically decidable. (I take it that the issue of which among alternative options would be chosen by someone under specified assumptions about that person's information and motivation regarding those options need not be in principle empirically undecidable; nor need it be empirically undecidable whether a social institution conforms to certain principles regarding the distribution of benefits and burdens.) For brevity we can speak of whether *Okin's model* fits a given institution. Yet whether an institution is just is surely a normative issue if anything is. If, then, the "is" above is that of identity, the question whether or not Okin's model fits a given social institution would be both a normative issue and one that is empirically decidable.

There is, I contend, no way to close off this possibility on the grounds of meaning alone once we concede meaning-value holism. Suppose we regard the identity claim as a definition offered within Okin's theory of justice. It is perfectly legitimate to dispute this definition on any number of grounds. For example, one might argue that the definition produces unacceptable conclusions about what is just. What one cannot do is argue that the definition is mistaken on the ground that the words used to specify Okin's model, since they have cognitive meaning and can be true or false, are by their intrinsic nature devoid of any normative meaning. Such reasoning would imply *that* there is a class of meanings that can be specified completely apart from any normative commitments, but this is just what meaning-value holism denies. The cognitive and normative import of any terms is to be determined holistically by reference to their place within an evolving theory, which is itself embedded within an evolving language. For this reason there can be no intrinsic barrier to terms acquiring normative force in virtue of their position within a theory of justice. Even if the terms function there to convey an empirically testable representation of social institutions, they are not thereby barred from the role of expressing normative commitment.

An immediate objection might be that this result is contrary to the weak thesis offered earlier, that, allowing for borderline cases, uses of language to express normative commitment can be distinguished from representational uses. Thus, the observation that women in our society do vastly more than men do in the day-to-day care of children does not itself express a commitment to any norms. This I have been willing to concede, but it is not a thesis about intrinsic meaning. The weak thesis does not preclude the possibility that some terms come to play both roles simultaneously. Potentially, this is true of the open sentence "X is an institution that conforms to principles that would be selected in Okin's reconstruction of the original position." In effect, meaning-value holism entails a normative realism in which moral claims can be true independently of their being recognized to be true.

Let me close this section by considering the kind of worry that many feminists have raised about realism in general. While recognizing its political advantages (the subordination of women can be claimed to be objectively wrong), it has the political disadvantage that moral truth is conceived as being potentially divorced from subjective experience and may thus be used as an instrument of patriarchy to devalue women's personal experience. Anne Seller expresses this concern as follows: "So the political problems of the rational-scientific epistemology are made more acute when questions of ideology and false consciousness are introduced. At best, the use of this epistemology appears to be profoundly undemocratic. At worst, it is an exercise in domination. . . . How do we know when we are not simply being sold someone else's ideology if we cannot rely on our own judgement?" (Seller 1988, 172). The objection is important for a number of related reasons. The most significant of these is that it is a *political* objection. A brand of meta-ethics is called into question on feminist grounds. In fact, it is not unusual for feminists to attack and to defend realism for political reasons.[25]

Anyone who is familiar with the literature on moral realism will know that political objections to a meta-ethical position are simply not raised outside of feminist philosophy.[26] There is in most of this literature the presumption that meta-ethics is a politically *neutral* inquiry into the meaning and logic of ethical discourse.[27] The very idea of bringing political considerations to bear on meta-ethical issues would be regarded in many quarters as based on a misunderstanding of the issues, if not a case of intellectual dishonesty. But it would be a profound mistake to answer the feminist worry on these grounds. Indeed, I want to argue that both the worry and the charge of irrelevance have their source in the same mistake.

The mistake is to suppose that our understanding of meaning and our normative commitments are not interdependent. It is to deny meaning-value holism. Quine has argued against the twin dogmas of verificationism and analyticity on the grounds that the factual and meaning components of language are inextricably intertwined. I have extended this holism with respect to evidence and meaning to apply to normative commitments as well. In this extended view, the value components are no more separable from the web of belief than those of fact and meaning.

This undermines the charge that meta-ethics is necessarily value neutral. But it also, at least potentially, undermines the charge that normative realism necessarily devalues personal experience and other sources of normative commitment. Whether it does or not depends how normative realism is conceived. Here I urge it as part of a feminist naturalized epistemology in which diverse feminist political commitments are internal to inquiry about models and norms. To suppose that realism about norms precludes the relevance of personal normative commitments to determining what really has value is of a piece with supposing that feminist political commitments are necessarily external to empiricist methods for testing the validity of models of nature. It is exactly in opposition to this form of fact-value dichotomy that I am advocating a feminist normative realism.

8. Conclusion: A Resolution of Apparent Paradoxes

My project here has been to develop a clear conception of feminist naturalized epistemology. Three potential paradoxes have stood in the way of making sense of such a conception. In each case Quine's insights have provided a basis for resolution. There is the seeming contradiction in making feminist political goals internal to empiricist methodology. The apparent inconsistency here is removed by recognizing that it is based on a untenable conception of empirical evidence. The move to naturalize feminist empiricism leads to a second problem: How is it possible for a feminist epistemology, which is indisputably normative, to be incorporated within science, which is purely descriptive? This problem is met by constructing from Quine's partial solution to Hume's problem of induction a normative interpretation of the way in which science explains itself.

The third potential paradox is the deepest. Science is able to explain and vindicate itself because contained within it are ends, however tentative and open to revision. Epistemology, contrary to what is often supposed, cannot be naturalized without reference to them. But how can these normative elements, which would be prominent in any feminist epistemology, be vindicated themselves without reference to some standpoint outside of science? If they cannot be, how can feminist epistemology, or indeed any epistemology, be fully naturalized?

The apparent paradox that naturalized epistemology presents at the this level is based on the supposed dichotomy between fact and value. While preserving a distinction between models and norms, I have tried to destroy this dichotomy in two stages. First, I have defended a fact-value holism in which models of nature can figure in the justification of norms and vice versa. Okin's revision of Rawls provided an example of how political epistemology might be naturalized in this regard. Second, I have drawn on Quine's critique of analyticity to show how, when his fact-meaning holism is added, a thoroughgoing meaning-value holism emerges, yielding a naturalistic form of normative realism. Again, Okin's theory of gender equality provides an important illustration.

There are a number of ironies in all this. Not the least of these is that if feminist epistemology can be naturalized in this way, Quine is fundamentally mistaken about the nature of value and the implications of his own holistic account of evidence and meaning. The epistemology defended here is, therefore, as much a critique of Quine's views as a vindication of them. It is also a critique of many feminist views, since, as we noted, neither feminist empiricism nor feminist normative realism has received widespread endorsement among feminist philosophers. Resistance to these ideas is due in large part, I believe, to the paradoxes that appear to be contained within them. My aim has been to show that these paradoxes are not real.

Notes

1. Two prominent examples of feminist empiricism are Longino (1990) and Nelson (1990).

2. The nature of that charge is elaborated in Harding (1989, 190).

3. See Campbell (1994, 1998). There as well as here I use "feminist political goals" to cover a broad range of political goals directed against the systematic subordination of women to men. Differences about which goals should count as feminist under this rubric will not affect the logic of the arguments to follow.

4. I develop these reasons in detail in Campbell (1994, 1998).

5. The labels, borrowed from Campbell (1994, 1998), apply to norms that determine the conditions for a good empirical test of a theoretical hypothesis. Predictive success requires that one observable outcome of the test must be predictable (or be within limits that are predictable) on the basis of the hypothesis being tested together with plausible auxiliary assumptions about the testing conditions and the theoretical background of the test. Explanatory power requires that, apart from the hypothesis being tested, there be no plausible alternative explanation for of the predicted outcome, should it be observed. These conditions are adapted from Giere (1984, 105).

6. Though I endorse this conception of objectivity, it begs the question "Why should empiricist norms in particular set the standard of objectivity?" I take up this question in section 4.

7. This is the opening sentence of his discussion of values in Quine (1974, 49). A similar view is expressed when he considers moral values in "On the Nature of Moral Values" (Quine 1981). But see Campbell and Hunter (2000).

8. See n. 7. Recently Quine has tempered his view slightly: "But [traditionalists] are wrong in protesting that the normative element, so characteristic of epistemology, goes by the board. Insofar as theoretical epistemology gets naturalized into a chapter of theoretical science, so normative epistemology gets naturalized into a chapter of engineering: the technology of anticipating sensory stimulation" (Quine 1992, 19). Still, this is a far cry from supposing that political and other contextual values can enter into determining the reliability of theoretical models in science prior to guiding their application.

9. Quine is typically represented as a coherentist, but this is a mistake if coherentism is conceived, as it normally is, to be an epistemology that is prior to science and hence one that explains the possibility of knowledge without appeal to science. Quine's epistemology might fit a naturalized coherentism, but then it would be inappropriate to compare it with foundationalism in the standard way.

10. The attempt to understand knowledge without appeal to science is explicitly rejected in "Epistemology Naturalized"(Quine 1969). But the groundwork for this move was already laid in "Two Dogmas of Empiricism" (Quine 1953). For a brilliant exposition of Quine's reasons for rejecting the possibility of a priori knowledge, see Harman (1967). I extend the argument in Campbell (1998, 145–52).

11. Quine is explicit in not rejecting the traditional concern of epistemologists to understand how evidence is related to theory. See, for example, Quine (1969, 83, 87; 1974, 1–4; 1981, 72; 1960, 1–5). Though the term "justification" does not appear in these passages, Quine can be interpreted along the lines sketched below as offering a naturalized understanding of how evidence justifies theory.

12. It is important to note that Quine says that natural selection provides a *partial* explanation. It can explain our knowledge of middle-sized objects in our immediate vicinity, since getting it roughly right about these would have correlated well with getting on with survival and reproduction when our innate similarity standards evolved. At the same time the theory explains its own limitations for vindicating instances of induction further afield. (Critics of evolutionary epistemology often fail to acknowledge this point.) But the foothold gained is a start. On the basis of a rough knowledge of ordinary things, we may be justified in moving beyond our innate "scientifically

unjustified similarity standard" to more refined methods of learning about the world. These in turn yield knowledge that both causes us to revise our understanding of ordinary things and calls for a deeper, more inclusive theory of cognitive activity to explain the reliability of our new inductions.

13. Though it receives less emphasis in his writing, Quine allows the possibility of socially evolved standards as well. See, for example, Quine and Ullian (1970, 47).

14. It seems clear that it isn't sufficient. An epistemology that incorporated a norm against the subordination of women to men but that implied that none were in fact subordinated would not be judged feminist by most of those who apply the label to themselves.

15. Note the passages already quoted from "Natural Kinds" (Quine 1969). Quine's realism is obvious there and in other passages in the same article. For example: "To trust induction as a way of access to the truths of nature . . . is to suppose, more nearly, that our quality space matches that of the cosmos. The brute irrationality of our sense of similarity, its irrelevance to anything in logic and mathematics, offers little reason to expect that this sense is somehow in tune with the world—a world which, unlike language, we never made" (125–26). But his realism is evident in more recent writing as well: "Dispositions to observable behavior are all there is for semantics to be right or wrong about. In the case of systems of the world . . . one is prepared to believe that reality exceeds the scope of the human apparatus in unspecifiable ways" (Quine 1992, 101). In the same work he makes an explicit link between realism (as conceived here) and objective knowledge: "The objectivity of our knowledge of the external world remains rooted in our contact with the external world, hence in our neural intake and the observation sentences that respond to it" (36). For other textual evidence of Quine's realism, see "On the Very Idea of a Third Dogma" (Quine 1981, 39), and "Five Milestones of Empiricism" (Quine 1981, 72).

16. The name is appropriate if we allow that facts are what true descriptions are about and values are what are expressed by normative claims. But the name should not be taken to imply that an ontology of facts and values is presupposed by this doctrine, which has been explained without reference to facts or values.

17. For critical discussion of whether internalism supports the fact-value dichotomy, see: McNaughton (1988, 20–24, 46–50); Goldsworthy (1992); and Campbell (1993). Recently I have defended a hybrid theory of moral judgment and argued that the internalism/externalism distinction is itself suspect (Campbell 1998, 169–75).

18. An excellent discussion of this argument with copious references to the relevant literature is Sayre-McCord (1988a).

19. I elaborate this point in section 7.

20. One might worry, is talk of functions inconsistent with naturalism? Whether it is or not depends, of course, on how functions are conceived. I subscribe to Wright's conception (Wright 1973). His view, which has gained some currency, especially in its application to biological functions, is roughly this: doing *y* is *x*'s function if *x*'s doing *y* is what explains why things of kind *x* exist. For example, circulating blood is the function of the heart, since in the past natural selection favored some organs that did this and hence their doing this explains why hearts exist today. So conceived, functions are hardly incompatible with naturalism. Allan Gibbard has developed conceptions of natural representation and normative commitment along these lines, understanding them to be biological adaptations with distinct functions (Gibbard 1990). Though for reasons given below I cannot agree with Gibbard's non-cognitivism, his view that the functions of models and norms are distinct biological adaptations is fully consistent with feminist naturalized epistemology as I am conceiving it.

21. This is the essence of Quine's critique of the first dogma in "Two Dogmas of Empiricism" (Quine 1953, 20–46).

22. In much of the interpretation to follow, I am indebted to Gilbert Harman's discussion (Harman 1967).

23. The primary argument for this step is to be found in Quine's indeterminacy of translation

thesis; see Quine (1960, 27, 54, 72, 206, 221), and his essay "Ontological Relativity" (Quine 1969, 26–68).

24. I take this to answer the argument from Grice and Strawson (1956) that there must be an analytic/synthetic distinction since students can learn to apply the distinction more or less consistently to an open class of cases.

25. Lorraine Code, for example, defends a qualified realism, which she prefers to call a "mitigated relativism," but her position too is based largely on political grounds: "Politically, feminists could not opt for an absolute relativism that recognized no facts of the matter—no objective, external reality—but only my, your, or our negotiated reality" (Code 1991, 319). Lisa Helke rejects both sides of the traditional debate, offering an alternative that she calls "the Corresponsible Option" (Helke 1988). In this case too the reason is political: "to construct epistemologies that are respectful and representative of the differences in women's experiences, without being glib, unreflective or uncritical about those differences" (17).

26. For an excellent introduction to this literature, see Sayre-McCord (1988b) and Darwall, Gibbard, and Railton (1992).

27. This presumption is challenged in Sherwin (1995).

References

Campbell, Richmond. 1993. "Critical Notice of Allan Gibbard, *Wise Choices, Apt Feelings*." *Canadian Journal of Philosophy* 23: 299–323.

———. 1994. "The Virtues of Feminist Empiricism." *Hypatia* 9: 90–115.

———. 1998. *Illusions of Paradox: A Feminist Epistemology Naturalized*. Lanham, Md.: Rowman & Littlefield.

———. 2001. "The Bias Paradox in Feminist Epistemology." In *enGendering Rationalities*, ed. S. Morgen and N. Tuana. New York: SUNY Press.

Campbell, Richmond, and Bruce Hunter, eds. 2000. *Moral Epistemology Naturalized*. *Canadian Journal of Philosophy*, supplemental volume 26.

Code, Lorraine. 1991. *What Can She Know? Feminist Theory and the Construction of Knowledge*. Ithaca: Cornell University Press.

Committee on the Ethical and Legal Issues Relating to the Inclusion of Women in Clinical Studies. 1994. In *Women and Health Research Vol. 1: Ethical and Legal Issues of Including Women in Clinical Studies*, ed. A. Mastroianni, R. Faden, and D. Bederman. Washington, D.C.: National Academy Press.

Darwall, Stephen, Allan Gibbard, and Peter Railton. 1992. "Toward *Fin de siecle* Ethics: Some Trends." *The Philosophical Review* 101: 115–89.

Fausto-Sterling, Anne. 1985. *Myths of Gender: Biological Theories about Women and Men*. New York: Basic Books.

Gibbard, Allan. 1990. *Wise Choices, Apt Feelinqs*. Cambridge, Mass.: Harvard University Press.

Giere, Ronald. 1984. *Understandinq Scientific Reasoninq*. 2d ed. New York: Holt, Rinehart, and Winston.

Goldsworthy, Jeffrey. 1992. "Externalism, Internalism, and Moral Scepticism." *Australasian Journal of Philosophy* 70: 40–60.

Grice, Paul, and Peter Strawson. 1956. "In Defense of a Dogma." *The Philosophical Review* 65: 141–58.

Harding, Susan. 1989. "Feminist Justificatory Strategies." In *Women, Knowledge, and Reality*, ed. A. Garry and M. Pearsall. Boston: Unwin Hyman.

Harman, Gilbert. 1967. "Quine on Meaning and Existence, I." *Review of Metaphysics* 21: 124–51.

Helke, Lisa. 1988. "Recipes for Theory Making." *Hypatia* 3: 15–29.

Hume, David. 1739. *A Treatise of Human Nature*. Reprint, 1978. Oxford: Clarendon Press.
Kim, Jaegwon. 1994. "What Is 'Naturalized Epistemology'?" In *Naturalizing Epistemology*, 2d rev. ed., ed. H. Kornblith. Cambridge: MIT Press.
Kornblith, Hilary, ed. 1994. *Naturalizing Epistemology*, 2d rev. ed. Cambridge: MIT Press.
Longino, Helen. 1990. *Science as Social Knowledge: Values and Objectivity in Scientific Inquiry*. Princeton: Princeton University Press.
McNaughton, David. 1988. *Moral Vision*. New York: Basil Blackwell.
Nelson, Lynn Hankinson. 1990. *Who Knows: From Quine to Feminist Empiricism*. Philadelphia: Temple University Press.
Okin, Susan Moller. 1989. *Justice, Gender, and the Family*. New York: Basic Books.
———. 1994. "Political Liberalism, Justice, and Gender." *Ethics* 105: 23–43.
Quine, W. V. 1953. *From a Logical Point of View*. Cambridge, Mass.: Harvard University Press.
———. 1960. *Word and Object*. Cambridge: MIT Press.
———. 1969. *Ontological Relativity and Other Essays*. New York: Columbia University Press.
———. 1974. *The Roots of Reference*. LaSalle: Open Court Publishers.
———. 1976. *The Ways of Paradox and Other Essays*. Cambridge, Mass.: Harvard University Press.
———. 1981. *Theories and Things*. Cambridge, Mass.: Harvard University Press.
———. 1992. *The Pursuit of Truth*. Cambridge, Mass.: Harvard University Press.
———, and J. S. Ullian. 1970. *The Web of Belief*. New York: Random House.
Sayre-McCord, Geoffrey. 1988a. "Moral Theory and Explanatory Impotence." *Midwest Studies* 12: 433–57.
———, ed. 1988b. "The Many Moral Realisms." In *Essays on Moral Realism*. Ithaca: Cornell University Press.
Seller, Anne. 1988. "Towards a Politically Adequate Epistemology." In *Feminist Perspectives in Philosophy*, ed. M. Griffiths and M. Whitford. Bloomington: Indiana University Press.
Sherwin, Susan. 1995. "Theory vs. Practice in Ethics: The Case Study of a Feminist Perspective on Health Care." In *Perspectives on Bioethics*, ed. W. Sumner. Toronto: University of Toronto Press.
Spanier, Bonnie B. 1995. *Im/partial Science: Gender Ideology in Molecular Biology*. Bloomington: Indiana University Press.
Tuana, Nancy. 1993. *The Less Noble Sex: Scientific, Religious, and Philosophical Conceptions of Women's Nature*. Bloomington: Indiana University Press.
Wright, Larry. 1973. "Functions." *Philosophical Review* 82: 139–68.

10

Quine and Feminist Theory

Jane Duran

Quine's work has often been viewed, from the platform of feminist theory, in terms of its commitment to holism or to communitarian accounts of knowledge acquisition, but a focus on Quine as naturalist is at least as instructive. I delineate areas of intersection between Quine and other thinkers or theories whose work has been considered of interest to feminists, such as pragmatism and the critical response to the Received View of positivism,[1] and I flesh out an account of what it is that Quine's rigorous empiricism and naturalism amount to. The chapter closes with a hint at future directions for feminist naturalized epistemology based on what Quine tells us about language acquisition.

The current contention that the work of Quine intersects with feminist theory requires specific articulation and development within the framework of feminist theorizing (Hankinson Nelson 1990, *passim*). It is not enough merely to point to such works as "Epistemology Naturalized" or "Two Dogmas" in order to substantiate this charge. Rather, there must be some specific detailing of what could be meant in the larger sense by the claim that feminist theory can use or build on some of Quine's work. In this chapter I shall be specific about the ways in which such use of his theory may be made.

Painting in very broad strokes, feminist theory, insofar as it has constructed a critique of science or a feminist epistemology, has been involved in a critique of notions such as universality, normativity, and the construction of theories that proceed by logical moves rather than by admission of evidence (Code 1990; Harding 1990; Hankinson Nelson 1990). Feminist theoreticians have often eschewed the "view from nowhere" thinking that has driven much of twentieth century epistemology, for it has often sought to disguise its origins under the pretense of universality, and it has frequently recommended cognitive moves for would-be knowers, regardless of who the knower is. It might be thought naively, then, that the author of a work such as *From a Logical Point of View* would have little to say that might benefit the feminist theorist, since presumably it may in fact be the logical point of view in which she has comparatively small interest. But those who have claimed that we can borrow from Quine have typically alluded, as I indicated above, to the attempt to naturalize epistemology, the notion of a scientific community, or the notion of some sort of holism (Hankinson Nelson 1990; Antony 1993; Duran 1991).

One can see in the body of Quine's work three themes or trends that catch the feminist eye. One is indeed holism—and this is in itself now the subject of a great deal of work (Fodor and LePore 1992). The notions that theories hang together, that their sentences are not subject to confirmability standing apart, so to speak, and that the body of science forms a continuum undercut the sorts of distinctions that used to prop up rigid positivism or logical empiricism, and in that sense holism is amenable to feminist use (assuming the latter theories to be androcentric in their construction because of the force of their airtight articulation, a stance that reinforces the alleged or purported view from nowhere). Another is the notion of community, and the subsidiary notion of language communities as the arbiters of intersubjectivity. This has already been the chief focus of work done on Quinean theory from a feminist perspective (Hankinson Nelson 1990). The third theme or trend is that of naturalization, and it is with this theme that I will largely be concerned. For the focus of the essay "Epistemology Naturalized" is not so much epistemology, but naturalization. And it is the ultimate reliance of Quinean theory on the world of the senses—perhaps somewhat unexpected when so much of the work is cast in terms of the first-order predicate logic—that provides the prompt that allows the feminist theorist to use Quine's work.

I

Reliance on the empirical as a sort of rough-and-ready arbiter of questions philosophical is a leading theme in Quine's thinking, and this we may take indeed to be the heart and core of his naturalism, a naturalism that, as has been indicated, feminists may well put to use. It occurs in most of the essays found in the three or four largest collections of Quine's work, and is the focus, of course, of "Epistemology Naturalized."[2] Quine's interest in the sciences stems from the fact that the sciences themselves are the theoretical offshoots of the sort of ballpark categorization with which we greet the world as children. Our efforts to acquire a language, our first essays at employing that language, and our preliminary trials at categorization all reflect our encounter with a sensory world. In "The Scope and Language of Science," Quine notes:

> Let us suppose that one of the early words acquired by a particular child is 'red.' How does he learn it? He is treated to utterances of the word simultaneously with red presentations; further, his own babbling is applauded when it approximates to 'red' in the presence of red. At length he acquires the art of applying the word neither too narrowly nor too broadly for his mother's tastes. This learning process is familiar to us under many names: association, conditioning, training, habit formation, reinforcement and extinction, induction. (Quine 1966, 218)

Quine's somewhat facetious "neither too narrowly nor too broadly for his mother's tastes" underscores the circumstances in which language is acquired for almost all human beings. Thus, from the outset, words are attached to space/time slices, the assumption is that the world impinges on us via our sensory receptors, and, as Quine also says in "Epistemology Naturalized," "[t]he stimulation of his sensory receptors is all the evidence anybody has had to go on" (Kornblith 1985, 24). This reliance on the notion that an individual is dependent upon her sensory receptors does, of course, undercut various takes on the view from nowhere.

Quine's interest in science and his strong empiricism constitute no more solid an orientation toward science than that of Carnap or any other of many important twentieth century philosophers. But it is along the lines of the rupture between Quine and those who share the Received View of the positivists that we can find the material that makes Quine's work so important for many other kinds of theorists, including feminists. For the difference between Quine and someone of Carnap's school has to do with the way in which each sees language—and hence the language of science—as linking up to the world, and what each makes of that linkage. What ultimately was ensconced as the Received View relied heavily on the notion of "correspondence rules": the idea was that every statement in the language of theory was wedded (by the law of the biconditional) to a concomitant statement in the language of observation. This notion in turn relied on a rigorously foundationalist epistemology in which privileged access played a major role. A theoretical stance of this type does, of course, purport to be both universally valid and strongly normative—and whether or not actual knowers can function in any capacity remotely resembling the theoretical account is deemed to be irrelevant.

A number of different arguments can be brought to bear against a system such as the Received View—one could, for example, focus on the development of the epistemology and ignore or pay short shrift to any other sorts of problems (Austin 1964, 111–13). But if one chooses to focus on the correspondence rules—or even a correspondence theory of truth, as some take Quine to be doing (Hankinson Nelson 1990, 92–98)—the arguments that immediately present themselves are that there could rarely be such a straightforward correspondence, and that attempts to find an ultimate "ground" for either theory or observation (a demarcated starting point) do not often work.

It is this tack, of course, that Quine has taken, and much of his work emphasizes the futility of trying to divorce our experience of the world from our theorizing about it. As a number of feminists have developed work with respect both to communitarian accounts of knowledge and to the particular experiences of the knower, Quine's twist becomes especially apt. To the hoary question of whether or not it is possible to cut off a potentially disconfirmable chunk of theory from the rest of the view, he replies:

> Might the molecular doctrine not be ever so useful in organizing and extending our knowledge of the behavior of observable things, and yet be factually false?
>
> One may question, on closer consideration, whether this is really an intelligible possibility. Let us reflect upon our words and how we learned them. . . .
>
> Sense data, if they are to be posited at all, are fundamental in one respect; the small particles of physics are fundamental in a second respect, and common sense bodies in a third. Sense data are *evidentially* fundamental: every man is beholden to his sense for every hint of bodies. The physical particles are *naturally* fundamental, in this kind of way: laws of behavior of those particles afford, so far as we know, the simplest formulation of a general theory of what happens. Common sense bodies, finally, are *conceptually* fundamental: it is by reference to them that the very notions of reality and evidence are acquired. . . . But these three types of priority must not be viewed as somehow determining three competing, self-sufficient conceptual schemes. Our one serious conceptual scheme is the inclusive, evolving one of science, which we inherit and, in our several small ways, help to improve. (Quine 1966, 235–39)

This undercutting of any attempt to separate theorizing, language, observation, and original experience is at the core of the Quinean project. It is this, of course, that is constitutive of his naturalization, since it represents a move away from the grand tradition of a priori conceptualizing—we encounter the world as infants and small children, we categorize, we learn to apply labels, and, perhaps as adults, we may do some work falling within the scope of the sciences. These projects, as it were, are merely part of a continuum, points along a path. The particle physicist is employing her senses in the same way in which she employed them when, as a small child, she learned to sort balloons by color. No hard-and-fast boundaries can be drawn between these sorts of events, and the failure to see this, according to Quine, has led to some murky and unsuccessful efforts at theory building.[3]

Quine is interested in the first-order predicate logic because variable-binding gives us precise answers to ontological questions. But for Quine, the creation of such sentences cannot be divorced from the experiencing of the entities about which they are constructed, or from the process of language learning (235–39).

II

As I have argued, it is Quine's reliance on the modes of our language learning and on the relationship between learning a term and obtaining intersubjective agreement on the term's use that gives his large-scale view its naturalism. Because the influence of his work has been so great, it is somewhat difficult for us at this point to come to grips with the force of the view against which he was arguing. But many adherents to the Received View posited a set of phenomenal data as prior to and independent of any use of language.[4] Although there were disagreements aplenty about this construct in the school of the Received View (Suppe 1977), epistemically the data had to have been posited as prior in order to obtain the linkage between the rigorously foundational epistemology needed to support such a view and the correspondence rules that make up the heart of the theory. In any case, Quine's work damages positivism as severely as it does precisely because of his refusal to allow any putatively bare phenomena a privileged standing independent of semantic categorization.

These notions—the lack of privilege of alleged divorced phenomena and the relatedness of phenomenal experience to language and language acquisition—are, of course, tied to those two other main tenets of Quine's work, the emphasis on community and what is referred to as "holism." As I have indicated, this tie-in is crucial for gynocentric or feminist thought. For the original language-learning community may indeed be small (in most cases, it is a dyad—the mother and child), but it is a community nonetheless. And the failure of any one sentence or term to attain stand-alone status—even those that Quine typifies as "occasion sentences"—indicates, as those referring to Quine's work now repeatedly emphasize, that there is a web, network, or whole grouping of beliefs, contentions, posit-bearing sentences, or theories that cannot reasonably be torn apart (Quine 1966).

It might be helpful at this point, in an effort to come to grips with Quine's naturalism and constructed empiricism, to contrast this important interlinkage of phenomena and the linguistic with some of the efforts of those associated with positivism. Fortunately, a body of historical evidence has come to bear on the weight that this debate carried even within positivist circles. Joia Lewis has attempted to come to terms with this issue with regard to the work of Moritz Schlick (Lewis 1988, 110–18), and it is an issue of no little importance in assessing the merits of, for example, contemporary labels such as "realist" and "instrumentalist" in application to the work of those holding the Received View (Duran 1994a). Lewis notes of Schlick that

> It is not well-known that Moritz Schlick, whose name is inseparable from the development of logical positivism, was extremely critical of positivism prior to the 1920s.
>
> His early criticisms of positivism, particularly the fact that it ignored the significance of the logical and conceptual in favor of the immediately experienced, became the issues that he then had to deal with. . . . Schlick identified intuition specifically with the act of sensing, with the fleeting moment before the one who is sensing has become consciously aware of what it is one is sensing. . . . Besides this strict identification of intuition with the act of sensing, Schlick also identified intuition with any philosophy that was 'anti-science' in attitude. (Lewis 1988, 110–11)

This citation, interestingly enough, reveals that in its beginnings positivism was entangled in a difficulty that dogged it for some time—how to delineate the notion that there were, in fact, sensory data that were conceptually prior to or independent of any attempts to ensconce them in language. Although Lewis is attempting to argue that Schlick at least to some extent misunderstood early, Machian formulations of positivistic views, her remarks here provide the framework for an interesting contrast with Quine's work, and show why it is that Quinean theory is regarded as such a breakthrough.

Whether one agrees or disagrees with Schlick's interpretation of one of the alleged chief tenets of positivism, the fact that the theoretical question arises here in the manner in which it does underscores the difficulty of the problem, and highlights its importance both for logical empiricism and for any view that followed it. Here Schlick attempts to focus on a level that might best fall under the rubric "preconceptual"—and in so doing, he adheres, as Lewis claims, to a notion of theorizing that values the "qualitative, sense-derived 'anthropomorphic elements'" over the scientific apparatus in which they later come to be embedded (Lewis 1988, 111).

It is, of course, just this sort of view against which Quine is writing. If our early experiences of the world are virtually inseparable from early attempts at language learning (particularly when we understand that the sensory experiences that we had before these attempts can almost never be recaptured at a later point), then it does not make sense to try to posit a chronological priority for one experience over the other. And if it does not make sense at an early point in our lives—when, as early "theoreticians," we may presumably be at our least language-tainted and most "preconceptual" stage—it certainly does not make sense at a later point, when as actual theoreticians, or sophisticated users of language, we cannot separate our phenomenal experiences from our language-based attempts at categorizing them. Thus, attempts at "one size fits all" categorizing seem doomed to failure.

To return to themes epistemological, some tendencies in positivism to at least separate the phenomena from conceptualization are, as I have indicated, at the heart of what enabled the positivists to adhere to a stringently foundationalist epistemology. There must be some assertion to the effect that phenomena are separate from conceptualization at some level, in order for us to be able to posit the phenomena as the "checkpoint" against which conceptualizations are matched, and the "first philosophy" nature of the requisite epistemology here virtually ensures that such an assertion will be strongly made. In other words, when we think of the correspondence rules at the core of logical positivism—the matched pairs of assertions in the observation language and assertions in the theoretical language linked by biconditionals—the one side of the biconditional relies on the other side as untainted, so to speak, in order for the formulation to make sense. Lindley Darden notes that "the philosopher of science must not lose sight of the distinction the positivists had viewed from their more static perspective of that which is to be accounted for and that which accounts for it" (Darden 1976, 247). Quine breaks down this distinction, doing it fatal damage, by his attack on the coherence of any separation between the experience and the conceptualization and his more pronounced attack on the distinction between the analytic and the synthetic.

Thus, one might be tempted to say that Quinean holism operates at more than one level. It is not only the case that Quine sees theoretical sentences in science as linked to each other, and thus not separable on the level of individual sentences meeting the world,[5] but it is also the case that language and sense data are so intertwined for Quine that the type of split that concerned Schlick and the positivists above is not a possibility, in Quine's view.[6] Quine's destruction of an important prop—perhaps the most important—for positivism or logical empiricism is related to the reading of Quine that bolsters what some have dubbed (currently, in any case) his "pragmatic" views.

III

The contemporary emphasis on American pragmatism is, I have argued elsewhere, not unrelated to a number of other philosophical events, and Quine is frequently cited in its articulation (Duran 1993).[7] Some areas of commonality between Quinean theory and pragmatism that come immediately to mind are the general denial of foundations, the emphasis on the experienced actuality of the language/world intersection, and the absence of interest in a priori speculation—areas that are, of course, important for feminist theory. The surge of interest in lines of thought that would not have drawn attention even as recently as fifteen years ago means that any theoretical stance divorced from a priori or universalizing considerations is probably more popular now than it would have been otherwise. Since a straightforward identification of Quine's empiricist position with pragmatism seems somewhat ludicrous, we must assume that what the commentators mean is that, again, there are large areas of intersection between these two types of theorizing, and that one can point to a number of areas in which Quine and at least some pragmatists have something in common.

Richard Rorty is himself one of the commentators who has mentioned Quine, and other contemporary American thinkers, in the same breath with the tradition of pragmatism espoused perhaps most strongly by John Dewey (Rorty 1979, 1983). But it is important to try to be very precise about what such a commonality could amount to, especially if it itself becomes useful for feminist theorizing. For the purposes of the work here, I am primarily concerned with two themes, the divorce from the a priori and the emphasis, or lack thereof, on universalizability.[8]

A strong emphasis on a priori theorizing and, in particular, a priori ontology construction has been a hallmark of Western philosophizing throughout its history. This emphasis is not found only in thinkers whom one might categorize as "rationalist"—Spinoza is a classic example—or who precede, chronologically, periods of time that are consonant with the rise of science. It is, in fact, this very tendency that accounts for some of the theoretical moves attempted by the positivists that I outlined in the previous section. The trial and error method of essaying an ontology as distinct from or prior to the use of language in some sense is still another instance of the strength of a priorism, and as we have seen, it has been a commonplace of philosophizing. Nothing of our experience of life indicates that this is feasible (hence much of Quine's own position on this matter). And yet the attractiveness of the view for theoretical purposes is such that it continually proves itself to be philosophical pyrite.

Quine's work, as we have seen, strongly attacks such a view. Hankinson Nelson captures this very nicely when she writes: "Questions of 'what there is' are always relevant to a background theory, and any particular 'theory form' can be interpreted 'anew' by picking a new universe of discourse over which to quantify. In short, the relationship between ontology and theory does not allow for the notion that we pick out an ontology (or discover one) and then decide what to say about the objects" (Hankinson Nelson 1990, 123).

It is this particular aspect of Quine's theorizing—and it is, of course, simply a corollary of his rigorous empiricism—that finds its most natural meshing with the work of the pragmatists, Dewey in particular. As Charlene Haddock Seigfried has argued, it also finds a solid home in feminism. This focus occurs so frequently in Dewey's work and with sufficient ubiquity that it is difficult to take any one articulation of it as paradigmatic. In addition to writing, rather tersely, that questions having to do with the priority of mind over matter and vice versa vanish "if the proper objects of science are nature in its instrumental characters"(Dewey 1929, 114–15), Dewey also wrote:

> This is the extent and method of my 'metaphysics':—the large and constant features of human sufferings, enjoyments, trials, failures, and successes together with the institutions of art, science, technology, politics, and religion which mark them, communicate genuine features of the world within which man lives. The

> method differs no whit from that of any investigator who, by making certain observations and experiments, and by utilizing the existing body of ideas available for calculation and interpretation, concludes that he really succeeds in finding out something about some limited aspect of nature. (Dewey 1927, 59)

This denigration of attempts at a priori ontology construction is perhaps the single leading characteristic of Dewey's thought, and it is no less so of Quine's—and, as Hankinson Nelson has indicated, it is crucial for work in feminist theory. That this is the case indeed constitutes one of the greatest reasons why the contemporary burgeoning of feminist epistemology finds a ready home both in American pragmatism and in Quinean theory and its offshoots, the naturalized epistemologies. And this large line of thought is, of course, related to the possibility of achieving universalizability, another desideratum of Western philosophy and one that springs in an obvious way from its Platonic and classical origins. The concept of the universal meshes to an extent with a priorism in the sense that, since empirical experience yields so little that is genuinely universalizable, we might tend to think that the home of the universal construct is a priori thought. But regardless of the strength of the relationship, we can examine the notion of the universal on its own merits and this, certainly, is one of the other great foci where Quinean theory, pragmatism, and feminist thought meet.

To obtain an accurate grasp of the universal is, indeed, to get at a sort of One True Account, and many contemporary commentators have been quick to note how Quine stands directly in a line of thinkers, beginning with James and Dewey, who attacked this possibility (Rorty 1983, xviii–xix). It is for this reason that Rorty notes:

> I think that analytic philosophy culminates in Quine, the later Wittgenstein, Sellars, and Davidson—which is to say that it transcends and cancels itself. . . . This . . . way of looking at language lets us avoid hypostatizing Language in the way in which the Cartesian epistemological tradition, and particularly the idealist tradition which built upon Kant, hypostatized Thought. For it lets us see language not as a *tertium quid* between Subject and Object, nor as a medium in which we try to form pictures of reality, but as part of the behavior of human beings. (Rorty 1983, xviii)

The notion of the universal is undergoing dismantling here because it is presumably only when language is seen as "Language" that we can get the concept of the universal at all. In other words, to return to the Platonic tradition, Plato sees language as Language—a scheme that points us on the path to the Forms and that lets us, in our best moments, come as close as we will ever come in this lifetime to obtaining an account of Virtue, Beauty, and so forth. (It is perhaps no accident that most translators employ such terms as "Beauty" to refer to the relevant Form and that Rorty tells us about something called "Language.") Many philosophers following the ancients have still seemed to think that language could do the work of Language—that it could hook up with the world in a way that would allow, at least on some occasions, for certainty, and from this connection and attachment we could get concepts of universal validity. Again, here we are given a one-size-fits-all view. Such a concept might be simple, like "red," or might be something like an occasion statement.[9]

But Quine undercuts attempts at getting to "red" in a very profound way not only because of his attack on the analytic/synthetic distinction, but also, as we have seen, because of his awareness of the circumstances in which humans learn language.[10] In other words, to return to the original Platonic line, Plato has no interest in or ignores the facts surrounding Phaedrus' use of language, Socrates' use of language, and the difficulty for getting at Love that such facts might indicate. But these facts cannot be ignored, and they are the empirical constraints of which Dewey and other pragmatists were well aware, so that Quine can, at least in some weak sense, be seen as the culminator of a line of argument moving directly from Dewey to his work and the work of, say, Donald Davidson.[11] Again the move against One True Account is useful for feminism and other related theories.

When Dewey reminds us of the importance of experience and of the weakness of a priori theorizing, an argument I examined in the preceding paragraphs, he is also reminding us of the uselessness of a search for universal constructs when that search is predicated on some view of language as having a nonhuman, hypostatized link to the world. Such a link can only be concocted, and is at variance with even a minimally accurate account of the ways in which humans come to learn language, or indeed, of the way(s) in which humans as a species came to possess language. In the quotation from "Half-Hearted Naturalism" that I cited earlier, Dewey notes that the hypothetical investigator "concludes that he really succeeds in finding out something about some limited aspect of nature"(1927, 59). The key word here is, of course, "limited." The investigator finds out nothing about some imagined realm that is the home of an all-encompassing concept such as "red"—or "justice."

IV

In the centenary issue of *Philosophical Review*, Philip Kitcher has an essay entitled "The Naturalists Return." In it he notes that a naturalistic bent seems to be overtaking analytic philosophy as a whole. "In recent years, confidence in conceptual analysis and in 'first philosophy' has begun to waver. . . . Some of the [theorists'] endeavors mark the return of epistemic naturalism, scorned by Frege and labeled as illicit philosophy by Wittgenstein" (Kitcher 1993, 55).

The naturalistic turn is, of course, a turn toward that which is "out there," so to speak, and is clearly related to the de-emphasis on the a priori that I have covered here previously. But more importantly, the naturalistic turn is part and parcel of a thoroughgoing empiricism, and in the sense that Quine has helped to promote or promulgate a naturalistic turn, this too is a theoretical construct of use to feminists.

In ethics, we write of a "naturalistic fallacy," *pace* G. E. Moore, because some concepts seem in need of conceptual analysis above and beyond whatever might be gleaned from the empirical—if anything. But it was precisely this emphasis on conceptual analysis at the expense of the empirical that led to the sort of theorizing against which Quine took a clear stand. Positivism, for example, has a clear-cut empirical orientation, but its empiricism is purchased at the cost of a tie-in to correspondence rules, and also at the cost of a finely-tuned analysis of what actually goes on when visual perception occurs.[12] Thus, positivism itself is engaged in "first philosophizing."

The naturalistic turn asks us to look at the intermingling of the evidence or data and of our conceptualizations. This sort of stance is inherently pragmatic, as I have indicated, but it is perhaps most directly related to certain core aspects of feminist theory. That this is the case has not always been easy for some feminists to see—many feminists have charged that virtually no projects smacking of mainstream epistemology or metaphysics could be related to feminist theorizing.[13] But the experience of women's lived lives is in fact a range of encounters that more or less, in most instances, precludes the kind of speculative theorizing that we associate with the Western tradition in the period leading up to the Enlightenment and that demands an empirical analysis of the world. It is not reason that is androcentric and male—what is masculinist about reason as employed throughout the Western tradition is its divorce from the everyday experience of life and its transcendental and a priori speculativeness. We might be inclined to characterize this desire for unifying views as related to male personality development, and indeed object-relations theory purports to inform us that this is the case (Chodorow 1985; Keller 1985). But even if we find ourselves unable to give any coherent theoretical account of the recurrent attempts in (male) theorizing to give some Grand Unified View, our own lived experience of life informs us that the freedom, leisure, and motivation to attempt to construct such a view are derived from the position of a privileged group or class. This is the kernel of truth in the charge that much theorizing is both white and male, and it also provides some explanatory back-up for the tendency of male theorists who are not white to look to other forms of philosophical theory construction to aid in the establishment of a view that deviates from this norm.[14]

Immersion in the world of mundane particulars has the effect of heightening one's senses. Just as certain tasks—driving, typing, cleaning—call for careful attention to visual and tactile data, a life that is lived in close proximity to a range of similar tasks makes one more aware (not less) of input from each and every one of the senses. Thus, a gynocentric worldview is perforce a view that is more sense-oriented than the androcentric view (a theme that recurs throughout various feminist epistemologies).[15] The appeal of Quine's theorizing, with its naturalistic bent, is exactly that—it is an appeal to a theoretical stance that is more sense-oriented and that takes more fully into account the circumstances under which we first come to learned behavior. This appeal also forms the basis for the feminist work on communities of knowers to which I alluded in the early portions of this chapter (Hankinson Nelson 1990, 14).

But aside from the emphasis on holism, however conceived, the Quinean emphasis on the actual raw data of the senses turns and propels the debate back to its preconceptual origins. This is obvious not only from the material previously quoted here that asks us to consider the circumstances under which linguistic terms are acquired, but from a stance as central as the attack on the analytic/synthetic distinction, since such an attack rests strongly on the notion that language use changes and has a flexibility and plasticity stemming from the actual circumstances of its employment.

Thus, the naturalistic turn on the whole, and Quine's previously cited remark that "[t]he stimulation of his sensory receptors is all the evidence anybody has had to go on" (Kornblith 1985), push us in a direction that is extremely valuable for feminist theory because it takes us thoroughly out of the realm of a priori theorizing. Those of us who were never inclined to be admirers of the rationalists can take heart in knowing that there is much in twentieth-century analytic philosophy that goes against Spinozistic attempts to think about more-than-"partial" causes or even Cartesian "clear and distinct" perceptions. It is this sort of theorizing—and the Platonic tradition that precedes it—that is wholly and thoroughly androcentric. Male stylistic aggression manifests itself in its universalizing and normative tendencies, and in its desire to divorce itself from and transcend the limitations of the body (Duran 1993).[16] The Quinean turn toward the natural, the empirical and the actual circumstances of the employment of one's sensory receptors, represents a move as far away from Grand Unified Theorizing as it is possible to make.

V

An overview of the intersection between Quine's work and portions of feminist theory, such as the one I have constructed in this chapter, must take into account the notion of the intersubjective at some point in order to complete its task. Fortunately—and not accidentally, I would claim—this notion is important, again, both for Quine's overall position and for feminism, especially insofar as one cares to address the notion of a feminist epistemology.

I have looked at some of Quine's work from the standpoint of its empiricism, from its relationship to the logical positivism of old, from the vantage point of what many take to be its meshing with pragmatism, and simply from the point of view of a sort of naturalism, which is a broadly applicable label. I have indicated that I would not, in general, address what many feminists have taken to be the two great areas of concern for feminism and Quinean theory (at least partially because these concepts have already been examined by others): the notion of holism with regard to theory construction, and the notion of a community of knowers, or an epistemic community (Hankinson Nelson 1990). But the latter notion is, indeed, almost inseparable from some of the points that I have made here, and it illuminates the nature of Quine's commitments on scores that we have already addressed, such as language acquisition and term matching.

To return one more time, then, to language acquisition and the notion of the intersubjective, I have focused thus far on the circumstances surrounding the acquisition. But note that, although it has not been the center of our attention, the view that Quine gave us was already constructed in such a fashion that a dyadic intersubjectivity lay at the heart of it. I noted Quine's delineation of the child's acquisition of the term "red." In almost all cultures, the child is in the hands of a female caretaker, and the caretaker—usually the child's mother—becomes the first significant person with whom the child has any interaction (this, of course, is at the heart of object relations theory). Thus, the relatively simple and unmarked appropriation of the term "red" by the child is already an instance of intersubjectivity.

Recall what Quine wrote on this score: "He [the child] is treated to utterances of the word simultaneously with red presentations; further, his own babbling is applauded when it approximates to 'red' in the presence of red" (Quine 1966, 218). This first instance of intersubjectivity is one that we encounter no difficulty in imagining, because it is within the realm of common human experience, and is also cross-cultural. All human cultures have at least some color words; colors, manifesting themselves in strong visual experiences, would be among the first words that children would learn in any situation. We not only experience no difficulty in imagining the child learning "red": we also can easily visualize the correctional situation in which the child mistakes another color, orange perhaps, for red.

Quine's quick adumbration of the experience of learning color terms is, in its own way, merely a conceptual shorthand for many of the learning experiences that take place throughout the rest of our lives. And this is no accident—it is because of his commitment to the inseparability of language and experience (as we saw at an earlier point) that he has been able to level critiques of views that do not adhere to this position.

Quine's view on these matters is far from opaque, and is ably articulated in one of his most recent pieces. Writing in 1993 in *Journal of Philosophy*, he remarked:

> I am with them [Hanson, Feyerabend, and Kuhn] in jettisoning traditional epistemology, but they have overreacted, neglecting significant distinctions. I shall argue for an intermediate position. I agree that the notion of a phenomenalistic conceptual scheme, ready and waiting for the positing of a physical world, is perverse. What are in fact noticed and remembered are usually physical things and events. These we capture in words and retain in memory, forgetting most sensory aspects of the scene. Physical conceptualization and nomenclature are the very tools of the systematic organizing of experience, the very tools of memory itself. (Quine 1993, 107)

When Quine remarks that what are "in fact noticed and remembered are usually physical things and events," he is merely highlighting the obvious: language forces us in this direction. And most of the learning that occurs during our formative years takes place in a dyadic context, and models or patterns itself, however more sophisticatedly, after the learning of color terms that the 24-month-old picks up from her caretaker.

Quine later goes on to tersely remark, in the same piece, that "sentences are learned from other speakers who are sharing the observations" (109). This key assertion, along with the concomitants, is fertile ground for feminist theorizing, for as I have argued in other places, a naturalized epistemology that purports or alleges to be feminist must have some accountability for the very modes in which the knowledge acquisition takes place (Duran 1991, 1993). It is no disparagement to theorizing to ask for precision; it merely helps us to focus on what may, at any given point of time, appear as a lacuna in the theory. A naturalized epistemology must provide for us a model of the process of acquiring knowledge, and contemporary naturalized epistemology—taking off from Quine—has at the ready not only the psychological theory to which Quine adverted in his early essay, but sociolinguistics, social anthropology, social psychology, and so forth.[17] Contemporary work in sociolinguistics alone fills in the blanks on Quine's contentions and underscores the dyadic nature of much concept acquisition.

As Louise Antony tells us, "[n]aturalized epistemology tells us that there is no presuppositionless position from which to assess epistemic practice, that we must take some knowledge for granted. The only thing to do, then, is to begin with whatever it is we think we know, and try to figure out how we came to know it: Study knowledge by studying the knower" (Antony 1993, 210). Everything that Quine has written leads us to this point, and underscores its importance. The circumstances of the learning of the sentences, or terms, cannot be ignored, nor can they be separated off from the initial experiences that gave rise to them. The term "holism" is normally reserved for the portion of Quine's work having to do with the confirmation or disconfirmation of scientific theories, but we can attach new meaning to it in this context. "Holism" now also reminds us of the interweaving of elements of conceptual structure that come to us in communitarian fashion. The theorist as naturalist in some measure sums up Quine's view. Feminism, underlining as it does the force of the experience of women's lives for theorizing, can make full use of this naturalistic worldview.

Notes

1. This use of the term "Received View" stems from Frederick Suppe, *The Structure of Scientific Theories* (Urbana-Champaign: University of Illinois Press, 1977).

2. I will be concerned here with essays found particularly in *Word and Object* (Cambridge, Mass.: Harvard University Press, 1960), and *The Ways of Paradox* (New York: Random House, 1966).

3. This debate is particularly pronounced in the commentary on Carnap and positivism. See in particular Joia Lewis, "Schlick's Critique of Positivism," in *PSA 1988*, Vol. I (East Lansing, Mich.: Philosophy of Science Association, 1988, 110–18).

4. Lewis believes that Schlick understood (or misunderstood) Mach in this way.

5. Hankinson Nelson provides strong emphasis on this part of Quine's work; see chapter 3 in Nelson (1990, 82–136).

6. See, for example, the section on observation sentences in chapter 2 of *Word and Object* (1960). Even for color terms such as "red," Quine notes that "[s]ome stimulus meanings are less susceptible than others to the influences of intrusive information" (40). The key phrase here is "less susceptible." There are no clear-cut boundaries between terms that fail to be susceptible and those that refer to the vagaries of language learning, problems of translation, etc.

7. An entire issue of *Hypatia* was devoted to the nexus of pragmatism and feminist concerns (*Hypatia* 8(2), 1993).

8. As has been indicated here, these themes are also found throughout feminist theory, particularly feminist epistemology, and a great deal of work has already been done to clarify these issues (see *Hypatia* 8).

9. The opening essays of *Word and Object* (1960) are particularly relevant here.

10. Rorty notes with regard to Quine: "On the question 'Does "rouge" mean "red"?', Quine tells us 'there is no fact of the matter even to *within* the acknowledge underdetermination of a theory of nature'" (Rorty 1983, 134).

11. Hankinson Nelson notes, for example, in an essay entitled "A Question of Evidence," which also appeared in the issue of *Hypatia* cited above, that Dewey claims that "[w]e move on . . . not because we answer questions but because we get over them" (Hankinson Nelson 1993, 173).

12. Michael Tye provides an overview of current work on visual perception with philosophical ramifications in *The Imagery Debate* (Cambridge: MIT Press, 1992).

13. In "Quine as Feminist," Antony notes that "I want to confront head-on the charges that mainstream epistemology is irremediably phallocentric. I believe that this impression is quite false, and its promulgation damaging not only to individual feminists—especially women—working within the analytic tradition, but also the prospects for an adequate feminist philosophy" (Antony 1993, 188).

14. I think here, for example, of the work of Cornel West with its emphasis on the American pragmatic tradition. See, for example, *Keeping Faith* (New York: Routledge, 1993).

15. Still another feminist take that may be of assistance here is the work of Patricia Hill Collins. Her *Black Feminist Thought* (New York: Routledge, 1991) is deservedly a classic, and does an extraordinary job of tying these themes together.

16. Acknowledgment for the use of this term here is due to Evelyn Fox Keller, whose work has been crucial in articulating these concepts.

17. I have dealt with naturalization from the standpoint of sociolinguistics in *Knowledge in Context* (Savage, Md.: Rowman and Littlefield, 1994b). The theoretical work in this book, although for the most part not overtly feminist, is intended as a continuation of the tasks of my previous volume.

References

Antony, Louise. 1993. "Quine as Feminist." In *A Mind of One's Own*, ed. L. Antony and C. Witt. Boulder, Colo.: Westview Press.

Austin, J. L. 1964. *Sense and Sensibilia*. New York: Oxford University Press.

Chodorow, Nancy. 1985. *The Reproduction of Mothering*. Berkeley: University of California Press.

Code, Lorraine. 1990. *What Can She Know?* Ithaca: Cornell University Press.

Collins, Patricia Hill. 1991. *Black Feminist Thought*. New York: Routledge.

Darden, Lindley. 1976. "The Heritage of Logical Positivism: A Reassessment." In *PSA 1976*, ed. the Philosophy of Science Association, 241 51. East Lansing, Mich.: PSA.

Dewey, John. 1927. "Half-Hearted Naturalism." Reprint, 1970. In *Guide to the Works of John Dewey*, ed. J. Boydston. Carbondale, Ill.: Southern Illinois University Press.

———. 1929. *Experience and Nature*. LaSalle, Ill.: Open Court Publishers.

Duran, Jane. 1991. *Toward a Feminist Epistemology*. Savage, Md.: Rowman & Littlefield.

———. 1993. "The Intersection of Pragmatism and Feminism." *Hypatia* 8(3): 159–71

———. 1994a. "Positivism's Heir." *Zeitschrift für allgemeine Wissenschaftstheorie*.

———. 1994b. *Knowledge in Context*. Savage, Md.: Rowman & Littlefield.

Fodor, Jerry, and Ernest LePore. 1992. *Holism: A Shopper's Guide*. New York: Basil Blackwell.

Harding, Sandra. 1990. *Whose Knowledge?* Ithaca: Cornell University Press.

Keller, Evelyn Fox. 1985. *Reflections on Gender and Science*. New Haven: Yale University Press.

Kitcher, Philip. 1993. "The Naturalists Return." *Philosophical Review* 101: 53–114.

Kornblith, Hilary, ed. 1985. *Naturalizing Epistemology*. Cambridge: MIT Press.

Lewis, Joia. 1988. "Schlick's Critique of Positivism." In *PSA 1988*, ed. the Philosophy of Science Association, 109–17. East Lansing, Mich.: PSA.

Nelson, Lynn Hankinson. 1990. *Who Knows: From Quine to a Feminist Empiricism*. Philadelphia: Temple University Press.

Quine, W. V. 1960. *Word and Object*. Cambridge, Mass.: Harvard University Press.

———. 1966. *Ways of Paradox*. New York: Random House.

———. 1993. "In Praise of Observation Sentences." *Journal of Philosophy* 90: 106–11.

Rorty, Richard. 1979. *Philosophy and the Mirror of Nature*. Princeton: Princeton University Press.

———. 1983. *Consequences of Pragmatism*. Minneapolis: University of Minnesota Press.

Seigfried, Charlene Haddock. 1993. "Shared Communities of Interest: Pragmatism and Feminism." *Hypatia* 8(3): 1–14.

Suppe, Frederick. 1977. *The Structure of Scientific Theories*. Urbana-Champaign: University of Illinois Press.

Tye, Michael. 1992. *The Imagery Debate*. Cambridge: MIT Press.

West, Cornel. 1993. *Keeping Faith*. New York: Routledge.

11

Feminist Naturalized Philosophy of Science

Lynn Hankinson Nelson

1. Introduction[1]

W. V. Quine's "Epistemology Naturalized" appeared in 1969. One might have thought that after more than thirty years, naturalized philosophy of science either would be part of the philosophical canon—just part of what the philosophy of science and epistemology *are* for practicing philosophers—or have long since disappeared from the philosopher's plate, no longer of interest to anyone. But not so. There continues to be intense interest in and debate about naturalized epistemology, and what it comes to.

My focus in this discussion is naturalized philosophy of science—as I see things, this is Quine's topic, and a discipline distinguishable from traditional epistemology.[2] Although there is comparatively less debate in the philosophy of science than in epistemology about the legitimacy of naturalized programs therein, considerable disagreement remains about what constitutes (genuine) naturalization.

What importance, for example, should naturalized philosophy of science attribute to the properties of individual scientists *qua* individuals (e.g., their cognitive or perceptual capacities or decision-making procedures) in explanations of episodes of theory adoption? What importance is appropriately attributed to "social" factors and processes, "internal" and/or "external" to science communities, in these episodes?[3] Disagreements about these issues have motivated debates about methodology in naturalized philosophy of science, as well as charges that one or more research programs claiming a naturalized approach is not (or not sufficiently) naturalistic.[4]

These and related issues shape my approach in this discussion, which aims to illustrate some elements and benefits of feminist naturalized philosophy of science.[5] I start from the assumption that although the methods and theories of naturalized philosophy of science are not forever fixed, it is both possible and appropriate to judge methodologies, and the research programs and analyses they shape, as sufficiently or insufficiently naturalistic—and, in relation to one another, as more or as less so. Three criteria for naturalization that have evolved in the discipline will figure in my arguments: commensurability with the actual history and contemporary practice of science;[6] grounding in scientific research that carries implications for a theory of theorizing (e.g., in empirical psychology, social psychology, cognitive science, evolutionary biology, and/or sociology);[7] and consistency of methodological principles (e.g., a consistent approach to the role of "social factors" in periods of consensus and dissent (Solomon 1994) and in episodes deemed progressive and less than progressive).[8]

These criteria do not, of course, constitute an algorithm for evaluating methodologies or research programs in the philosophy of science. Evaluations based on commensurability with scientific practice rely on more specific views about historical and contemporary science—for example, that particular episodes (the Darwinian or plate tectonic revolutions) or sciences (physics and/or biology) are paradigmatic. Evaluations based on the grounding of a methodology in scientific research rely on assumptions about *which* sciences or disciplines produce findings most relevant to a theory of science—assumptions in turn interdependent with general views about cognitive agents and agency. Naturalists who assume individualism may look to empirical psychology, while those who emphasize the social nature of scientific practice may instead emphasize research in social psychology. The third and most recently identified criterion presumes a relationship between naturalism and consistency of methodological principles. This presumption is motivated by the suspicion that inconsistent principles—for example, the "arationality" principle advocated in Laudan (1977)—represent an unnaturalistic imposition of philosophical proclivities. In Laudan's case, this proclivity is for viewing rationality in individualistic terms, which is compromised by the influence of some (or most) "social factors" (Solomon 1994; cf. Nelson 1990, 1995).

In general, the arguments advanced for these criteria have assumed that the degree to which a methodology is naturalistic is a function of the degree to which it does not force or facilitate "excessively rationalized" reconstructions of historical and contemporary scientific practice. But however we parse "excessively rationalized," the philosophy of science cannot avoid reconstruction altogether. Judgments of episodes of theory adoption as "progressive," for example, involve reconstructions of events that we take to make the most overall sense of the cases in question. Even a single episode can be reconstructed differently by philosophers who agree that the episode is progressive and who take a naturalistic approach to it.[9]

My arguments for feminist naturalized philosophy of science build on two implications of these considerations. I contend that the interdependence of broad criteria, methodologies, and the current state of science and science scholarship at the core of Quine's argument for naturalizing the philosophy of science is part of what makes this research program promising at the present time, a claim to which I give specific content below. I also appeal to the view that methodologies can be judged as sufficiently or insufficiently naturalistic in light of current views about historical and contemporary scientific practice, the nature of theorizing and human cognitive capacities, and the criterion of consistency. I claim that a research program that uses the practices of feminist scientists and results in feminist science scholarship as resources can better satisfy these criteria than research programs not so informed. That said, the methodology I advocate builds substantively on developments in both feminist and naturalized philosophies of science, and I use the next section to discuss the relationship between the research program I propose and others in naturalized philosophy of science.

Methodology Naturalized

Research programs in the discipline that are quite different in their details share a common root in Quine's proposal that the philosophy of science be naturalized. The core of Quine's argument is his claim that the philosophy of science is continuous with science and should be pursued as such. The continuity Quine claims is twofold. First, the philosophy of science should draw on current research and theories in the sciences (and abandon the pretense of providing an "extra-scientific" explanation or justification for science), and its own methods and theories are to be judged by the standards, such as explanatory power, used to assess theories and research in the sciences proper. Second, like the sciences, the philosophy of science is normative, using criteria such as empirical success to judge whether an episode of theory adoption in science is progressive and a decision to pursue a particular line of research is warranted.[10] Naturalism so understood is nontrivial; it takes the goal of science and naturalized philosophy of science to be the construction of theories that organize, explain, and predict experience, with efforts and results evaluated on the basis of how effectively they help us *to do* these things.

The foregoing suggests the view that the deep and significant argument of Quine's "Epistemology Naturalized" is not that a particular science or research program should serve as the primary resource (or site) for the philosophy of science but, rather, for the continuities just outlined. In practice (and in keeping with what Quine envisioned), empirical psychology and cognitive science have served as primary resources. The rationale is straightforward. As Quine puts the point, all the evidence any of us has for what goes on comes via our sensory receptors; hence we look to empirical psychology and evolutionary biology for at least a partial account of the relationship between the firings of these and the generation of hypotheses, theories, and research programs. It is also understandable that empiricist theories of science and knowledge, including naturalized versions thereof, have taken the individual to be the locus of knowledge. Sensory receptors are features of individuals, not of groups.

But although understandable, these emphases are not dictated by naturalism but, rather, by assumptions about cognitive agents and agency that shape expositions of naturalism. In recent years, the relative lack of attention to the social processes and contexts in which research programs and theories develop and are adopted has been criticized by some philosophers of science as decidedly *un*-naturalistic, and consistently so by feminist philosophers of science. Although the details of these criticisms vary, a common feature is an argument that theory construction and choice, the design and evaluation of experiments, and the identification and weighing of evidence are not appropriately parsed as the achievements of individual scientists *qua* individuals, and cannot be explained or evaluated by reference solely or primarily to the perceptual or cognitive capacities thereof.[11] From this view, although naturalized philosophy of science will draw on empirical psychology and cognitive science, explanations of, say, theory adoption are not *themselves* forthcoming from these sciences.

Feminist naturalized philosophy of science, as I seek to develop it, starts out from the view that the philosophy of science is continuous with science in the ways earlier outlined. It is subject to the criteria for naturalization accepted in the discipline and expected to contribute to their refinement, and takes the results and implications of the practices of feminist scientists and feminist science scholarship as among its primary resources. The importation of insights, questions, results, and theories from these areas of science and science scholarship is not different in kind from the importation of results in cognitive science, empirical psychology, evolutionary biology, linguistics, sociology, and history of science, upon which feminists, like their colleagues, also draw. But until there is a modicum of consensus concerning the implications of the practices of feminist scientists and the results of feminist science scholarship for a theory of science, work is done and remains to be done by "feminist" in "feminist naturalized philosophy of science."

2. A Social and Normative Philosophy of Science

The characteristics I have attributed to feminist approaches to science are reflected in three methodological principles, which I next outline.[12] Two build from a view of the nature of evidence; the third, on a view of the primary loci of explanations of scientific practice. I claim that these methodological principles satisfy the criteria of commensurability with scientific practice, grounding in relevant scientific theories and research, and consistency—and better satisfy them than do many current alternatives. In terms of their empirical and normative import, these principles constitute a further naturalization of the philosophy of science.

Modest and Inclusive Holism

A widely recognized implication of four decades of research in the philosophy of science is that hypotheses, sentences of theories, and sentences expressing methodological or broad metaphysical commitments do not, in Quine's words, "face the tribunal of experience" individually (1693, 41), but do so as part of a larger body of current theory. This larger body is, for Quine and Pierre Duhem, all of science;[13] for those who recognize a role for "auxiliary" statements and theories it is some significant part of science; for Kuhn it is the disciplinary matrices that define normal science communities; and for semantic theorists it is the background assumptions that mediate the relationship between models and domains.[14]

A widely recognized implication of more than two decades of feminist and other critical science scholarship is that social beliefs and values have informed various sciences: they have shaped the research questions identified and pursued, the design and interpretation of experiments, the broad and specific ontological and methodological commitments, and the theories generated. Significant disagreement remains, however, concerning the implications of such episodes, including whether they can or should be construed as bad science and/or as idiosyncratic, or whether or not they reflect something of broader significance about science.

I suggest the following methodological principle:

> The evidence supporting a specific theory, hypothesis, or research program is constituted by observation, itself largely structured as current theories would have it, *and* other current theories, inclusive of those informed by social beliefs and values.

In other words, there are two kinds of evidence for individual theories, research projects, methodologies, and claims. One of these is, as traditional empiricism would have it, experience parsed in terms of observation sentences—though not, as traditional empiricism would have it, "pre-theoretic" observations. The second is constituted by bodies of accepted methods, standards, and theories—though not, as other versions of holism would have it, exclusive of those informed by social beliefs and values.[15] In this view, evidential warrant is constituted by both empirical success and integration within a body of accepted research, standards, and theories.

This account of evidence constitutes an alternative to models of evidential relations that construe evidence narrowly (e.g., as exhausted by "data" or observation sentences) and relegate other theories and methodological and metaphysical commitments recognized to figure in the adjudication of an individual theory or hypothesis to a realm of "background assumptions" or "auxiliary" theories. It also constitutes an alternative to theories of evidence that presume a sharp distinction between observation sentences and theoretical sentences, as it maintains that observation sentences are structured by bodies of current theories and standards. And it constitutes an alternative to theories of evidence that demand a hard and fast boundary between good science and social values and beliefs. It is significant because it provides an account of how, without these several distinctions, theories and research programs are constrained by their observational consequences.

I have advanced two lines of argument for this account of evidence.[16] One builds on Quinean holism: the thesis that individual sentences, including observation sentences, have empirical content only as part of a body of theory.[17] This view of empirical content is the core of Quine's argument that a substantial body of theory is the unit of empirical significance, i.e., that it is such bodies that yield observational conditionals and figure in the adjudication of any particular hypothesis or theory. What I add to Quine's argument is that holism is best understood as taking the *evidence* for a specific claim or theory to include *both* the observational consequences of that claim or theory (together with the larger theory or theories within which it is embedded) *and* the relationship of the claim or theory in question to other accepted theories, methods, and standards.[18]

I build on feminist science scholarship to maintain that the kinds of claims or theories that can constitute evidence include those informed by social beliefs and values—not just in episodes in which scientific practice fails to adhere to standards taken to be constitutive of good science, but when, with the obvious exception of "value neutrality," such standards are met. The case study summarized in the next section is representative in demonstrating that social beliefs and values can do more than motivate the formulation of research questions, the application of results, or the choice between theories in cases in which that choice is not dictated by available evidence. It demonstrates that such beliefs and values can be *integrated* in research questions, experiments, methodologies, and ontologies that, with the obvious exception of value neutrality, meet general and discipline-specific standards for good science.

The relationships between this view of evidence and the developments in both mainstream and feminist philosophy of science earlier outlined constitute grounds for my claim that this principle meets the criterion of commensurability with scientific practice, a claim for which the case study will provide further support. This principle has additional virtues.

The narrow construals of evidence to which it is opposed—construals that limit evidence to "data" and/or rule out a role in good science for theories and claims informed by or expressive of politics and (non-constitutive) values—allow and perhaps encourage excessively rationalized reconstructions of historical and contemporary science. They encourage us, in our approach to cases deemed progressive (cases in which the theory adopted is empirically successful, leads to new lines of research, and so on), to ignore or downplay the role of social beliefs and values in informing or shaping the theory and/or contributing to its adoption and pursuit.[19] So, for example, the identification by feminist scientists of androcentrism in various sciences is described by advocates of a science/politics dichotomy as "just good science," and its relationship to feminist politics denied, even though this line of reasoning forces *implausible explanations* of the theories and methodologies feminists have criticized.

Narrow construals of evidence do, on the other hand, encourage the search for explanations incorporating social beliefs and values for non-progressive science—for these are research programs that are, by hypothesis, inadequately supported by evidence narrowly construed. So, for example, efforts in nineteenth-century craniometry to establish sex, race, and class differences in intelligence are often construed as bad science, hence providing no insights into (real) science, on the grounds that they were based (inappropriately) on social and political views. According to the view of evidence I am advocating, this research was indeed non-progressive—not because social and political views and values constituted part of its evidential warrant, however wrongheaded we may *now* see those views to have been—but because its observational consequences were not borne out.

I claim that inclusive holism sustains the empiricist norms of explanatory power and empirical success, a claim supported by the case study outlined in the next section. But one question this account of evidence immediately raises is how broad a body of theory and results needs to be considered in the assessment of a specific research program or theory. So far, I have mentioned "other currently accepted theories." This reflects the full scope of the holistic claim and the view, defended in the discussion of case studies, that demarcation will be case specific.

Evidential Independence

Holism, as so far explicated, implies that research can be judged as enjoying substantial evidential warrant precisely because its categories and assumptions are deeply integrated in a large body of accepted theory, both within and beyond the sciences. Indeed, I have elsewhere used cases involving such commensurabilities to claim that there was substantial evidential warrant for the hypotheses feminists have criticized in order to counter claims made by critics of feminist science scholarship that the cases to which feminists draw attention are (1) idiosyncratic; (2) unambiguously "bad science"; and (3) that their identification was the result of "science as usual"—that is, unrelated to feminism. Instead, cases like the "man, the hunter" theory of human evolution, and hypotheses like that positing a role for prenatal androgens in the development of "male brains," represented *logical extensions* of bodies of research and assumptions that, in some if not most cases, were not concerned to *establish* gender differences, and that do not, in any obvious sense, constitute *bad* science.[20] Given the prevalence of the assumptions in question, it is just implausible to blame individual scientists for "not knowing better" or, given the *content* of the assumptions in question, to argue that feminism had nothing to do with the eventual identification of them.

I still advocate holism and continue to think that Quine's arguments for the interdependence of science, "common sense," and philosophy—arguments that rely on the same core argument concerning empirical content—are sound and useful for feminist theorizing about science, although I have argued that his view about what constitutes "common-sense" theorizing and theories needs to be expanded.

But I am concerned that an implication of my earlier formulations of holism is that the *strength* of the evidential warrant for a specific hypothesis is (solely) a function of the *amount* of theories and empirical results with which it is compatible and from which it can claim support. As the example of assumptions of gender dimorphism indicates, feminist science scholarship has shown that assumptions that are widely held and consequential for research in a variety and substantial number of disciplines can and should be challenged.

So holism needs to be refined in ways that make it possible to draw distinctions concerning the nature of the evidence that supports a hypothesis, either of the observational or theoretical type, on grounds other than sheer amount. Here I find recent work by Alison Wylie to be particularly promising. In an extensive analysis of the role of evidence in feminist research initiatives in archaeology, Wylie refines and extends the notion of "evidential independence" proposed by Ian Hacking, and the notion of "evidential distance" proposed by Helen Longino and Ruth Doell (Wylie 1996). I propose to use Wylie's analysis to explicate a holistic account of evidence that distinguishes the strength of the evidence provided by empirical successes and inter-theoretic integration on the basis of evidential independence. But it is important to note at the outset that the model of evidential relations Wylie is using is much closer to the contextual empiricism that Longino advocates. That is to say, those things that figure in Wylie's model are data, hypotheses, and auxiliary assumptions, rather than sentences of theories and observation sentences. Wylie also uses "evidence" in a narrower sense than I, to refer to data—albeit "data . . . [that are] richly interpreted to stand as evidence" (1996, 326).

In her analysis, Wylie demonstrates that archaeologists, including feminist archaeologists, sometimes employ norms of evidential independence that parallel the notions developed by Hacking, Longino, and Doell. One such norm invokes "vertical independence," which attributes more significance to archaeological data "that are *in no sense dependent* for their characteristics or patterns of interaction upon interactions [that constitute the subject of the reconstructive hypothesis under evaluation]" (327). Archaeologists who make use of this norm, Wylie argues, are citing "precisely the kind of independence that Hacking stresses, and that Longino and Doell also explore using the term 'distance'":

> *[V]iz.*, independence between the constituents and the conclusions of an inference that runs on what amounts to a vertical axis from some element of a data base to claims about its linkage to (and significance as evidence of) some aspect of the cultural past. Longino and Doell's concept of "distance" also covers

> considerations of independence in this sense. [They maintain that] the less a description of a fact is a direct consequence of the hypothesis for which it is taken to be evidence, the more distant that hypothesis is from its evidence. (327)

The intuition Wylie shares with Hacking, Longino, and Doell is that data or observations that enjoy "vertical" independence from a hypothesis in the ways just outlined constitute stronger evidence than those that do not. More specifically, she maintains, such independence "ensures that, while observations are clearly 'loaded with theory' (as Hacking puts it, 1983, 185), it is by theory that has no connection with the subject under investigation, on current understanding of the relevant subject domains" (328).

Wylie also develops and extends Hacking's notion of "horizontal independence." In explicating this notion, Hacking uses microscopes as his example. The security of observations made using microscopes is ensured, Hacking argued, "by the fact that different physical theories and experimental arrangements detect the same microscopic bodies, or structural features of bodies" (328). In archaeology, Wylie argues, horizontal independence is often displayed in the "congruence" of results yielded by *independent* resources, and that such independence "can be as important in determining the credibility of any given bit of evidence on the vertical dimension" (328). As examples involving both kinds of independence, Wylie cites cases in which feminists in archaeology have used independent (and, at times, "non-archaeological") resources of both the conceptual and empirical sort to challenge assumptions projecting a sexual division of labor onto the cultural past, assumptions that in turn shaped hypotheses and the interpretation of data (328–32).

So I suggest a second methodological principle concerning evidence:

> Evidence for a specific hypothesis or theory (whether constituted by empirical results or by inter-theoretic integration) that enjoys vertical or horizontal independence from that hypothesis or theory constitutes stronger evidence than that which does not enjoy such independence.

That is, the degree of evidential warrant for a hypothesis or theory is in part a function of the independence of the empirical results and bodies of theories that constitute this warrant.

A Social Empiricism

The third principle I advocate concerns the focus of philosophical studies of science.

> The appropriate loci of philosophical analyses of science are science communities, with the standards, theories, and practices of such communities the appropriate loci of philosophical explanations and evaluations of scientific practice.

This principle constitutes an alternative to methodologies that take scientists *qua* individuals as their loci. I contend that the epistemological primacy of science communities is an implication of a holistic account of evidence.

The theories and standards that holism recognizes as constituting part of the evidence for specific hypotheses and theories are not the "property" or achievement of the scientist who uses them, but the products of collective efforts to explain and predict experience, themselves undertaken within, and structured and constrained by, traditions of inquiry. Even construals of evidence that limit it to "data" or observation sentences cannot plausibly construe the "auxiliary" or "background" theories and standards that mediate the relationship of these to particular theories or models in individualistic terms.[21]

I claim more controversially that holism dictates that observation, the second component of evidence, is best parsed as social, and this constitutes my most significant break with traditional empiricist accounts of evidence. One consequence of a holistic account of empirical content—but, I should add, a consequence of the more general developments that led to the demise of logical positivism—is that there is no determinate list of sensory stimulations from which a particular claim is derived or derivable (Quine 1960, 1969).[22] The observations an individual or a community will countenance as evidence for a theory are themselves for the most part structured by a larger body of accepted theory. In this view, the experiential evidence we garner for our theories consists of observations of *features of the world*—features posited by the bodies of theory that are established and maintained by communities, experienced as communal standards of observation and the world as experienced ordain, and justified on the basis of their contribution to our ability to make sense of the world.

It is the social nature of both kinds of evidence that forms the core of my argument that philosophical reconstructions, explanations, and assessments of science should take science communities, rather than scientists *qua* individuals, as their primary loci.

The nature and implications of the shift in focus I recommend are perhaps most clear when contrasted with alternatives. One such alternative, advocated by Quine, would have us construe observation as the "triggerings of exteroceptors," evidence as observation so defined, and the subject matter of naturalized philosophy of science as the relationship between the triggerings of exteroceptors and "stimulatory situations" (Quine 1990, 1993). According to this view, empirical psychology will serve as the primary resource for naturalized philosophy of science, and individualism, of a fashion, will be preserved.

The view I am advocating incorporates the naturalized account of the relation between stimulatory situations and the triggerings of exteroceptors as a part of a general theory of science, and I assume that results in empirical psychology will also constitute a part. But there is more for a naturalized philosophy of science to do. We must explain episodes of theory generation and adoption, and the explanations we generate must have room for the role of bodies of accepted theory, science education, experiments and instruments, research traditions, peer review and funding mechanisms, and other features of the world. Such explanations, of course, presuppose some account of the triggerings of exteroceptors in response to stimulatory situations. But most of their content will be at the level of both the esoteric posits of science and the less esoteric posits of ordinary life. There is no reason to think that we could *start from* the triggerings of exteroceptors and build to explanations of these posits and our theory building involving them.[23] There *is* reason to think that the kinds of explanation afforded by empirical psychology will only emerge apace with these higher-level explanations. It is at this higher level, the level at which we engage in explanations and evaluations of episodes of *theory formation, adoption, and change*, I am arguing, that the appropriate loci of our analyses are science communities, for the reasons earlier cited and illustrated by the case study in the next section.[24]

This shift in focus will mean that sciences and research programs that can provide insight into the social processes through and by which knowledge is generated—social psychology, for example—will serve as our primary resources. The shift also brings a concomitant change in our normative questions, from those built on the assumption that the discernment and evaluation of evidential relations is in principle a solitary undertaking to questions about whether or not the social processes that currently characterize scientific practice—those involving the recruitment of scientists, peer-review mechanisms, and so on—are the processes that *should* be at work—i.e., are likely to produce the *best* theories and research programs—and, if not, what changes should be made.

As modest holism would have it, the parameters of the communities serving as the loci of philosophical analyses will be case specific, a function of shared or partially overlapping research questions and traditions, standards, theories, and methodologies. In some cases, the relevant community will be a narrowly defined scientific discipline; in others, a research community or tradition traversing more than one discipline or science; in still others, the effect one tradition or science has on another (e.g., the strong influence Sociobiology has had on research in the social sciences); and at times, two or more communities whose theories conflict. In the case study summarized below, I followed Richard Burian and Miriam Solomon in using institutional factors (the existence of disciplines, journals, departments, and professional associations), the core research questions of disciplines, research collaborations, published results, citations, and conferences to identify relevant communities and bodies of evidence.

Beyond the emphasis on the role of shared bodies of theory and standards, inclusive of those informed by social beliefs and values, I have left the designation of "social factors" imprecise. This open-endedness reflects the view that *naturalized* philosophy of science must allow the details of individual episodes to dictate which, if any, of the many kinds of social factor cited in recent science scholarship were of import, in what ways, and to what degree, rather than adopting methodological principles that prejudge this question.

In their broad outlines, the changes I recommend in philosophical methodology—the shift in focus from individuals to communities and the abandonment of the commitment to a hard and fast boundary separating good science from social beliefs and values—are commensurate with other recent work in naturalized and feminist philosophy of science to develop a social empiricism (e.g., Longino 1990; Solomon 1994). As I see things, a holistic and inclusive theory of evidence is the most substantive basis for social empiricism and a normative philosophy of science. I use the case study to which I now turn to argue that when evidence is construed holistically, science communities are not the "closed systems" that sociologists of knowledge suggest, evidence is communal *and* substantive, and research programs and theories—including those in which social beliefs and values are integrated—can be assessed on the basis of their evidential warrant.

3. Case Study

Organizer hypotheses emerged in endocrinology and empirical psychology in the late 1970s and early 1980s, particularly in research concerned with sexual differentiation of the rat brain, and were subsequently extended into investigations of other species, including some primates. Most attributed what Robert Goy and Bruce McEwen described as an "organizing effect" to androgens that mitigates what they call "the intrinsic tendency [of the fetus] . . . to develop according to a female pattern of body structure and behavior" (Goy and McEwen 1980). One effect that was attributed to testosterone was right-hemisphere lateralization, and some organizer hypotheses posited testosterone as the cause of right-hemisphere dominance in human males, and this dominance as the biological foundation for sex-differentiated visual-spatial and mathematical abilities. The formulation I consider is representative of this group and was first advanced by Norman Geschwind and Peter Behan in 1982.[25]

In a study reporting a correlation between left-handedness, immune-system disorders, and learning disabilities, Geschwind and Behan proposed the effects of testosterone *in utero* as an explanation of "the biological foundations of laterality"—by which they meant right-hemisphere lateralization in human males (Geschwind and Behan 1982, 5099). The evidence they cited for this hypothesis came from several sources. Their own study and others found left-handedness, immune-system disorders, and learning disabilities to be more common in men and boys. Four additional studies reported asymmetries in human fetal brains. One, Chi et al. (1977), reported that two convolutions of the right hemisphere, in areas earlier linked to language, develop several weeks earlier than corresponding convolutions of the left. Another, Ounsted and Taylor (1972), used results indicating that convolutions in areas of the brain associated with language were more common in boys in the first year of life as evidence of a sex difference caused by testosterone *in utero*, and related both to sex-differentiated lateralization.[26] A fifth study cited by Geschwind and

Behan, Diamond et al. (1981), had reported that two areas of the cortex of male rat brains are 3 percent thicker on the right side than the left (an asymmetry not found in female rats), and had proposed that the thickness was caused by androgrens and related to right-hemisphere lateralization. The evidence provided by Diamond et al. for this hypothesis included the ability to reverse the lack of asymmetry in female rat brains by removing the ovaries at birth; other studies reporting sex differences in asymmetries in weight, structure, and size of the hemispheres in rats and some primates; and studies in empirical psychology linking areas of the right cerebral cortex in male rodents to spatial integration and preference.

Building on these results and hypotheses, Geschwind and Behan proposed that the differential rate of development in human brains reported by Chi et al., Ounsted and Taylor, and others was caused by testosterone slowing the development of the left hemisphere, and further proposed that this slower development was the foundation of right-hemisphere lateralization. They did not link lateralization to mathematical ability in the study;[27] but two years later they appealed to a study in empirical psychology that reported "a marked excess of males" among mathematically gifted children as further evidence that testosterone causes right-hemisphere lateralization.[28]

In the 1980s, feminist biologists criticized this and other hypotheses linking right-hemisphere lateralization and mathematical abilities to testosterone. Of this specific formulation, they pointed out that no causal mechanism was identified for the relationship posited between testosterone and the slower development of the left hemisphere; that the research of Diamond et al. had established a thickness in small areas of male rodent brains but not a relationship between that thickness and lateralization; and that the hypothesis of sex-differentiated lateralization to which Diamond et al., Ounsted and Taylor, and Geschwind and Behan appealed remained controversial in empirical psychology. Finally, they pointed out that the study by Chi et al. cited by Geschwind and Behan had in fact reported differential development in the hemispheres of both male and female brains, and also stated that investigators could find no sex differences in 507 human brains of between ten and forty-four weeks gestation.[29]

In arguments challenging the evidence for organizer hypotheses more generally, feminist biologists criticized the emphasis on the organizing effects of androgens and challenged various hypotheses concerning their effects, pointing to continuous conversions of some forms of sex hormones to others as presenting difficulties for both. They also challenged the linear explanatory model that the organizer hypotheses presumed, and in particular the extrapolation of the model to humans, citing experimental results indicating complex and often non-linear interactions between cells, and between cells and the maternal and external environments, during every stage of fetal development. Finally, they pointed out that hypotheses positing sex-differentiated lateralization themselves rely on controversial hypotheses concerning sex differences in cognitive abilities. Many questioned the rationale for looking for a biological foundation for the sex differences alleged, given that a substantial body of research documents significant differences in relevant socialization, that differences among males and among females appear to be more significant than the differences between the genders, and that studies claiming to establish such differences typically assume that gender is a sufficient variable and use criteria for cognitive abilities that are themselves controversial.

On the basis of these several lines of critique, feminist biologists concluded that organizer hypotheses of the sort Geschwind and Behan proposed lacked evidential warrant and that their driving force was largely political.[30]

Considered in isolation, Geschwind and Behan's hypothesis does appear to lack evidential warrant. Given the nature of the topic, the gender stereotypes informing it, the staggering number of explanations proposed in the history of science for alleged sex differences in cognitive abilities, and the misstatement or misrepresentation of the results of Chi et al., its driving force can be seen, as many feminist biologists did see it, as largely political. But in my initial analyses of this case, I argued that when evidence is taken to include *both* empirical results *and* integration within a body of accepted research, standards, and theories, Geschwind and Behan's hypothesis is revealed to have enjoyed substantial evidential warrant at the time it was proposed, notwithstanding the results of Chi et al. This is not to say, I argued, that social beliefs and values did not constitute part of its evidential warrant; construing evidence holistically reveals that these had a role both more subtle and pervasive than an analysis focusing on this hypothesis in isolation would reveal (Nelson 1990, 1995).

Results, hypotheses, and core research questions in three research traditions provided evidential support for this hypothesis. The core questions, standards, and theories of neuroendocrinology—the discipline within which Geschwind and Behan were working—concern relationships among hormones, neural events, and behavior, and there is a long-standing commitment to sexual dimorphism and to designating hormones, and mechanisms and lines of fetal development, as "male" and "female." *Given* these commitments, males and females appear to provide a "natural" baseline for investigating the relationships with which the discipline is concerned, and sex differences have functioned as support for its core hypotheses positing such relationships. That is to say, Geschwind and Behan's investigation and hypothesis fell well within the parameters of neuroendocrinology. Further, the prevalence of some cognitive and other disabilities among boys and men revealed by their research provided additional warrant for the investigation of the effects of hormones on neuro-organization and function.

In addition, research based on a male/female dichotomy—and extending this dichotomy to hormones, lines of fetal development, neuro-organization, and behavior—had yielded results in closely allied disciplines and research collaborations. Research in reproductive endocrinology two decades earlier had led investigators to posit a "male" rodent brain as resulting from the influence of androgens and a "female brain" as resulting from their absence.[31] And, as indicated by the studies that Diamond et al. and Geschwind and Behan cited, investigations in endocrinology and empirical psychology (most involving rats) had linked androgens to morphological sex differences in the brain, to "cognitive capacities" (e.g., maze-negotiating abilities), and to behavior (e.g., "aggression" in laboratory animals). Studies in psychology claiming to establish clear sex differences in cognitive abilities in humans, and in particular differences in visual-spatial and mathematical abilities, were also numerous in the 1970s and 1980s. And research into cerebral dominance involving collaborations across these disciplines and neuroanatomy, research in which Geschwind had been involved, had found structural and functional asymmetries in the human brain. By 1979, three years before Geschwind and Behan's proposal, two landmark studies in reproductive endocrinology could claim that sexual differentiation of brain morphology and function was established, and called for further investigations into its mechanisms.[32]

When evidence is construed holistically, Geschwind and Behan's hypothesis is revealed to represent the synthesis of core research questions, current hypotheses, and experimental results in three research traditions, aspects of which reflected cultural assumptions about sex differences (e.g., that males have superior spatial and mathematical abilities, that there is a biological foundation for these sex differences, etc.). So viewed, their hypothesis enjoyed substantial evidential warrant.

A Dissenting Community

However, an analysis of the evidence appealed to by feminist biologists critical of this hypothesis also reveals a substantial role for unquestioned assumptions about gender and a fair dose of androcentrism in the research providing evidential warrant for Geschwind and Behan's hypothesis. Recall that feminist biologists criticized the emphasis organizer hypotheses place on the effects of so-called male hormones. Androcentrism characterized research into fetal development more generally.[33] At the time, research concerned with sexual differentiation of the brain had been characterized by an emphasis on the effects of male hormones, and much of the research ostensibly concerned with human fetal development had been devoted to the sex-determining function of the Y chromosome and the H-Y antigen in the organization of the primitive gonad into the testes, and to the subsequent effects of testosterone on the developing brain and somatic sex organs. Until the mid and late 1980s, when as Anne Fausto-Sterling describes it "a positive role for estrogen began to creep into parts of the literature" in fetal development, what research there had been into the role of estrogens had been largely devoted to the question of why the developing male embryo was not feminized by them. But well into the 1980s, relatively little was known about the directions or mechanisms of female fetal development (Fausto-Sterling 1987). Even with the creeping in of interest that Fausto-Sterling notes, a survey of articles and textbooks indicates that the conflation of male fetal development with human fetal development has been widespread.[34]

In the research background earlier summarized, gender dimorphism, inclusive of social connotations, was also commonly imposed on other species, as well as objects that are not sexed. The association of males with activity and of females with passivity has been pervasive in research into fetal development in endocrinology and empirical psychology. These associations have shaped descriptions of laboratory animal behavior and facilitated extrapolations of that behavior to human behavior. One reason why so little was known about the mechanisms or directions of female fetal development was that it had been conceptualized as occurring passively in the "the absence of instructions" from sex hormones designated as male (Fausto-Sterling 1987)—a methodological commitment John Money calls "the Adam principle, the principle that you have to do something to get a male" (quoted in Fausto-Sterling 1987).

The commitment to sexual dimorphism and to extending it to biological entities and processes was also pervasive. Androgens and estrogens, for example, were consistently designated as respectively "male" and "female," even though males and females produce both (it is the amounts that differ); the circulating form of progesterone, which is metabolized to testosterone, the major androgen, is also metabolized to estradiol (the major estrogen); and among the three families of sex hormones, there are continuous conversions of some forms to others. The difficulties in isolating the effects of these hormones, and the role of the assumption of sexual dimorphism and presuppositions about gender in the interpretation of research results involving them, are attested to by the reversal of claims that an "organizing effect" on fetal rat brains that researchers had attributed to androgens and linked to rodent behavior they described as "masculine" is now attributed to estrogen converted from testosterone by brain cells (Fausto-Sterling 1987).

Feminist biologists have provided detailed analyses that demonstrate that conclusions can not be drawn on the basis of research apparently establishing the organizing and activating effects of androgens, given that a similar amount of research has not been devoted to the effects of estrogen and the mechanisms and directions of female fetal development. They have also demonstrated that androcentric descriptions of behavior, and the imposition of gender on biological entities and process, facilitated unwarranted extrapolations of explanatory models positing linear causal relationships from hormones to neural events to cognitive capacities and behavior from rodents to humans.[35]

In my initial analysis of this case, I offered the following assessment. First, notwithstanding the problems feminist scientists have identified, the organizer hypothesis is *not* plausibly written off as bad science. There was substantial evidence for it, constituted both by research traditions and experimental results in several disciplines and by widely accepted assumptions, within the relevant sciences and the broader social community, about gender differences and their source in biology. In 1981, the year before Geschwind and Behan proposed their formulation of the organizer hypothesis, a number of the articles in a special issue of *Science* devoted to sex differences took sexual differentiation of the brain and its source in the organizing effects of androgens as *established* for many species and as *well supported* for humans.[36]

Second, viewed in light of the research questions, results, and theories brought to bear by feminist scientists, that hypothesis is revealed to be considerably less promising than its proponents took it to be, and aspects of the research background providing its evidential warrant are problematic in the ways just outlined. It might not be reasonable to expect endocrinologists in the 1970s and early 1980s to know and consider sociological studies suggesting alternative explanations for the sex differences alleged, to know of the critiques offered by psychologists of research into sex differences in cognitive abilities and lateralization, or even to know of the several levels of critiques offered by feminist colleagues in biology. But relevant studies and critiques were sufficiently publicized by the late 1980s to make it reasonable to expect those pursuing biological explanations for sex differences to show why such explanations constituted or were likely to constitute better explanations than sociological explanations, and to attend to the unwarranted imposition of gender, and the critiques of the commitment to sexual dimorphism and of its imposition on biological entities and processes, the lack of research into female fetal development, and so on. And while holism does not take the borrowing of hypotheses criticized by feminist biologists to be itself problematic, I argued that those key to the rationale of organizer hypotheses—hypotheses positing sex differences in lateralization and in cognitive abilities—would need to be confirmed, and the substantial problems in the research to date involving them would need to be resolved, to warrant future organizer hypotheses.

Finally, I argued that this case, along with others focused on by feminist scientists, carried implications for the role of social beliefs and values in science. The role of androcentrism, of gender dimorphism, and of the impositions of gender and its social connotations on other species and biological entities and processes just outlined, *and* the identification of these factors by feminist scientists, demonstrate that social beliefs and values can be integrated in research questions, experiments, methodologies, and ontologies that meet general and discipline-specific standards. Such cases indicate that neither the role of social and political factors of various kinds, nor that of values, can serve as a litmus test for good science or be ignored in philosophical theorizing about science.

Geschwind and Behan's hypothesis lost support among biologists because they failed to identify the causal mechanisms it proposed. Given this and the misstatement of the results claimed by Chi et al., some scientists have objected to my assessment that the hypothesis did enjoy evidential warrant. I think the proper response to this objection is along the lines of "hindsight is always 20/20." Darwin had no mechanism to explain inheritance, but we don't find the provisional acceptance of natural selection pending the discovery of that mechanism unwarranted. Had a mechanism been found in the present case, it is likely that, despite Chi et al.'s results, Geschwind and Behan would have been credited with synthesizing what was in fact a broad spectrum of results and hypotheses, and with providing a biological explanation for sex differences in cognitive abilities—an explanation in which there continues to be considerable interest in biology and psychology.

Two other objections were common. Given that this hypothesis is no longer viewed as viable, some argued, it is rather like the hypotheses that intelligence is a function of brain size and that both are differentiated by class, race, and sex—of historical interest, perhaps, but not a case that provides insights into science. In a more generalized version of this objection, scientists and philosophers committed to a hard and fast boundary between good science and values often maintain that this case and others that feminists cite as demonstrating relationships between on the one hand, social values and beliefs, and on the other, research questions, methods, and theories in science, are idiosyncratic, or cases of bad science, or both. One formulation of such criticisms maintains that the problems feminist scientists identified could be recognized by anyone "practicing good science."

Responses to some of these objections are straightforward. Neither this case nor craniometry is idiosyncratic: three decades of science scholarship have revealed numerous cases, both historical and current, in which social values and beliefs are integrated in research questions, the design of experiments and interpretation of results, and theories. As much to the point, organizer hypotheses have been taken seriously by a substantial number of scientists, with research assuming or proposing them published in science journals, the focus of special issues of *Science*, and so on. They have been taken seriously because they represent a logical extension of broader bodies of accepted research questions, standards, and theories—much of which remain in place in the present case. If we take the integration of social beliefs and values as a litmus test, the amount of research and results we would need to designate this case as bad science is far more than one or even several hypotheses, and extends well beyond research specifically devoted to establishing or explaining sex differences in women's and men's cognitive abilities.

Finally, this case is not one in which scientists without social values or preconceptions about gender were, *on that basis*, able to recognize the role of such beliefs and values in their colleagues' research. I undertook a detailed analysis to show that what feminist scientists appealed to reveals the conscious integration of theories and results in their scientific disciplines with theories and results produced by an evolving community of feminist scientists and science scholars, *and* that it was such integration, as well as their scientific backgrounds, that led to the identification of the problems in this research and to the identification of alternative models (Nelson 1996).

I take the broader implications of this case to be the following. First, explanations and reconstructions that focused on individual scientists and/or that excluded the social beliefs and values integrated in the research within which organizer hypotheses developed would be *empirically inadequate*. And explanations and reconstructions of the identification of these factors that excluded the role of an evolving body of feminist science scholarship analyzing relationships between gender and science, undertaken by and publicized among feminist scientists and science scholars, would be similarly inadequate.

Second, a substantial benefit of holism is that it provides the basis for the kinds of assessment just concluded. In this case, holism allowed for distinguishing between the "local" body of theories and standards that constituted evidence for the organizer hypothesis, and the broader body of theories and standards brought to bear by feminist scientists, in light of which aspects of the former are problematic. Such analyses and discriminations are necessary if we are going to be able to distinguish successful from unsuccessful science, and both from bad science (i.e., science characterized by the flagrant violation of norms, the ignoring of relevant and available results, and the like). What is good but unsuccessful science can be seen to be so because it can be seen to fit with local theories and standards, but to fail when the scope of holism is enlarged.

Third, while there is no algorithm in the foregoing for demarcating evidence and communities, there are guidelines. I used the core research questions of disciplines and research traditions, research collaborations, published results, citations, and conferences to identify relevant communities and bodies of theory, and the latter to assess evidential warrant.

Finally, as Ruth Bleier argued some years ago—an argument I earlier criticized but now see is correct (Nelson 1990)—when we look carefully at the assumptions, studies, and citation patterns of research seeking or claiming to find a hormonal basis for sex differences in fetal brains, and attempting to link such differences to alleged sex differences in cognitive abilities, the research results themselves (the "data," if you will) are small relative to the number of *borrowed hypotheses* supporting organizer hypotheses, and often these hypotheses are themselves not well supported (Bleier 1984). There are also cases of circular citations, in which research groups attribute "results" to another group, which in turn credits them with the results.

For example, two years after they proposed their organizer hypothesis, Geschwind and Behan cited a study in empirical psychology that reported "a marked excess of males" among mathematically gifted children as further evidence that testosterone causes right-hemisphere lateralization, a study undertaken by Benbow and Stanley in 1983 (Geschwind and Behan 1984). But *that* study cited Geschwind and Behan's 1982 paper as establishing the existence of the sex differences in question. In this and other instances involving the research in question, the norm of "evidential independence" reveals that although organizer hypotheses emerged from within a broad body of research, both they and aspects of that body enjoyed less evidential warrant than simply adding up such research studies would suggest.

4. Methodology Naturalized and Normative

I began this discussion with the claim that naturalized philosophy of science is not traditional epistemology. It is also not one of the sciences. It is a discipline that takes the sciences as its subject matter, hence the distinction, but is also continuous with them as it can claim no "higher" norms for assessing theories and practices, whether of common sense, philosophy, or the sciences, than those that evolve apace with our efforts as laypersons, philosophers, and scientists to explain and predict experience. For empiricists, these norms at least include empirical success and explanatory power. Both the distinction and the continuity argue for the normative function of naturalized philosophy of science, one I will parse in terms of the methodological shifts I advocate.

As a discipline, naturalized philosophy of science attempts to explain and evaluate the efforts made within the sciences to construct empirically adequate theories, recognizing such theories as the goal of science. Like the sciences, its methods and research focuses are those that prove (or that we assume will prove) most effective in achieving its goals.

Accordingly, we find philosophers of science, but usually not practicing scientists, concerned with providing general accounts of evidence and of cognitive agency. Scientists could, of course, engage in such research, just as philosophers of science could pursue degrees in science. But for the most part, the questions and research that philosophers of science pursue, like those scientists pursue, presuppose a tradition of inquiry and the core research questions, categories, unresolved issues, and overlapping bodies of theory that constitute their discipline.

My assessment of the evidential warrant for the organizer hypothesis and of aspects of the research background within which it emerged are obviously different from those of the scientists directly involved because I considered theories, research, and questions of a broader reach. And while these included the criticisms that feminist scientists have leveled, I did not always concur with the conclusions reached by these scientists. Both differences are traceable to the methodological principles I utilized, and these in turn to developments within my own discipline. Scientists claim and attribute results in a more individualistic manner than I assumed in my analysis and recommend for naturalized philosophy of science. Similarly, many construe evidence as exhausted by empirical success and remain committed to the view that research and theories in which values are integrated cannot constitute good science. I have recommended that philosophers of science part company with scientists on each of these issues.

If we begin from the view that the goal of science is to generate theories—presumably the best possible ones—that organize, explain, and predict our experience, and that the goal of the philosophy of science is to produce theories that explain and evaluate these efforts, then the shifts in methodology I recommend suggest two sets of deeply related questions. We should ask whether the social processes that characterize science—those involving the recruitment and education of scientists (for example, peer review mechanisms), the ways in which research is reported and disseminated, and the differences in prestige that separate specialties and sciences—do or do not contribute to that goal. For example, do current mechanisms for peer review ensure that the most promising research is published and/or funded, or are they such that very good research, if it challenges entrenched models or powerful networks, will not receive funding? That science has achieved empirical success, and substantial empirical success, is not debatable—but this does not mean that the theories and research programs it has generated are the best that might be generated.

As we turn to individual cases, our questions about the social processes that characterize science will take on more specific content. The case just considered suggests that we should ask if the processes that characterize science education and recruitment, or the current standards governing scientific practice, are likely to foster awareness among scientists of the social values and beliefs they bring to science, or of those integrated in the research questions and theories of their disciplines. Does science education as currently organized preclude study in the humanities and, if so, is it reasonable to expect scientists to be experts on social policy or to be in a position to assess the impact of their highly-specialized endeavors on the broader social community, and vice versa? How do prestige hierarchies among the sciences and specialization have an impact on the directions of research? Do they contribute to cases such as that just considered in which unquestioned assumptions about gender deeply inform research in biology, and in which a substantial body of research in the social sciences relevant to the existence and explanation of sex difference is not considered by those positing biological explanations of these? Or, to take a more extreme case, do these hierarchies contribute to the confidence among some geneticists engaged in sociobiology that they can *do* sociology and anthropology, and recommend social policy?

Let me be very clear here. From the point of view of the holistic account of evidence I have advocated, *the questions just listed about social processes are simultaneously questions about bodies of evidence*. If we locate our work in naturalized philosophy of science, our work to identify and answer questions about the social processes and bodies of evidence that characterize science will involve empirical research, rather than armchair reasoning. And the answers that bench scientists give to these and other questions we identify will need to be part of what we consider. But when we disagree, such disagreements should be pursued. And if, as philosophers of science, we conclude that our answers are more empirically warranted than those scientists offer, we should advocate changes in scientific understandings and practices.

I am arguing, of course, that given that the goal of both the philosophy of science and science is the production of theories that explain and predict our experience, philosophical analyses of science will be by their very nature normative. This is an obvious consequence of construing evidence holistically—but it is no less obviously a consequence of empiricism.

Notes

1. This discussion builds on and extensively revises "Feminist Naturalized Philosophy of Science" (*Synthese* 104(3): 399–421). Earlier versions were presented to the Nordiskt Nätverk för Feministisk Epistemologi och Feministisk Vetenskapsteorito, the Institutionen för Filosfi och Vetenskapsteorito at Umeå Universitet, the Philosophy departments at the University of Pennsylvania and the University of Missouri-St. Louis, and the Center for Philosophy of Science at the University of Minnesota. I am grateful to members of these audiences for challenging and insightful criticisms.

2. Following Burian (1993), I take "disciplines" to be "organized and institutionalized bodies of research focused around a core group of questions" (387–88).

3. (1) The issues are more complex than these questions suggest. Some recent arguments for "socializing" the philosophy of science raise questions about individualistic construals of "cognitive capacities" (e.g., Longino 1990; Maffie 1991; and Nelson 1990). (2) The distinction between factors "internal" and "external" to science is at least controversial. Similarly, the denotation of "social factors" varies widely in the recent literature, as do views about whether some or all of the things so designated are epistemologically significant. I will contend that a *naturalistic* philosophy of science must allow the details of individual cases to determine which, if any, "social factors" were of import, how, and to what degree, and not prejudge this issue (cf. Burian 1985; Maffie 1991; Nelson 1990; Solomon 1994; and Stump 1992).

4. See, e.g., Downes (1993); Fuller (1988); Giere (1988); Maffie (1990, 1991); Nelson (1990, 1997); Solomon (1994); and Stump (1992).

5. Cf. Campbell (1998) and Chapter 9 of this volume for different arguments for naturalizing the philosophy of science, epistemology, and moral epistemology.

6. See, e.g., Giere (1988); Laudan (1984b); Nelson (1990); Solomon (1994); and Stump (1992).

7. See, e.g., Giere (1988); Kornblith (1985); Maffie (1991); Nelson (1990); Quine (1969); Solomon (1994); and Stump (1992).

8. See, e.g., Nelson (1990) and Solomon (1994). Cf. Downes (1993); Fuller (1988); and Stump (1992).

9. Compare, for example, the different accounts of the plate tectonic revolution provided in Giere (1988); Solomon (1994); and Thagard (1992).

10. My claim that naturalized philosophy of science as Quine advocates it is normative is, of course, controversial, and will be supported in my larger discussion. See other chapters in this volume.

11. See, e.g., Addelson (1983); Downes (1993); Fuller (1988); Harding (1983); Longino (1990); Maffie (1991); Nelson (1990, 1993); Potter (1993); Solomon (1994); and Stump (1992).

12. It is the rejection of relativism *and* the insistence on relationships between science, values, and sociopolitical contexts that I claim to be characteristic of feminist approaches to science. The holistic view of evidence I next advocate is a different empiricist model from those used by feminists who construe evidence narrowly and locate values in "background assumptions" (e.g., Longino 1990).

13. As I note below, Quine has long maintained that a "relative" or modest holism suffices (Quine 1960, 1981c) and has recently described "a tempering of the extreme holism" advocated in "Two Dogmas of Empiricism" (Quine in Borradori 1994, 36).

14. Some may object that this construal of issues subsumes "the semantic view" under a view it rejects and claims to replace. I cannot here defend my retention of the notion of theories.

15. My use of "theory" to denote methodological commitments and standards reflects the view that these, like parts of theories narrowly construed, are sentences (Nelson 1990, 1995).

16. Nelson (1995).

17. Quine (1963, 1981b, 1981c). In a line of reasoning similar to that I will take below, Quine maintains that while the stimulus conditions of an occasion sentence (i.e., an observation sentence)

may be specifiable, the specification will be by reference to the behavior of a *community* with the empirical content determined in part by the theories that community maintains (Quine 1960, 35–45). Note that while a notion of "observation sentences" has been, in Quine's words, "dredged out," the sentences so designated are theoretical and the empirical content an observation sentence *holds for an individual* is partly determined by the theories and standards generated by a community.

In apparent contrast, Quine has also defined an observation sentence in terms of *individuals*, and specifically as a sentence that "*taken as an undivided whole* commands [an individual's] assent consistently or dissent consistently when the same global sensory stimulation is present" (Quine 1981b, 26, emphasis added; cf. Quine 1990, 1–8). But Quine also maintains in these later discussions that *observation sentences share terms with theory*—indeed, it is on the basis of such connections, he notes, that observation is "relevant to scientific theory"—and that when viewed *analytically*, observation sentences are "theory-laden" (Quine 1990, 7). It is when viewed holophrastically (i.e., taken as a whole and "as conditioned to stimulatory situations") that Quine maintains that such sentences are "theory-free" (7).

Hence, the shift in *focus* in these definitions—from communities to individuals—is really a shift from viewing sentences analytically to holophrastically, and does not change the fact that the empirical content an observation sentence holds *for an individual*—the stimulatory situations in light of which she or he will assent to or dissent from it—is determined in part by a body of accepted theory.

18. I retain evidence as a technical notion. In contrast, Quine describes observation, and "evidence, if that was observation," as the "temporally ordered set of all those of [a subject's] exteroceptors that triggered on [an] occasion," and maintains that, so defined, both evidence and observation "drop out" as technical notions. "We can make do instead," he maintains, "with the notion of observation sentences" (Quine 1990, 2). See n. 17.

19. See n. 2.

20. See, e.g., the case studies undertaken in Nelson (1995); cf. Longino (1990).

21. This is demonstrated in, for example, Solomon (1994).

22. See n. 17.

23. That is, once we acknowledge (as Quine himself insists) that we can expect no sameness of physical state (i.e., not the triggering of the same exteroceptors) among similarly placed observers or for the same observer on individual occasions in response to some "fixed range of stimulations," that the *stimuli* that shape our positing of objects, events, and causal relationships *include* the sentences constituting the methods, core questions, and theories of established traditions of inquiry, and that decision-making and other cognitive processes take place within and are constrained by such traditions, it is clear that the emphasis on individuals for naturalized accounts of theory generation and adoption is misplaced.

24. I have argued that research and analyses undertaken by feminist science scholars further the case for our needing such higher level explanations and the case for taking communities as their primary loci (Nelson 1990, 1995). In a line of reasoning I will pursue in the case study, feminist scientists and scholars have documented ways in which social arrangements and processes, including divisions in cognitive labor and authority, have affected both the directions and the content of scientific knowledge (e.g., Addelson 1983; Keller 1985; Potter 1993; and Tuana 1988).

25. In summarizing this research, its theoretical background, and feminist critiques of both, I draw most heavily on a special issue of *Science* (Vol. 211, 1981) focusing on sex differences (in particular, Ehrhardt and Meyer-Balhburg 1981; MacLusky and Naftolin 1981; and Wilson et al. 1981), and also on Bleier (1984, 1988); Chi et al. (1977); Diamond et al (1981); Fausto-Sterling (1985, 1987, 1993); Geschwind and Behan (1982, 1984); Geschwind and Galaburda (1984); Gorski et al. (1978); Gorski (1979); Harris and Levine (1965); and Hubbard et al. (1979).

26. In addition to Chi et al. and Ounsted and Taylor, Geschwind and Behan cited Le May and Culebras (1972); Wada et al. (1975); and Galaburda and Kemper (1979).

27. But, in describing this study a year later in *Science*, Geschwind suggested that the effects of testosterone *in utero* can produce "superior right-hemisphere talents such as . . . mathematical talent" (Kolata 1983, 1312).

28. Geschwind and Behan (1984, 221); the study they cited was Benbow and Stanley (1983).

29. Representative critiques are found in Bleier (1984, 1988); Fausto-Sterling (1985); and Hubbard et al. (1979); overviews of aspects of the debate concerning organizer hypotheses are provided in Longino (1990) and Nelson (1990).

30. See the works cited in n. 29.

31. Harris and Levine (1965); cf. Fausto-Sterling (1987). Harris and Levine also investigated the role of estrogens, but this represented an exception rather than the rule, as I outline below. Overviews are provided in Bleier (1984, 1988) and Fausto-Sterling (1985, 1987, 1993).

32. The first of these studies announced that "the concept of the sexual differentiation of brain function is now well established" (Gorski et al. 1978, 334); the second called for a search for "a clear morphological signature of sexual differentiation in the brain" (Gorski 1979, 114).

33. I rely here primarily on Bleier (1984, 1988); Fausto Sterling (1985, 1987, 1993); Hubbard et al. (1979); and the special issue of *Science* (Vol. 211, 1981) focusing on sex differences —in particular, Ehrhardt and Meyer-Balhburg (1981); MacLusky and Naftolin (1981); and Wilson et al. (1981)—Geschwind and Galaburda (1984); Gorski et al. (1978); Gorski (1979); and Harris and Levine (1965).

34. In MacLusky and Naftolin's 1981 overview of the current state of research into the effects *in utero* of sex hormones on the central nervous system, for example, the subject is presented in these general terms, but the authors move on in the next sentence and subsequent discussion to the effects of androgens secreted by the testes on the development of the central nervous system.

35. See the works cited in n. 33.

36. Thus, for example, the introductory section of one article states "[w]hile the role of social learning is much greater in human behavior than in subhuman mammals [for which the existence of sex differences in neuro-organization is no longer a question], there is sufficient evidence to suggest that biological factors influence psychosexual differentiation in human beings" (Ehrhardt and Meyer-Bahlburg 1981, 1312).

References

Addelson, Kathryn Pyne. 1983. "The Man of Professional Wisdom." In *Discovering Reality*, ed. S. Harding and M. Hintikka.

Alcoff, Linda Martín, and Elizabeth Potter. 1993. *Feminist Epistemologies*. New York: Routledge.

Benbow, C., and J. Stanley. 1983. "Sex Differences in Mathematical Reasoning Ability: More Facts." *Science* 222: 1029–31.

Birke, Lynda. 1986. *Women, Feminism, and Biology*. New York: Methuen.

Bleier, Ruth. 1984. *Science and Gender: A Critique of Biology and Its Theories on Women*. New York: Pergamon Press.

———, ed. 1988. *Feminist Approaches to Science*. New York: Pergamon Press.

Borradori, Giovanna. 1994. *The American Philosopher: Conversations with Quine, Davidson, Putnam, Nozick, Danto, Rorty, Cavell, MacIntyre, and Kuhn*. Trans. Rosanna Crocitto. Chicago: University of Chicago Press. 1994.

Burian Richard. 1993. "Technique, Task Definition, and the Transition from Genetics to Molecular Genetics." *Journal of the History of Biology* 26(3): 387–407.

Campbell, Richmond. 1998. *Illusions of Paradox: A Feminist Epistemology Naturalized*. Lanham, Md.: Rowman & Littlefield.

Chi, J. G., E. C. Dooling, and F. H. Giles. 1977. "Gyral Development of the Human Brain." *Annals of Neurology* 1: 86–93.

Diamond, M. C., G. A. Dowling, and R. E. Johnson. 1981. "Morphologic Cerebral Cortical Asymmetry in Male and Female Rats." *Experimental Neurology* 71: 261–68.

Downes, Stephen M. 1993. "Socializing Naturalized Philosophy of Science." *Philosophy of Science* 60: 452–68.

Ehrhardt, A. E., and H. F. L. Meyer-Bahlburg. 1981. "Effects of Prenatal Sex Hormones on Gender-Related Behavior." *Science* 211: 1312–18.

Fausto-Sterling, Anne. 1985. *Myths of Gender: Biological Theories about Women and Men*. New York: Basic Books.

———. 1987. "Society Writes Biology/Biology Constructs Gender." *Daedalus* 116: 61–76.

———. 1993. "The Five Sexes: Why Male and Female Are Not Enough." *The Sciences* 33(2): 20–24.

Fuller, Steve. 1988. *Social Epistemology*. Bloomington: Indiana University Press.

Geschwind, N., and P. O. Behan. 1982. "Left-handedness: Association with Immune Disease, Migraine, and Developmental Learning Disorder." *Proceedings of the National Academy of Sciences* 79: 5097–100.

———. 1984. "Laterality, Hormones, and Immunity." In *Cerebral Dominance: The Biological Foundations*, ed. N. Geschwind and A. M. Galaburda.

Geschwind, N. and A. M. Galaburda, eds. 1984. *Cerebral Dominance: The Biological Foundations*. Cambridge, Mass.: Harvard University Press.

Gilbert, Scott, et al. 1988. "The Importance of Feminist Critique for Contemporary Cell Biology." In *Feminism and Science*, ed. N. Tuana. Bloomington: Indiana University Press.

Giere, Ronald N. 1988. *Explaining Science: A Cognitive Approach*. Chicago: University of Chicago Press.

Gorski, R. 1979. "The Neuroendocrinology of Reproduction: An Overview." *Biology of Reproduction* 20: 111–27.

Gorski, R., J. H. Gordon, J. E. Shryne, and A. M. Southam. 1978. "Evidence for a Morphological Sex Difference Within the Medial Preoptic Area of the Rat Brain." *Brain Research* 148: 333–46.

Goy, R., and B. McEwen. 1980. *Sexual Differentiation of the Brain*. Cambridge: MIT Press.

Haraway, Donna. 1984. "Primatology is Politics by Other Means." In *Science and Gender: A Critique of Biology and Its Theories on Women*, ed. R. Bleier.

Harding, Sandra. 1983. "The Visibility of the Sex/Gender System." In *Discovering Reality*, ed. S. Harding and M. Hintikka.

Harding, Sandra, and Merrill Hintikka, eds. 1983. *Discovering Reality*. Dordrecht: Kluwer Academic Publishers.

Harris, G. W., and S. Levine. 1965. "Sexual Differentiation of the Brain and its Experimental Control." *Journal of Physiology* 181: 379–400.

Hubbard, R., M. S. Henifin, and B. Fried, eds. 1979. *Women Look at Biology Looking at Women: A Collection of Feminist Critiques*. Boston: G.K. Hall.

Keller, Evelyn Fox. 1985. *Reflections on Gender and Science*. New Haven: Yale University Press.

Kinsbourne, M. 1980. "If Sex Differences in Brain Lateralization Exist, They Have Yet to be Discovered." *The Behavioral and Brain Sciences* 3: 221–42.

Kolata, G. 1983. "Math Genius May Have Hormonal Basis." *Science* 222: 1312.

Kornblith, Hilary, ed. 1985. *Naturalizing Epistemology*. 1st ed. Cambridge: MIT Press.

Laudan, Larry. 1984. *Science and Values*. Berkeley and Los Angeles: University of California Press.

Longino, Helen E. 1990. *Science as Social Knowledge*. Princeton: Princeton University Press.

Longino, Helen E., and Ruth Doell. 1983. "Body, Bias, and Behavior: A Comparative Analysis of Reasoning in Two Areas of Biological Science," *Signs* 9: 206–27.

MacLusky, N. J., and F. Naftolin. 1981. "Sexual Differentiation of the Central Nervous System." *Science* 211, 1294–311.

Maffie, James. 1990. "Recent Work on Naturalized Epistemology." *American Philosophical Quarterly* 27(4): 281–93.

———. 1991. "What is Social about Social Epistemics?" *Social Epistemology* 5(2): 101–10.

Nelson, Lynn Hankinson. 1990. *Who Knows: From Quine to a Feminist Empiricism*. Philadelphia: Temple University Press.———. 1993. "Epistemological Communities." In *Feminist Epistemologies*, ed. L. Alcoff and E. Potter. New York: Routledge.

———. 1995. "A Feminist Naturalized Philosophy of Science." *Synthese* 104(3): 399–421.

———. 1997. "Empiricism Without Dogmas." In *Feminism, Science, and the Philosophy of Science*, ed. L. H. Nelson and J. Nelson.

———, and Jack Nelson, eds. 1996. *Feminism, Science, and the Philosophy of Science*. Dordrecht: Kluwer Academic Publishers.

Potter, E. 1993. "Gender and Epistemic Negotiation." In *Feminist Epistemologies*, ed. Alcoff and Potter.

Quine, W. V. 1960. *Word and Object*. Cambridge, Mass.: Harvard University Press.

———. 1963. "Two Dogmas of Empiricism." In *From a Logical Point of View*. 2d rev. ed. New York: Harper & Row.

———. 1969. "Epistemology Naturalized." In *Ontological Relativity and Other Essays*. New York: Columbia University Press.

———. 1981a. *Theories and Things*. Cambridge, Mass.: Harvard University Press.

———. 1981b. "Empirical Content." In *Theories and Things*.

———. 1981c. "Five Milestones of Empiricism." In *Theories and Things*.

———. 1981d. "On the Nature of Moral Values." In *Theories and Things*.

———. 1981e. "On the Very Idea of a Third Dogma." In *Theories and Things*.

———. 1990. *Pursuit of Truth*. Cambridge, Mass.: Harvard University Press.

———. 1993. "Three Indeterminancies." In *Perspectives on Quine*, ed. R. Barrett and R. Gibson. Oxford: Blackwell.

Reiter, R. R., ed. 1975. *Toward an Anthropology of Women*. New York: Monthly Review Press.

Science 211, 1981.

Slocum, S. 1974. "Woman the Gatherer: Male Bias in Anthropology." In *Women in Perspective*, ed. S. Jacobs. Urbana-Champaign: University of Illinois Press.

Solomon, Miriam. 1994. "Social Empiricism." *Noûs* 28(3): 325–43.Spanier, B. 1987. "Gender and Ideology in Science: A Study of Molecular Biology." *NWSA* 3(2): 167–98.

———. 1996. *Im/Partial Science: Gender and Molecular Biology*. Bloomington: Indiana University Press.

Stump, David. 1992. "Naturalized Philosophy of Science with a Plurality of Methods." *Philosophy of Sciences* 59: 456–60.

Tanner, N., and A. Zihlman. 1976. "Women in Evolution." *Signs* 1: 585–608.

Thagard, Paul. 1992. *Conceptual Revolutions*. Princeton: Princeton University Press.

Tuana, Nancy. 1988. *Feminism and Science*. Bloomington: Indiana University Press.

Wilson, J. D., F. W. George, and J. E. Griffin. 1981. "The Hormonal Control of Sexual Development." *Science* 211: 1278–84.

Wylie, Alison. 1996. "The Constitution of Archaeological Evidence: Gender Politics and Science." In *The Disunity of Science*, ed. Peter Galison and David J. Stump. Stanford: Stanford University Press.

Bibliography

Selected Works by W. V. Quine

Quine, W. V. 1960. *Word and Object*. Cambridge, Mass.: MIT Press.
———. 1963. *From a Logical Point of View*. 2d ed. New York: Harper & Row.
———. 1963a. "On What There Is." In *From a Logical Point of View*.
———. 1963b. "Two Dogmas of Empiricism." In *From a Logical Point of View*.
———. 1966. *The Ways of Paradox and Other Essays*. New York: Random House.
———. 1966a. "Foundations of Mathematics." In *The Ways of Paradox and Other Essays*.
———. 1966b. "On Mental Entities." In *The Ways of Paradox and Other Essays*.
———. 1966c. "Mr. Strawson on Logical Theory." In *The Ways of Paradox and Other Essays*.
———. 1966d. "Necessary Truth." In *The Ways of Paradox and Other Essays*.
———. 1966e. "Posits and Reality." In *The Ways of Paradox and Other Essays*.
———. 1966f. "The Scope and Language of Science." In *The Ways of Paradox and Other Essays*.
———. 1966g. "Truth by Convention." In *The Ways of Paradox and Other Essays*.
———. 1966h. "The Ways of Paradox." In *The Ways of Paradox and Other Essays*.
———. 1969. *Ontological Relativity and Other Essays*. New York: Columbia University Press.
———. 1969a. "Epistemology Naturalized." In *Ontological Relativity and Other Essays*.
———. 1969b. "Natural Kinds." In *Ontological Relativity and Other Essays*.
———. 1969c. "Ontological Relativity." In *Ontological Relativity and Other Essays*.
———. 1969d. "Speaking of Objects." In *Ontological Relativity and Other Essays*.
———. 1970. "Grades of Theoreticity." In *Experience and Theory*, ed. L. Foster and J. W. Swanson. Cambridge, Mass.: MIT Press.
———. 1978. "Facts of the Matter." In *Essays on the Philosophy of W. V. Quine*, ed. R. W. Shahan and C. Swoyer. Norman: The University of Oklahoma Press.
———. 1981. *Theories and Things*. Cambridge, Mass.: Harvard University Press.
———. 1981a. "Empirical Content." In *Theories and Things*.
———. 1981b. "Five Milestones of Empiricism." In *Theories and Things*.

———. 1981c. "On the Nature of Moral Values." In *Theories and Things*.
———. 1981d. "Responses." In *Theories and Things*.
———. 1981e. "Things and Their Place in Theories." In *Theories and Things*.
———. 1981f. "On the Very Idea of a Third Dogma." In *Theories and Things*.
———. 1985. *The Time of My Life*. Cambridge, Mass.: MIT Press.
———. 1987. *Quiddities: An Intermittently Philosophical Dictionary*. Cambridge, Mass.: Harvard University Press.
———. 1986. "Autobiography of W. V. Quine." In *The Philosophy of W. V. Quine*, ed. Lewis Edwin Hahn and Paul Arthur Schilpp. La Salle, Ill.: Open Court.
———. 1990. *Pursuit of Truth*. Cambridge, Mass.: Harvard University Press.
———. 1990. "Three Indeterminacies." In *Perspectives on Quine*, ed. R. Barrett and R. Gibson. Cambridge, Mass.: Blackwell.

Feminist Analyses of Quine and of Feminist Appropriations of Quine

Addelson, Kathryn Pyne. 1993. "Knower-Doers and Their Moral Problems." In Alcoff and Potter, *Feminist Epistemologies*.
Alcoff, Linda Martín. 1987. "Justifying Feminist Social Science." In *Feminism and Science*, ed. Nancy Tuana. Bloomington: Indiana University Press.
Alcoff, Linda Martín, and Elizabeth Potter, eds. 1993. *Feminist Epistemologies*. New York: Routledge.
Antony, Louise. 1994. "Quine as Feminist: The Radical Import of Naturalized Epistemology." In *A Mind of One's Own*, ed. Louise Antony and Charlotte Witt. Boulder, Colo.: Westview.
Babbitt, Susan. 1993. "Feminism and Objective Interests." In Alcoff and Potter, *Feminist Epistemologies*.
Campbell, Richmond. 1994. "The Virtue of Feminist Empiricism." *Hypatia* 9.
———. 1998. *Illusions of Paradox: A Feminist Epistemology Naturalized*. Lanham, Md.: Rowman & Littlefield.
———. 2002. "The Bias Paradox in Feminist Epistemology." In Tuana and Morgen, *Engendering Rationalities*.
Clough, Sharyn. Forthcoming. *Beyond Epistemology*. Savage, Md.: Rowman & Littlefield.
Code, Lorraine. 1995. *Rhetorical Spaces*. New York and London: Routledge.
Dalmiya, Vrinda, and Linda Martín Alcoff. 1993. "Are 'Old Wives' Tales' Justified?" In Alcoff and Potter, *Feminist Epistemologies*.
Duran, Jane. 1991. *Toward a Feminist Epistemology*. Savage, Md.: Rowman & Littlefield.
———. 1998. *Philosophies of Science/Feminist Theories*. New York: Westview Press.
Harding, Sandra. 1986. *The Science Question in Feminism*. Ithaca: Cornell University Press.
Hoagland, Sarah Lucia. 2002. "Resisting Rationality." In Morgen and Tuana, *Engendering Rationalities*.
Longino, Helen E. 1990. *Science as Social Knowledge*. Princeton: Princeton University Press.
Nelson, Jack. 1995. "The Last Dogma of Empiricism?" In Nelson and Nelson, *Feminism, Science, and the Philosophy of Science*.
Nelson, Lynn Hankinson. 1990. *Who Knows: From Quine to a Feminist Empiricism*. Philadelphia: Temple University Press.
———. 1993. "Epistemological Communities." In Alcoff and Potter, *Feminist Epistemologies*.

———. 1993. "A Question of Evidence." *Hypatia* 8 (2). Reprint, 2002. In *Siblings Under the Skin: Feminism, Social Justic,e and Analytic Philosophy*, ed. S. Clough. Aurora, Colo.: The Davies Group.

———. 1993. "Who Knows? What Can They Know? And When?" *Reason Papers* 18. Reprint with revisions, 1986. In *Women, Knowledge, and Reality*, 2d ed., ed. A. Garry and M. Pearsall. New York and London: Routledge.

———. 1995. "The Very Idea of Feminist Epistemology," *Hypatia* 10 (3). Reprint with revision, 1999. In *Is Feminist Philosophy Philosophy?*, ed. E. Bianchi. Evanston: Northwestern University Press.

———. 1995. "A Feminist Naturalized Philosophy of Science," *Synthese* 104(3).

———. 1996. "Empiricism without Dogmas." In Nelson and Nelson, *Feminism, Science, and the Philosophy of Science*.

Nelson, Lynn Hankinson, and Jack Nelson. 1994. "No Rush to Judgment." *Monist* 77.

———. 1995. "Feminist Values and Cognitive Virtues." *PSA II*.

———. 2000. *On Quine*. Belmont, Calif.: Wadsworth.

———. 2002. "Logic from a Quinean Perspective: An Empirical Enterprise." In *Representing Reason: Feminist Perspectives on Logic*, ed. M. Haas and R. J. Falmagne. New York: Rowman & Littlefield.

———, eds. 1996. *Feminism, Science, and the Philosophy of Science*. Dordrecht: Kluwer Academic Publishers.

Potter, Elizabeth. 1993. "Gender and Epistemic Negotiation." In Alcoff and Potter, *Feminist Epistemologies*.

———. 1996. "Underdetermination Undeterred." In Nelson and Nelson, *Feminism, Science, and the Philosophy of Science*.

Rouse, Joseph. 1996. *Engaging Science*. Ithaca : Cornell University Press.

Tuana, Nancy. 2002. "Material Locations: An Interactionist Alternative to Realism/ Social Constructivism." In Tuana and Morgen, *Engendering Rationalities*.

Tuana, Nancy, and Sandra Morgen, eds. 2002. *Engendering Rationalities*. Albany: SUNY Press.

Index

Contributors

KATHRYN PYNE ADDELSON is Mary Huggins Gamble Professor in the Philosophy department at Smith College. In 1994, she was honored as "woman philosopher of the year" by the Eastern Division of the Society for Women in Philosophy. She is the author of two books and a number of articles in journals and feminist anthologies.

LOUISE ANTONY is a professor of Philosophy and Women's Studies at Ohio State University. She is the author of many articles in the philosophy of mind, the philosophy of language, epistemology, and feminist theory. She is co-editor with Charlotte Witt of *A Mind of One's Own: Feminist Essays on Reason and Objectivity*, and with Norbert Hornstein of *Chomsky and His Critics*.

RICHMOND CAMPBELL is a professor and Chair of the Philosophy department at Dalhousie University, Halifax, Nova Scotia, and an editor of *Canadian Journal of Philosophy*. He is the author of *Illusions of Paradox: A Feminist Epistemology Naturalized* and co-editor of *Paradoxes of Rationality and Cooperation: Prisoner's Dilemma and Newcomb's Problem*. His publications include articles in logic, philosophy of science, philosophy of mind, moral epistemology, and feminist theory.

LORRAINE CODE is Distinguished Research Professor in Philosophy at York University in Toronto, and cross-appointed to the Graduate Programs in Social and Political Thought and in Women's Studies. In addition to numerous articles and four co-edited volumes, she is the author of *Epistemic Responsibility* (1987), *What Can She Know? Feminist Theory and the Construction of Knowledge* (1991), and *Rhetorical Spaces: Essays on (Gendered) Locations* (1995); and General Editor of an *Encyclopedia of Feminist Theories* (2000). Her editorial contribution to the Re-Reading the Canon Series, *Feminist Interpretations of Hans-Georg Gadamer*, is due to be published in 2003. As a Canada Council Killam Research Fellow (1999–2001), she is writing a book with the working title "Responsible Knowing, Ecological Imagining, and the Politics of Epistemic Location."

JANE DURAN is Fellow in the department of Philosophy at the University of California at Santa Barbara, where she is also a lecturer in the Humanities. She received her BA from the University of California at Berkeley, and her Ph.D. from Rutgers. She is the author of *Philosophies of Science/Feminist Theories*, *Toward a Feminist Epistemology*, and numerous journal articles in epistemology, the philosophy of science, and feminist theory.

MAUREEN LINKER received her Ph.D. in philosophy from the City University of New York, Graduate Center in 1996. She is currently an assistant professor of Philosophy at the University of Michigan, Dearborn where she teaches logic, epistemology, and feminist theory. Her research focuses on conceptions of "reasonableness" in law and science. She has papers in *Criminal Law Quarterly*, the anthology *Women Succeeding in the Sciences: Theory and Practice Across the Disciplines*, published by Purdue University Press, and a forthcoming article in *Social Epistemology* on realism and the science wars. Email: mlinker@umich.edu.

JACK NELSON is Vice Chancellor of Academic Affairs and professor of Philosophy at the University of Washington, Tacoma. He is a co-author of *The Logic Book* (Macmillan). He is co-author with Lynn Hankinson Nelson of *On Quine* (Wadsworth 2000), "Feminist Values and Cognitive Virtues" (*PSA* II, Summer 1995), "No Rush to Judgment" (*Monist* 77, October 1994), and "Logic from a Quinean Perspective: An Empirical Enterprise" (in *Representing Reason*, forthcoming). He is co-editor with Lynn Hankinson Nelson of *Feminism, Science, and the Philosophy of Science* (Kluwer 1996). They are currently working on *Empiricism Reconstituted: The Project and Legacy of W. V. Quine*.

LYNN HANKINSON NELSON is a professor of Philosophy at the University of Missouri, St. Louis. She is co-author with Jack Nelson of *On Quine* (Wadsworth 2000), "Cognitive Virtues and Feminist Values" (*PSA II* Summer 1995), "No Rush to Judgment" (*Monist* 77), and "Logic from a Quinean Perspective: An Empirical Enterprise." She is co-editor with Jack Nelson of *Feminism, Science, and the Philosophy of Science* (Kluwer 1996). They are currently working on *Empiricism Reconstituted: The Project and Legacy of W. V. Quine*. She is the author of *Who Knows: From Quine to a Feminist Empiricism*, and guest editor of a special volume of *Synthese* on "Feminism and Science" (*Synthese* 104 [3]).

PHYLLIS ROONEY is an associate professor of Philosophy at Oakland University in Michigan. Much of her work is in feminist epistemology, and she has special interests in reason and gender. She has published papers in *Hypatia*, *American Philosophical Quarterly*, *Philosophical Forum*, *Metaphilosophy*, *Proceeding of the Philosophy of Science Association*, in *Epistemology: The Big Questions*, edited by L. M. Alcoff (Blackwell 1998), and in *Feminists Doing Ethics*, edited by P. DesAutels and J. Waugh (Rowman and Littlefield 2001). She is currently working on two book projects: an introduction to feminist epistemology and a book on reason and gender.

PAUL A. ROTH is currently professor of Philosophy at the University of Missouri, St. Louis and chaired the department for six years. His primary areas of research and writing are on Quine and on various issues in the philosophy of social science, particularly those related to issues of meaning and explanation. He is author of *Meaning and Method in the Social Sciences* (Cornell 1987) and co-editor of the forthcoming *Guidebook to the Philosophy of Social Science* (Blackwell 2003). Forthcoming publications include "Mistakes" (*Synthese*) and "Beyond Understanding" (in the *Guidebook to the Philosophy of Social Science*). His primary non-academic activity consists in driving his daughter to various activities.